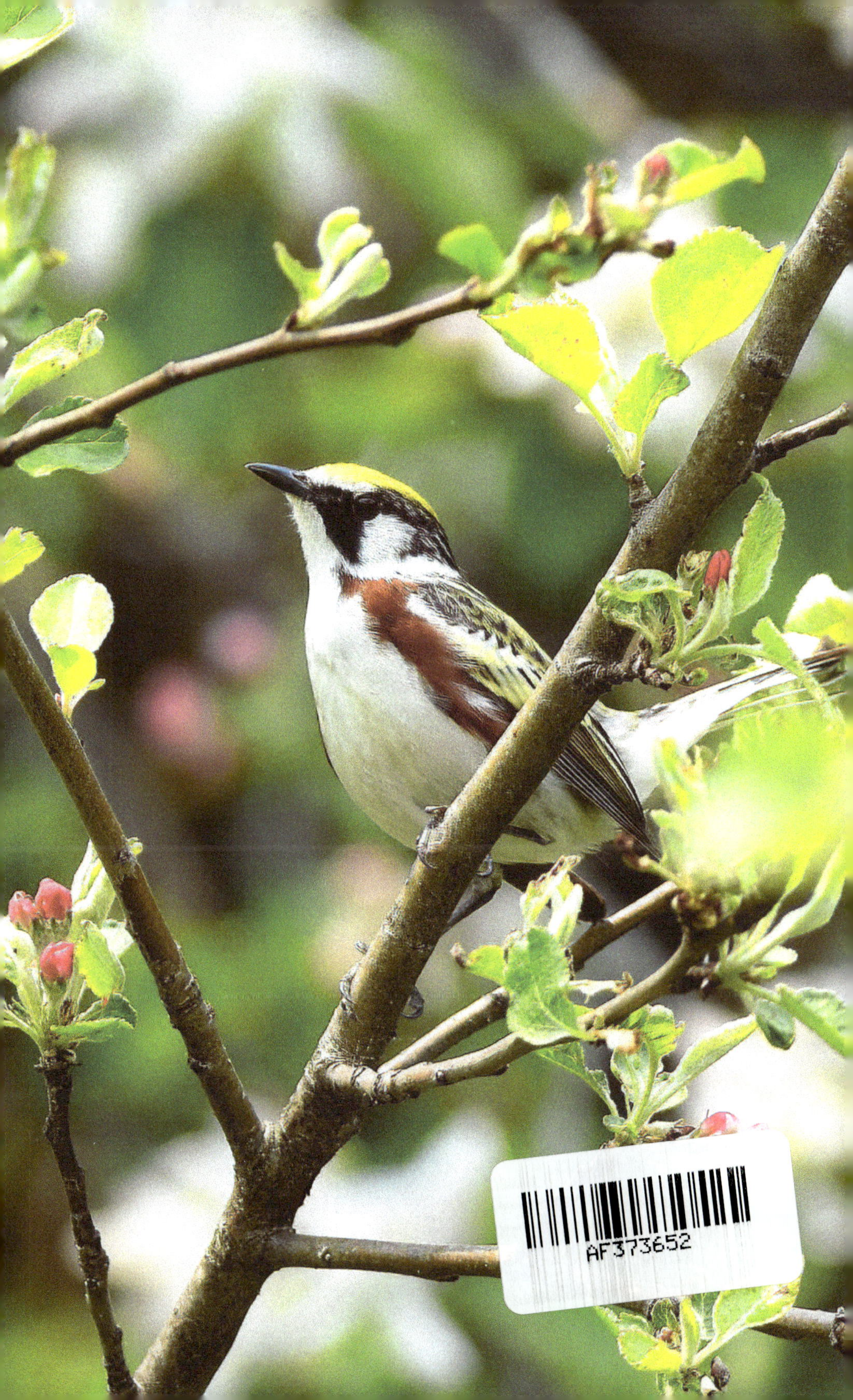

AF373652

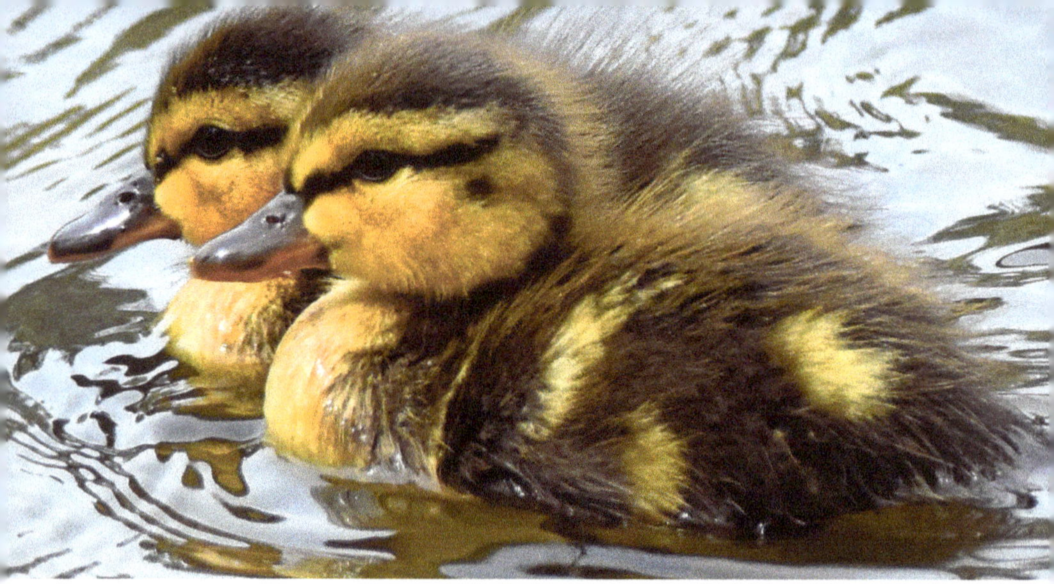

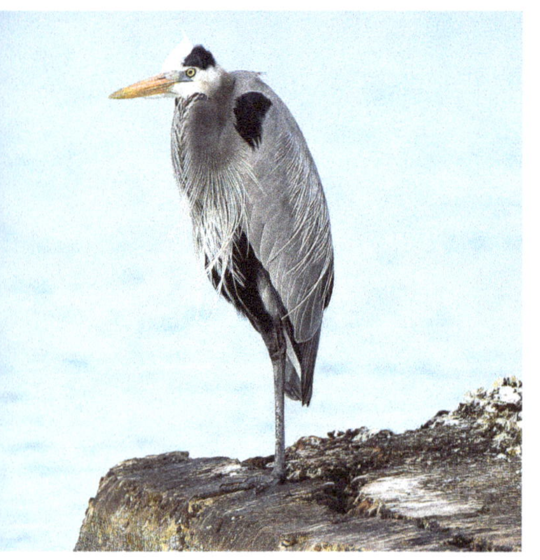

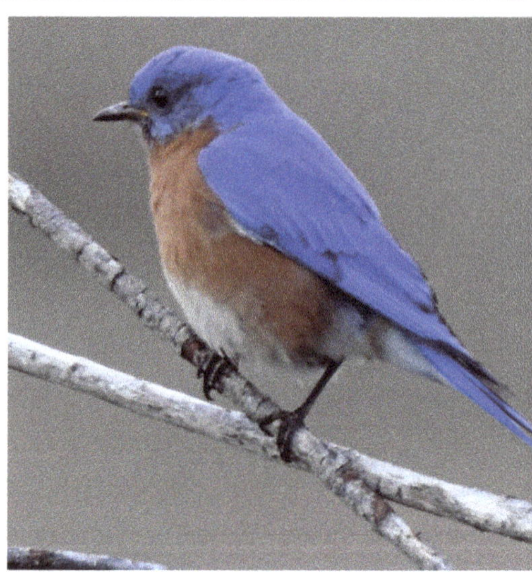

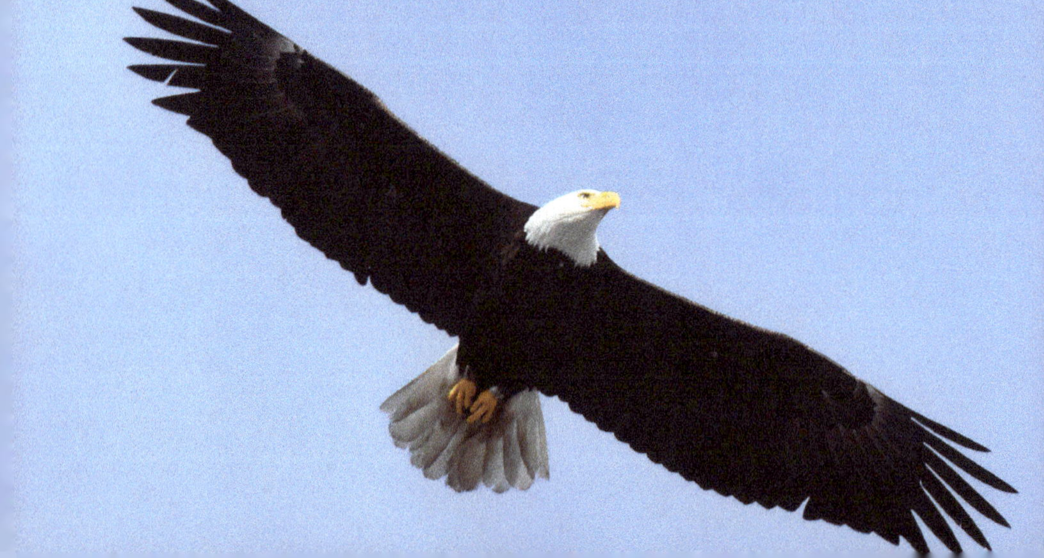

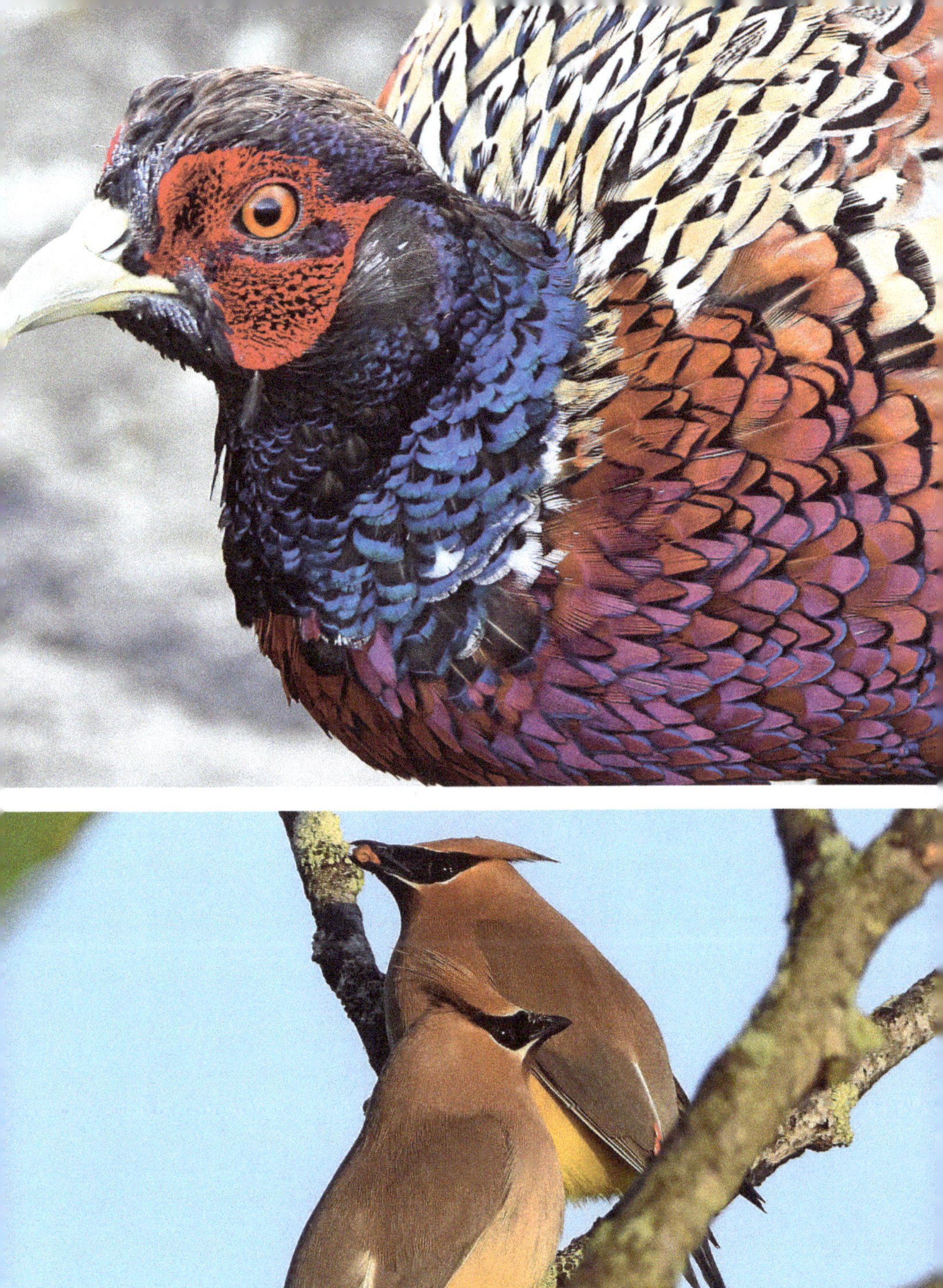

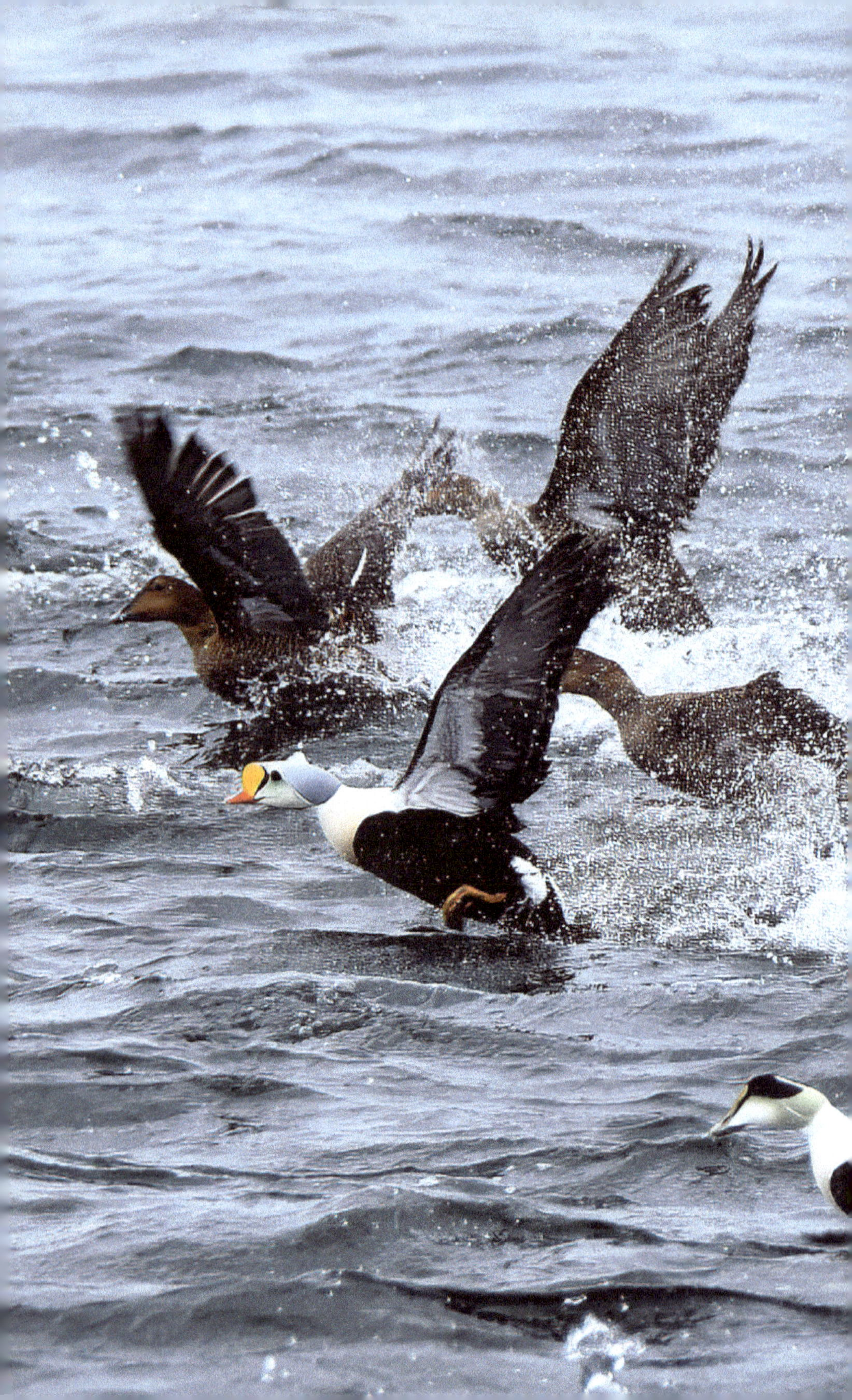

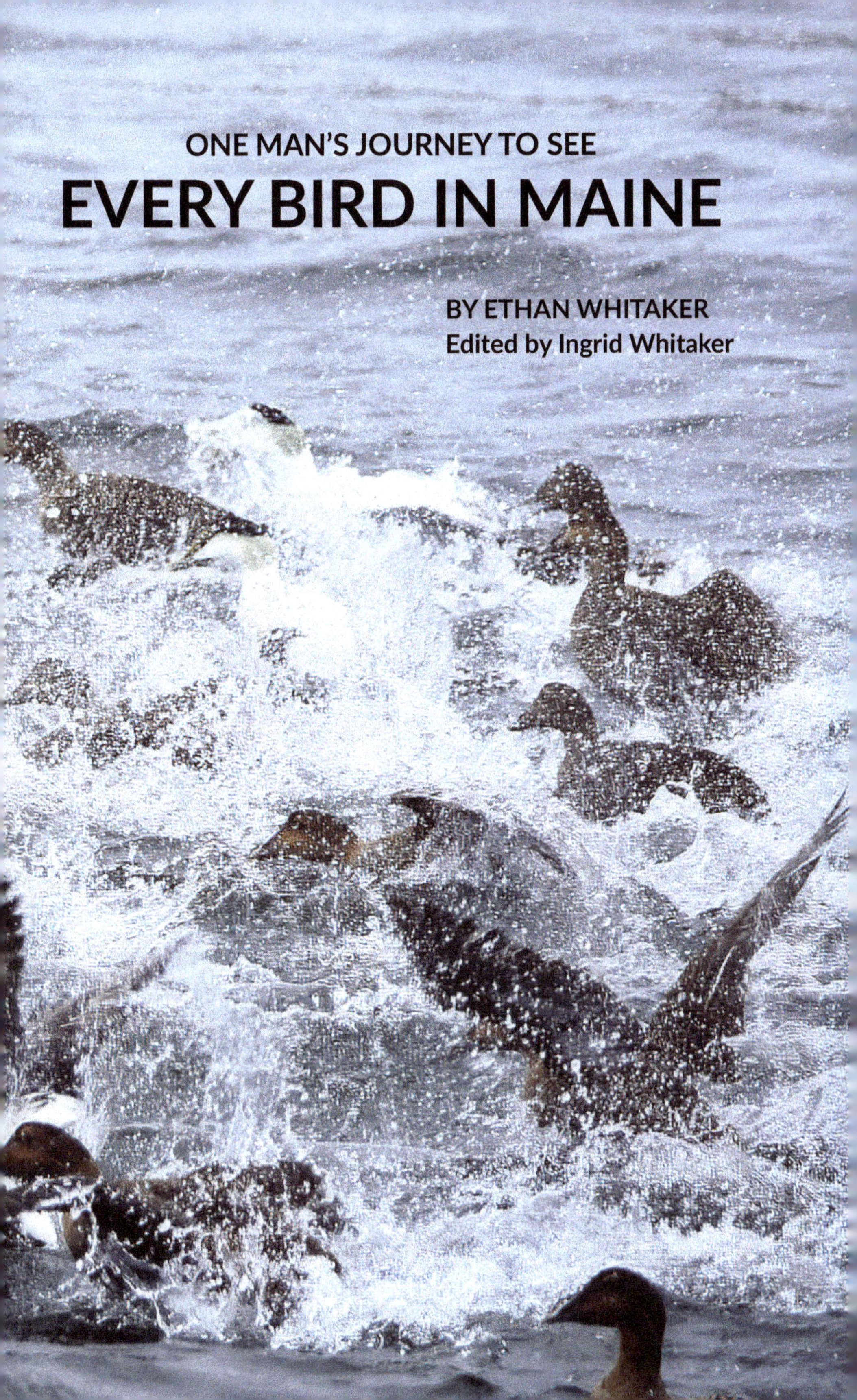

ONE MAN'S JOURNEY TO SEE
EVERY BIRD IN MAINE
BY ETHAN WHITAKER
Edited by Ingrid Whitaker

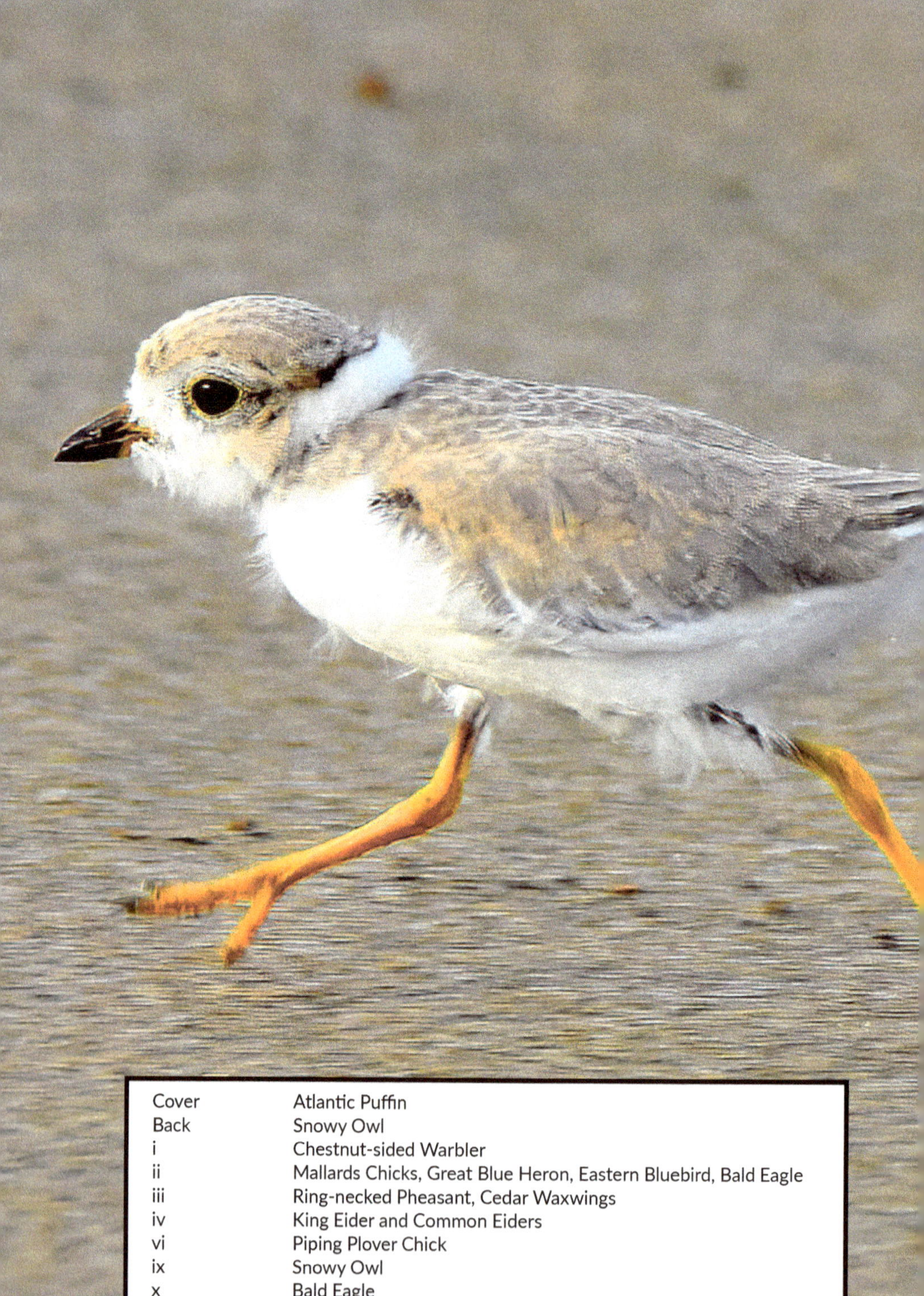

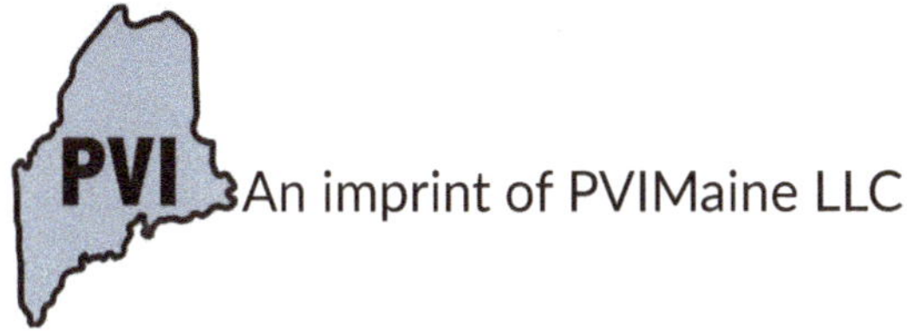
An imprint of PVIMaine LLC

Every Bird in Maine
One Man's Journey to See Every Bird in Maine
A Photographic Account of a Maine Big Year in Birding

By Ethan J Whitaker
Edited by Ingrid J Whitaker

Library of Congress Cataloging-in-Publication Data

ISBN: 979-8-9856205-1-1 (paperback)
ISBN: 979-8-9856205-0-4 (hardcover)
ISBN: 979-8-9856205-2-8 (kindle)
ISBN: 979-8-9856205-3-5 (epub)

Requests for Information:
Mail: PVIMaine LLC
attn: Ethan Whitaker
117 Cushman Point Rd
Wiscasset, Maine 04578

Phone: 1-207-671-2006

E-Mail: ewhitaker@PVIMaine.com

To Ingrid:

*She got me into the field birding,
and she's the reason I return home.*

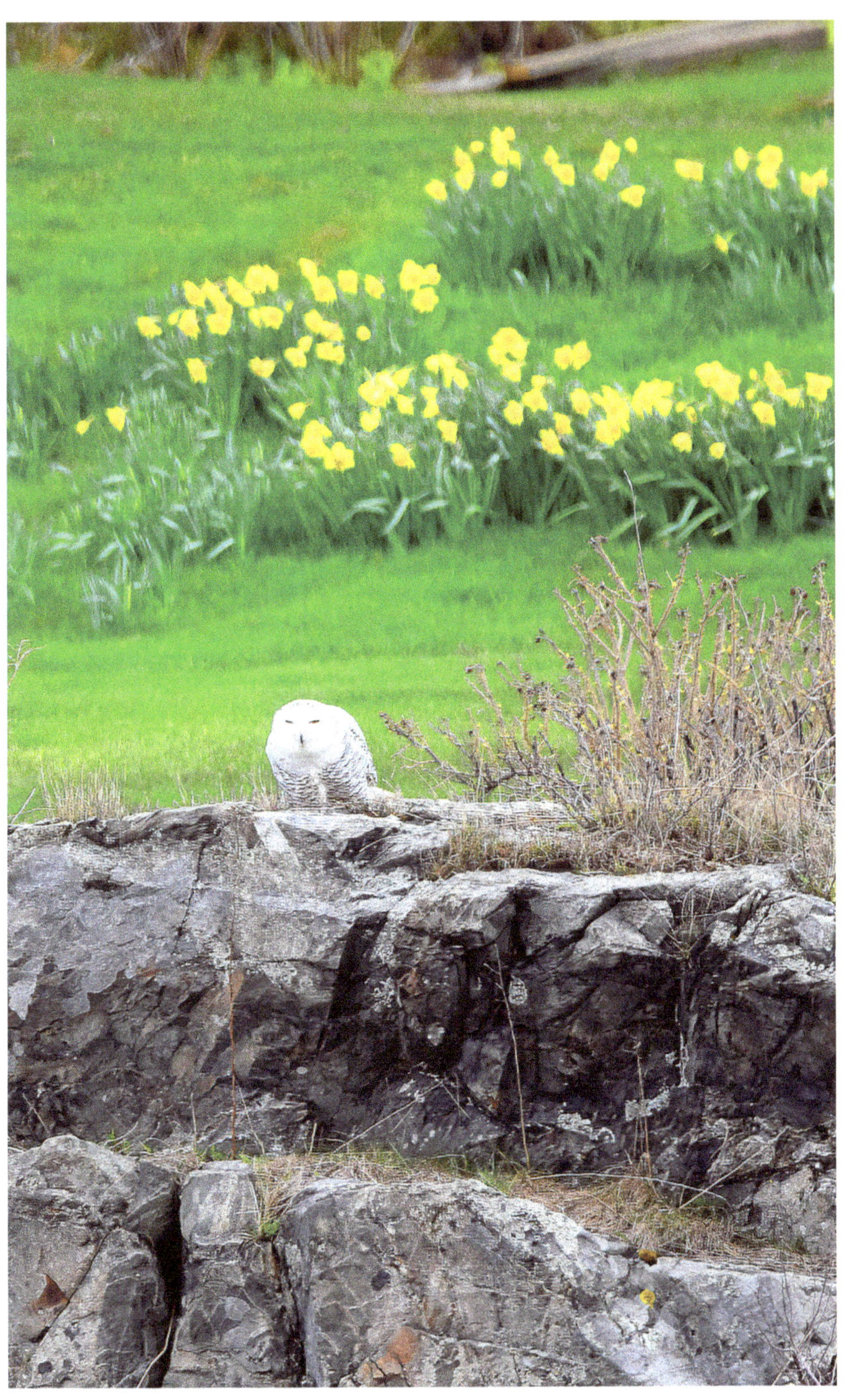

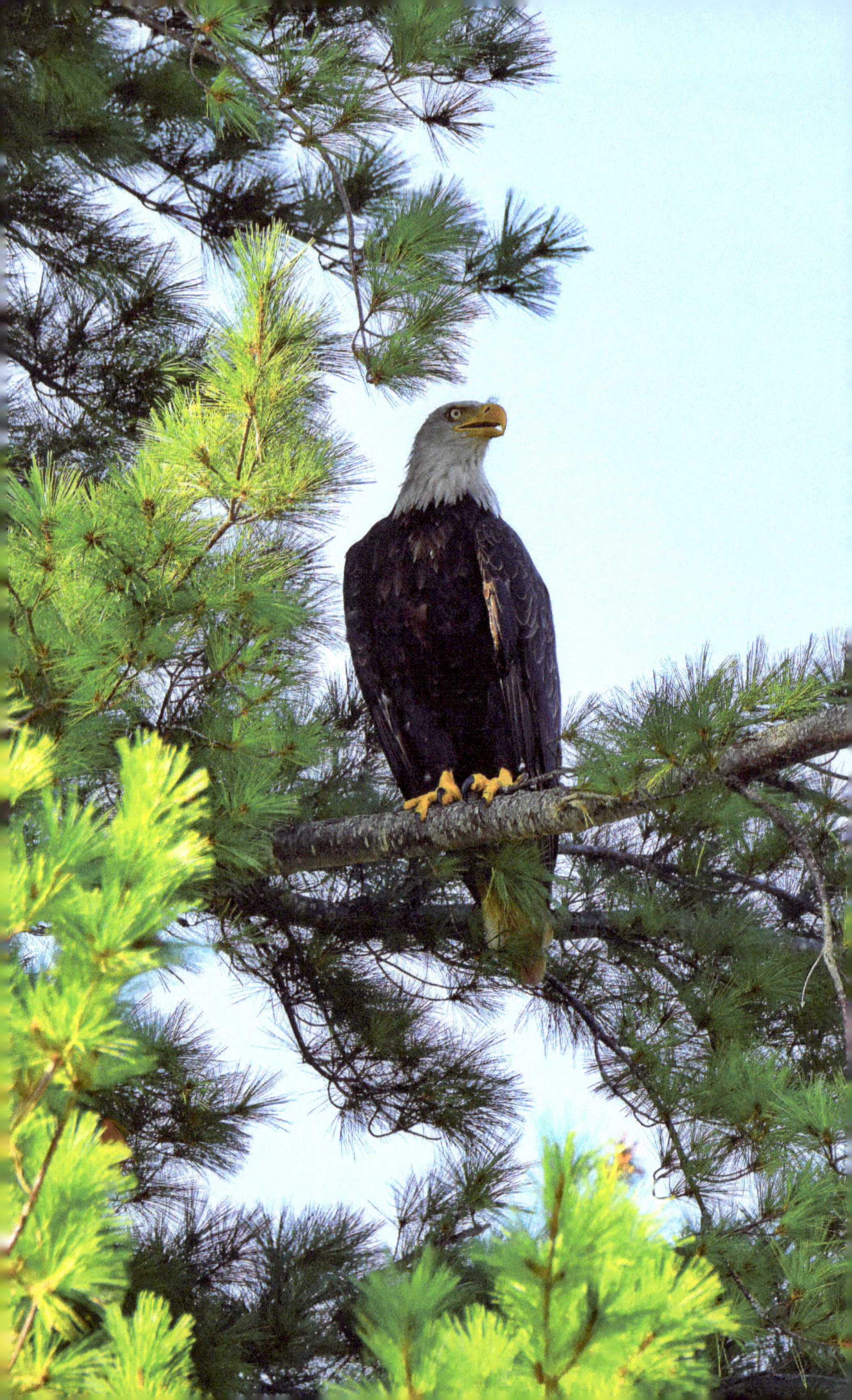

CONTENTS

Every Bird in Maine ... Why?

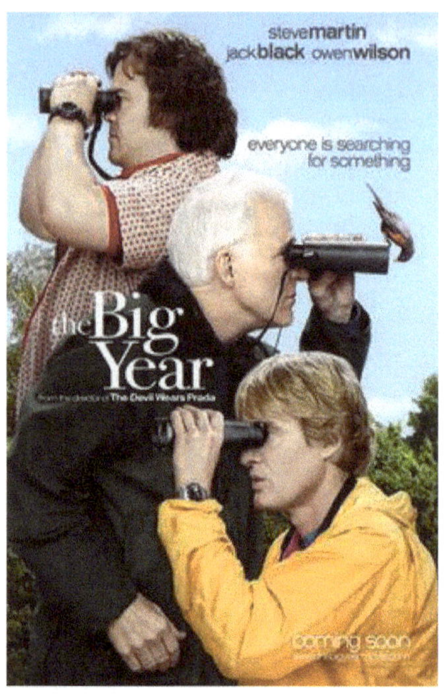

In 2011, 20th Century Fox released *The Big Year*, a comedy starring Steve Martin, Owen Wilson and Jack Black. The movie was characterized as a box office failure and was quietly retired to the rear of various movie streaming services.

One evening while watching HBO, I stumbled across *The Big Year* and thoroughly enjoyed the story of three 'competitive' birders, striving to see the highest number of North American bird species in a calendar year.

At the time, my knowledge of birds consisted of those that visited my feeders and the Bald Eagles and Ospreys that patrolled the river by my Wiscasset home.

A few months later, in February of 2013,

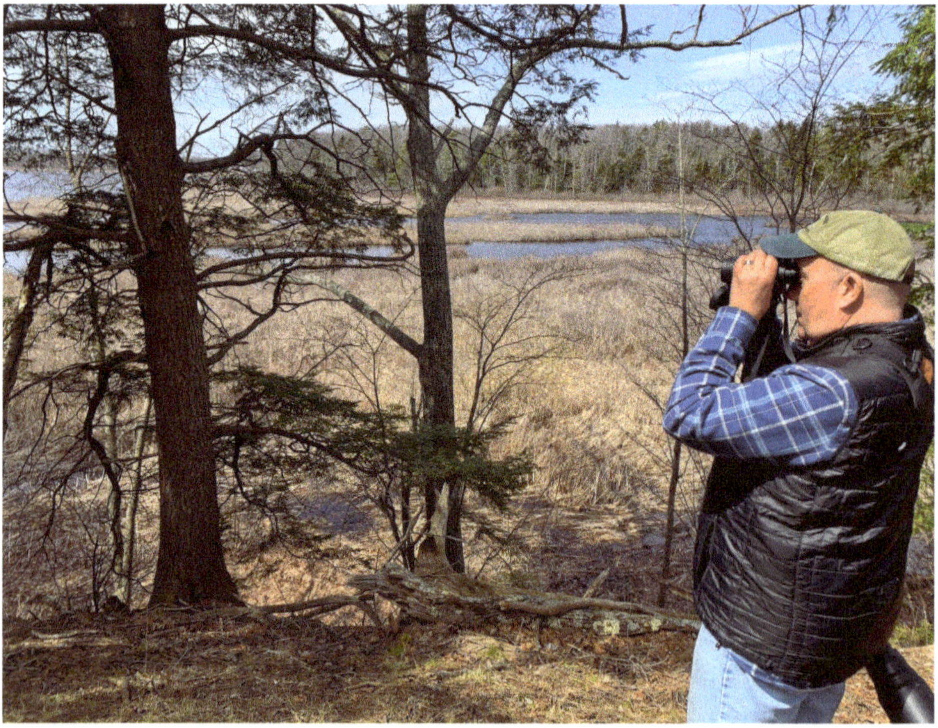

I met Ingrid, a beautiful 4th grade teacher who was also a birder. I was smitten from the moment I met her.

In a desperate effort to impress Ingrid, on our second date I took her to a marsh where I had seen dozens of Snowy Egrets the previous September. I had no idea that they had all migrated south four months earlier.

Despite my birding ignorance, Ingrid continued to date me, and we married a year and a half later. Over time, our shared birding excursions became far more successful.

Ingrid patiently taught me how to identify different species, bought me a decent pair of binoculars, took me to birding festivals and slowly created a birding addict.

In 2015 we began taking our vacations at birding hotspots in Texas, California, and Arizona. I was rushing out the door every time a rare bird was spotted and spending all of my free time in marshes, bogs and shorelines.

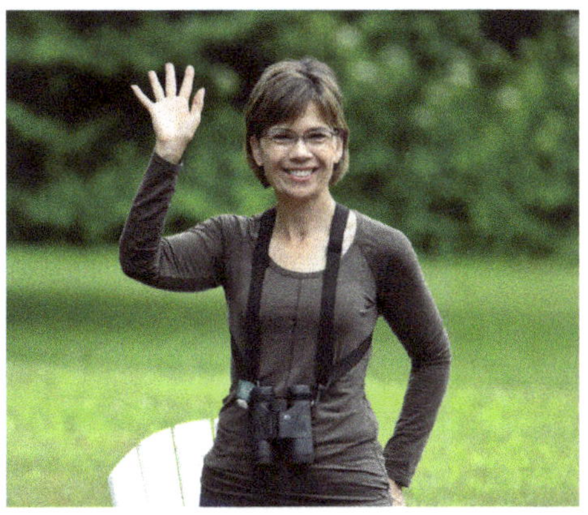

A few years later, I asked Ingrid how she would feel about me doing a 'Maine Big Year' in 2021, spending an entire calendar year seeing how many species of birds I could find. To do it right, I'd have to retire early, get my bad knees replaced, and spend even more time training for my Big Year.

Ingrid immediately said, "I think you should do it!!!"

This book is a memoir of my Maine Big Year adventure. The state record sat at 317 species. Could I find 318?

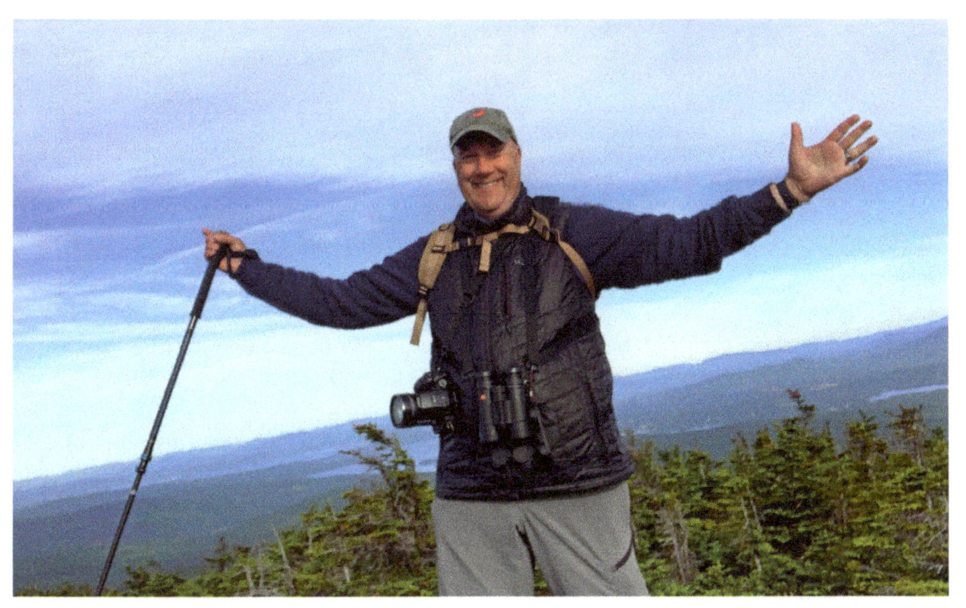

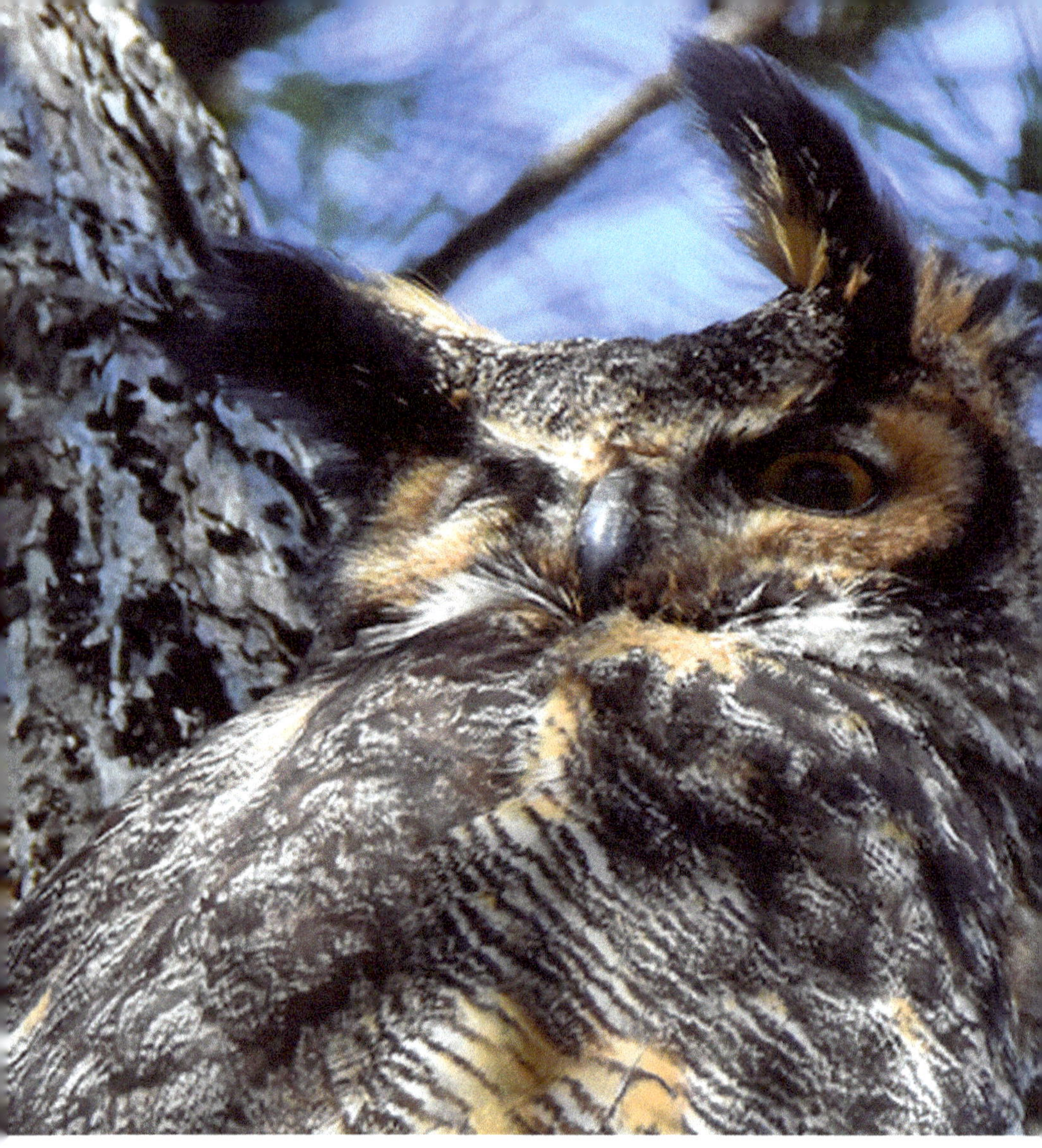

As expected, I didn't sleep too well the night of December 31. Ingrid and I had been planning my Maine Big Year since 2018, and the adrenalin was really pumping.

An hour before dawn, I headed out to Sprague Hall in Cape Elizabeth. A grange hall, it abuts hayfields where we have seen and heard owls over the years.

As I turned my black 2019 Subaru Crosstrek into the parking lot, I could hear a Great Horned Owl calling. To hear a bird, any bird, in a moving car with the windows rolled up is remarkable, clearly the owl was very close.

Hoo Hoo-Hoo Hoo Hoo

Hoo Hoo-Hoo Hoo Hoo

It was too dark to see him, but upon getting out of the car I could tell the Great Horned Owl was in a tree right above me.

Then, from across the road, a second owl, perhaps his mate called back:

Hoo Hoo-Hoo Hoo Hoo.

For the next twenty minutes I listened to the melodious duet:

Hoo Hoo-Ho Hoo Hoo Hoo Hoo-Hoo Hoo Hoo"

Although I was unable to see the Great Horned Owls that morning, one rarely does, I was able to record their vocalization and that counts!

Throughout the rest of the year I observed and heard a number of other Great Horned Owls, including a pair of owlets at a Portland cemetery in May.

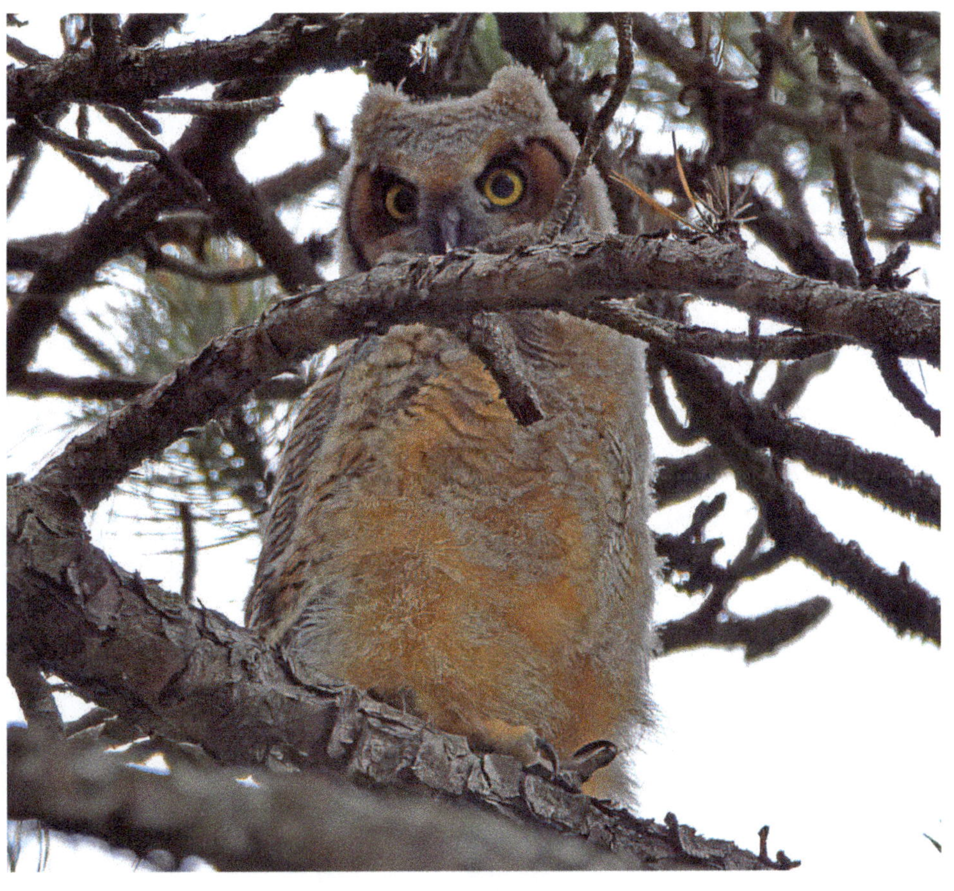

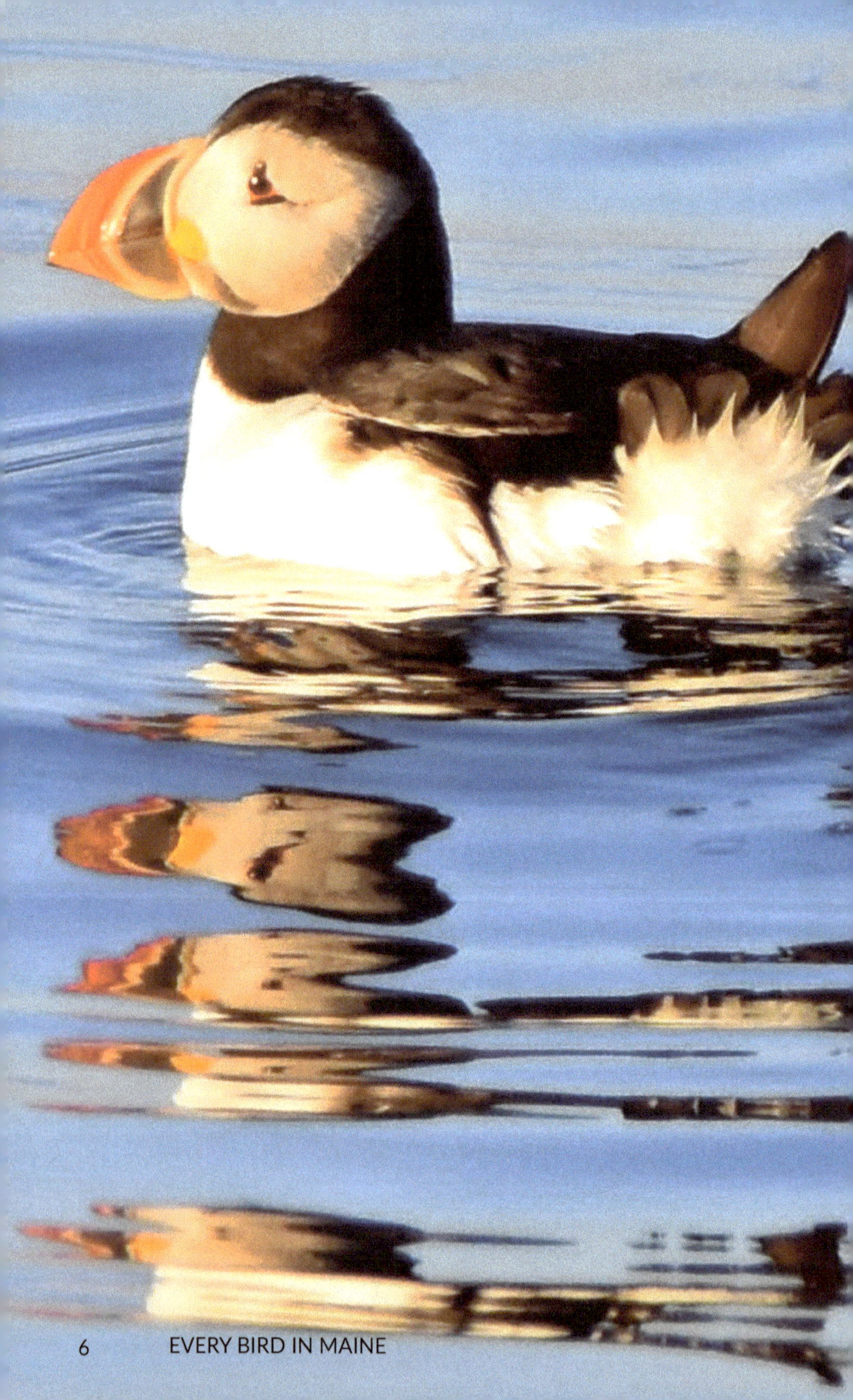

  EVERY BIRD IN MAINE

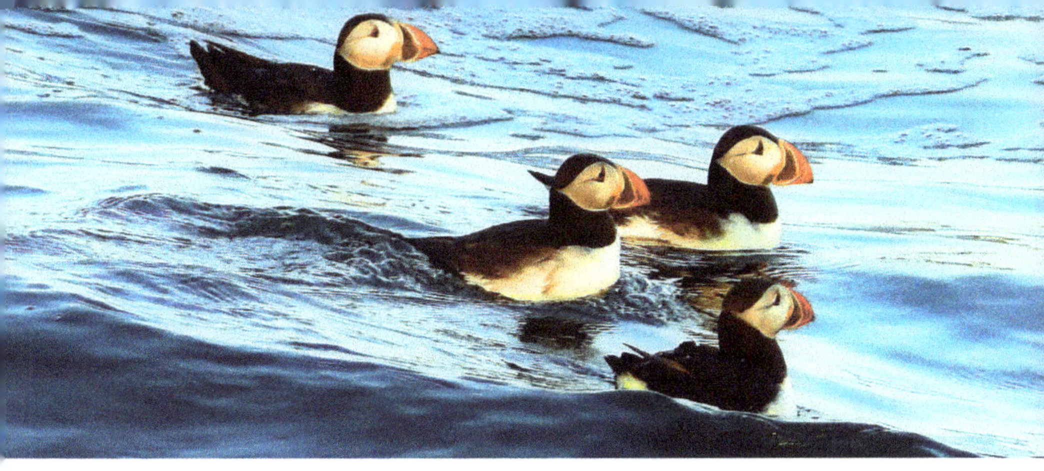

Alcids are ocean birds that fly both above and below the water.

While Maine boasts several Alcid species, the Atlantic Puffin is the star of the show.

Eastern Egg Rock was once home to a thriving Puffin colony, but by the 1880's egg hunters had completely eradicated the population.

In 1973, the Rockland based Project Puffin began transplanting young Atlantic Puffins from Newfoundland to Eastern Egg Rock. By 1981, a small number of Puffins began

nesting there. Today, approximately 200 pairs breed on the island, a world renowned seabird recovery success, and one of Maine's more unique tourist attractions.

Atlantic Puffin (February 21)

Alcids

During my Maine Big Year, Ingrid and I made numerous trips to the Puffin sanctuary on Eastern Egg Rock as well as the other nesting islands at Matinicus Rock and Machias Seal Island. While we were never able to land and walk on the islands, we enjoyed watching these flying footballs as they carried mouthfuls of herring to the underground borrows where their young were maturing.

Atlantic Puffins fish by sight, swimming under water using their wings as paddles, almost flying.

Puffins can seize multiple fish in a single dive, holding the first ones with a muscular tongue while catching additional fish with a razor sharp bill.

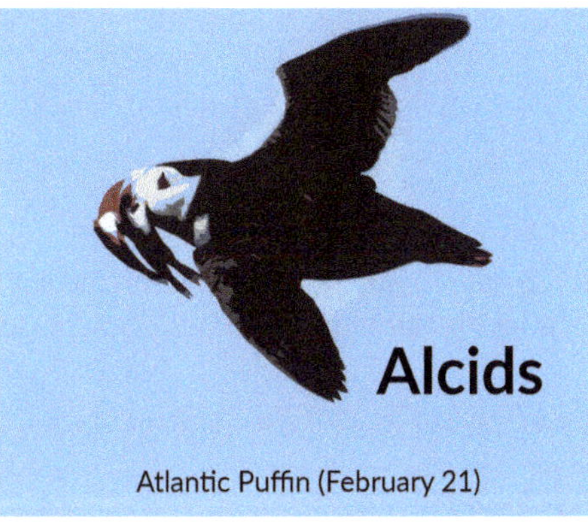

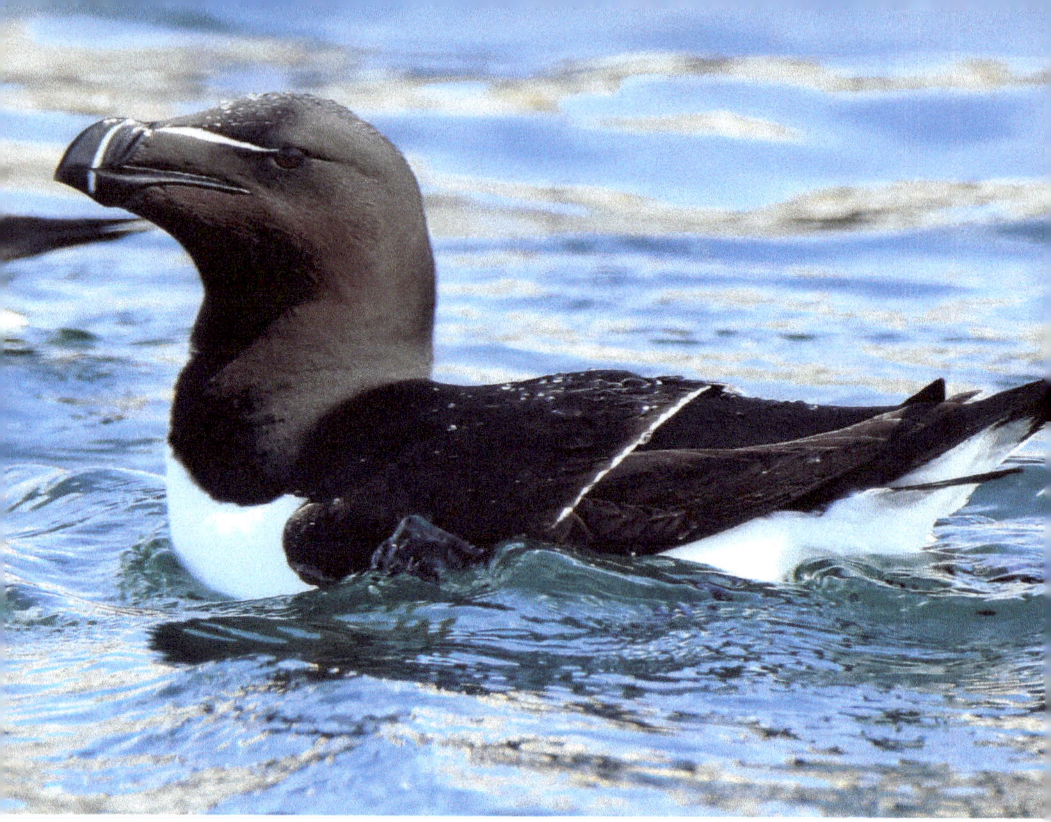

The Atlantic Puffin's white downy face turns ashen once the breeding season is over. This can be quite surprising when one comes upon a Puffin with a 5-o'clock shadow during the winter.

While other Maine Alcid species are not as cute and entertaining as the Atlantic Puffin, they are no less interesting and beautiful in their own way. No one looks better dressed for a formal event than a Razorbill in breeding plumage.

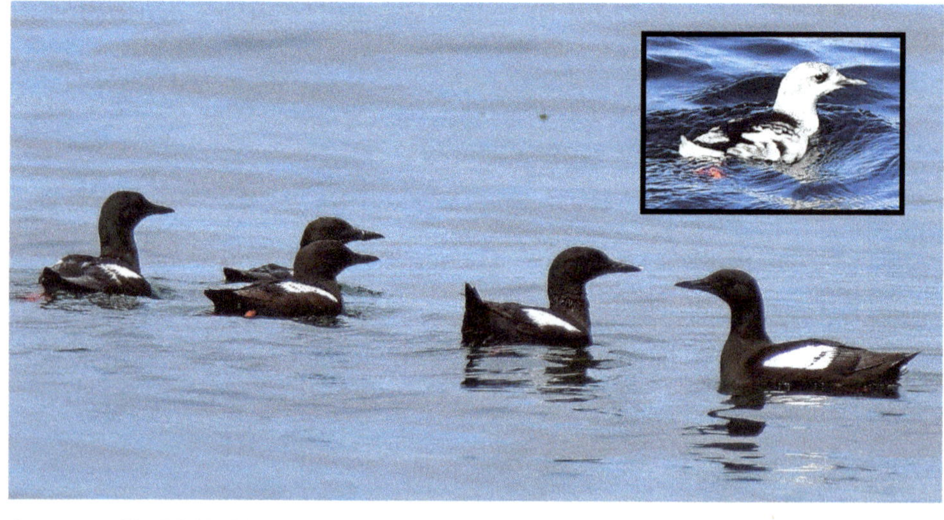

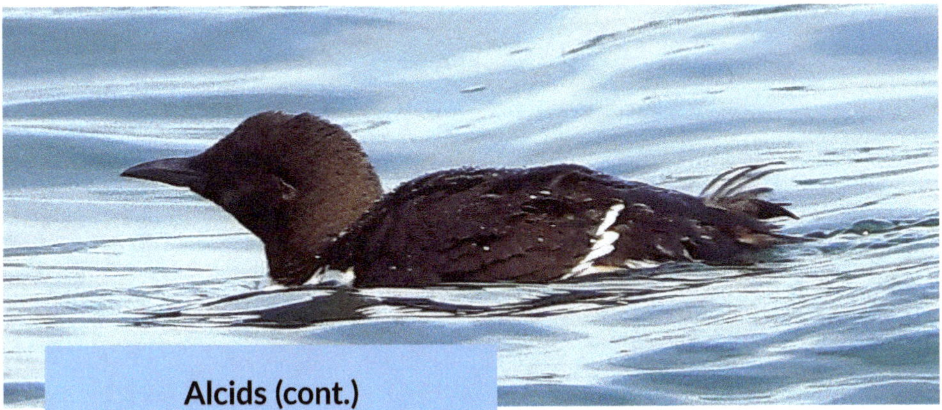

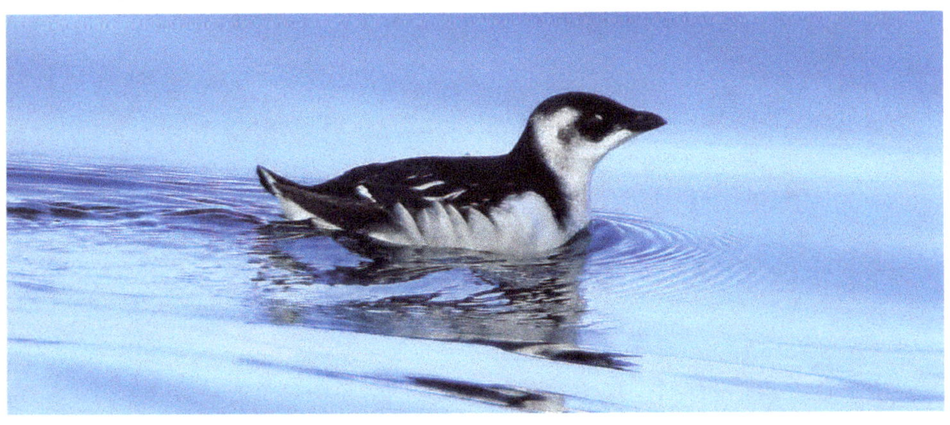

Alcids (cont.)

CLOCKWISE FROM TOP LEFT
Razorbill (January 4)
Thick-billed Murre (January 15)
Common Murre (January 13)
Dovekie (January 13)
Black Guillemot (Breeding)
INSET Black Guillemot (January 1)

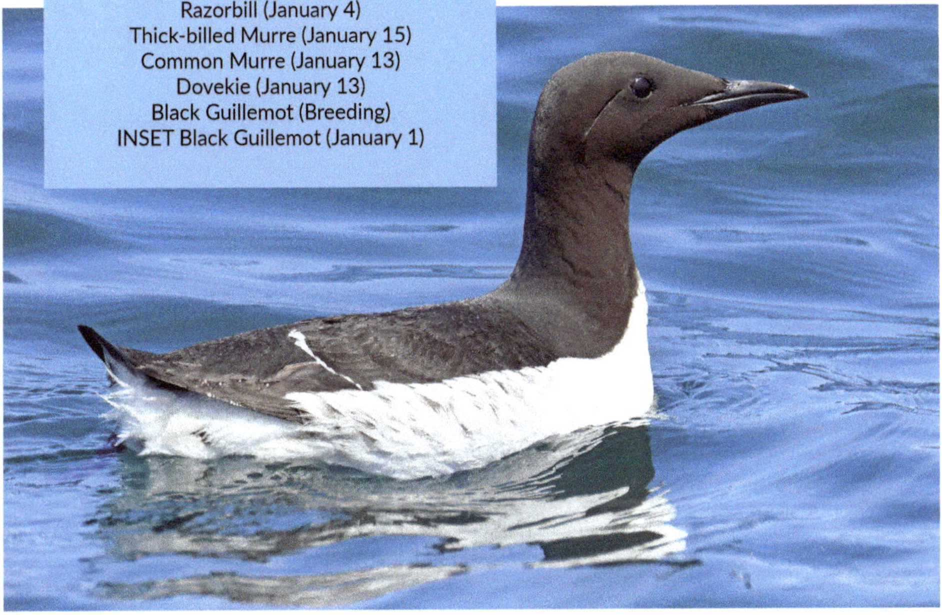

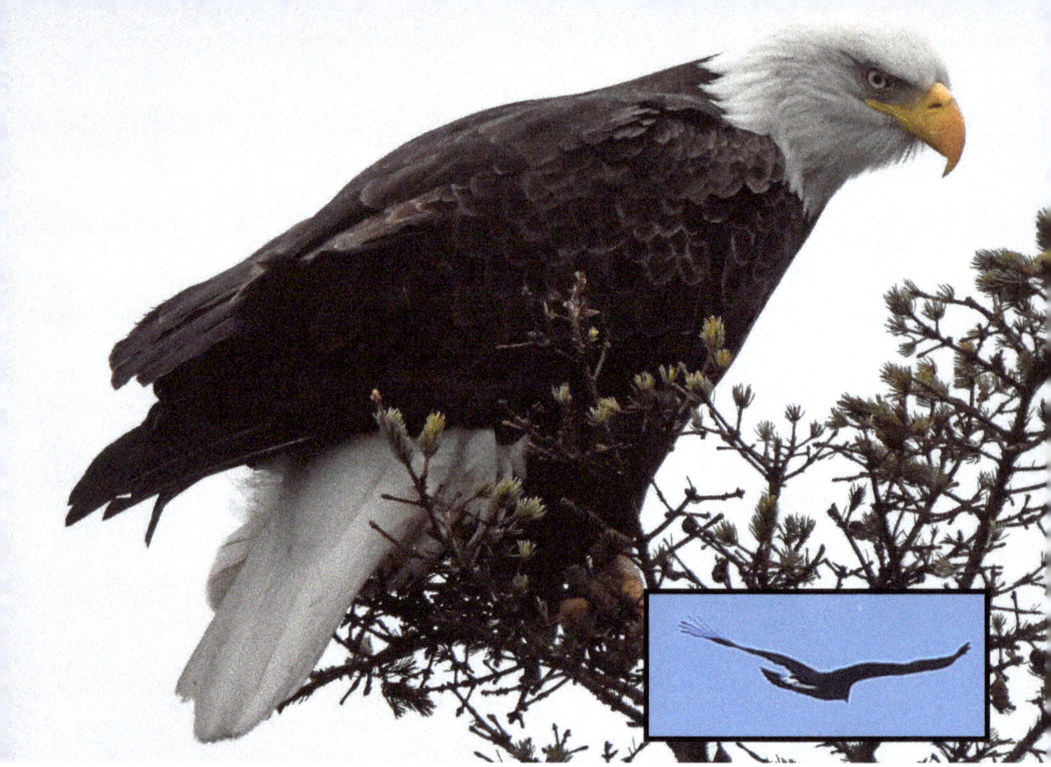

Living along the coast, we see lots of Bald Eagles, especially during the winter.

Eagles nest near rivers and lakes all over the state of Maine, but they need open water to find the fish they require to survive.

When the lakes freeze over, eagles move to the coast, often taking up residence in Osprey nests abandoned for the winter.

One of my greatest birding thrills has been watching returning Ospreys drive much bigger Bald Eagles away. Repeated attacks and parries take place, often over several days, until the Eagles give up and move on.

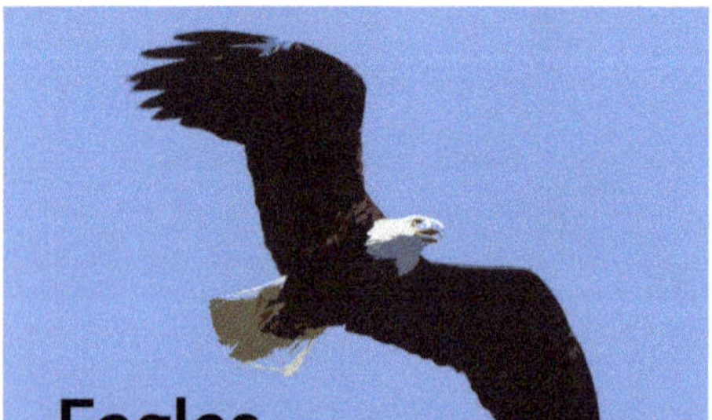

TOP Bald Eagle (January 4)
INSET Golden Eagle (November 1)
RIGHT Steller's Sea Eagle (December 31)

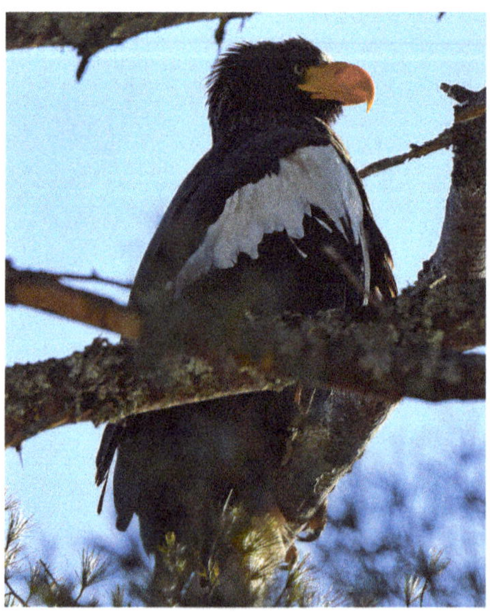

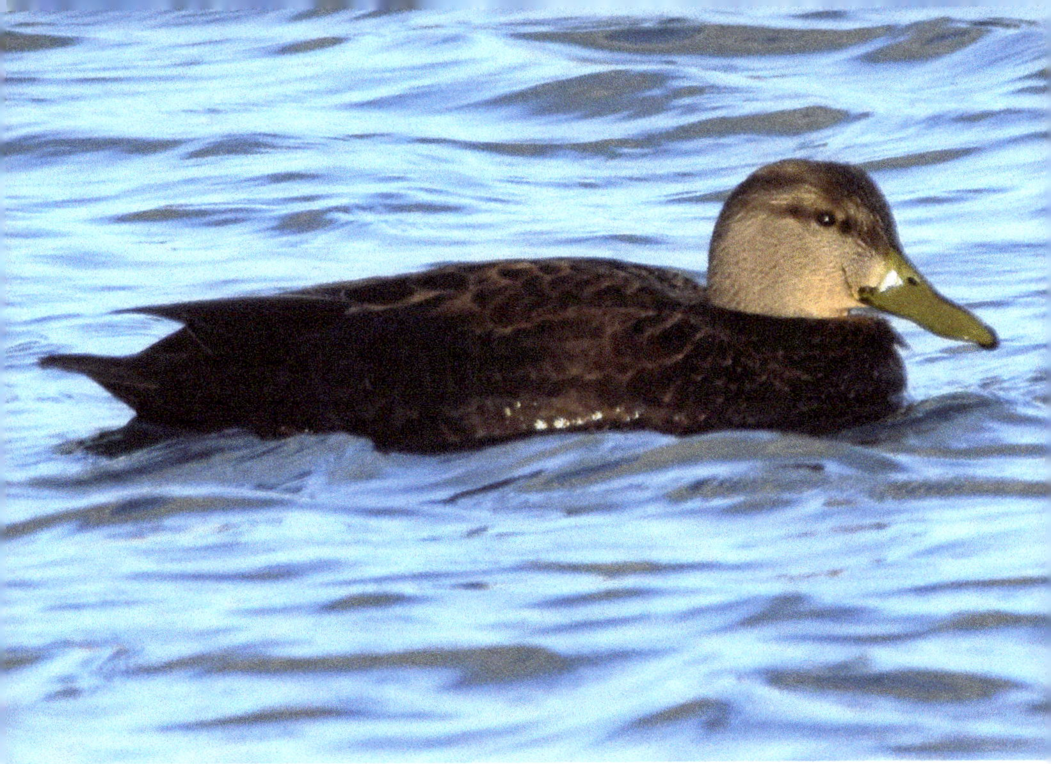

When I was a child, my mom read Robert McCloskey's *Make Way For Ducklings* to me at least once a week. I heard it so many times that I could re-cite the duckling's names "Jack, Kack, Lack, Mack, Nack, Ouack, Pack, and Quack", long before I could read their names.

And that was my complete knowledge of Ducks until I started exploring the rivers of Maine in my 30s.

I noticed the large white male ducks swimming with their brown mates.

I noticed tiny black and white ducks bobbing up and down in the water.

And I noticed a funny red-headed duck with a brush back haircut reminiscent of an army drill sergeant.

After I became a birder I learned that the large ducks were Common Eiders; the tiny bobbers were Buffleheads; and the brush cut was a Red-breasted Merganser.

I had just scratched the surface.

While Mallards are still Maine's most prevalent duck, the American Black Duck is closely related and also found in great numbers.

Mergansers are diving ducks that have tiny teeth along the edges of their bills which helps them grasp fish, frogs and salamanders.

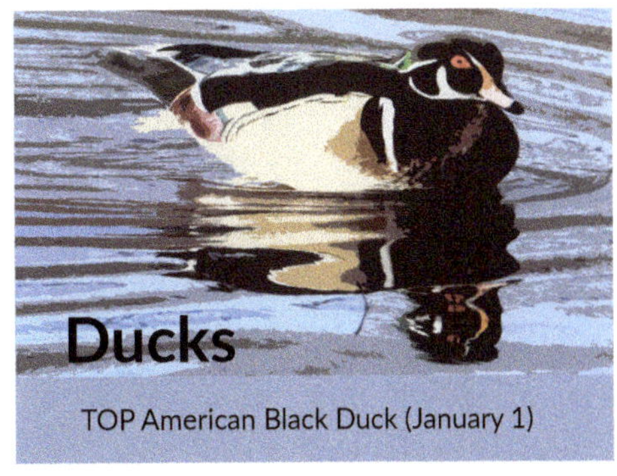

TOP American Black Duck (January 1)

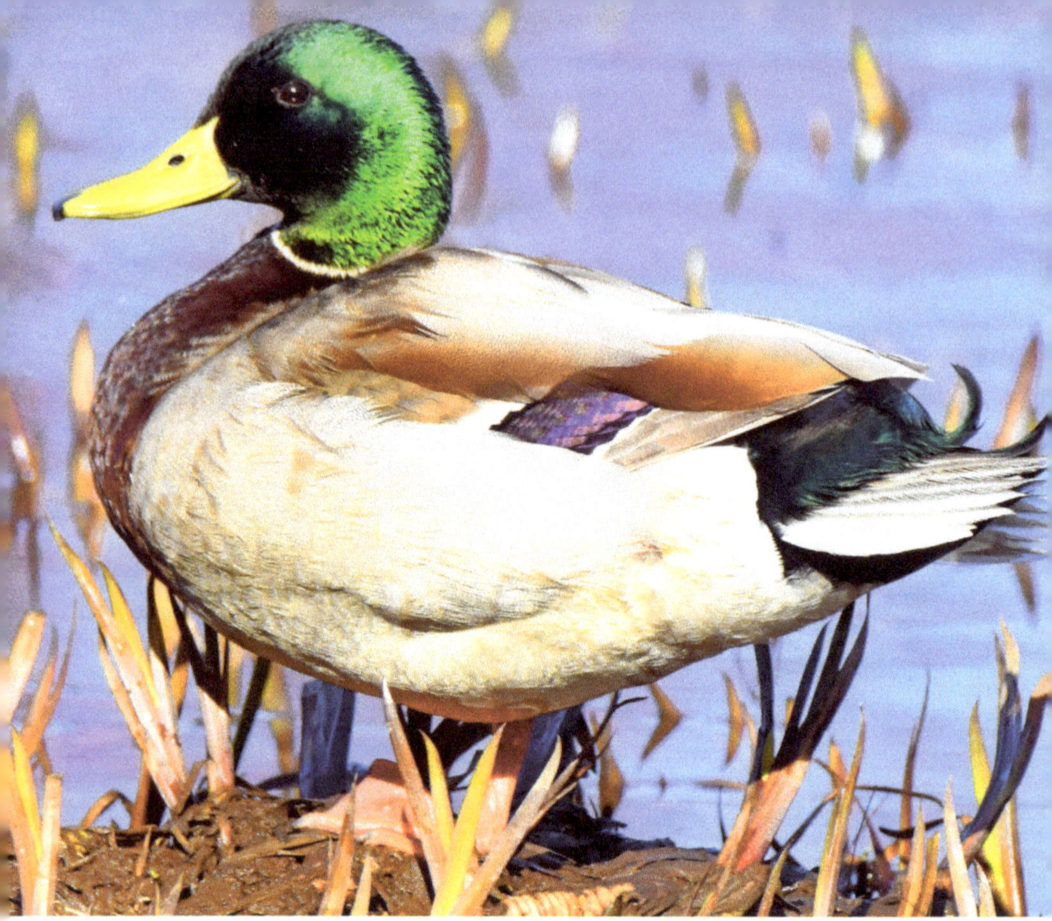

The smallest of these is the Hooded Merganser or "Hoodie" for slang.

Hoodies are Ingrid's favorite Maine duck, and we are thrilled when they return each fall to share the winter with us.

The biggest and ironically least common is the Common Merganser. Common Mergansers love fresh water and have black heads and necks with an

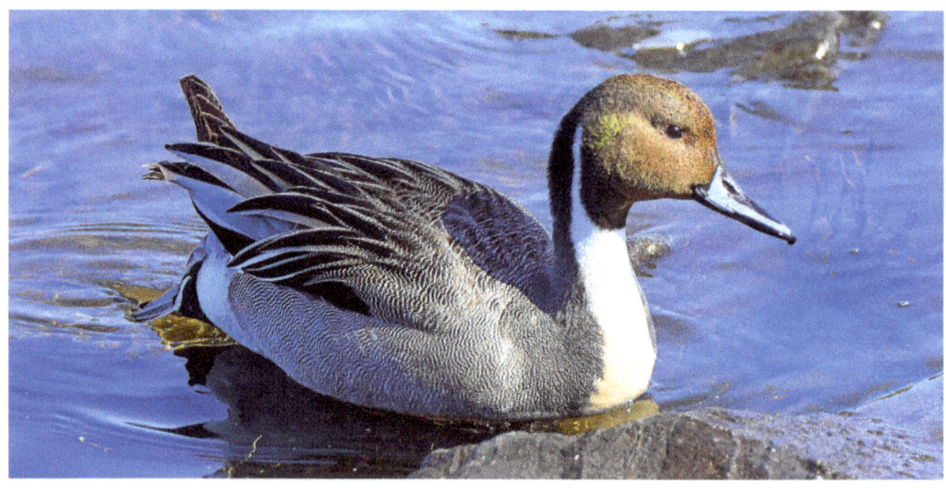

iridescent green gloss. The rest of their bodies are white and black, an absolutely stunning bird.

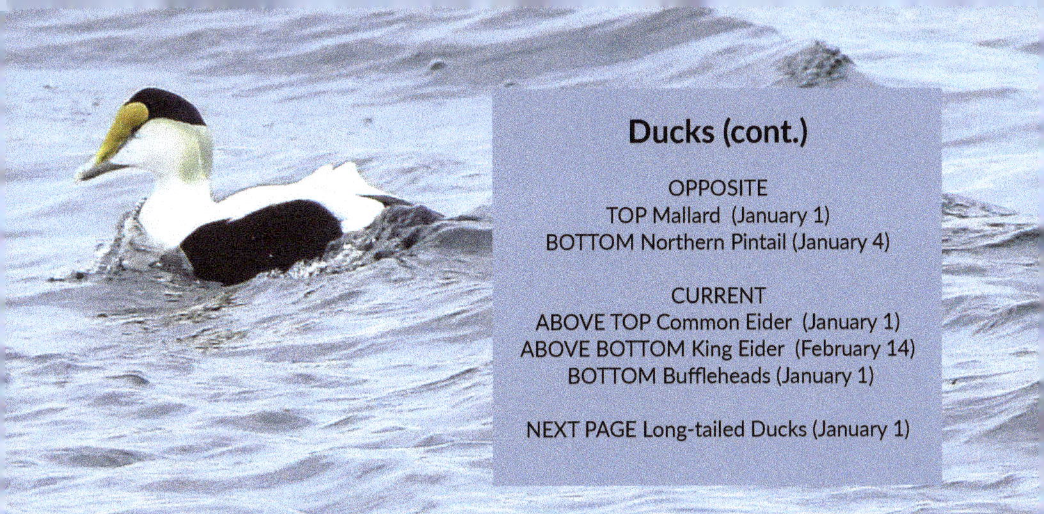

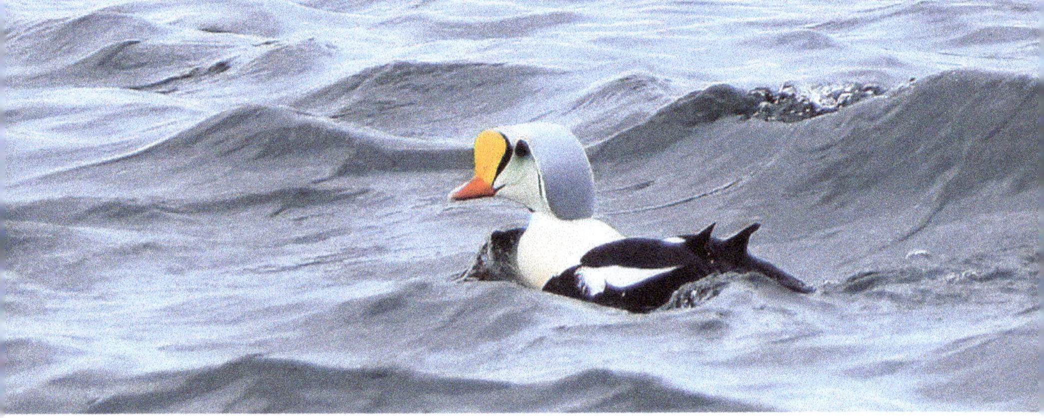

The Long-tailed Duck is a rather goofy looking sea bird. The male Long-tail has a pink bill, white cap, brown face and a (you guessed it) Long Tail!

Prior to the turn of the century, the Long-Tailed Duck's official name was "Old Squaw", which is said to have been Sexist, Ageist and Racist all at the same time.

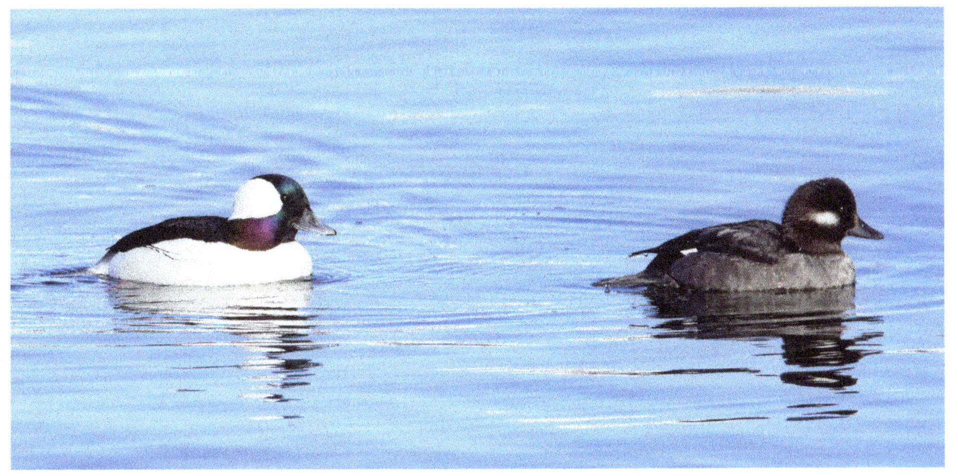

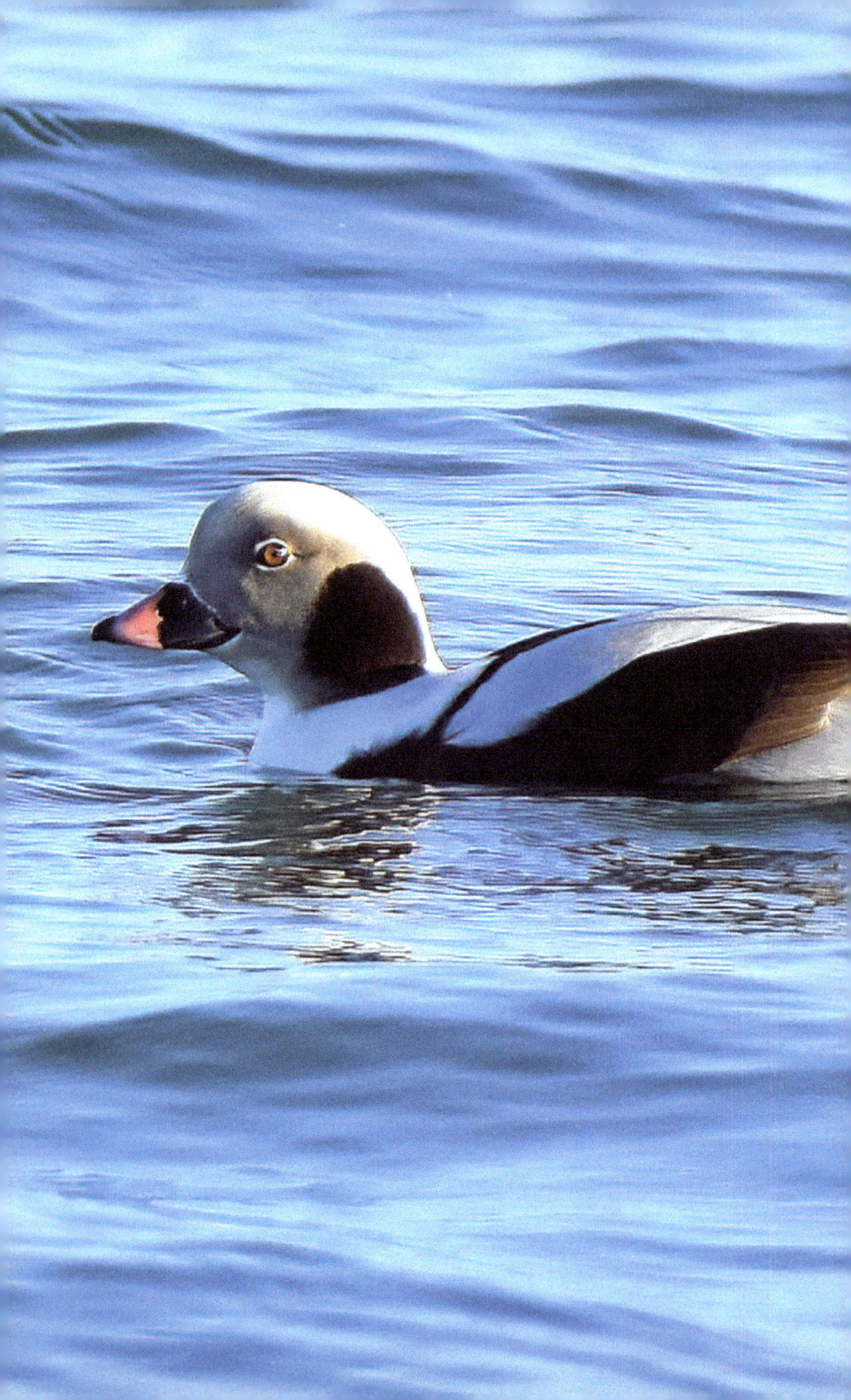

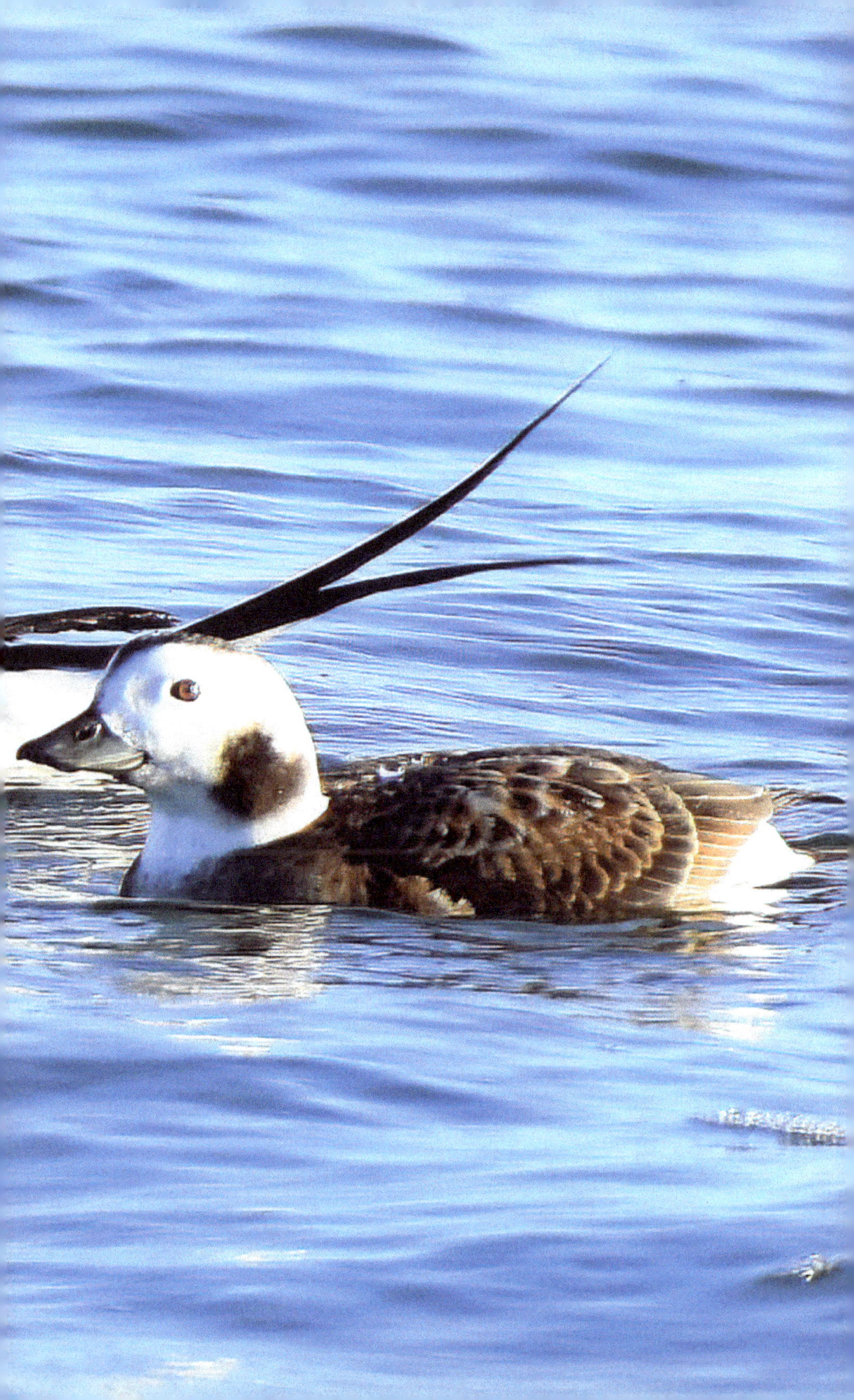

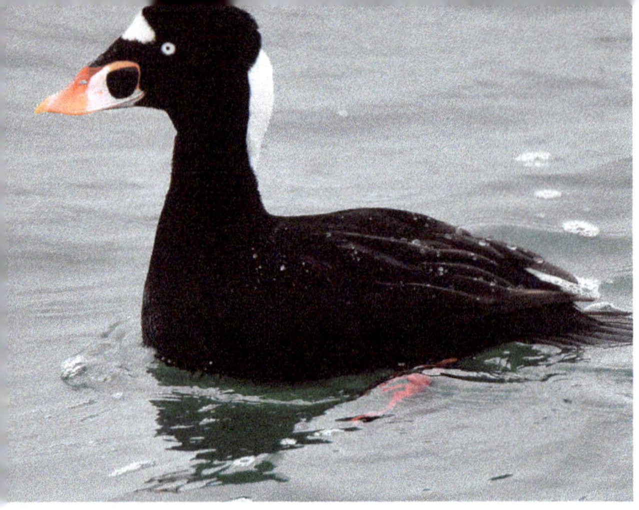

Ducks are divided into two different types, diving ducks and dabbling ducks. Dabblers feed primarily at the surface, often submerging their heads to get to vegetation. As you might expect, Divers swim beneath the surface to find mollusks, crustaceans, fish and shellfish.

One fascinating family of diving ducks is the stocky Scoters.

Often seen in winter near wave-rocked shorelines, scoters thrive in the maelstrom of waves and undercurrents.

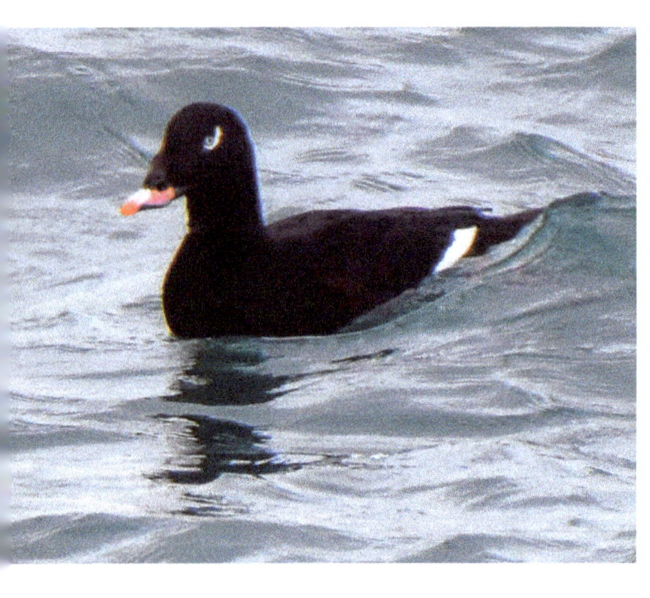

Scoters are great fun to watch as one is convinced they will be crushed against the rocks as each wave slams into an outcrop a few feet away.

A moment later the bird will pop up unharmed, often with a clam in it's mouth.

Mallard and Black Ducks, both dabblers, submerge their heads, necks and even upend themselves to find plant material to consume.

On occasion Mainers will see dabbling ducks feeding at the surface with just their bills submerged, stirring up and consuming organic material. These are the Teal.

Green-Winged and Blue-winged Teal, breed in small numbers in Maine, but for the most part we see them during migration.

While Green-winged Teal often

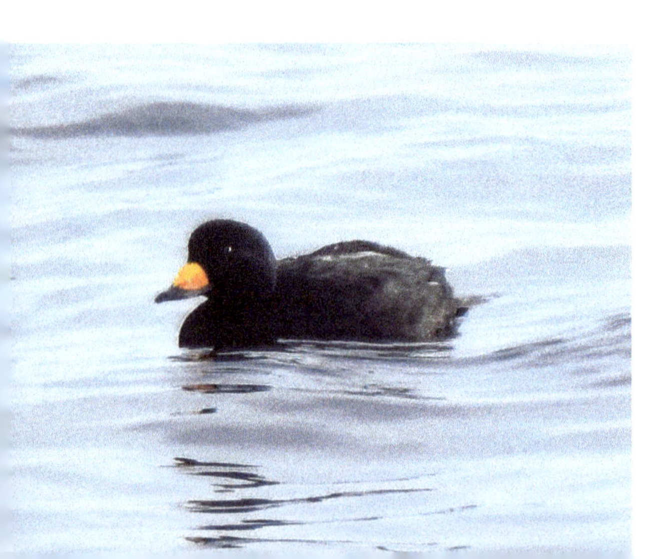

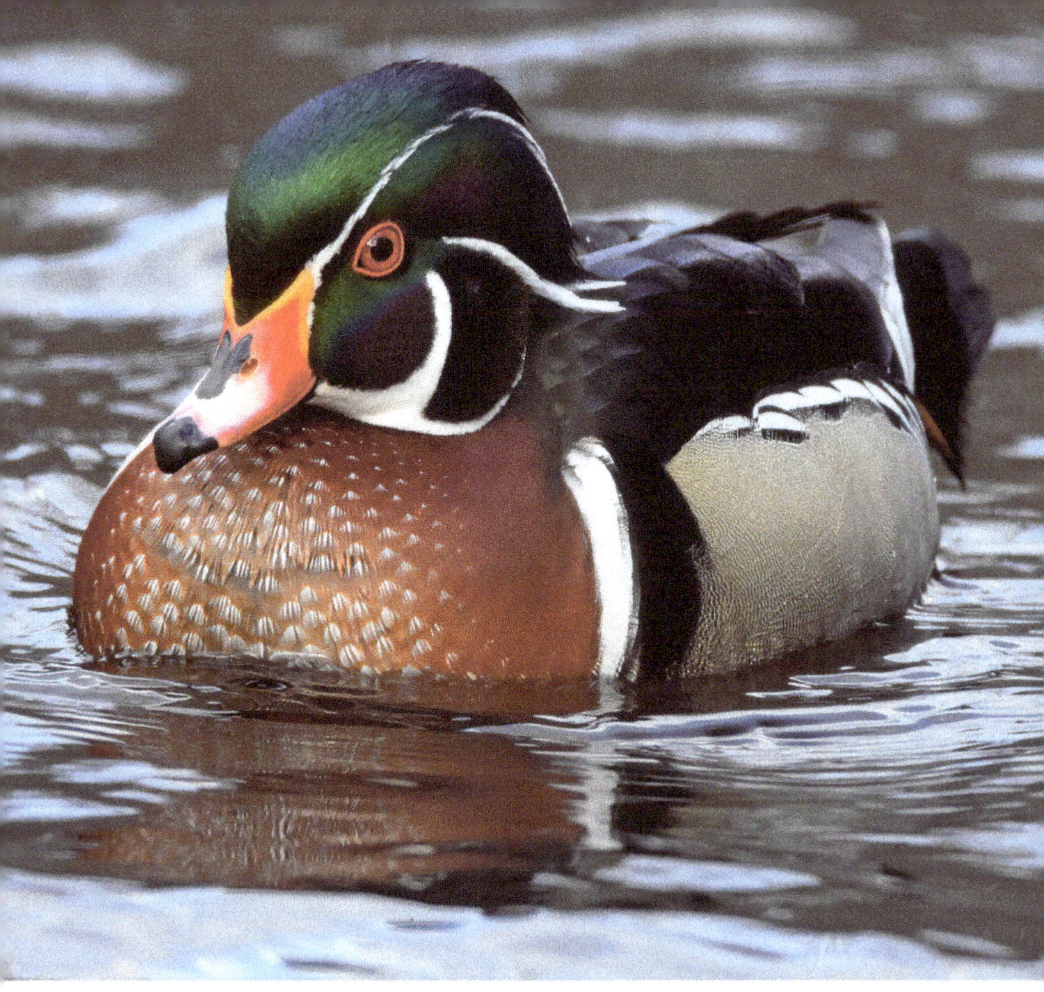

appear in flocks, I generally only see one or two Blue-winged Teal at a time.

Ring-necked Ducks are a poorly named but handsome duck. While they sport a narrow chestnut ring around the base of the neck, one has to have super powers to see it.

Instead, their most prominent feature is a bold blue and white ring at the end of the bill. It really should be called the "Ring-billed Duck".

Then there is the Harlequin Duck, a stunningly patterned sea duck seen along the coast in the winter. It is named after the brightly dressed character "Harlequin" from 16th century Italian comedies. A bit of an obscure reference in my opinion, but well deserved.

Ducks (cont.)

OPPOSITE
TOP Surf Scoter (January 2)
MIDDLE White-winged Scoter (Jan 1)
BOTTOM Black Scoter (January 1)

CURRENT
ABOVE Wood Duck (January 25)

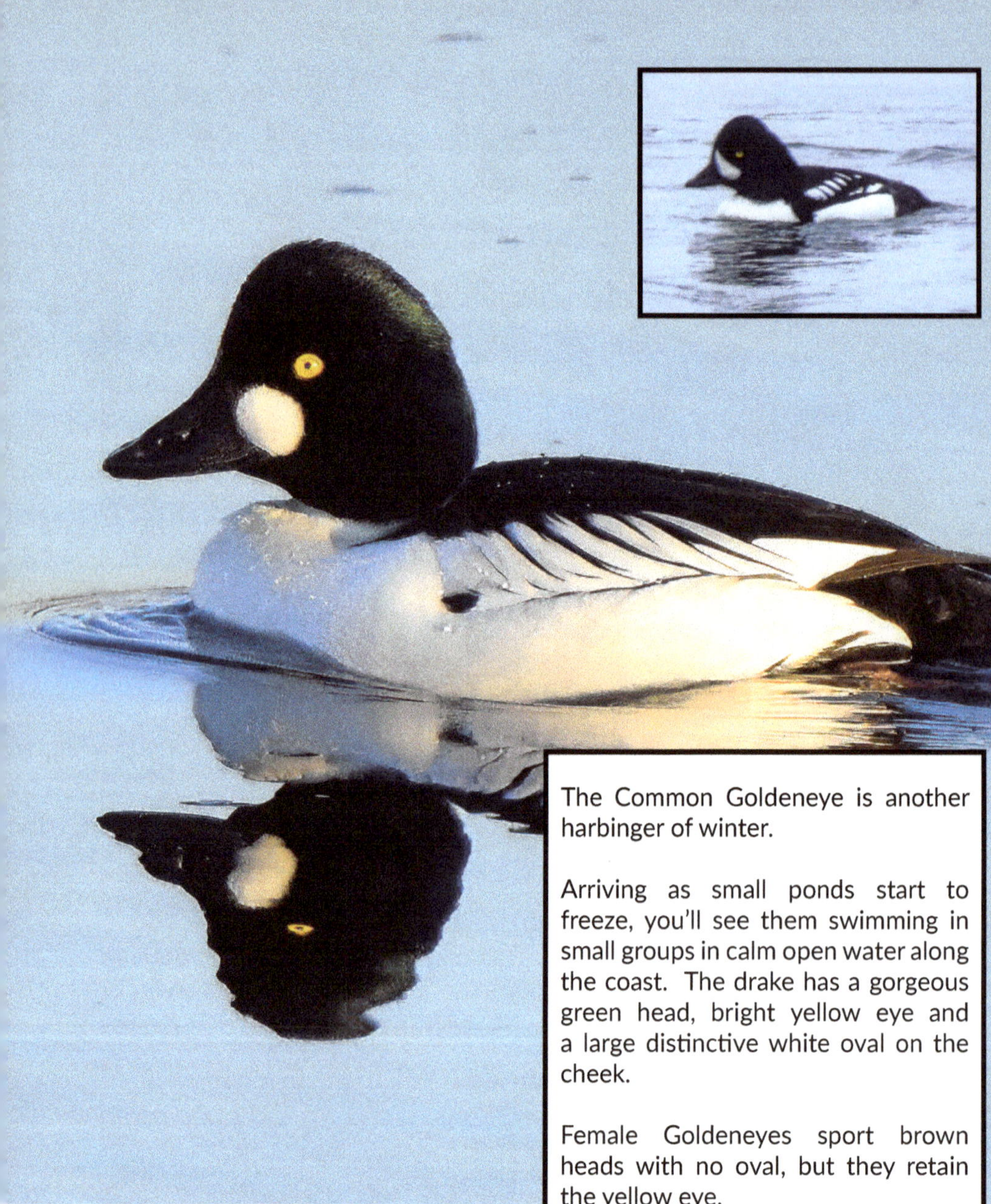

The Common Goldeneye is another harbinger of winter.

Arriving as small ponds start to freeze, you'll see them swimming in small groups in calm open water along the coast. The drake has a gorgeous green head, bright yellow eye and a large distinctive white oval on the cheek.

Female Goldeneyes sport brown heads with no oval, but they retain the yellow eye.

On occasion, one will be studying a raft of Common Goldeneyes (yes, a flock of ducks on the water is called a raft) and might notice a male Goldeneye with a white tear drop in place of the white spot. Consider yourself very lucky, you've found a rare Barrow's Goldeneye!!!

Ducks (cont.)

LEFT Common Goldeneye (January 2)
INSET Barrow's Goldeneye (January 8)

OPPOSITE
TOP Hooded Merganser (January 1)
MIDDLE Common Merganser (Jan 5)
BOTTOM Red-breasted Merganser (Jan 1)

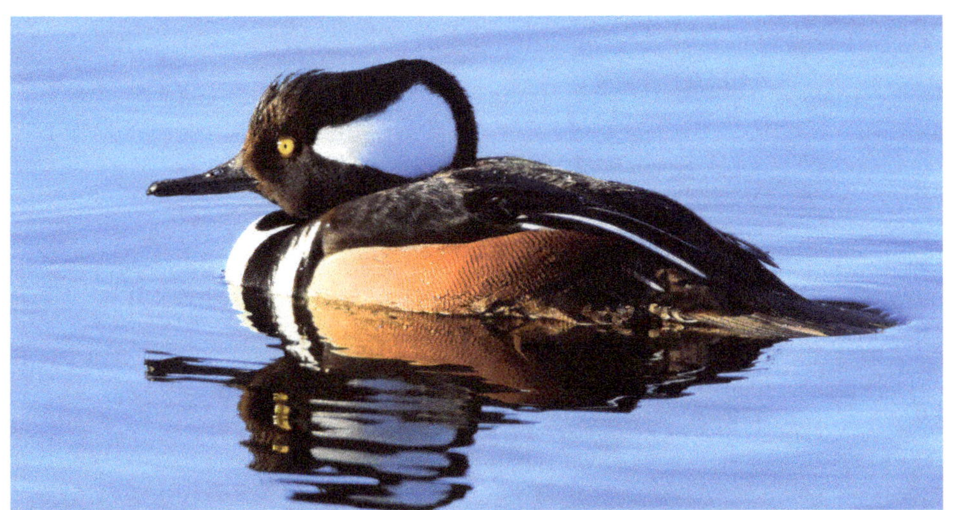

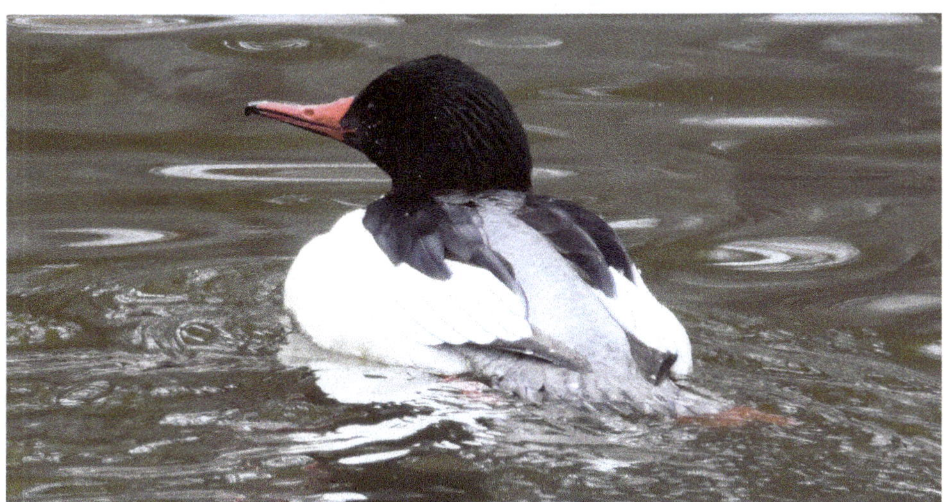

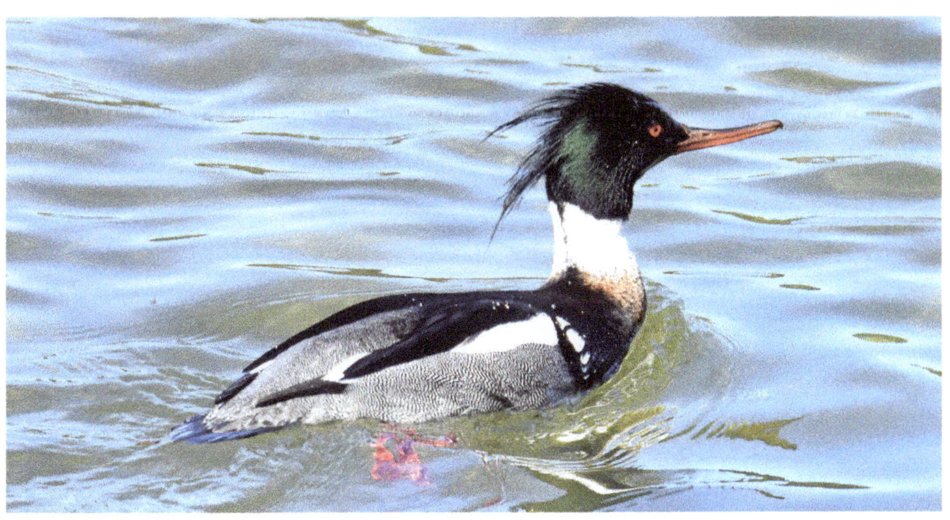

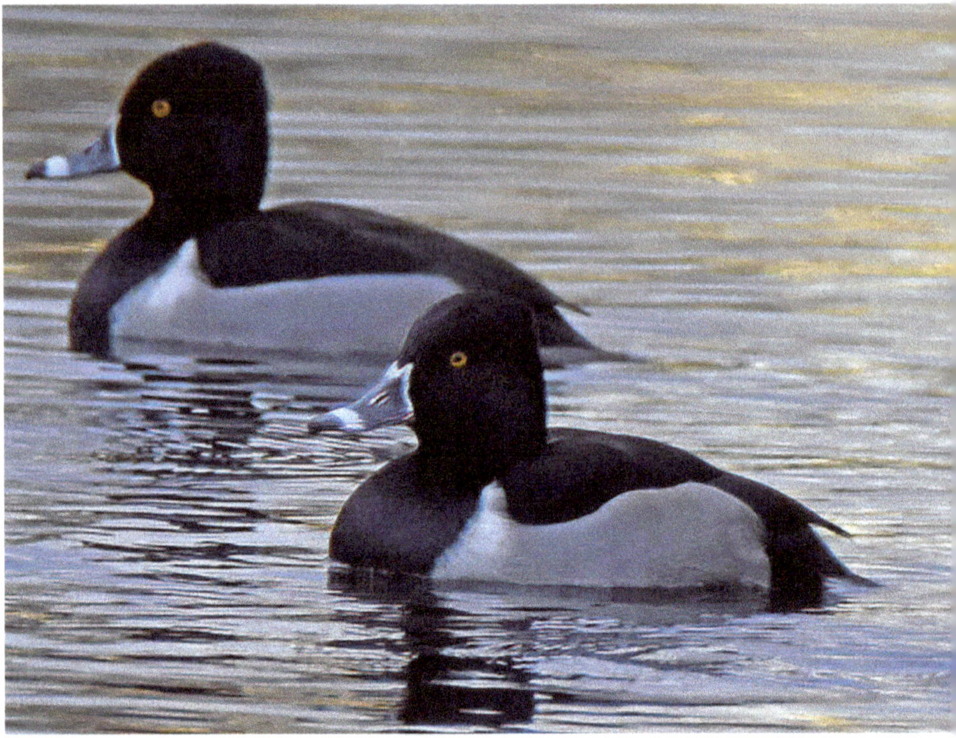

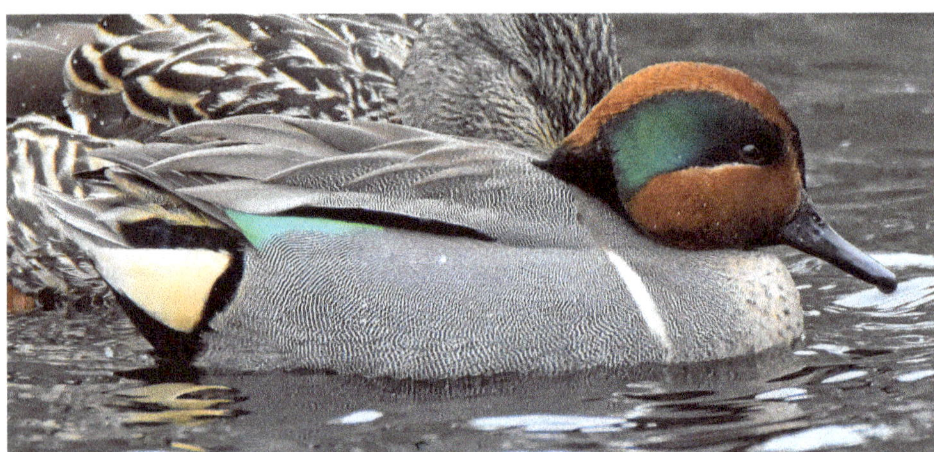

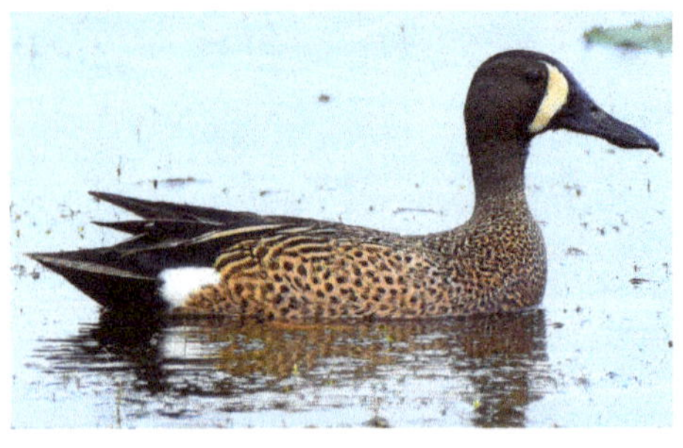

Ducks (cont.)

CLOCKWISE FROM TOP
Ring-necked Duck (January 7)
Harlequin Ducks (January 1)
Blue-winged Teal (April 1)
Green-winged Teal (January 4)

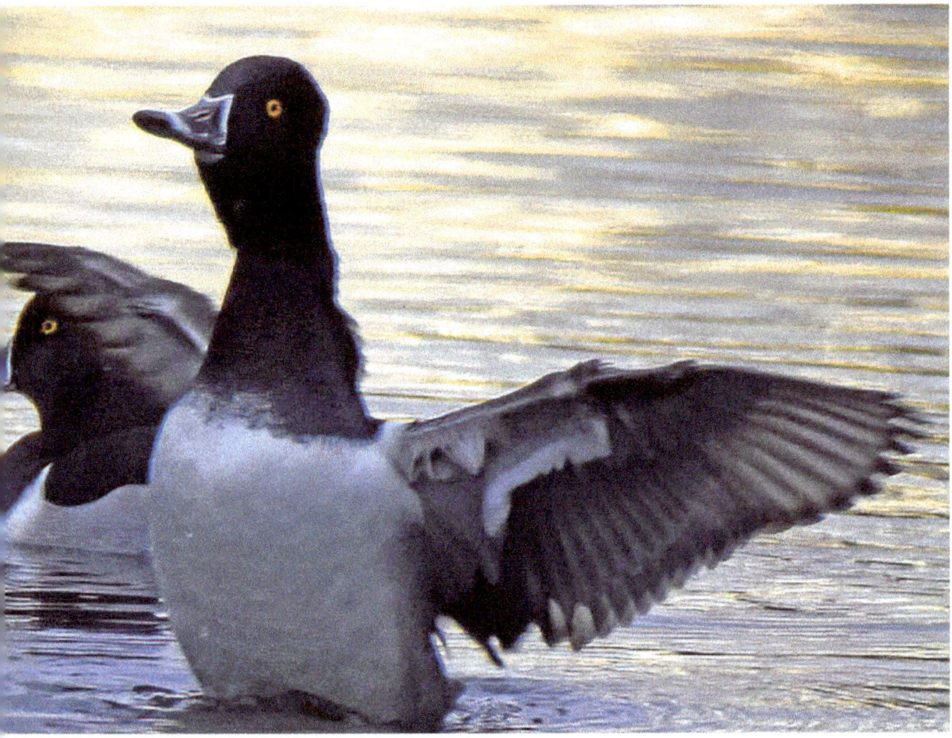

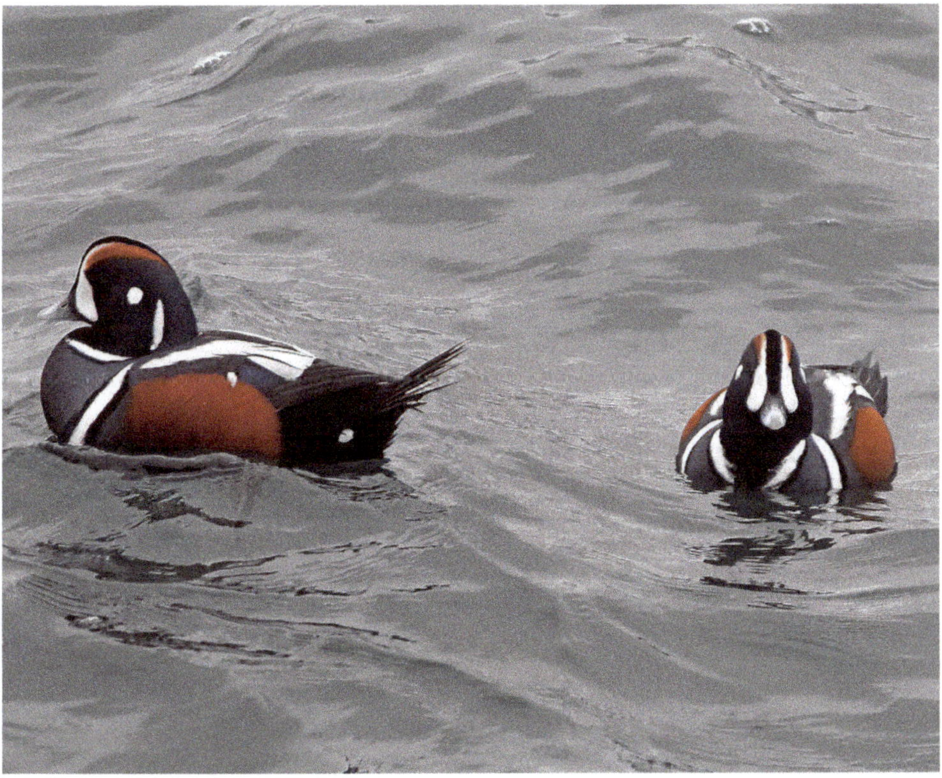

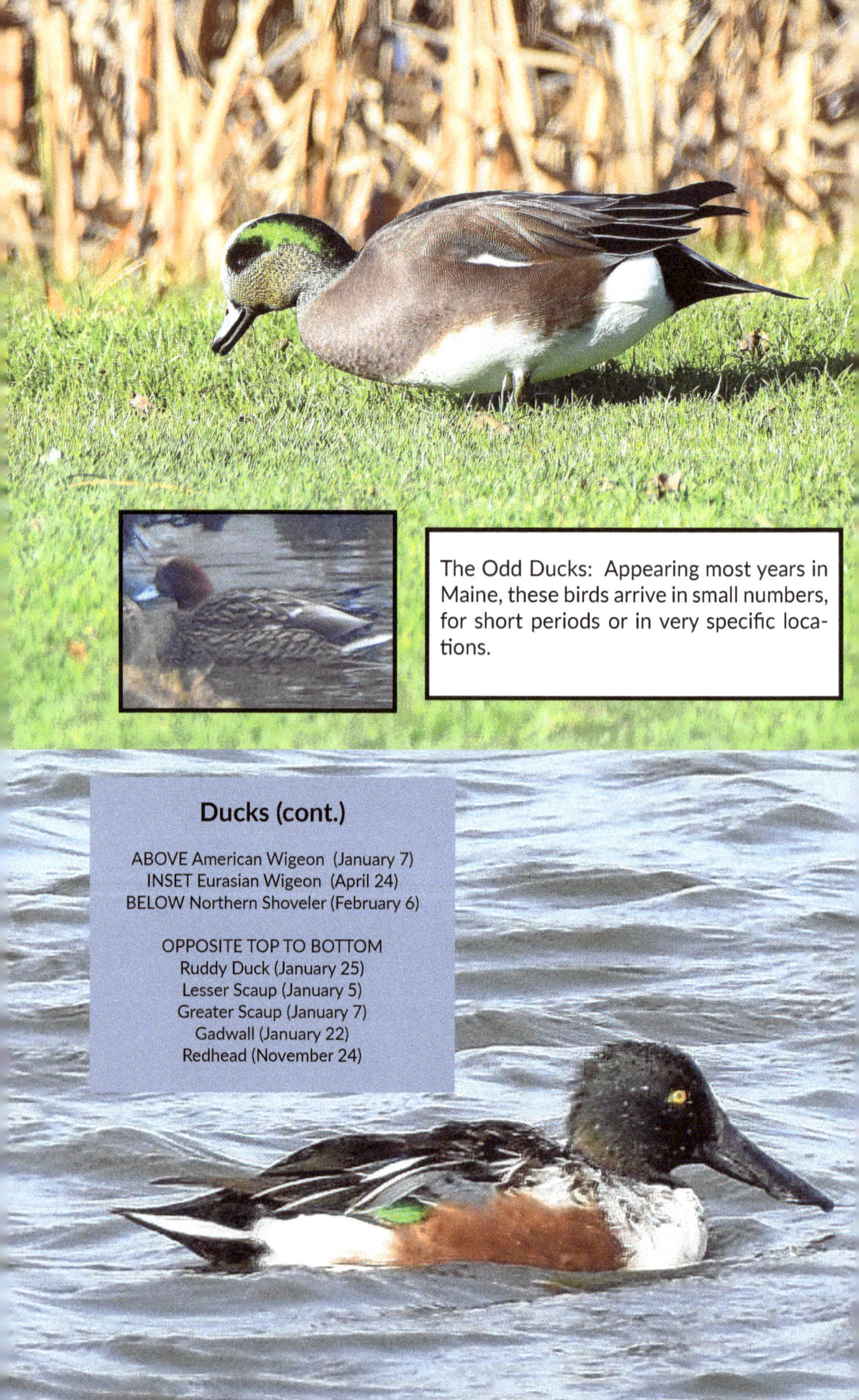

The Odd Ducks: Appearing most years in Maine, these birds arrive in small numbers, for short periods or in very specific locations.

Ducks (cont.)

ABOVE American Wigeon (January 7)
INSET Eurasian Wigeon (April 24)
BELOW Northern Shoveler (February 6)

OPPOSITE TOP TO BOTTOM
Ruddy Duck (January 25)
Lesser Scaup (January 5)
Greater Scaup (January 7)
Gadwall (January 22)
Redhead (November 24)

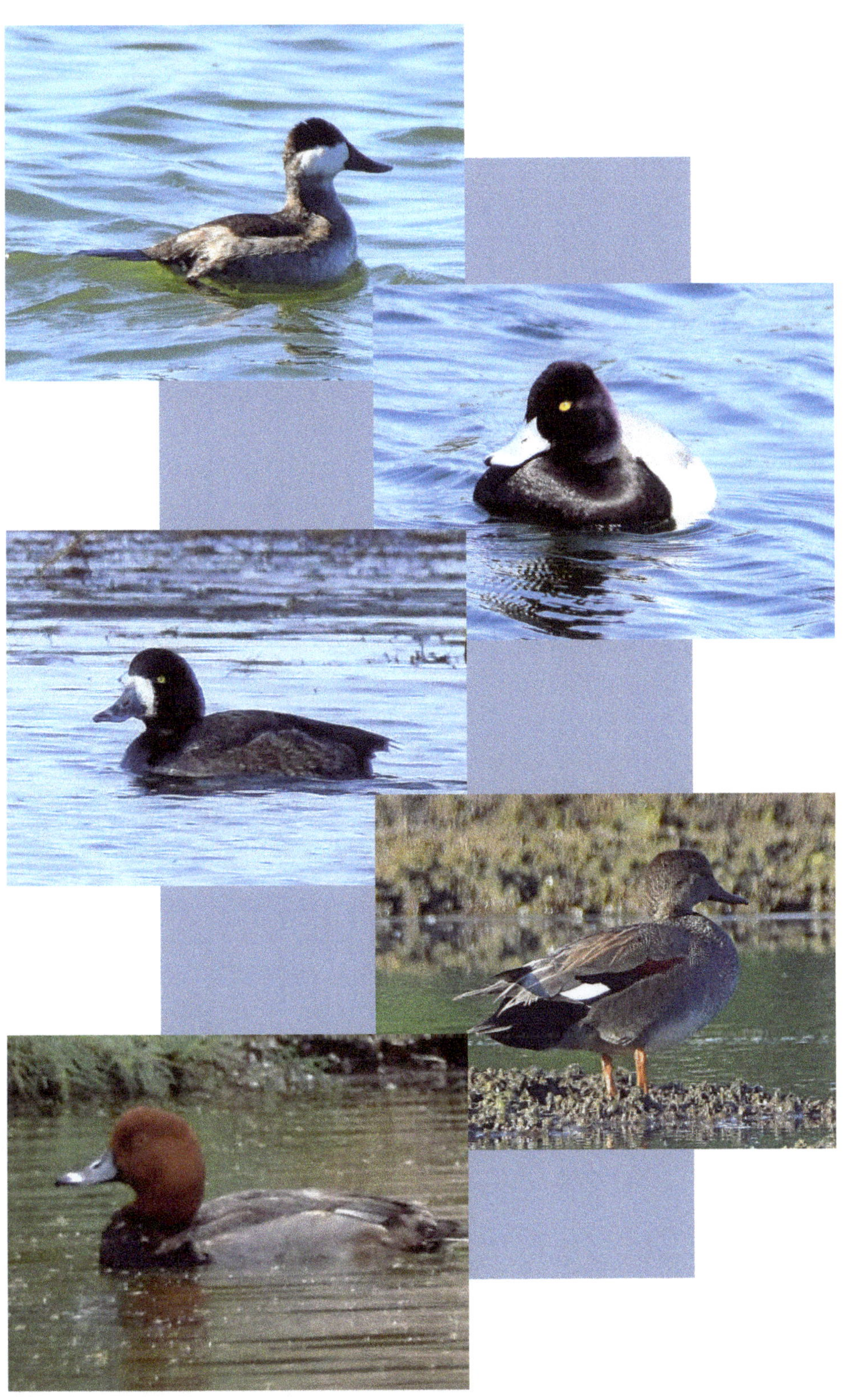

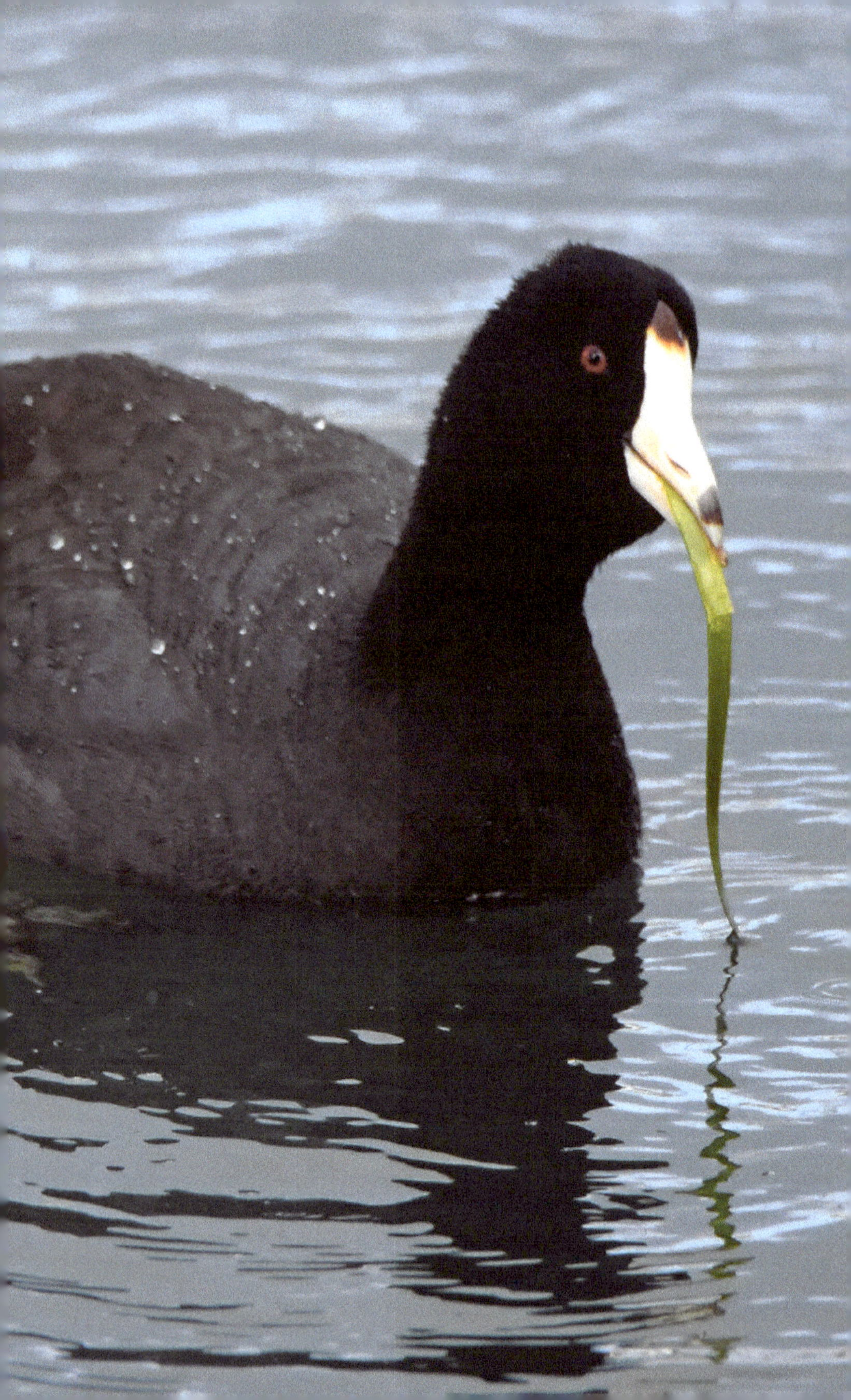

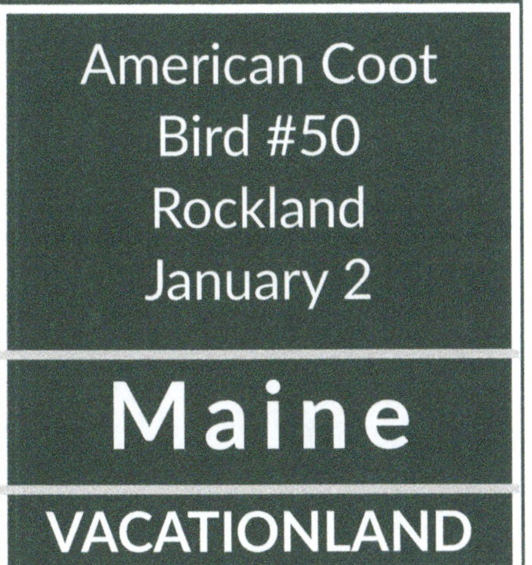

If you live in the western United States, you're probably familiar with the American Coot, a black, goofy looking duck-like bird. It nods its head as it swims, walks on land with large yellow feet sporting lobes along its toes, and makes a variety of clucks, grunts and cackles.

Each year, generally in the fall, a Coot or two will show up in Maine, birds migrating south that have gotten a bit off course.

When an American Coot was reported on the second day of my Maine Big Year along the Mid-coast, I jumped in the car and headed to Rockland.

The bird was reported feeding in an old quarry off of a dirt road. Unfortunately, natural berms coupled with high snow banks made the quarry invisible from the road. It was ridiculous how long it took me to find a great big hole in the ground filled with water.

Finally, after five minutes scanning with my binoculars, I found my quarry in the quarry. An American Coot was swimming along the edge of the distant ice.

Not a very satisfying view but countable and my first rare Maine bird of the Big Year.

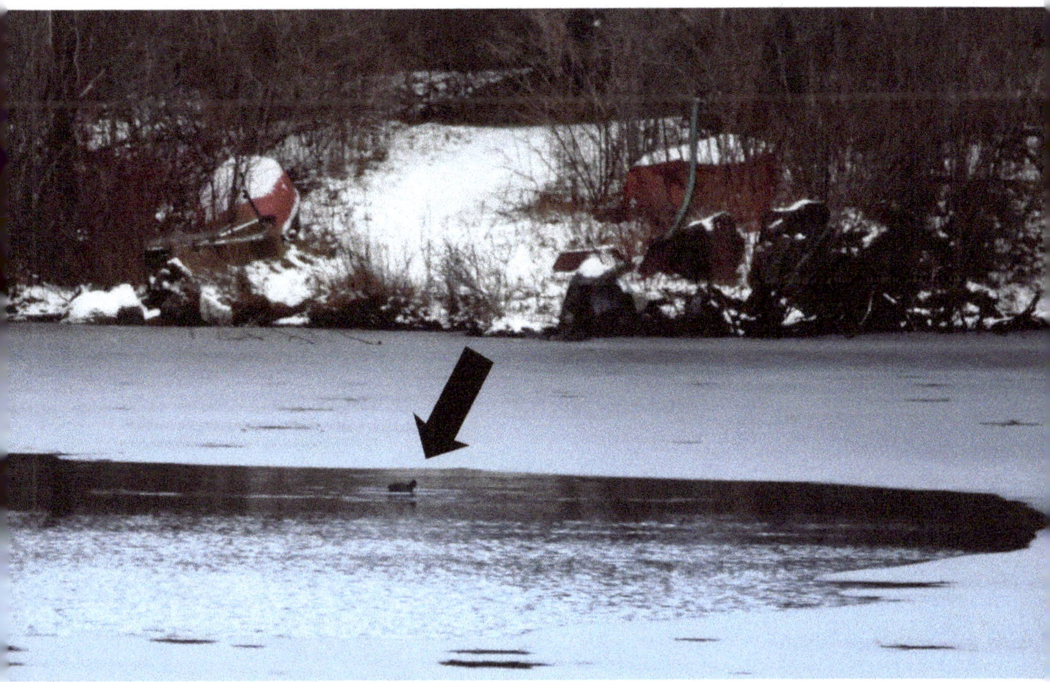

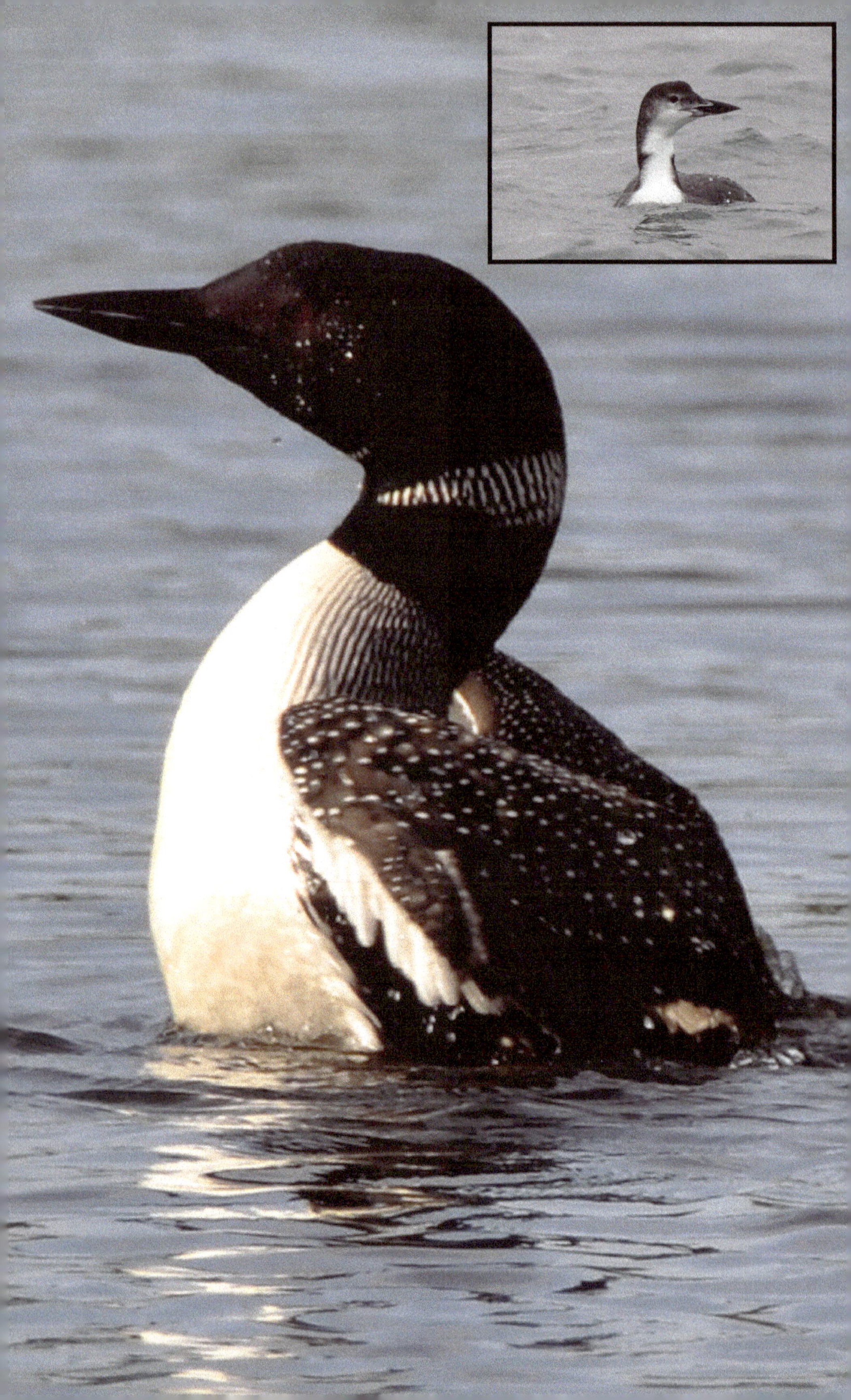

The call of the loon on a peaceful lake is a ubiquitous symbol of summer in Maine. The Common Loon, in its elegant summer plumage, adorns Maine license plates, tourist brochures, and t-shirts. The rest of the year it assumes a much less impressive, drab gray appearance.

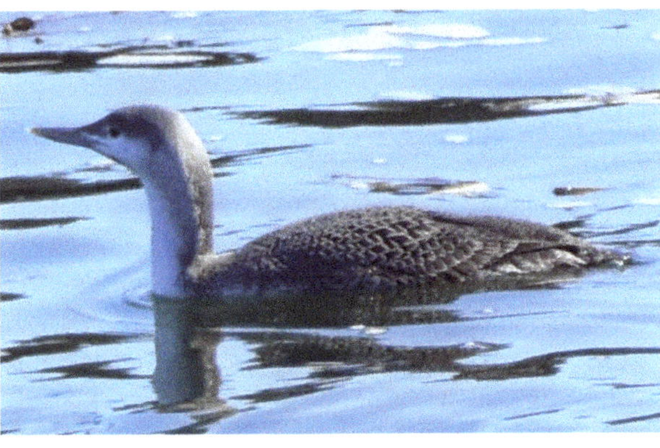

When Maine lakes and ponds begin to freeze, these "plain" loons move to the coast, spending winter on saltwater bays and harbors. In winter it's common to see two or three at a time floating on the river by our Mid-coast home. After sunset, we are occasionally treated to a loon calling, a truly eerie sound on a dark cold night.

During these cold months, a smaller, sleeker loon will occasionally surface near our dock. The Red-throated Loon is a somewhat rare along the coast but a regular visitor to Wiscasset.

In mid-October Ingrid and I piled onto a Boothbay Harbor Whale Watch boat with fifty other birders to look for deep

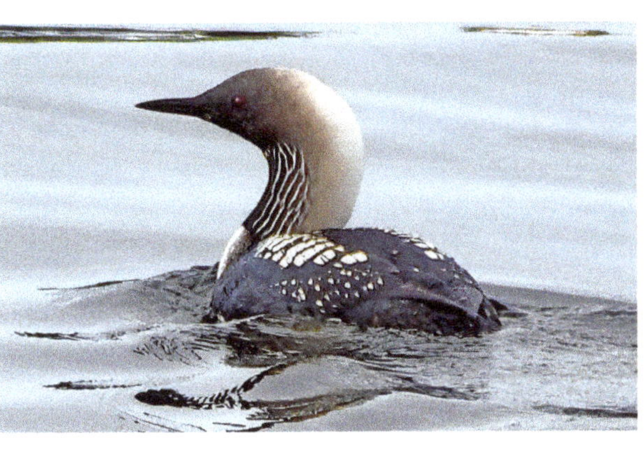

sea birds. We hadn't been moving for five minutes when the boat erupted in excitement, a Pacific Loon was swimming right beside us, while we were still in the harbor.

A Pacific Loon, as you might imagine does not belong in the Atlantic. However, every year a handful of these birds leave their Arctic breeding grounds and fly east instead of west. This particular Pacific Loon was still in its stunning breeding plumage, something I had never seen before.

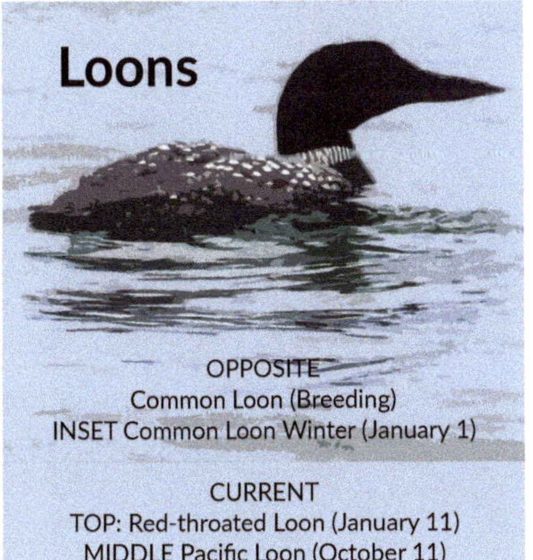

Loons

OPPOSITE
Common Loon (Breeding)
INSET Common Loon Winter (January 1)

CURRENT
TOP: Red-throated Loon (January 11)
MIDDLE Pacific Loon (October 11)

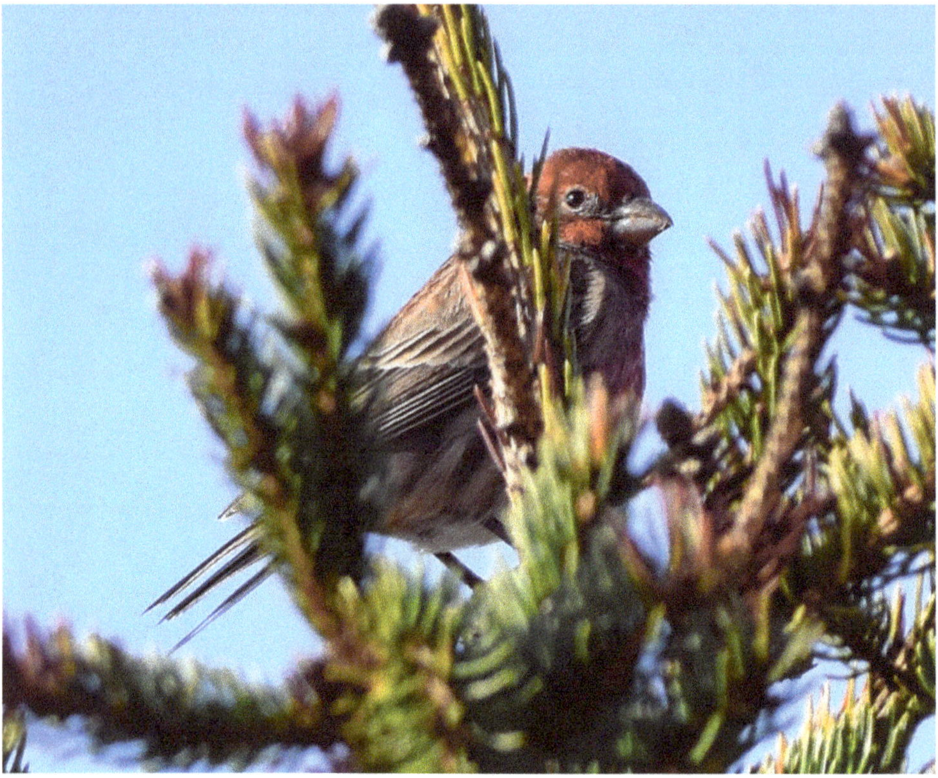

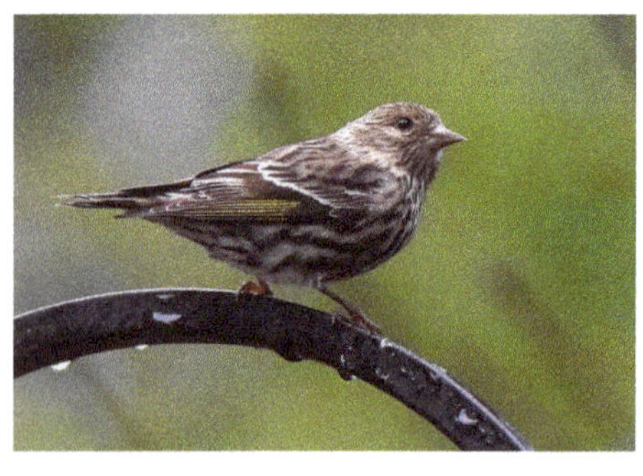

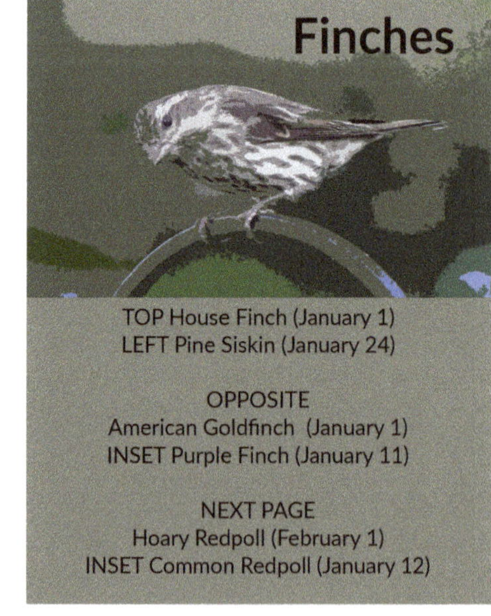

TOP House Finch (January 1)
LEFT Pine Siskin (January 24)

OPPOSITE
American Goldfinch (January 1)
INSET Purple Finch (January 11)

NEXT PAGE
Hoary Redpoll (February 1)
INSET Common Redpoll (January 12)

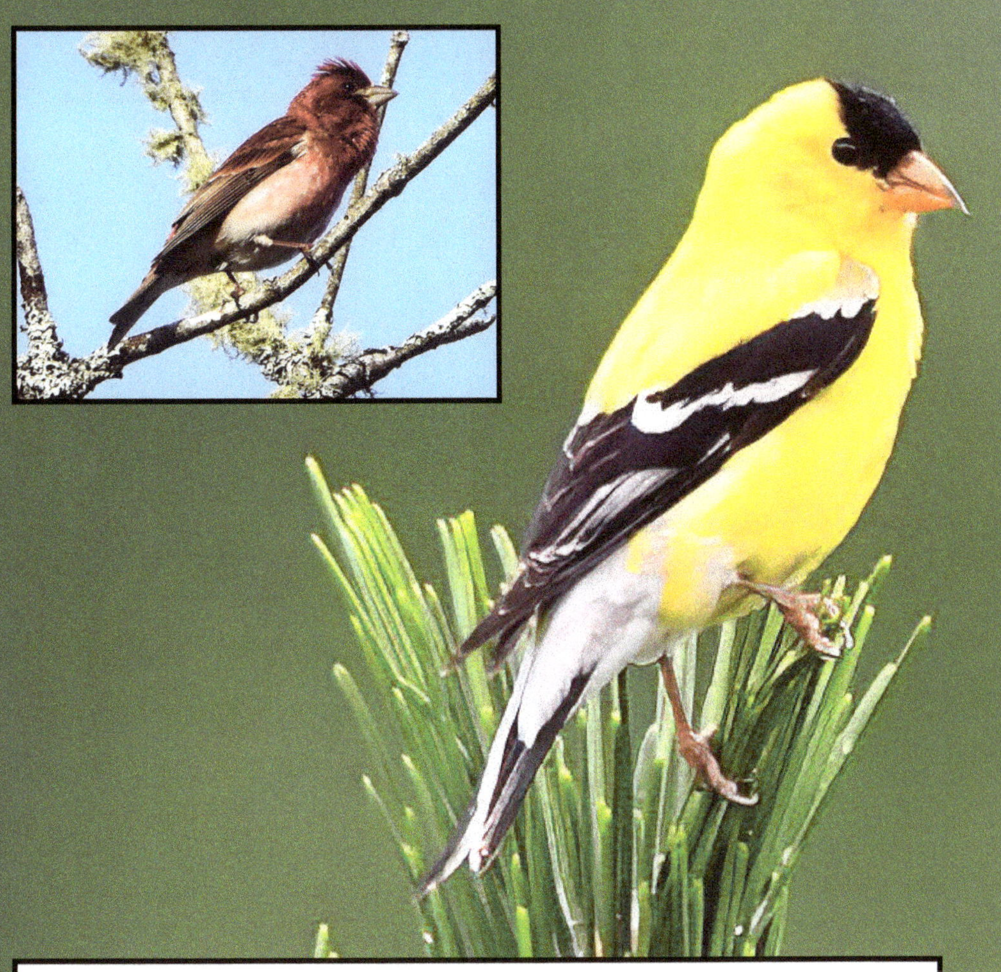

If you feed birds in Maine, every year you are guaranteed hundreds of American Gold-finches and a maybe few House Finches. Some years, that is all you will see.

Other years you may have Purple Finches, Pine Siskins, Redpolls, Grosbeaks, and Cross-bills.

Why the difference? Three words: CANADIAN SPRUCE CONES!!!

Each fall, the Winter Finch Report (by Tyler Hoar), discusses the abundance of spruce cone crops across the boreal forest in Ontario, Quebec, and Newfoundland. It is seized upon by birders as a predictor of the coming winter's Finches.

The number of cones at the top the trees in Canada's enormous Boreal Forest can fluctu-ate from year to year. In a poor cone year, birds will flock south looking for food and our feeders. This is commonly called an irruptive year. In a non-irruptive year, a good cone crop will keep the finches close to their breeding ground in Canada.

My Maine Big Year benefited by a record interruption year, over the 2020-2021 winter, with millions of Finches, Pine Siskins, Redpolls and related species flooding into Maine and parts south. This is sometimes called a "Superflight Year."

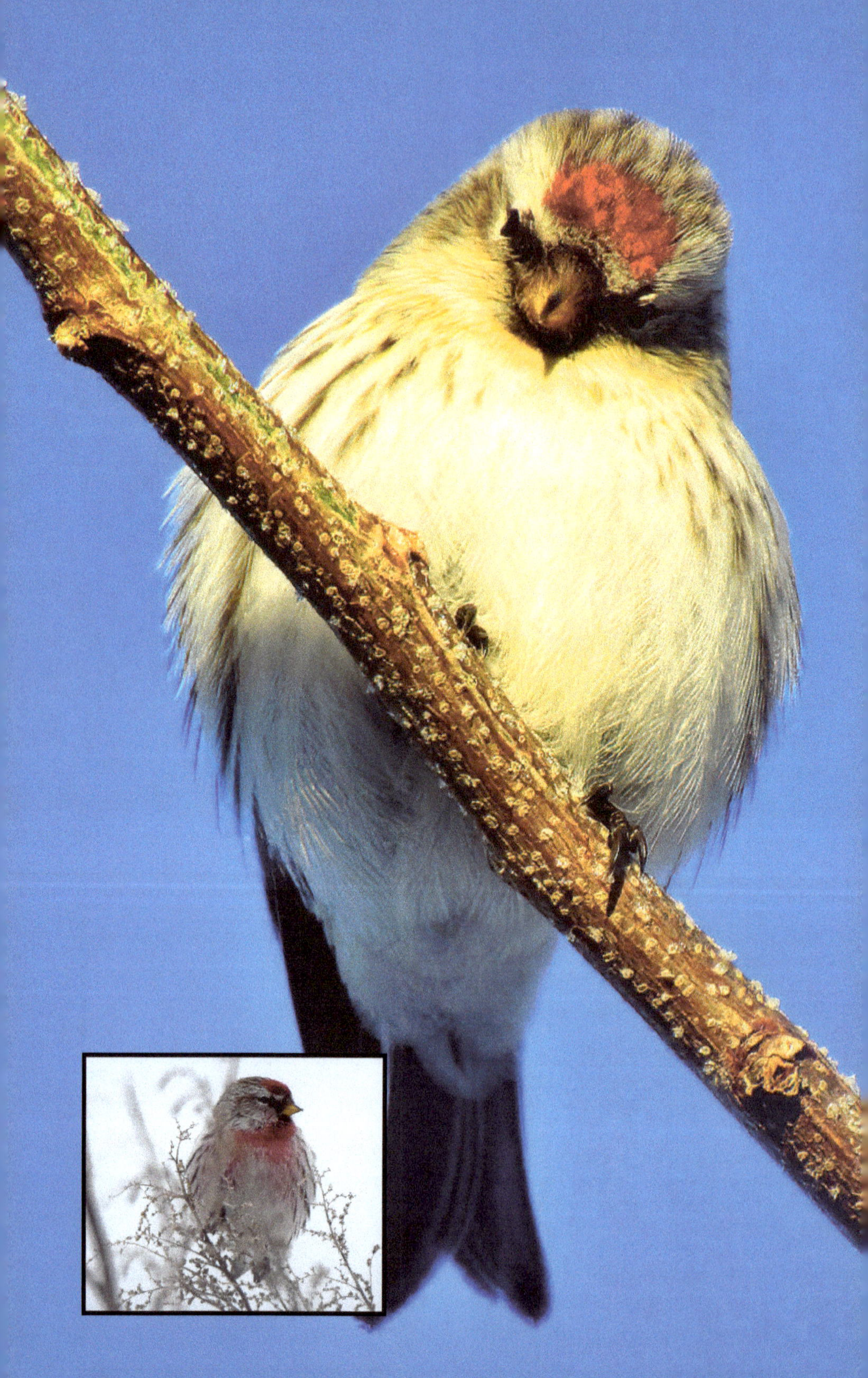

It was 8:30 in the morning on November 28, 2020, thirty-three days before the start of my Maine Big Year when a Rock Wren was found feeding on ocean rocks near an Ogunquit restaurant. I was in the car 10 minutes later.

A bird of the arid American West, the

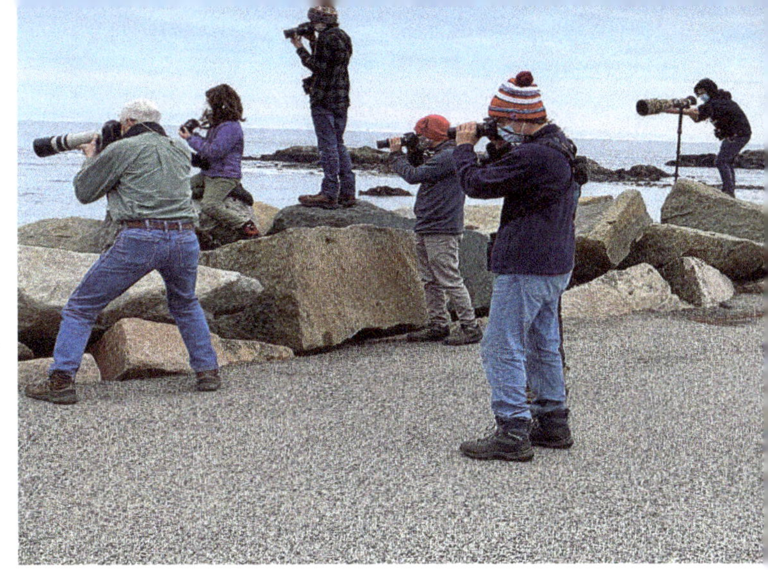

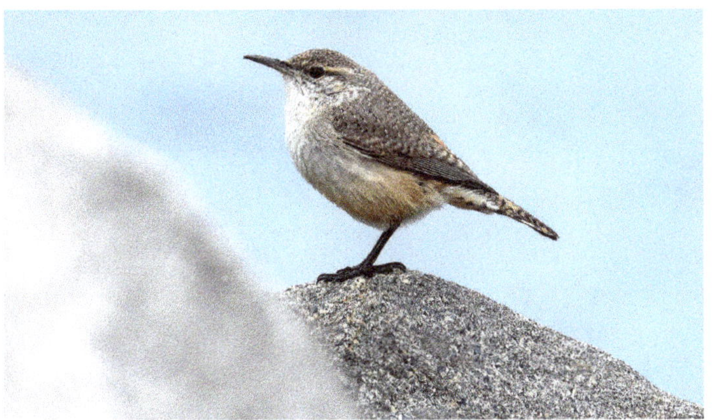

Over a month later, on day four of my Maine Big Year, I returned to Oqunquit, and the Rock Wren was still on the same rocks. Somehow it had stayed warm, dry and was getting enough to eat.

Rock Wren is so well adapted to the desert that it never drinks water. Instead, it gets all of the moisture it needs from food.

What was it doing on the coast of Maine in November?

Like so many other western rarities that appear, this Rock Wren was a mystery. Perhaps changing weather patterns in the West traps birds in the jet stream and then deposits them in Maine.

Whatever the reason, dozens of birders showed up to see this remarkably tame bird hopping within a few feet of us.

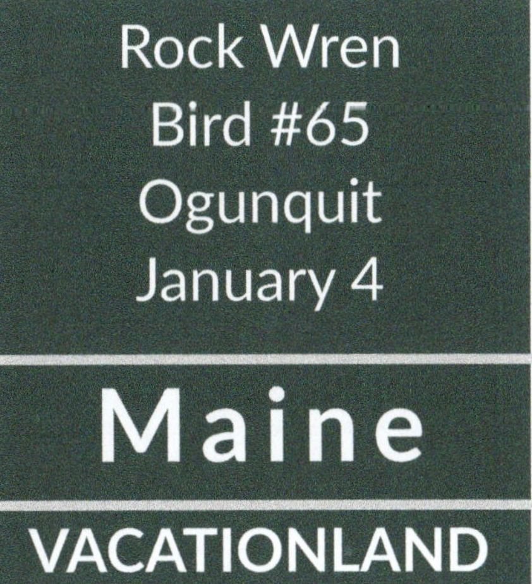

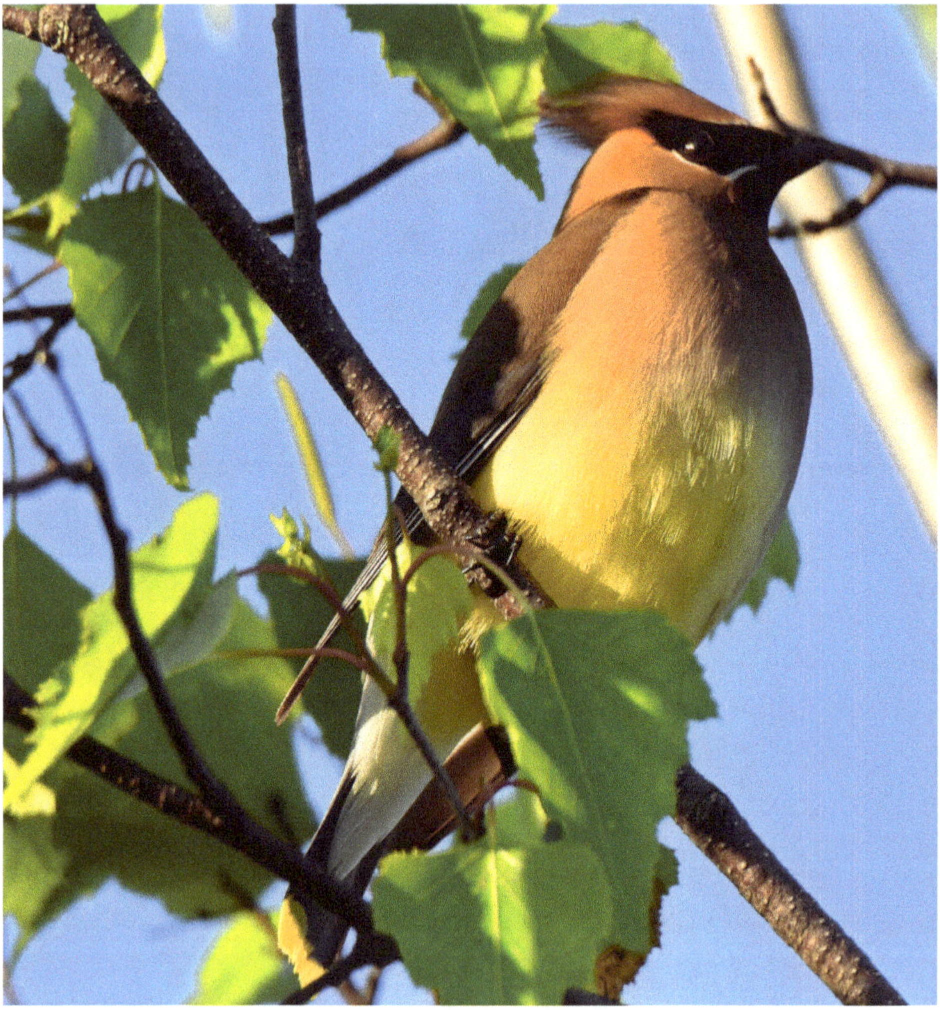

Cedar Waxwings are berry eating birds that travel in flocks. When they come upon a tree or bush filled with fruit, they consume every crab apple, holly and sumac berry. Cedar Waxwings are such gluttons that they may be temporarily unable to fly after an eating binge.

In Maine, their cousin the Bohemian Waxwing is much more rare. I only saw a couple flocks of them during the entire Big Year.

Cedars tend to be brown with yellow bellies while Bohemians are more gray overall with rufous and white markings on their wings.

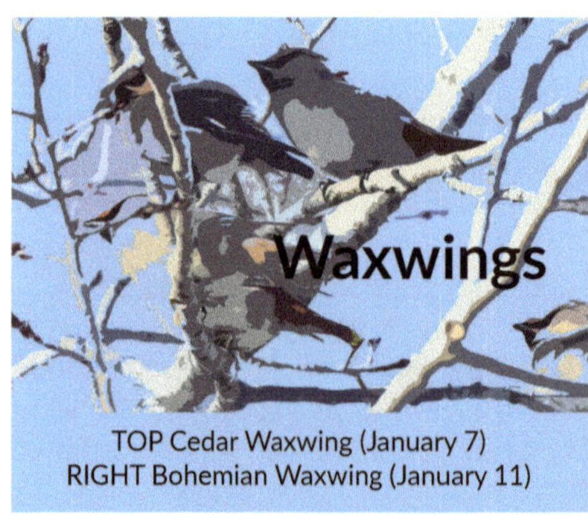

TOP Cedar Waxwing (January 7)
RIGHT Bohemian Waxwing (January 11)

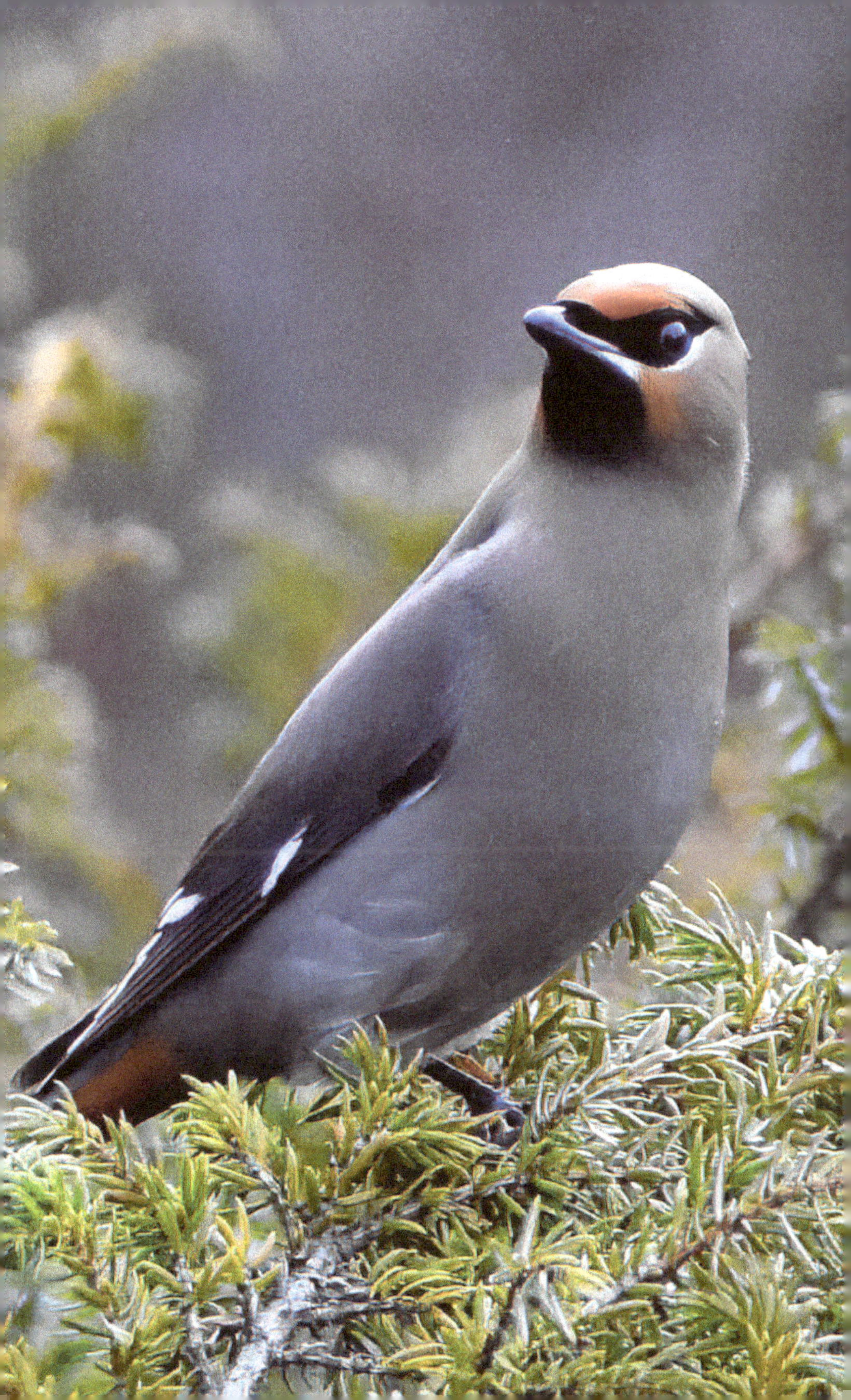

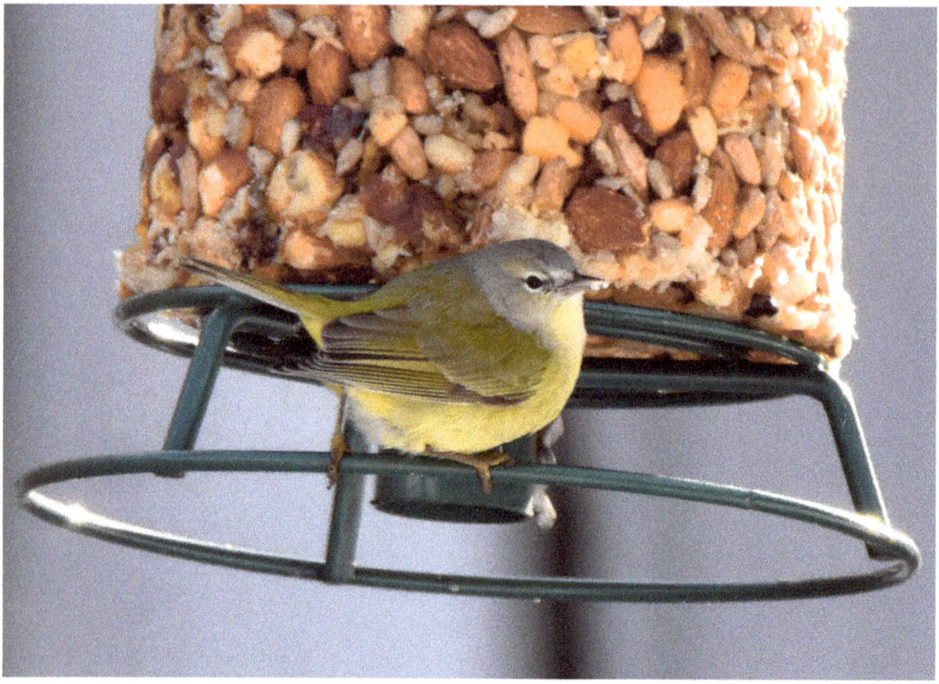

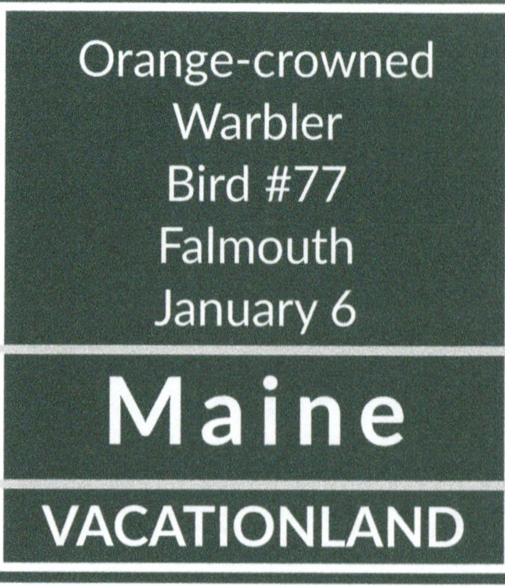

Before beginning my Maine Big Year, I read everything I could on Big Year efforts. The "experts" all emphasized: "Chase the rare birds when they appear." There will be plenty of time to find your more common Chickadees and Blue Jays.

Thus when I heard that an Orange-crowned Warbler was at a residential feeder north of Portland, I asked the owner if I could come see it and get my "year-tic" for this rarity.

While understandably reluctant to have every Tom-Dick-and-Birder showing up at his house, the owner graciously let me park in his driveway for 90 minutes until the Orange-crowned showed up.

While sitting silently in a very cold car with the windows rolled down may not be everyone's cup of tea, I had a great time watching a variety of birds visit his feeder.

Just as I was about to take a bio-break, a gray/greenish-yellow bird showed up, and for five minutes I photographed this healthy and very lost young warbler.

He left the feeder and kindly perched above my car. I could just make out the splotch of orange on his head.

Orange-crowned
Warbler
Bird #77
Falmouth
January 6

Maine

VACATIONLAND

The Belted Kingfisher is the only one of the world's 114 Kingfishers found in Maine.

A year-round resident, these dive bombing fish eaters often make their presence known with their long penetrating rattle as they fly from perch to perch.

The Belted Kingfisher raises its young in long burrows at the water's edge. After the young fledge in late summer, they can be seen (and heard) playfully chasing each other around lakes and ponds throughout the state.

Unlike most birds, the female Belted Kingfisher is actually more colorful than its male counterpart, sporting a bright rust/orange breast.

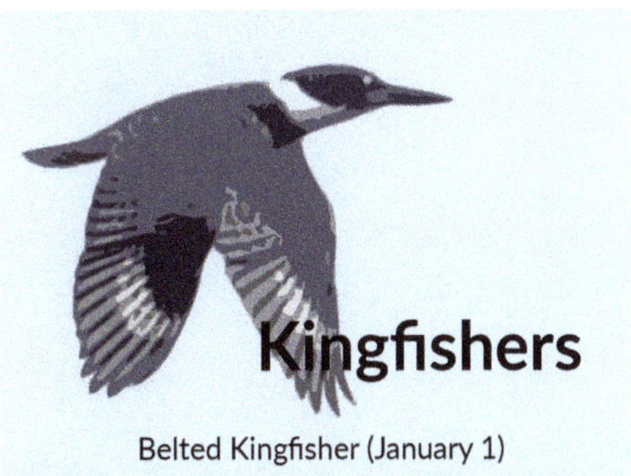

Belted Kingfisher (January 1)

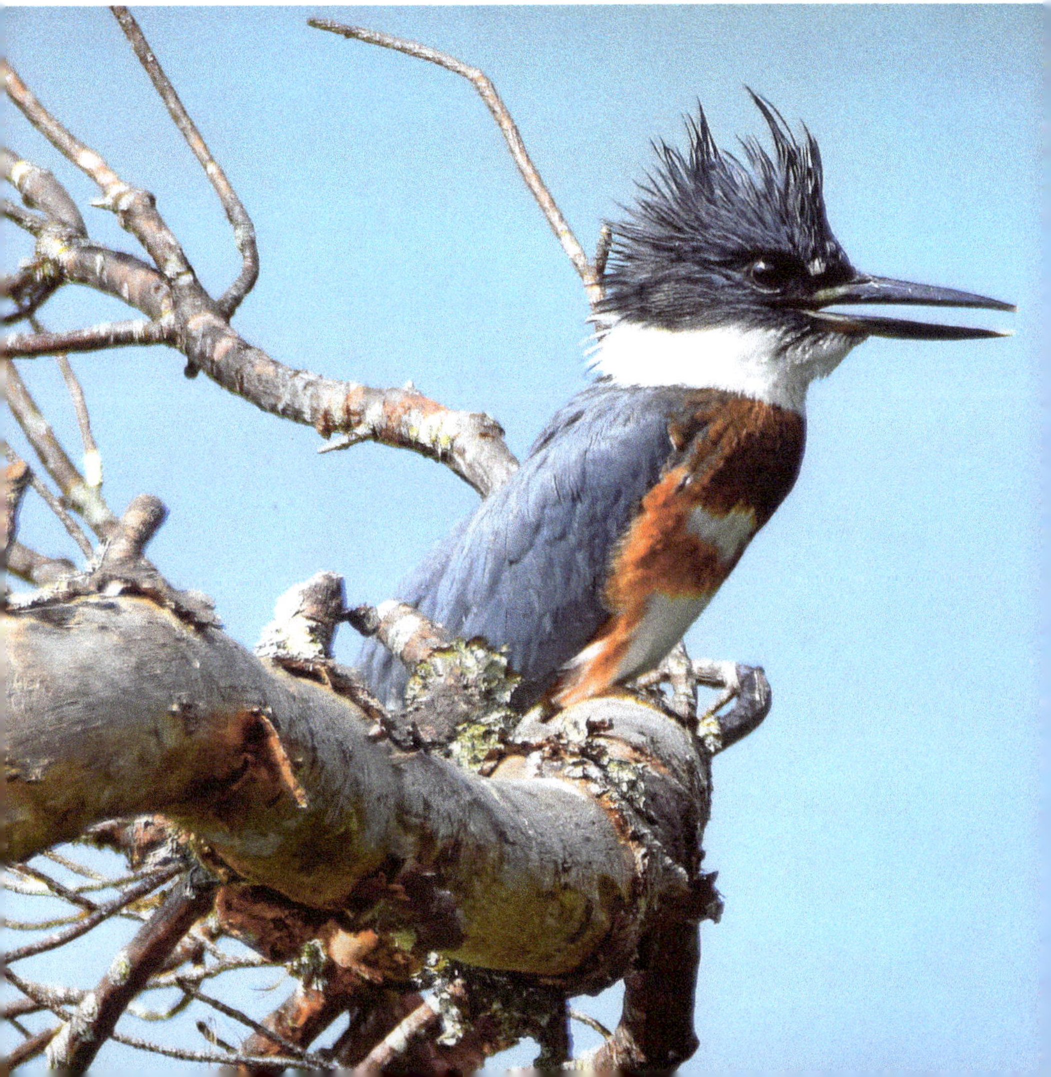

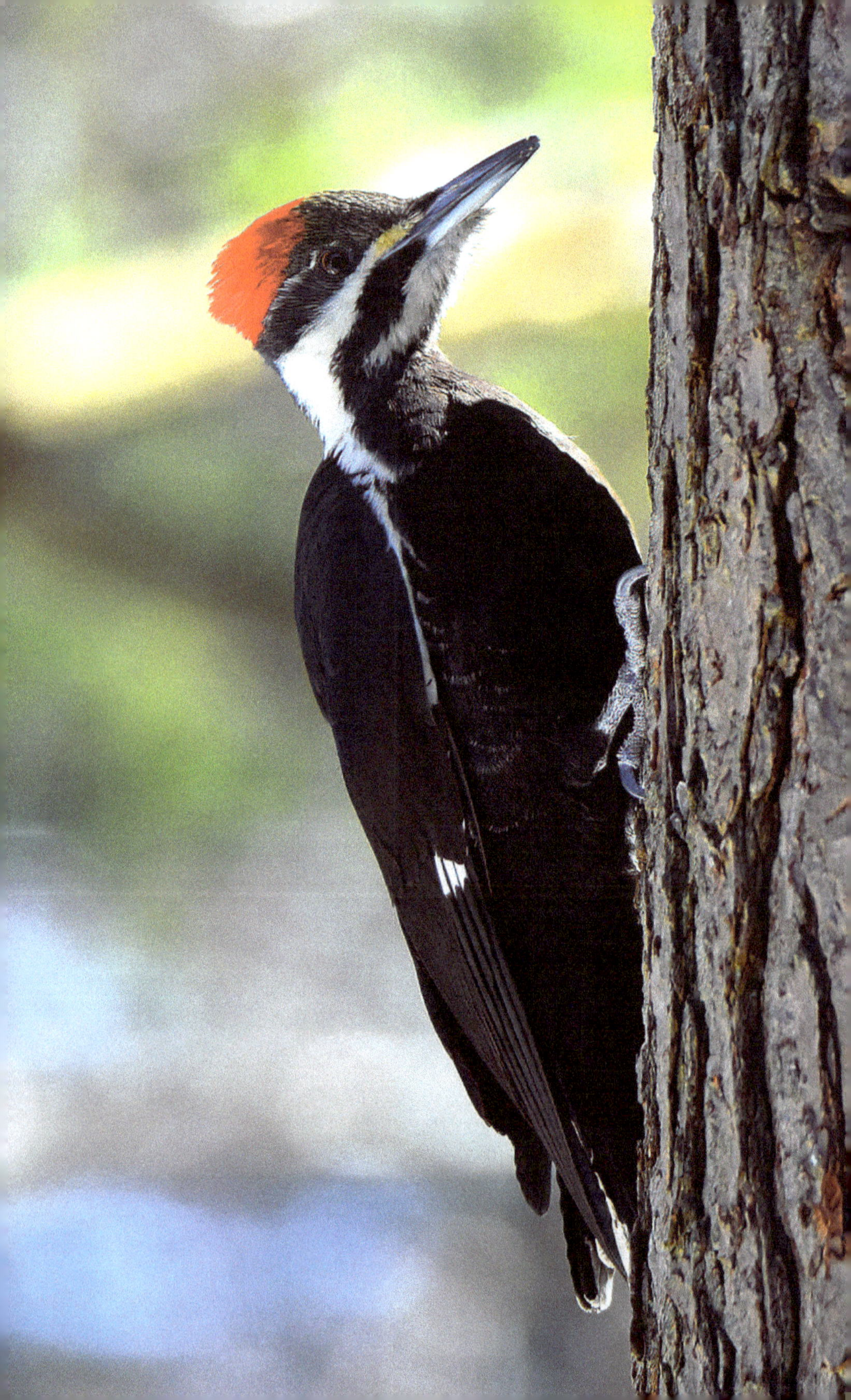

There are nine different wood-peckers found in Maine: the very common Hairy and Downy Woodpeckers, the less common but still readily found Northern Flicker and Pileated Woodpecker, the wonderfully named Yellow-bellied Sapsucker, the southern migrant Red-headed and Red-bellied Woodpeckers, and Maine north woods residents Black-backed and Three-toed Woodpeckers.

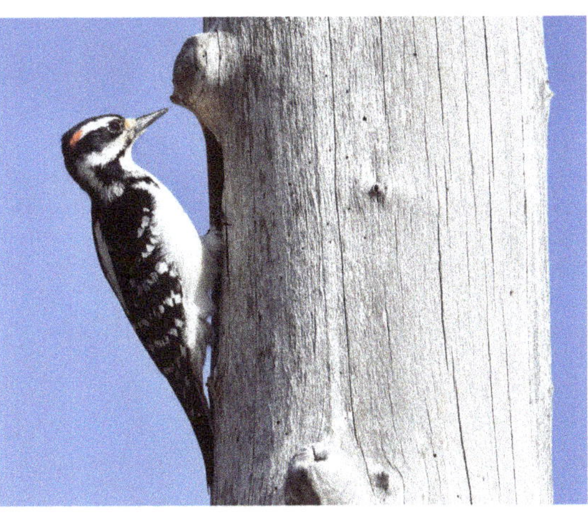

My favorite by far is the Pileated, a crow sized bird with a bright red cap and a black and white body, which looks like a tuxedo.

Some days when I'm birding in the woods, the stillness will be broken by a blood curdling scream, the unique and unmistakable cry of a Pileated Woodpecker. I have to admit that its cry can be unnerving when I'm alone.

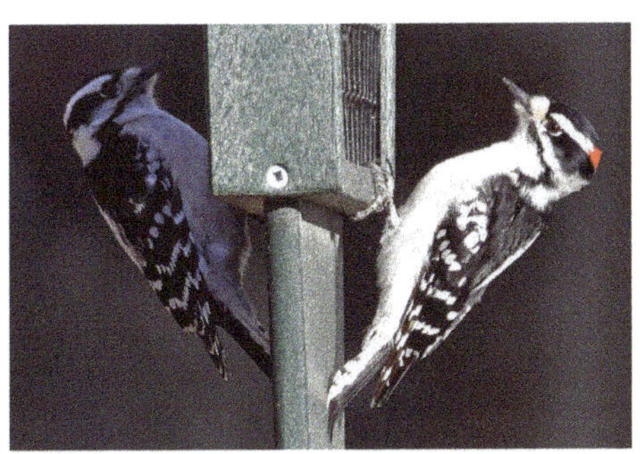

To see one in the air is just as intimidating. Their long, pointed bill and enormous wings are very impressive as they glide through the woods. I've had one fly within a few feet of me (he didn't know I was there) and the adrenalin rush was incredible.

Watching a Pileated drum on a tree for insects is equally inspiring. Its head can take an impact of 1,000 times the force of gravity. Coupled with a chisel-like bill, it sprays wood chips as it works. Once a hole is drilled away, a Pileated's enormous tongue (it wraps internally around the skull) is used to extract insects.

A tree that has been assaulted by a Pileated Woodpecker will have deep rectangular shaped holes in a line, up and down and left and right across the trunk. These holes often become nesting sites for other birds such as Northern Saw-whet Owls.

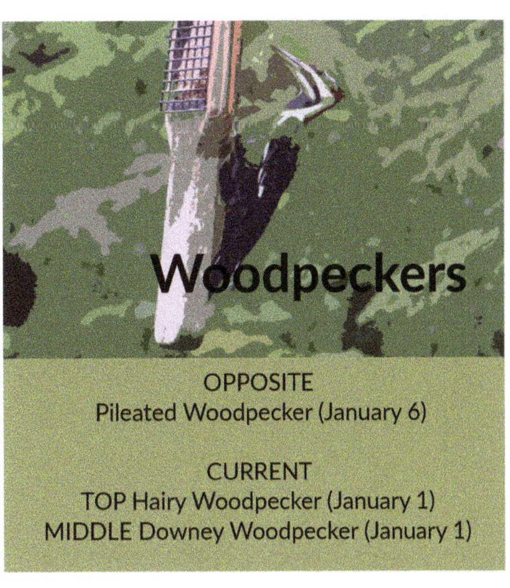

OPPOSITE
Pileated Woodpecker (January 6)

CURRENT
TOP Hairy Woodpecker (January 1)
MIDDLE Downey Woodpecker (January 1)

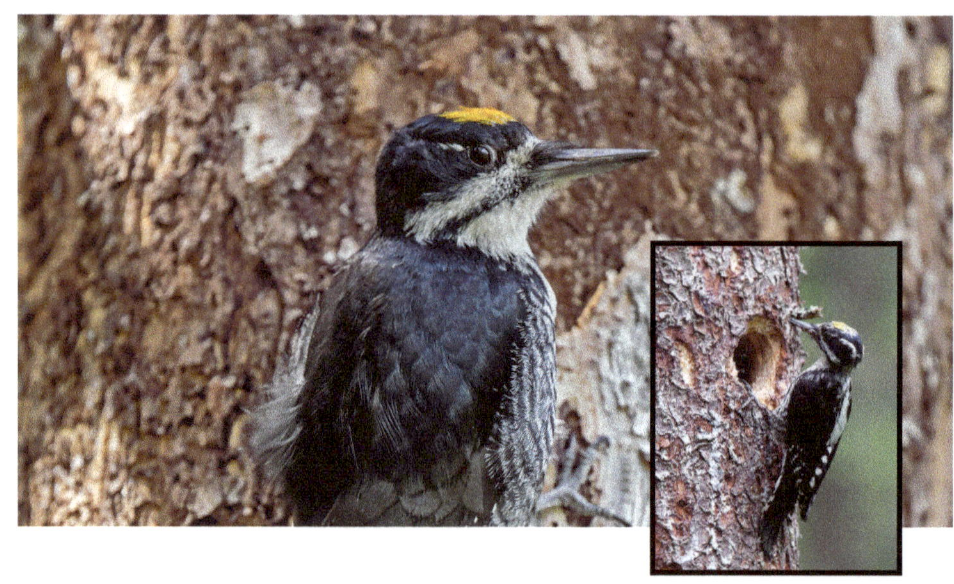

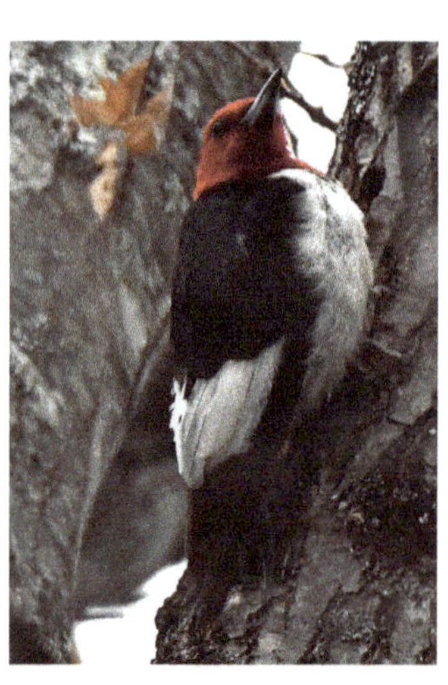

Woodpeckers (cont.)

TOP Black-backed Woodpecker (May 27)
INSET
American Three-toed Woodpecker (August 3)
ABOVE Red-headed Woodpecker (Nov 26)
RIGHT Yellow-bellied Sapsucker (January 31)

OPPOSITE
TOP Northern Flicker (January 5)
BOTTOM Red-bellied Woodpecker (Jan 2)

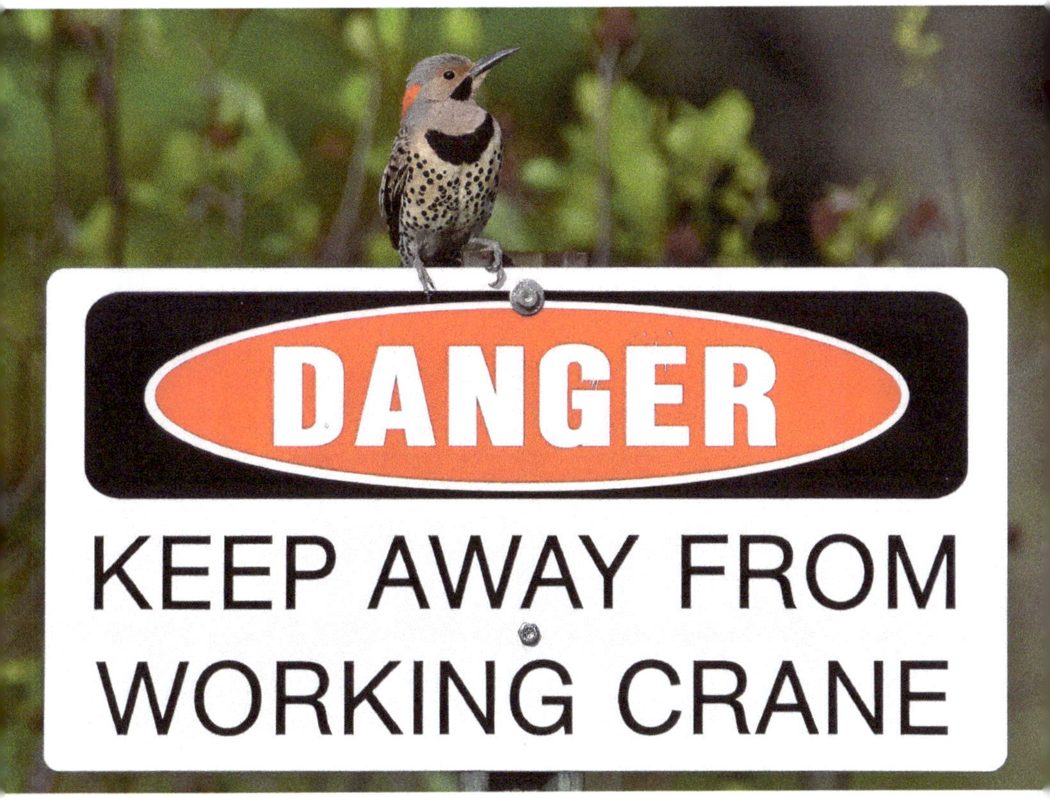

DANGER
KEEP AWAY FROM
WORKING CRANE

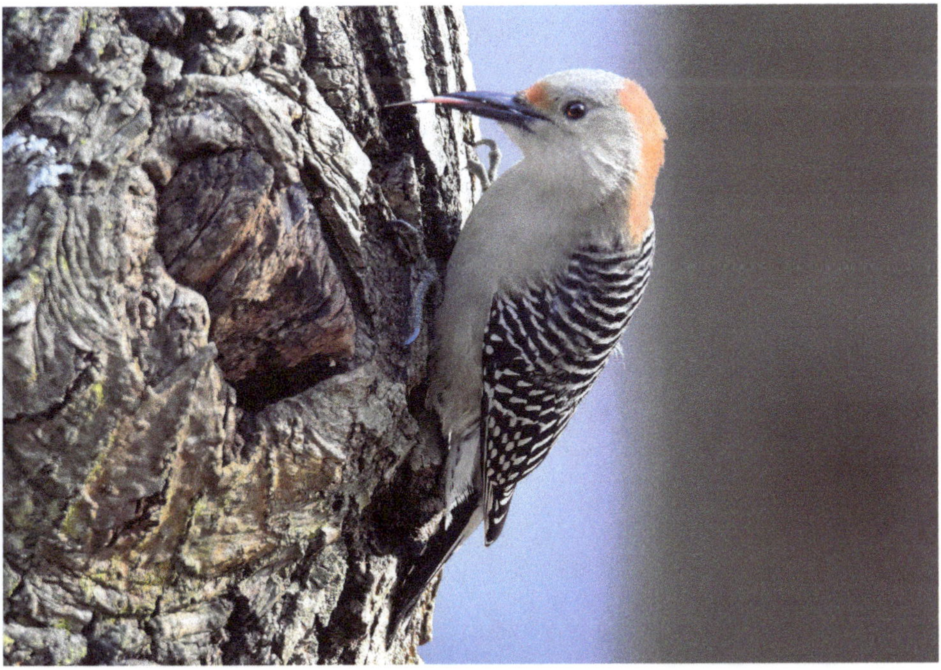

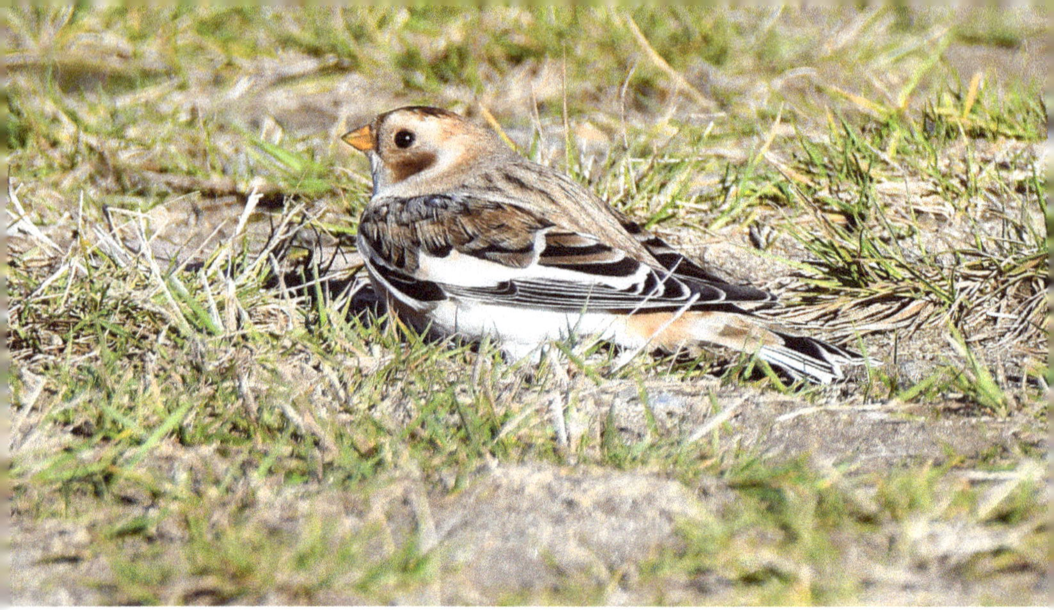

The rusty-white Snow Bunting breeds in the Arctic and winters all across the northern regions of the United States.

We've seen them on beaches, eating salt at the side of the road, on the steps of Ingrid's elementary school, resting on a rock outside a popular restaurant, on a dairy farm manure pile, and on the local high school's soccer field.

It is one of our favorite birds.

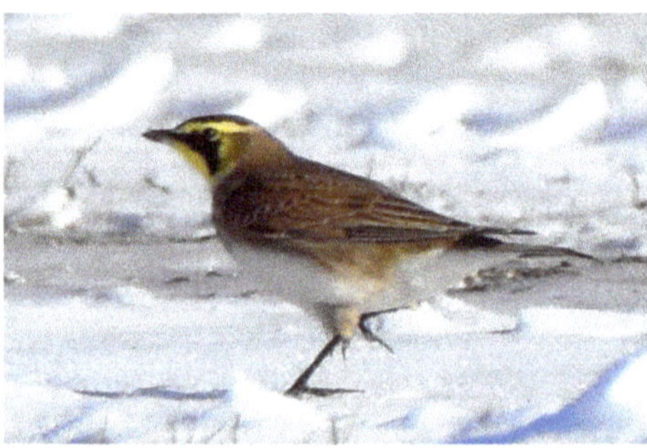

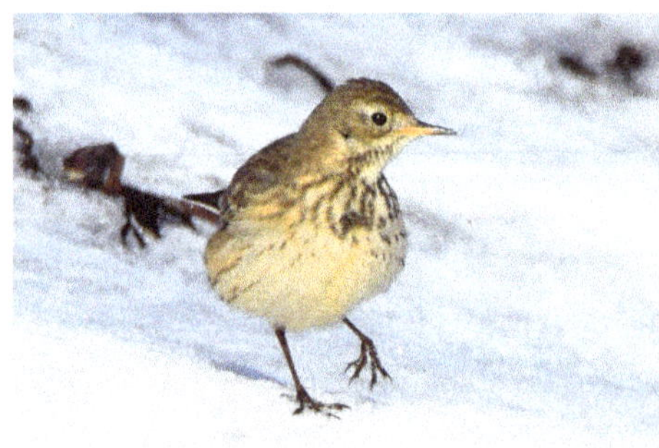

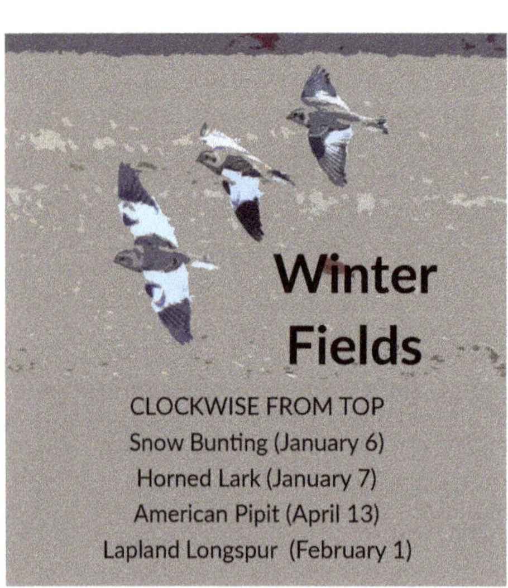

CLOCKWISE FROM TOP
Snow Bunting (January 6)
Horned Lark (January 7)
American Pipit (April 13)
Lapland Longspur (February 1)

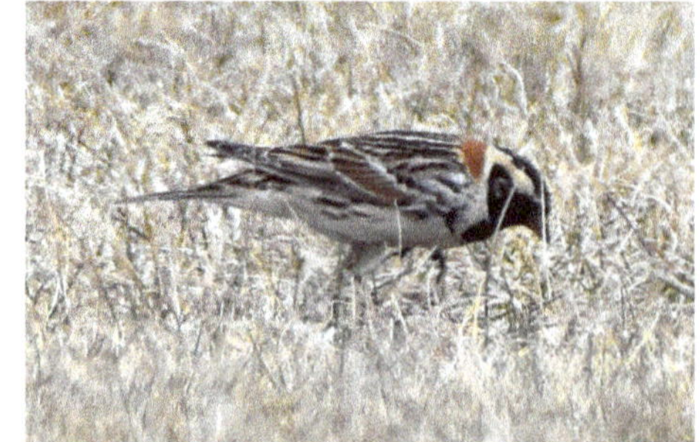

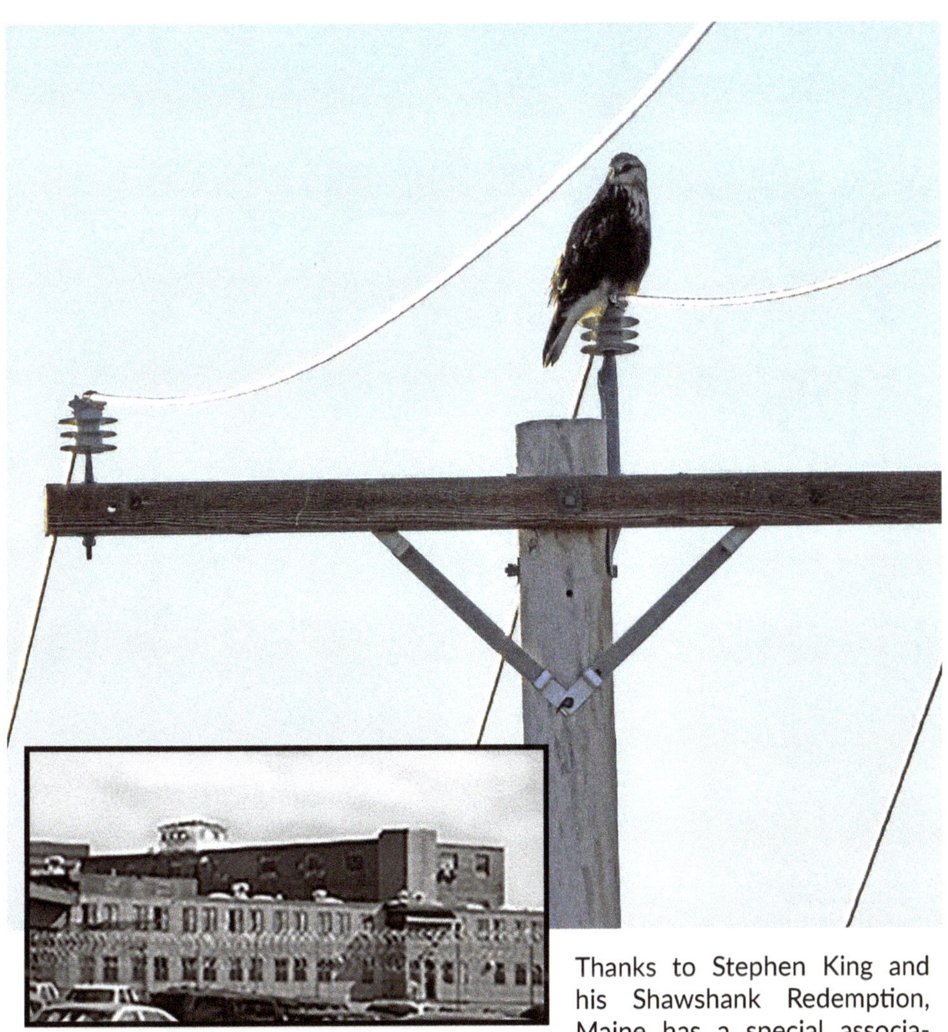

Thanks to Stephen King and his Shawshank Redemption, Maine has a special association with prisons. But like most Mainers, I've had little in the way of interaction with the Prison System.

This all could have changed when a Rough-legged Hawk appeared on a power line in front the Maine Correctional Center in Windham.

Stopping your car in front of a State Prison, scanning the area with binoculars and then taking photographs with a high powered telephoto lens is a whole new kind of stupid, but this is what one does during a Big Year!!!!

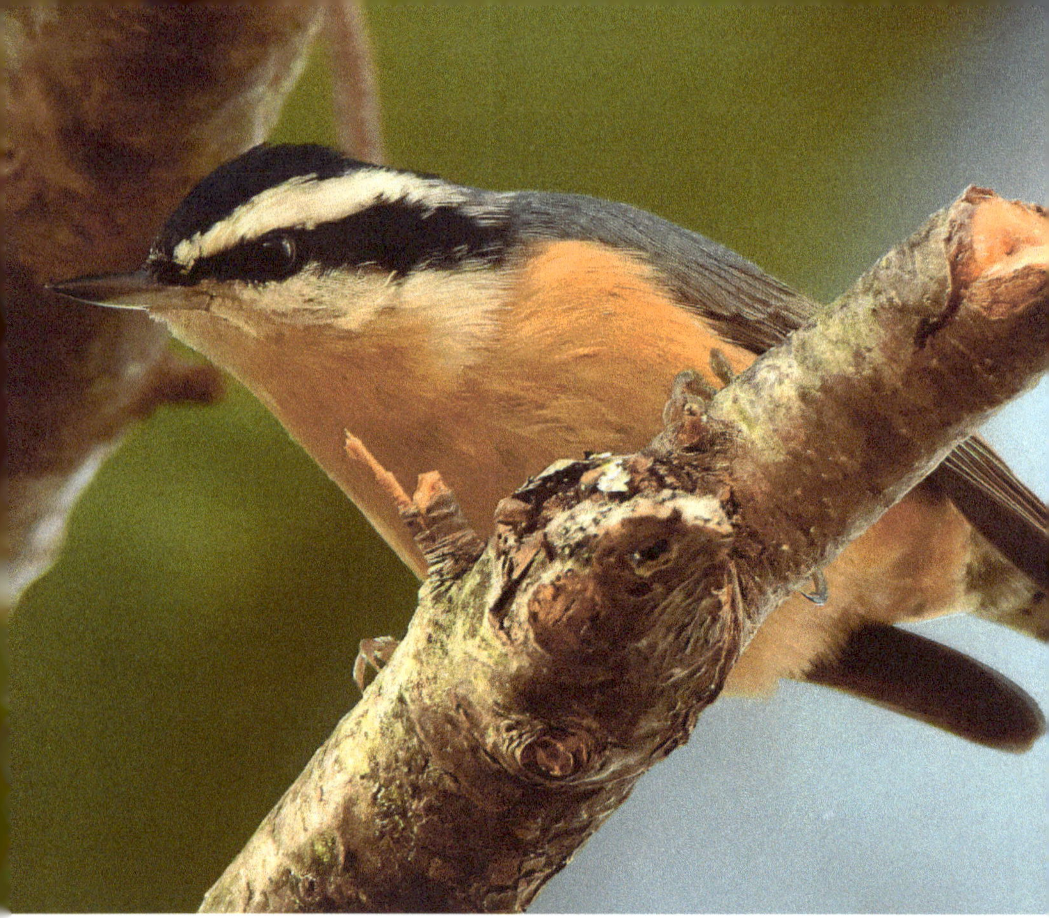

Every birder has a "Spark Bird", the species that "sparks" one's interest in birding, generally a single sighting that changes one's life.

Mine was the Red-breasted Nuthatch, a common Maine bird that had been coming to my feeders for decades.

Ingrid dragged me to the Acadia Birding Festival shortly after we started dating. During one of our field sessions, the guide played the song of the Red-breasted Nuthatch to demonstrate the territorial passion of this bird.

Within a few minutes the bird arrived, and boy, was he angry!

It was the coolest thing I had ever seen. Birds communicate with each other, have emotions, and even interact with humans.

I wanted to learn more, to see more, I was hooked!!!

Nuthatches

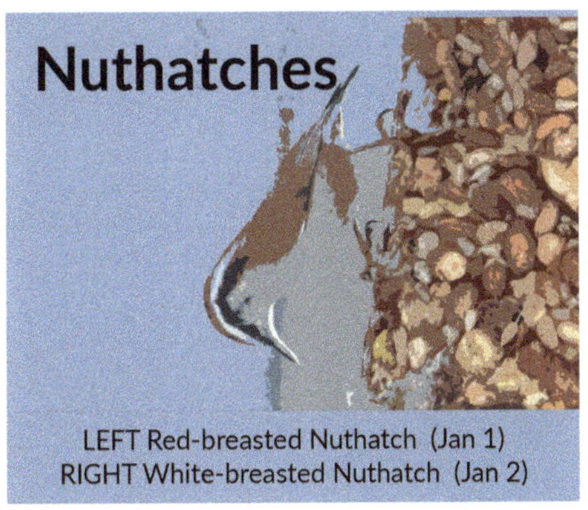

LEFT Red-breasted Nuthatch (Jan 1)
RIGHT White-breasted Nuthatch (Jan 2)

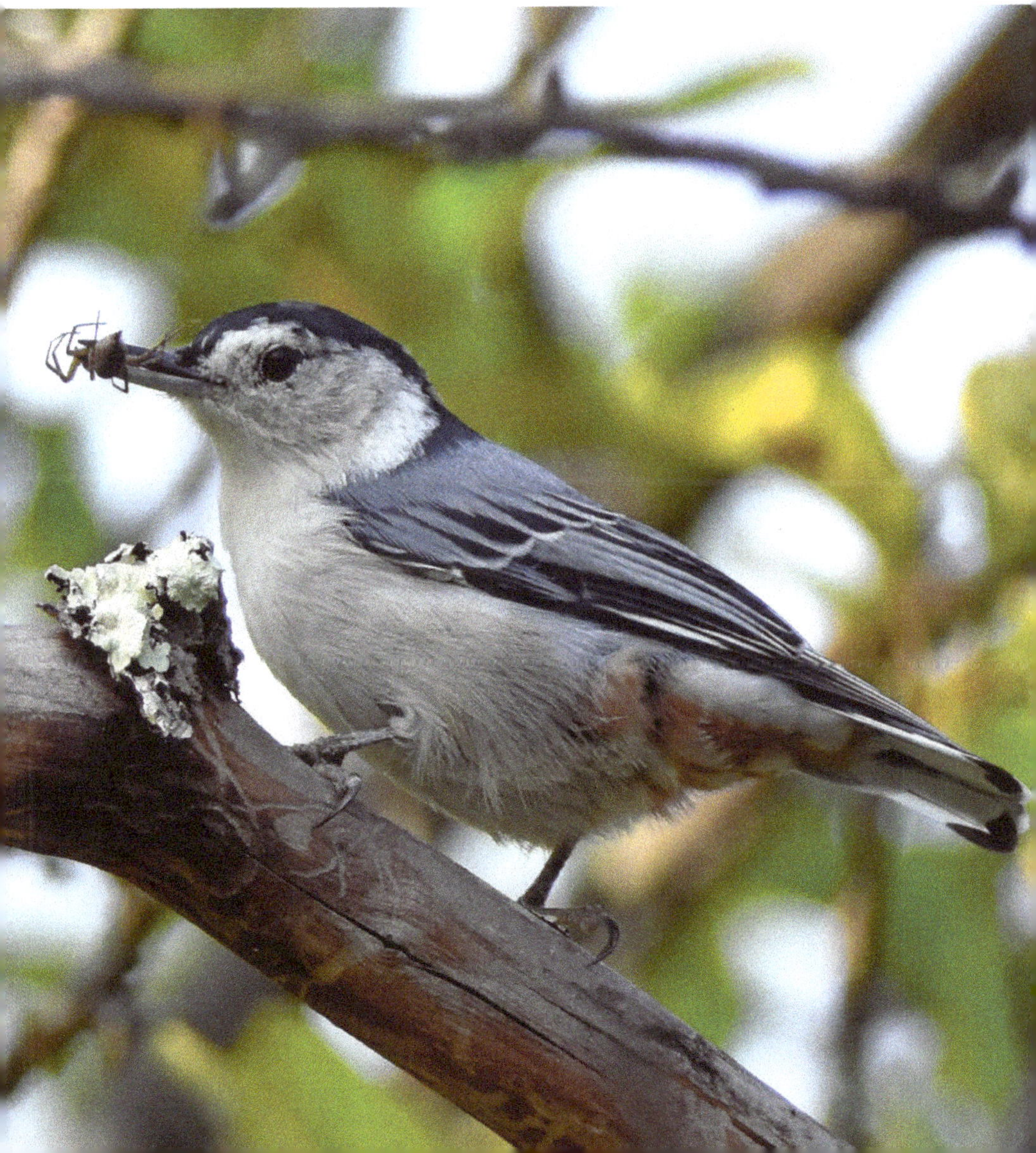

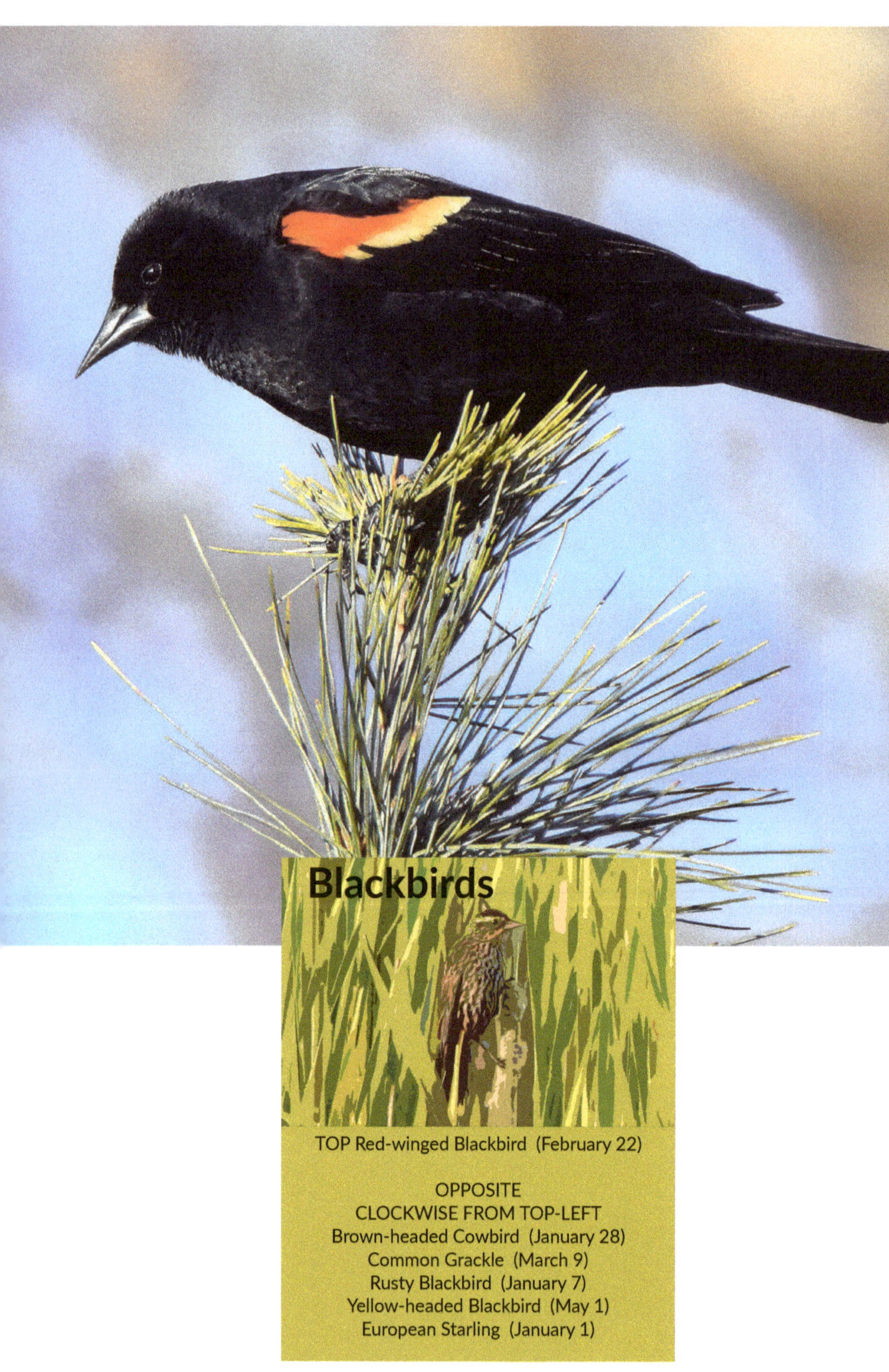

TOP Red-winged Blackbird (February 22)

OPPOSITE
CLOCKWISE FROM TOP-LEFT
Brown-headed Cowbird (January 28)
Common Grackle (March 9)
Rusty Blackbird (January 7)
Yellow-headed Blackbird (May 1)
European Starling (January 1)

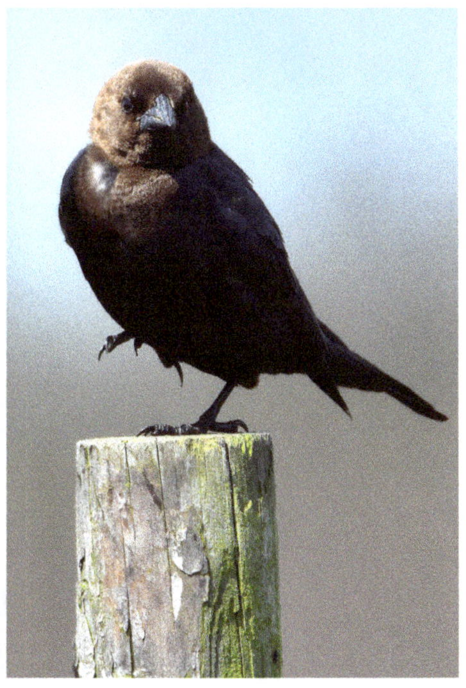

It's late February in Maine, and it's cold.

A foot of snow still remains on the ground and it will be a long time before we see the first daffodil blooms. But for Maine birders, this is when the first sign of spring arrives.

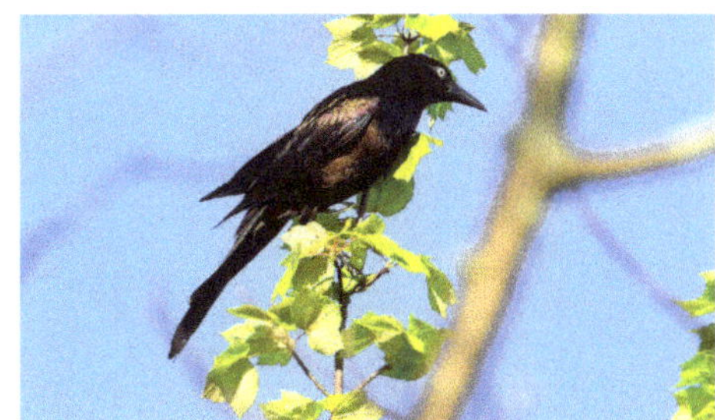

The male Red-wing Blackbirds migrate early, to stake out the best territory in the cattails. When the females arrive in a month, they will be attracted to the best bachelor pads.

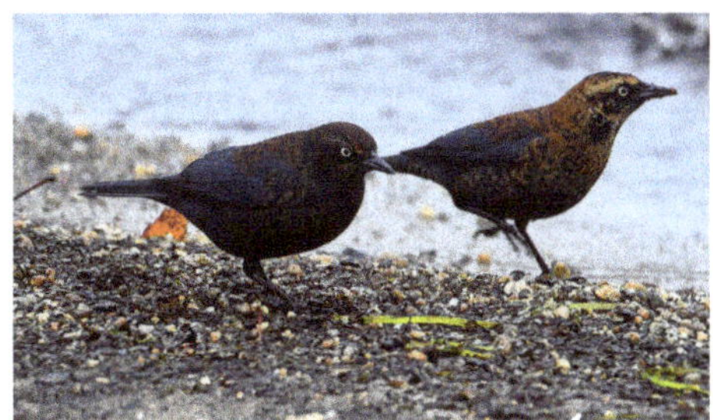

Red-winged Blackbirds are polygamists and will mate over and over. Thus, males will sing their *conk-la-ree* song repeatedly to attract female attention.

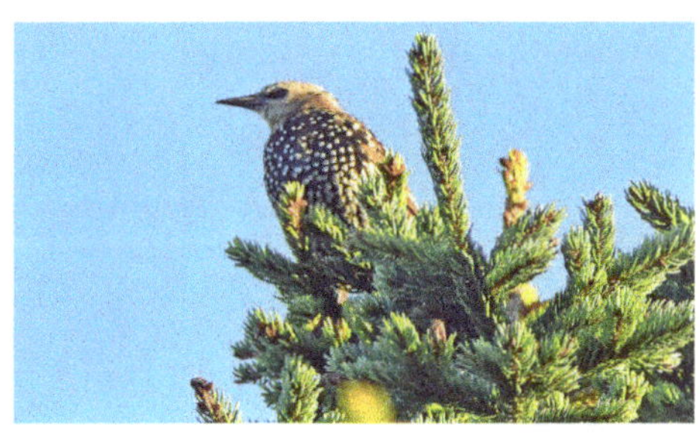

When the seemingly endless Maine winter is at its worst, a stunning black-bird with a red and yellow patch on its wing, singing in the reeds, is a wel-comed first sign of spring!!!

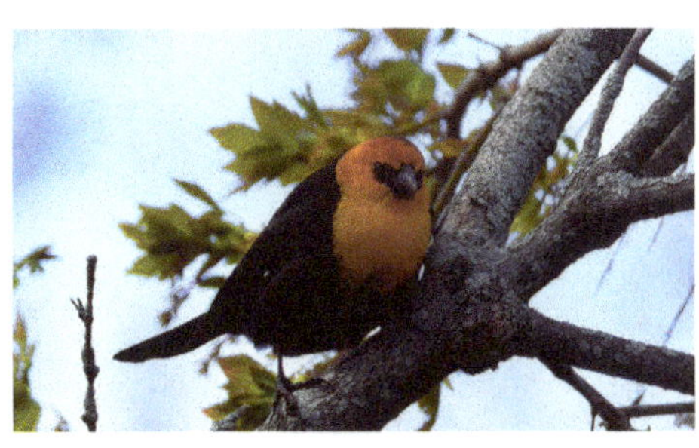

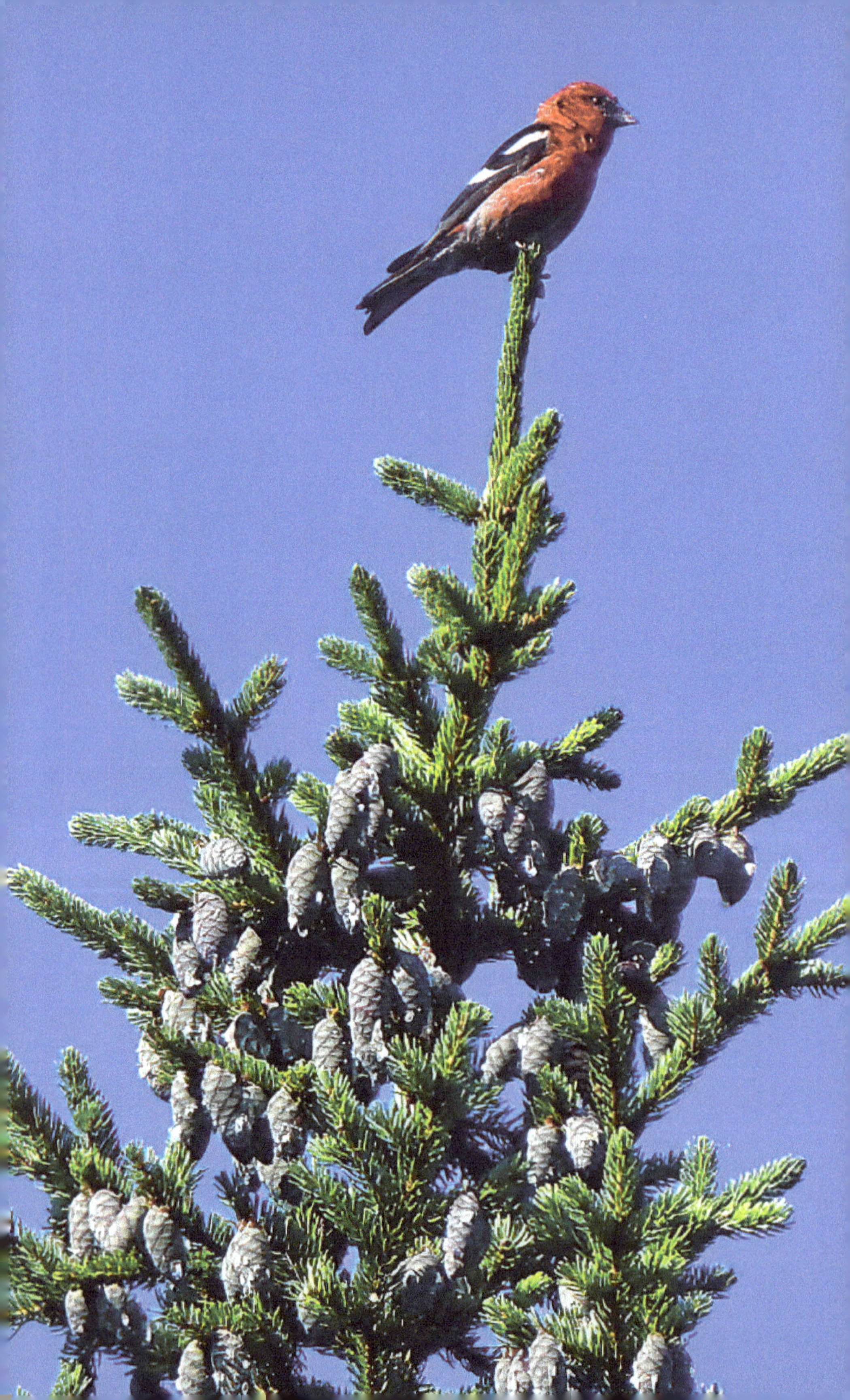

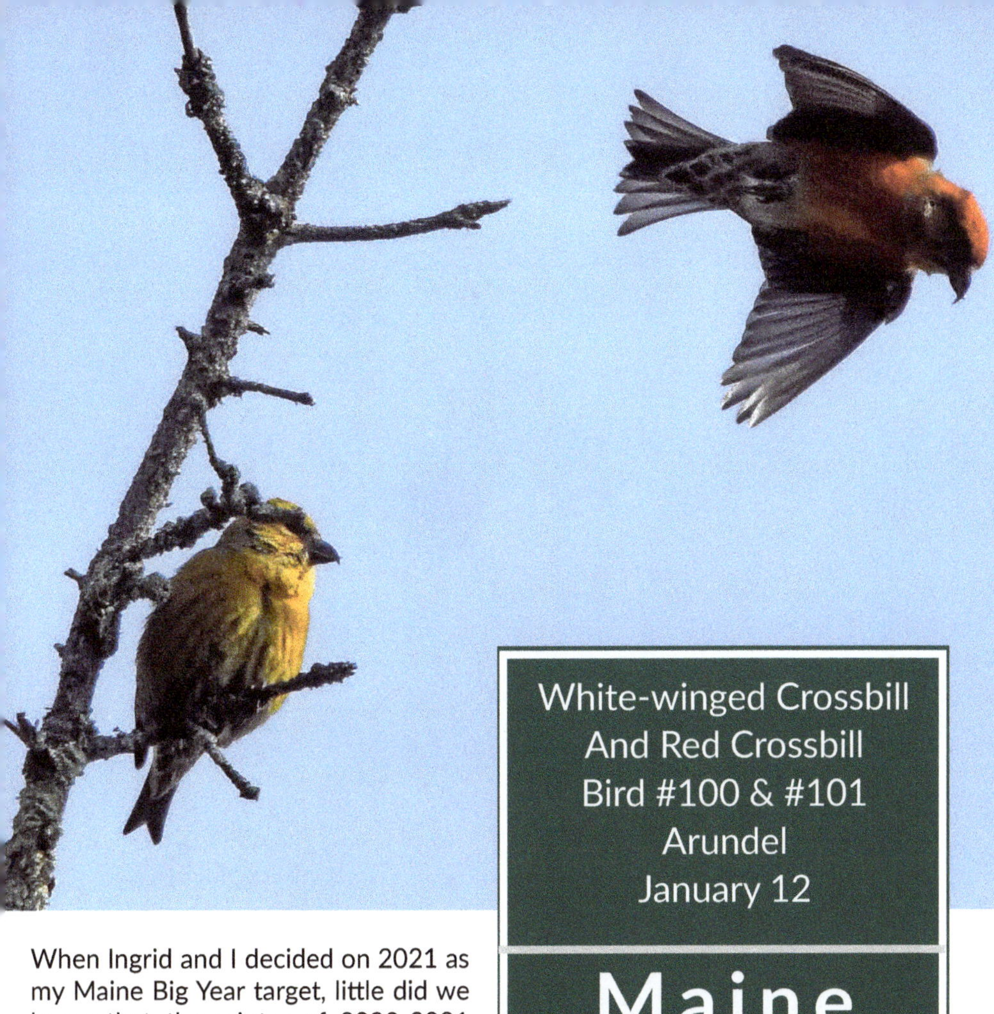

When Ingrid and I decided on 2021 as my Maine Big Year target, little did we know that the winter of 2020-2021 would be a "Superflight Year." It was the biggest irruption of northern finches and their allies in recent history. Species that normally reside in Canada's Spruce Forests moved south in search of food.

A perfect storm of feast and famine made this a banner year, affecting Redpolls, Grosbeaks, Siskins, Crossbills, and of course, Finches. Other irruptive species, like Blue Jays, Bohemian Waxwings, and Red-breasted Nuthatches, also migrated in incredible numbers. Basically, there is not enough food to support them, so they all spilled out of Canada into the lower 48 states.

This was both good and bad for my Maine Big Year. Purple Finches and Pine Siskins were blown south of the State (bad), while Crossbills and Redpolls stopped in southern Maine and were easy to find (good).

In mid-January I found large flocks of Red Crossbills and White-winged Crossbills in a Kennebunkport cemetery. They were at the tops of enormous spruce trees, buzzing and trilling as they fed on spruce cones.

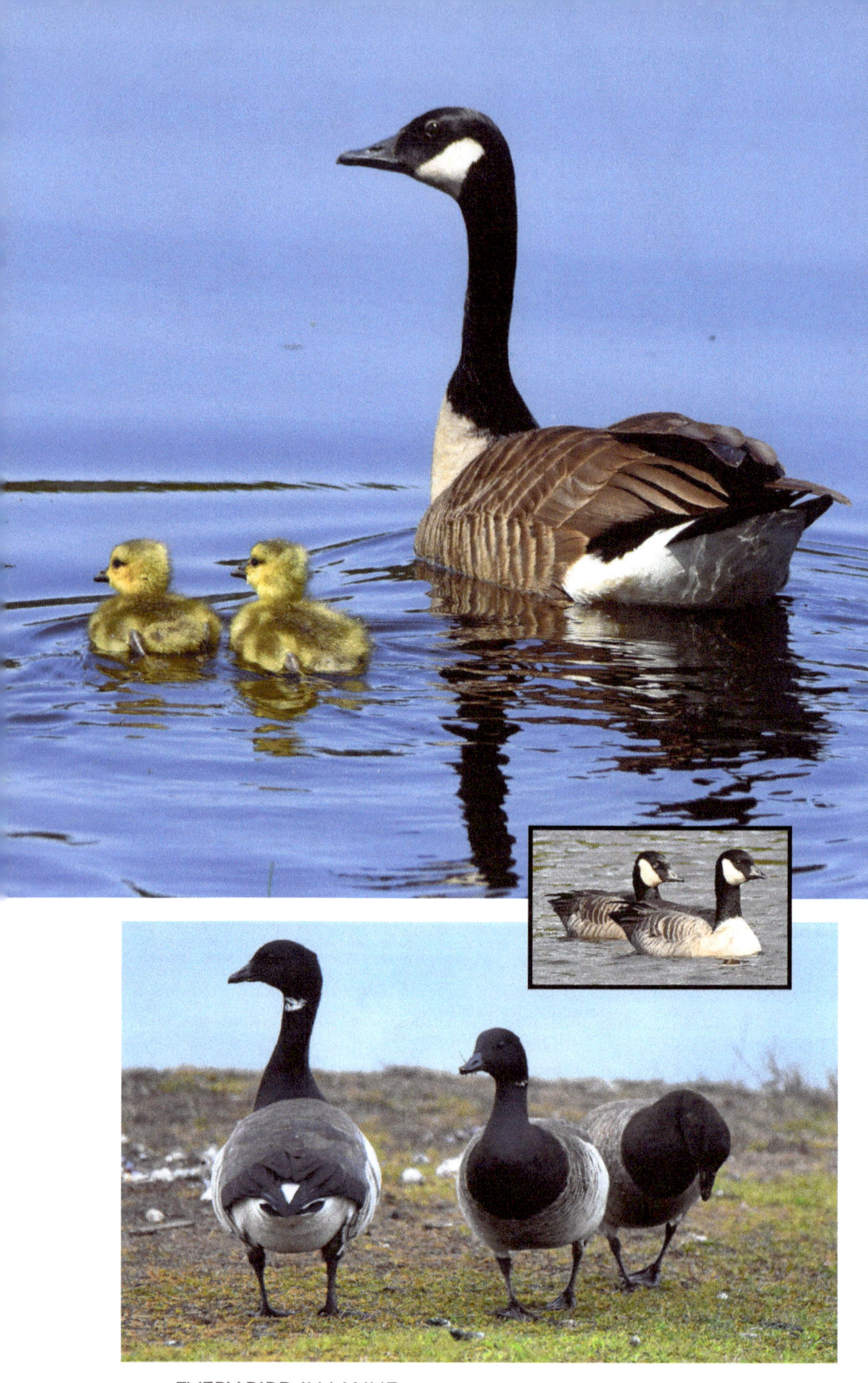

     EVERY BIRD IN MAINE

When we think of Geese, most of us immediately think of Canada Geese, and there are lots of them in Maine.

However, on occasion, other types of Geese stop by for a visit.

Brant, a small goose that winters along the mid-Atlantic, often appear on a beach in Cape Elizabeth.

A Snow Goose or two shows up in Maine's farm fields each year, a far cry from the millions that join enormous flocks in the Mid-West.

Stray Geese like the Pink Footed and Barnacle (from Iceland/Greenland) and Mid-West Birds, like Greater White-fronted and Cackling, appear every few years.

But mostly, it's the Canada Geese, lots and lots of Canada Geese. Watch where you step!!!

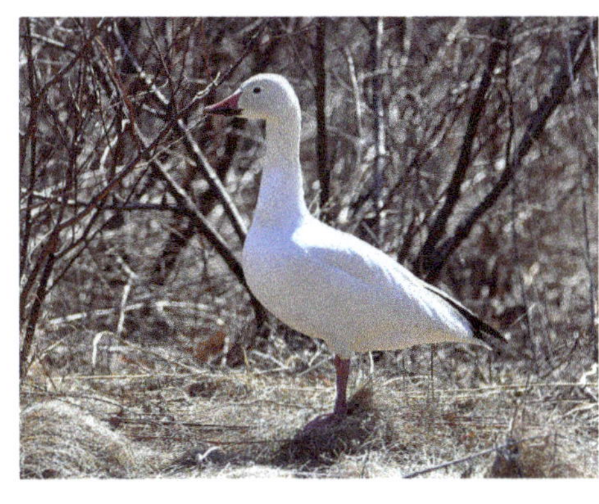

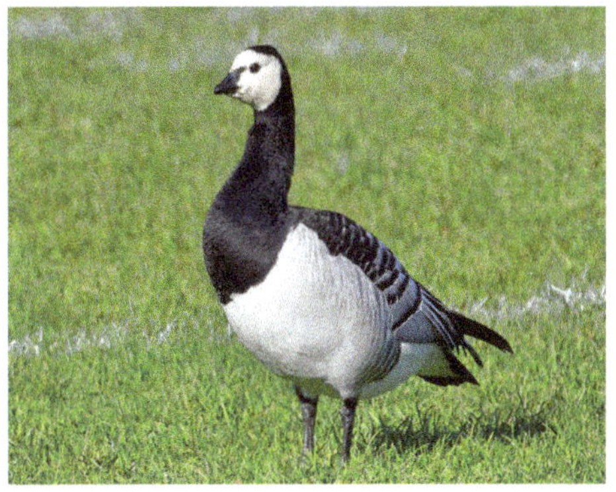

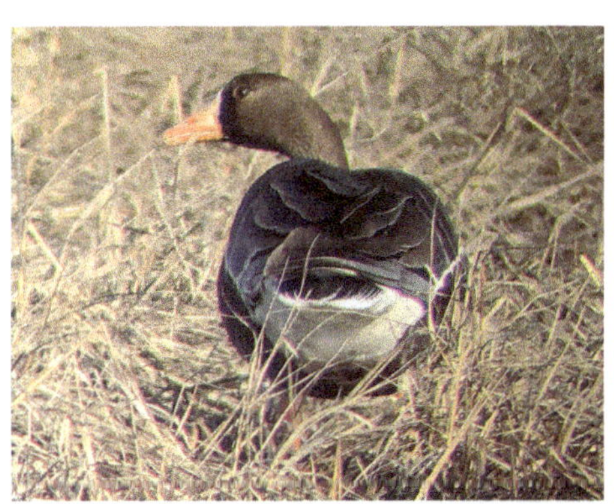

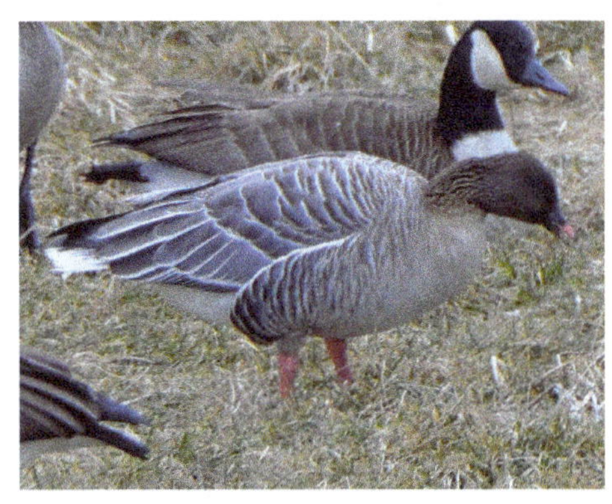

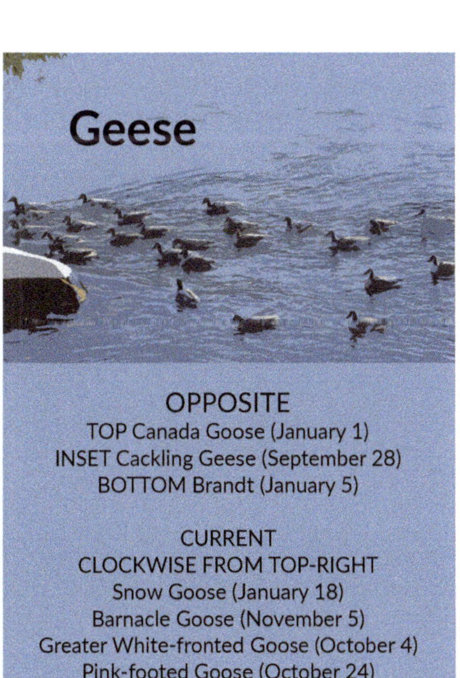

Geese

OPPOSITE
TOP Canada Goose (January 1)
INSET Cackling Geese (September 28)
BOTTOM Brandt (January 5)

CURRENT
CLOCKWISE FROM TOP-RIGHT
Snow Goose (January 18)
Barnacle Goose (November 5)
Greater White-fronted Goose (October 4)
Pink-footed Goose (October 24)

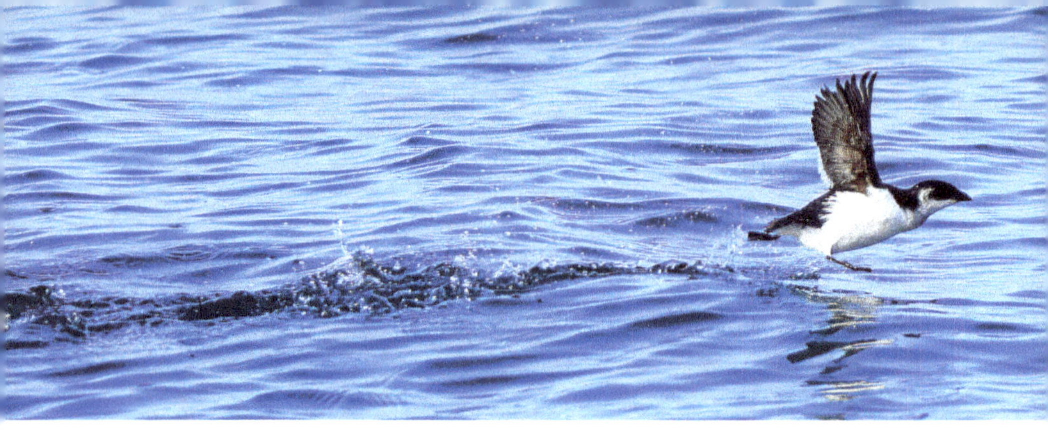

When I decided to do a Maine Big Year, I knew I'd have to make at least one winter off shore trip to look for sea birds.

I talked to a couple of lobster men about riding out with them, but they really didn't seem too excited about a clumsy birder getting tangled up in their trap lines.

Then Ingrid suggested that I ride the Mohegan Island Ferry out and back (25 miles round trip) and see what I could see. Monhegan is a summer artist and tourist colony, but in the winter it shrinks to a few hearty residents that are supplied by a single daily ferry.

January is not exactly the nicest time to be out on the ocean in Maine, as it can be deadly. I watched the weather reports and found an unseasonably warm day (40 degrees), with calm seas and headed out.

The ferry captain knew what I was doing and let me sit up in the bow. About halfway out, the boat was surrounded by the elusive Dovekie, a small relative of the Atlantic Puffin.

Dovekies are only found near shore after winter storms and generally only seen with high powered scopes. That day dozens were popping up around the boat, often only a few feet away.

As I leaned over trying to get a once in a life time photo of a Dovekie, the Captain taped the horn, and said "Ethan, look a Bald Eagle."

Eagles are a wonderful bird, but we see them daily in Maine. All I could do is wave as the startled Dovekies flew away.

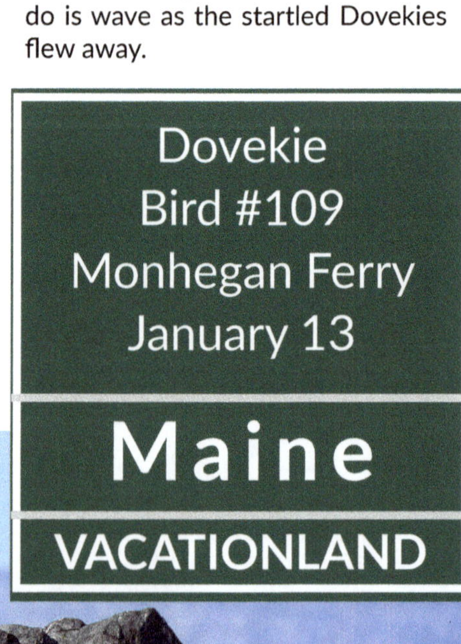

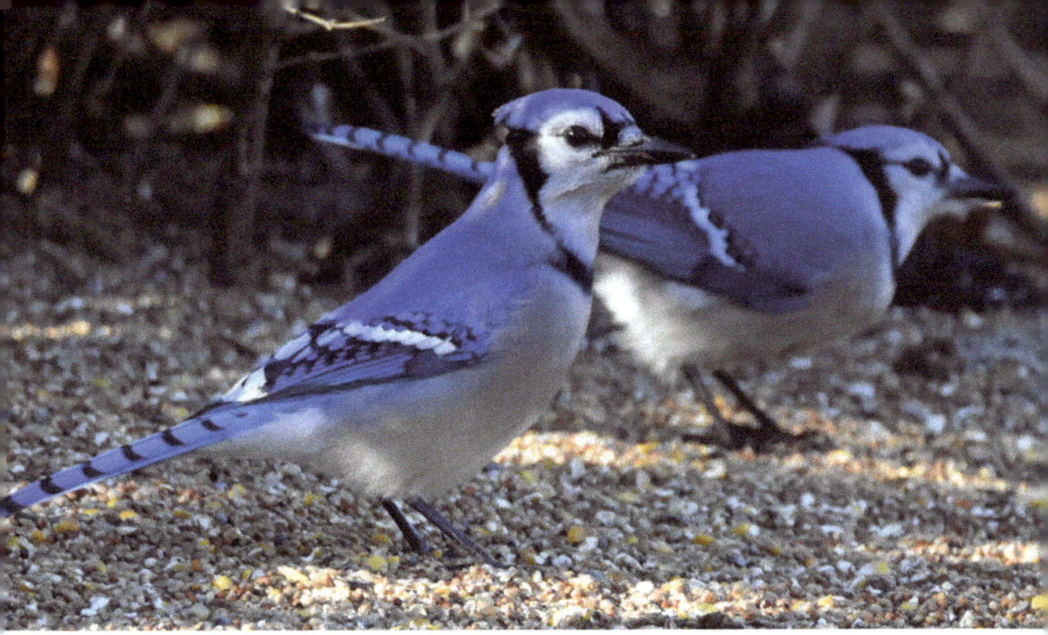

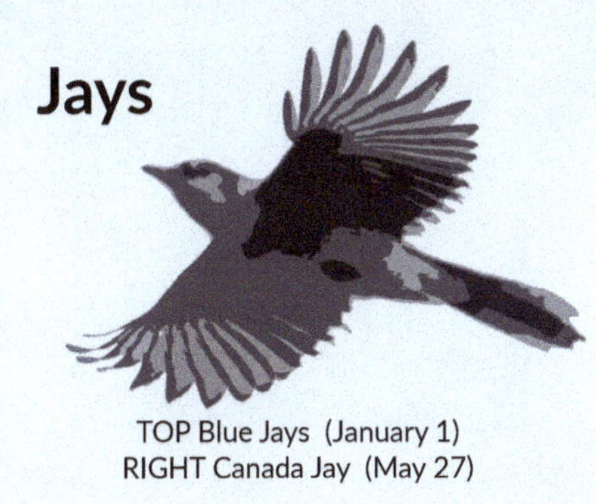

Jays

TOP Blue Jays (January 1)
RIGHT Canada Jay (May 27)

Ingrid and I have a special place in our hearts for the Canada Jay, also called the Gray Jay, Whiskey Jack, Camp Robber, Lumberjack, Meat Bird, Venison Hawk, Moose Bird, Gorby Bird and Gooney Bird.

In years past it was our "White Whale", a bird we wasted countless hours trying to find, but it always ended up evading us.

To add insult to injury, Alpine Skiers and Hikers in Maine's mountains are often visited by groups of these little rascals, stealing food whenever they have a chance. But could Ingrid and I find them???

Then one day on a dirt road in Rangeley, Ingrid and her husband Ahab finally got their Moby Dick as they were surprised by four very curious Canada Jays.

Ingrid fed them pieces of her peanut butter sandwich which they gobbled right up just a few feet away.

Since then we've had no problem finding these scoundrels. I was visited by them numerous times during the Maine Big Year.

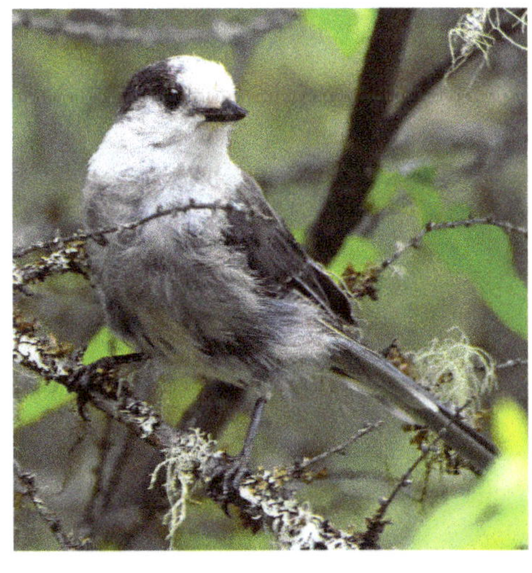

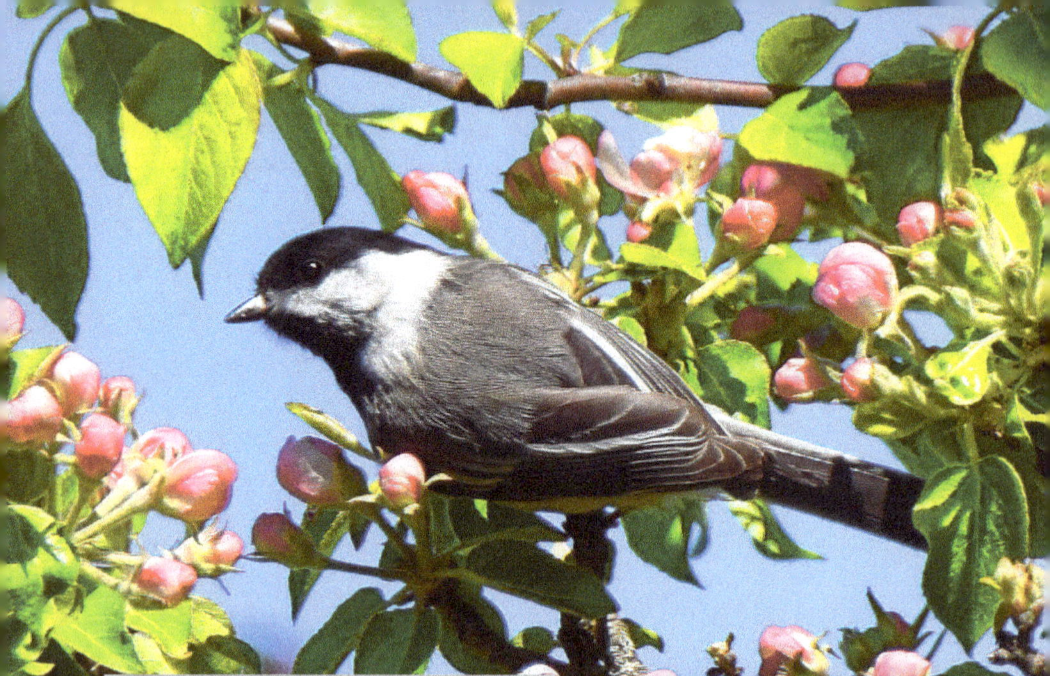

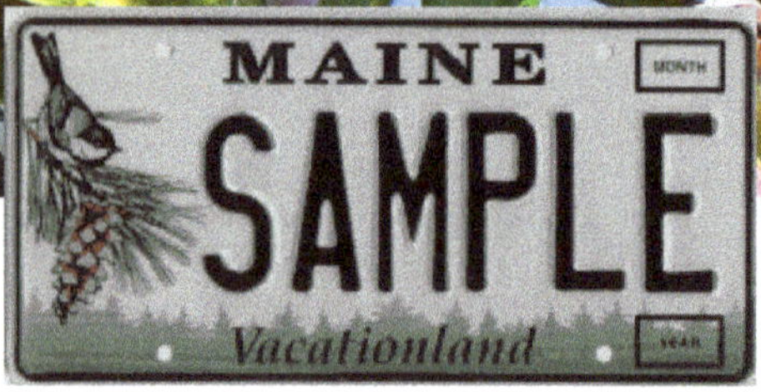

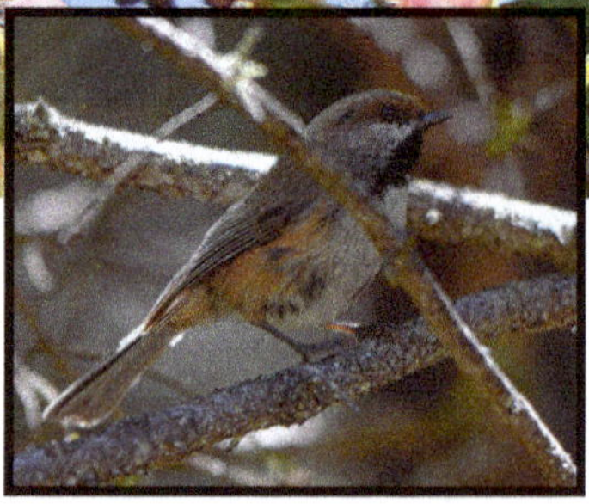

The Chickadee is the Maine State Bird, but which Chickadee? In 2019, the Maine State Legislature actually took up this all-important question.

To quote Maine Audubon's Nick Lund, "It's not a bird. It's a family of birds. So, it would be like saying the state dog is a dog. Or the state pizza is pizza."

The Black-capped Chickadee is a resident of the entire state, curious, vocal (*chick-a-dee-dee-dee*) and social.

But in the Maine north woods, moving through the spruce trees, the Boreal Chickadee, its ginger colored cousin, resides.

In the halls of the Maine Legislature, State Representative Betty Austin offered a bill to make the ubiquitous Black-capped Chickadee the state bird.

Apparently it was decided that the legislature had more important issues to resolve, and the "Chickadee Bill" was withdrawn.

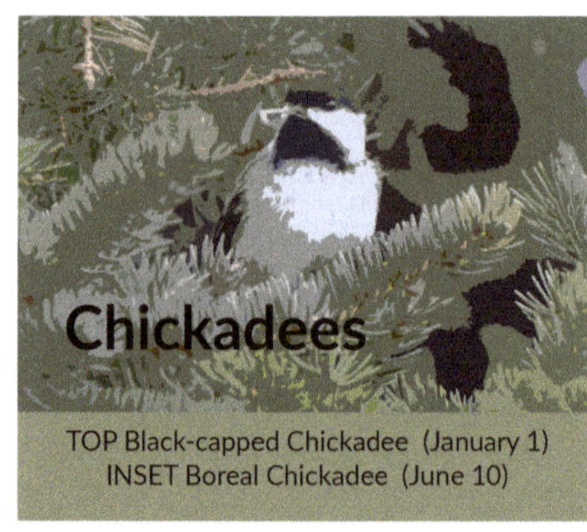

TOP Black-capped Chickadee (January 1)
INSET Boreal Chickadee (June 10)

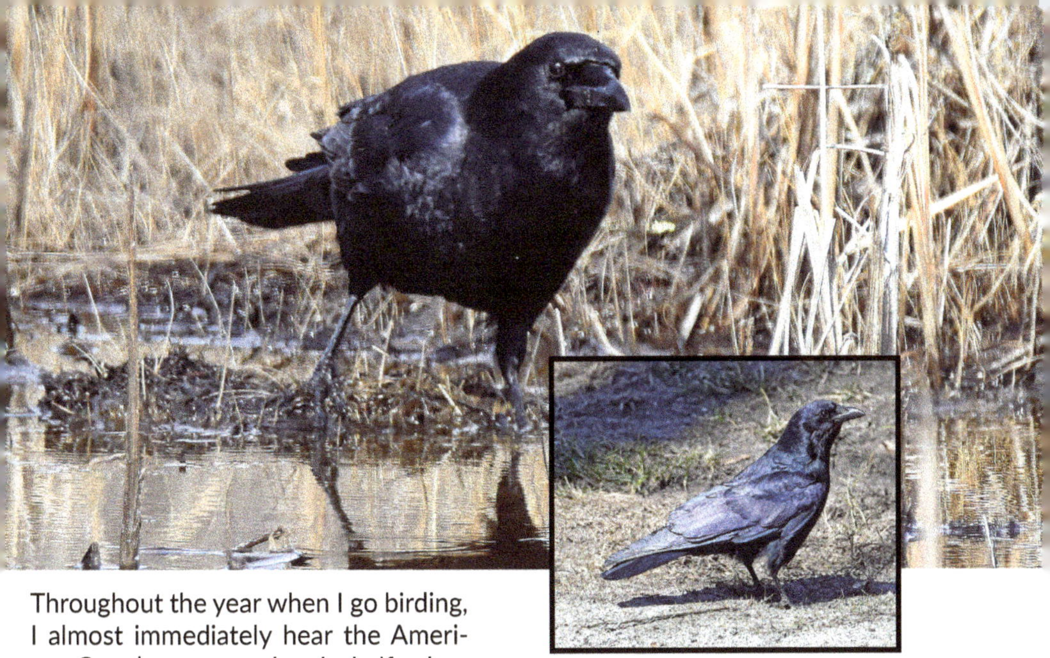

Throughout the year when I go birding, I almost immediately hear the American Crow's *caw* sound and a half a dozen familiar vocalizations.

However, around shopping centers and convenience stores, particularly in the warmer months, there is a slightly smaller Crow, the Fish Crow. The further south one goes along the eastern seaboard the more Fish Crows you'll find.

Identifying a Fish Crow can be challenging as the two crow species are practically identical. To the trained eye, the Fish Crow is a little smaller, and its legs are shorter. Also, the Fish Crow in the right light can have a blue sheen and tends to lean forward, its body parallel to the ground.

The only definitive way to tell the difference is through their vocalization. The Fish Crow makes a nasal *cahrr* sound.

The Common Raven dwarfs both Maine Crows in size. Further, it sports a wedge shaped tail and an enormous beak. It is commonly said that, "The Crow has a head with a beak and the Raven has a beak with a head."

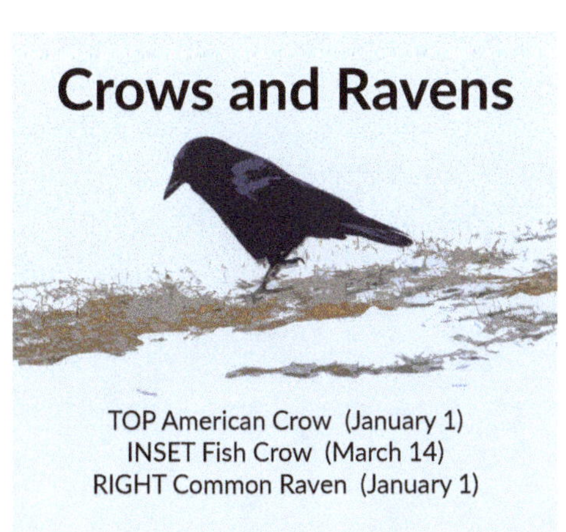

Crows and Ravens

TOP American Crow (January 1)
INSET Fish Crow (March 14)
RIGHT Common Raven (January 1)

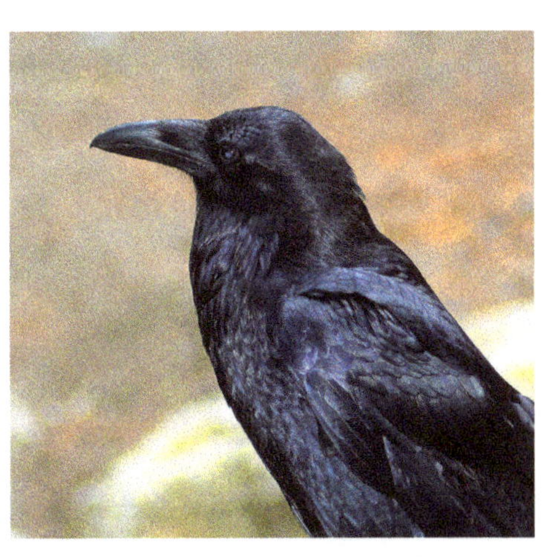

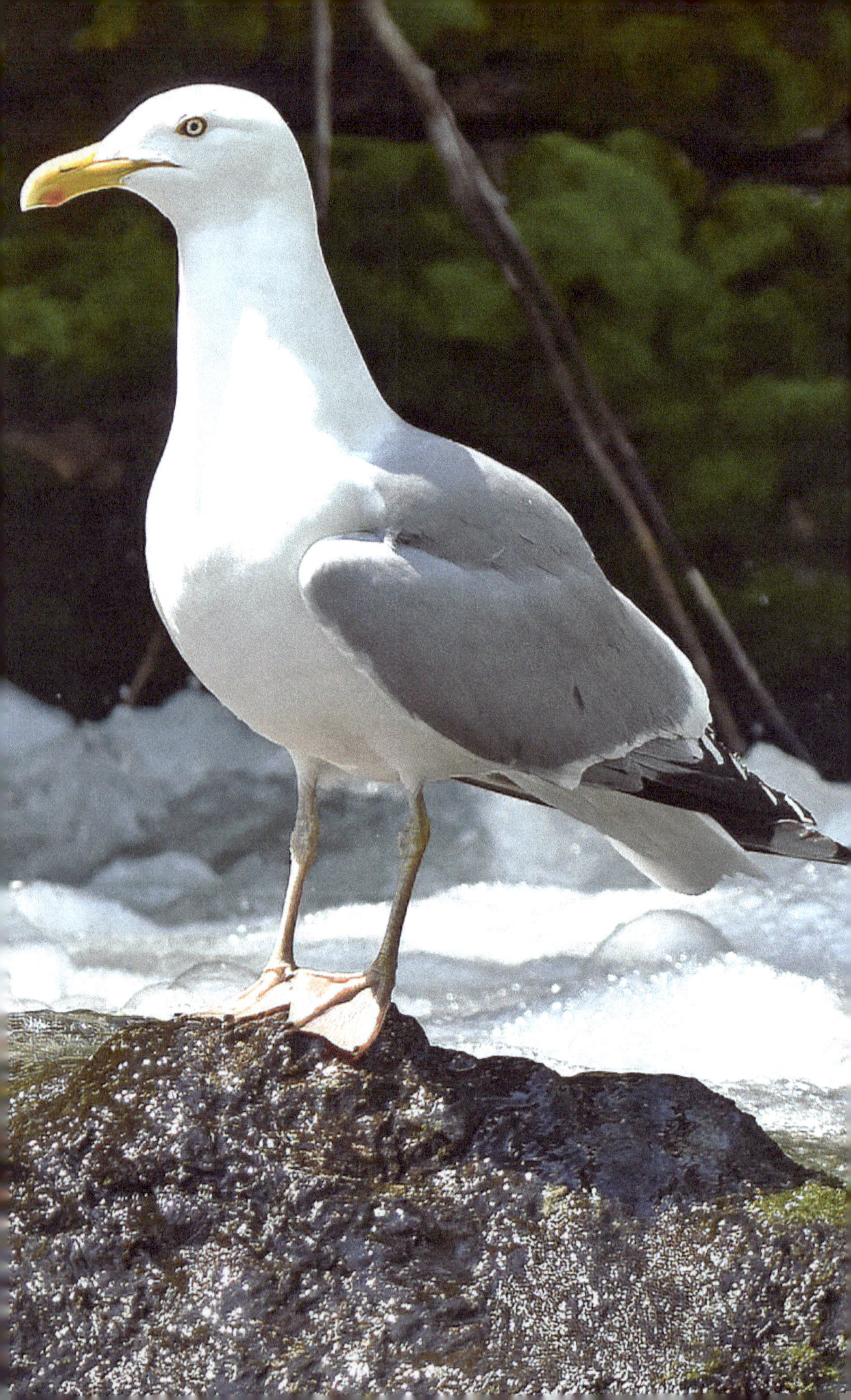

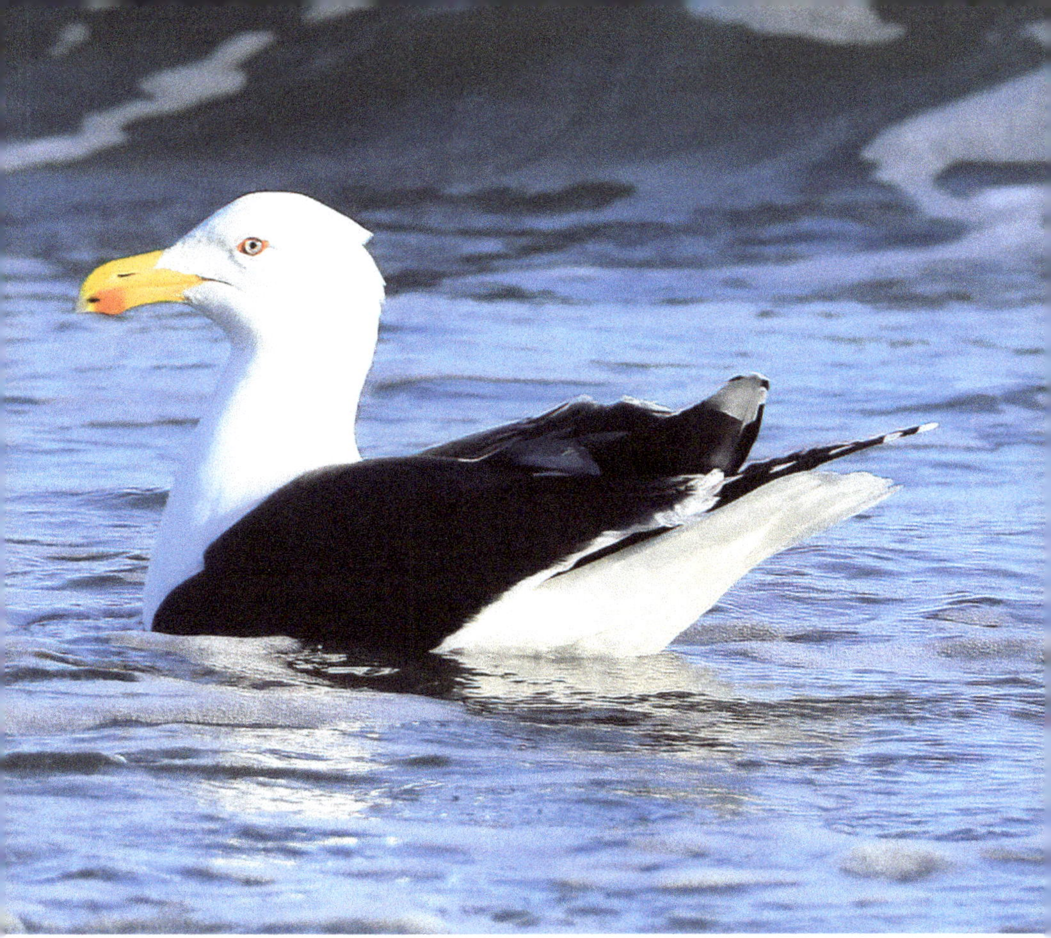

Nothing triggers a birder more than the term "seagull". That's because there is no such thing as a "seagull". It's a term we've heard and perhaps used our whole lives, but there is no such bird, nor is there even a family of birds called "seagull".

The white, gray and black birds that we see at the beach, a fast food parking lot or the local landfill are more appropriately called "gulls".

World-wide, there are about 100 species of gulls with sixteen having been identified in Maine.

The most common of these are the Herring Gulls (the bird that steals your French fries at a clam shack on a hot summer day), the Ring-billed Gulls (the two dozen birds congregating in the center of the grocery store parking lot), and the Great Black-backed Gull (the large bird stealing those French fries from other gulls). The "Big Three" are year-round residents of Maine.

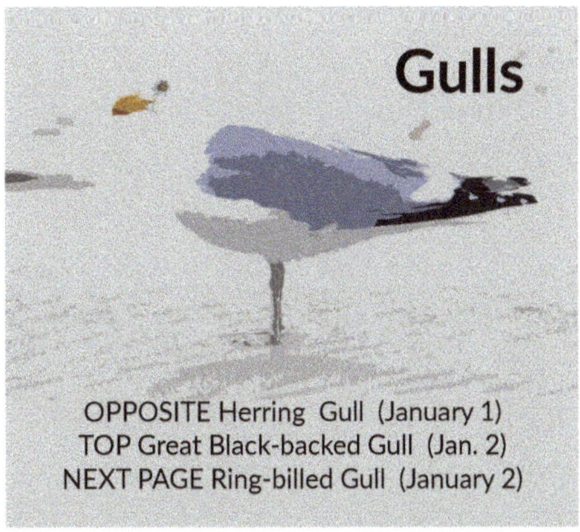

OPPOSITE Herring Gull (January 1)
TOP Great Black-backed Gull (Jan. 2)
NEXT PAGE Ring-billed Gull (January 2)

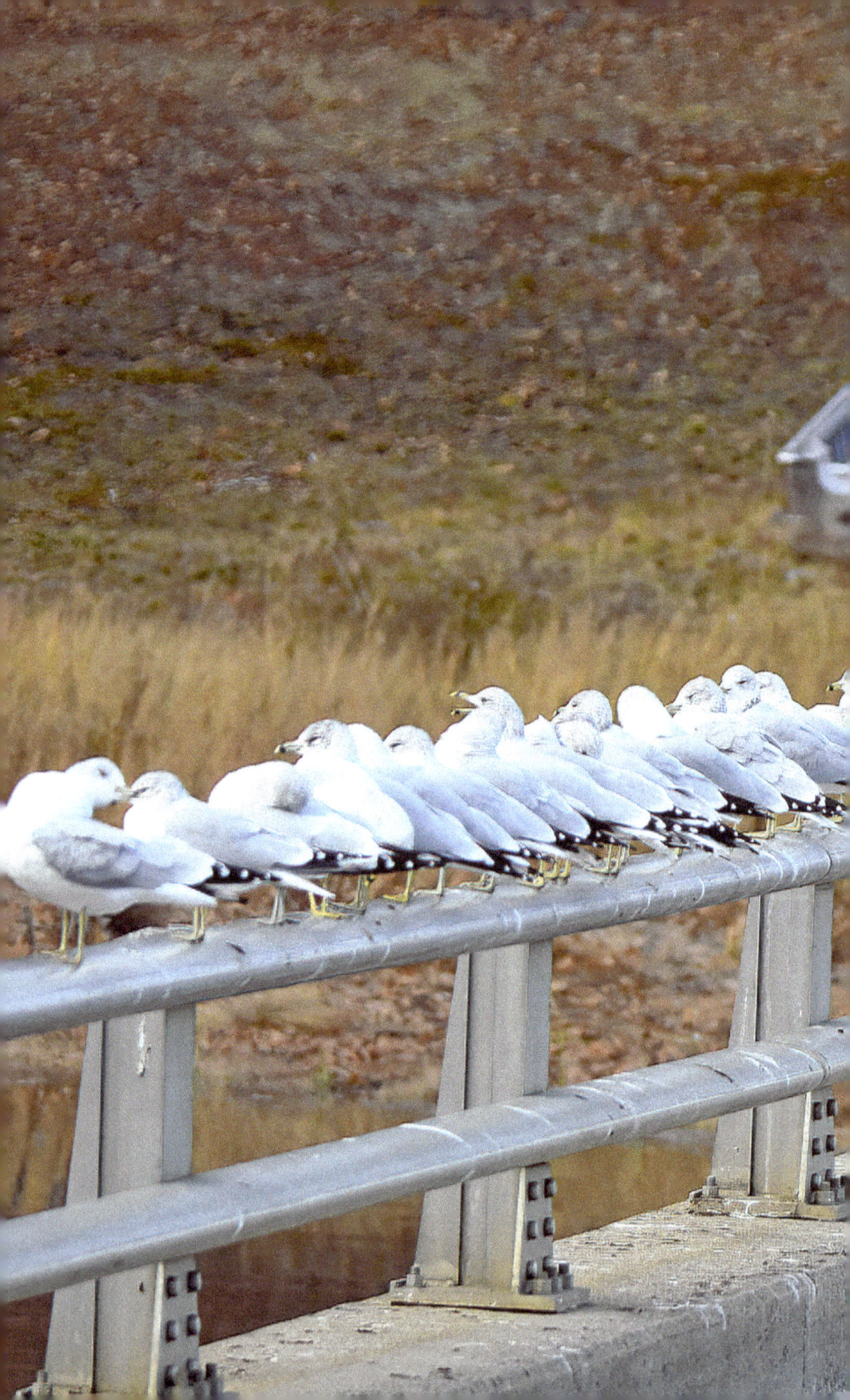

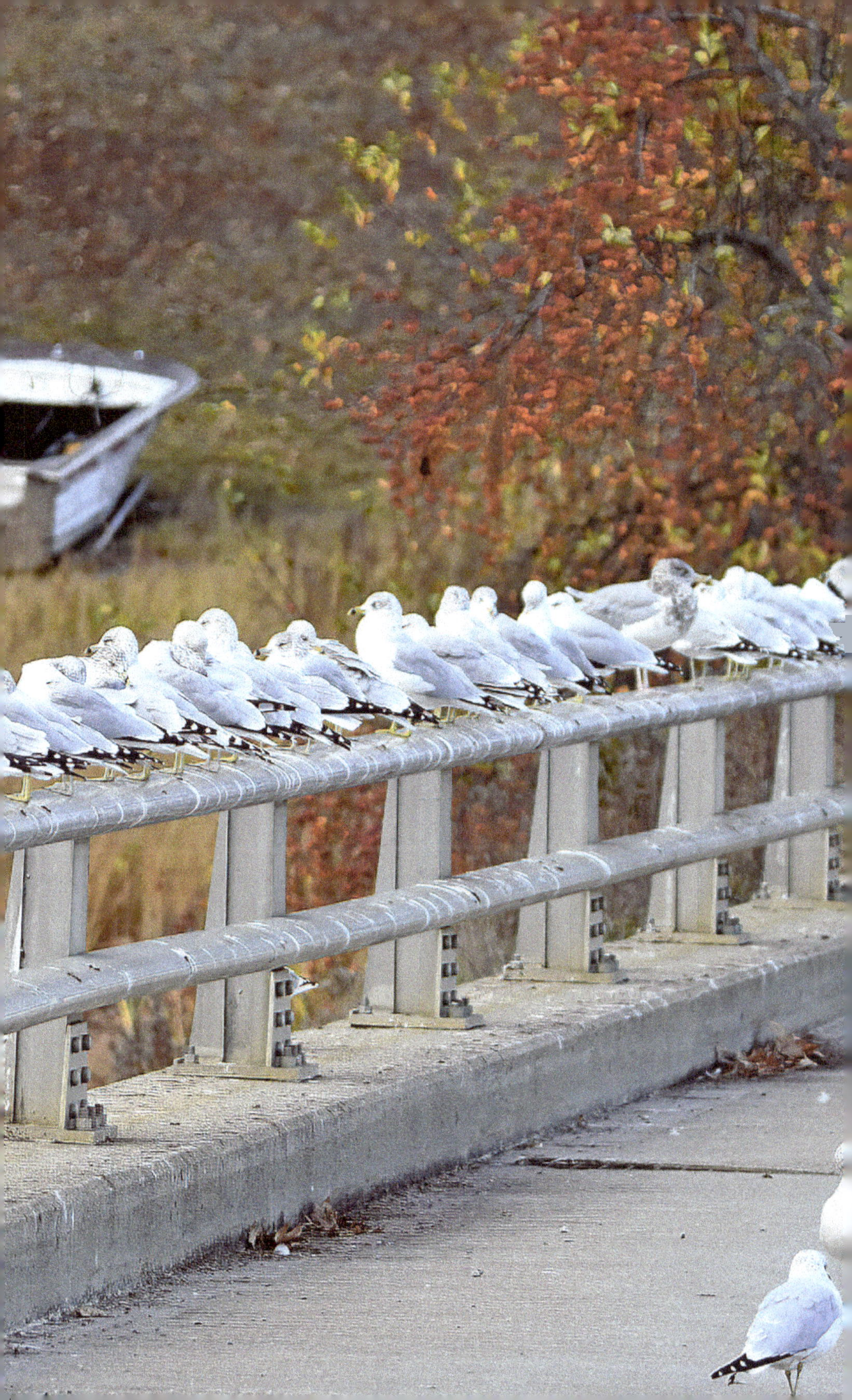

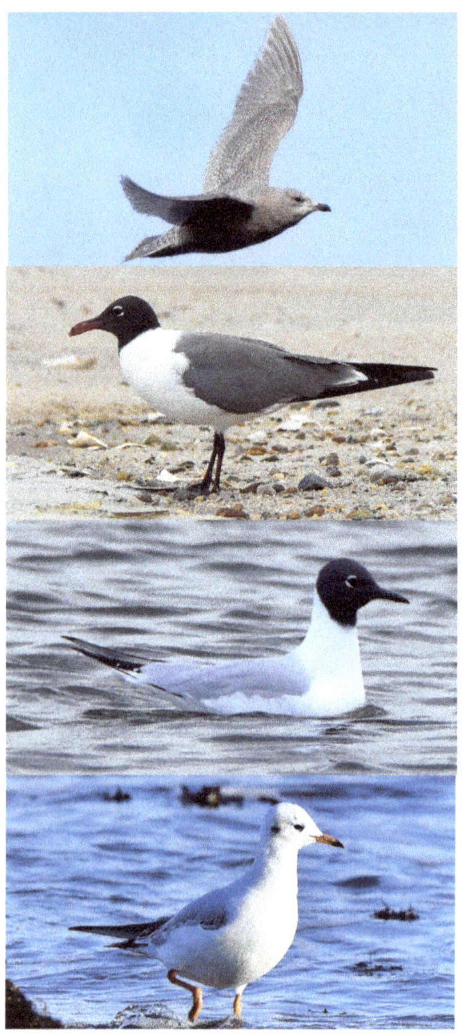

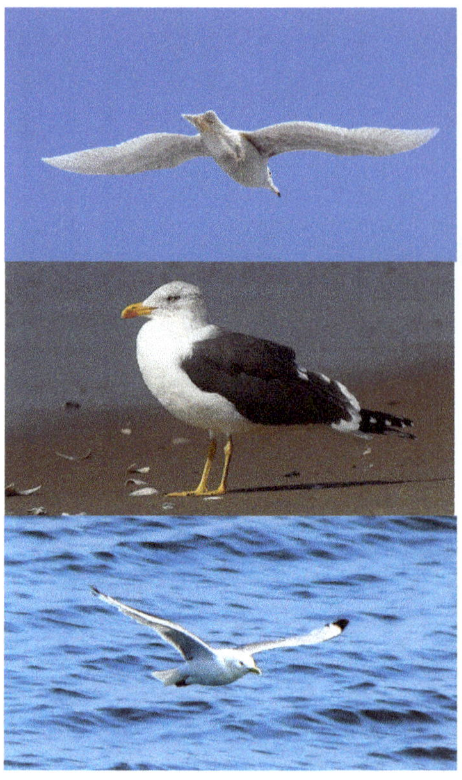

version of the Great Black-backed but with yellow legs.
• Black-legged Kittiwake, a Canadian Maritime bird that occasionally drops down into the states.

Gulls also take on different appearances when they are juveniles, and again in years two, three and adulthood, during molting and in various seasons. Identification is difficult and the handful of birders who specialize in the minute details are somewhat fanatical.

Bonaparte's and Laughing are smaller gulls that move in and out of the state with the seasons. These species also have stunning black heads while breeding and white heads (with a large gray fake eye spot) the rest of the year. The best way to tell the difference: "Laughers" have red bills and Bonaparte's have black bills.

Other Gulls seen sporadically:
• Iceland and Glaucous Gulls, comparatively white birds without black on their wing tips.
• Lesser Black-backed Gull, a smaller

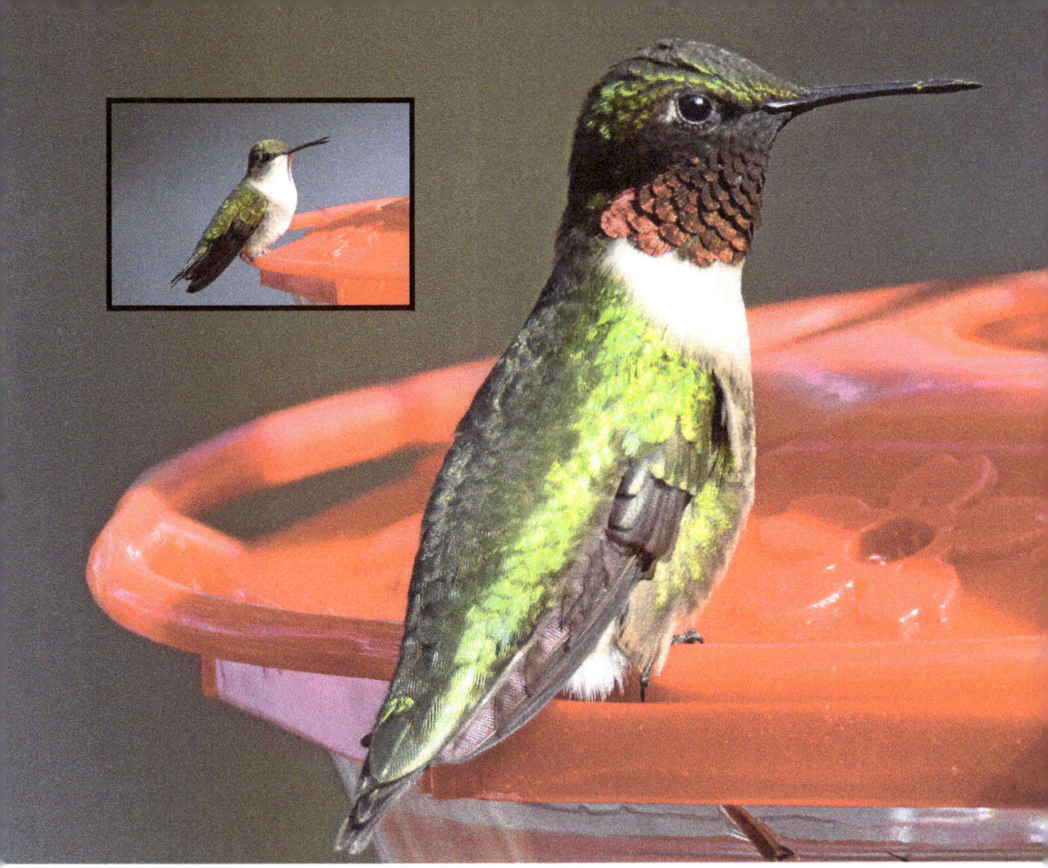

There are 359 species of Hummingbirds in the world, twenty-one of which are found in the United States. Of these, only one, the Ruby-throated Hummingbird, is regularly found in Maine.

Most of the North American hummingbird species migrate in the spring from South America through Mexico and Texas and then into the West. The Ruby-throated Hummingbird is the only one that migrates over the Gulf of Mexico, a flight that takes 18 to 22 hours in one incredible effort.

Afterwards, the Ruby-throateds move north up the Eastern seaboard into Maine. They arrive each year during the first week in May and depart around Labor Day.

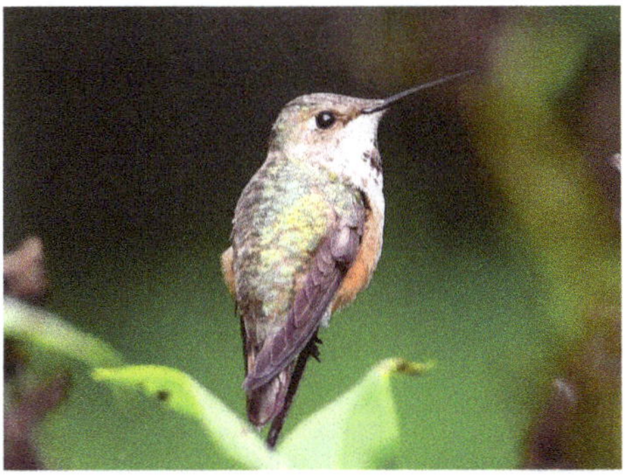

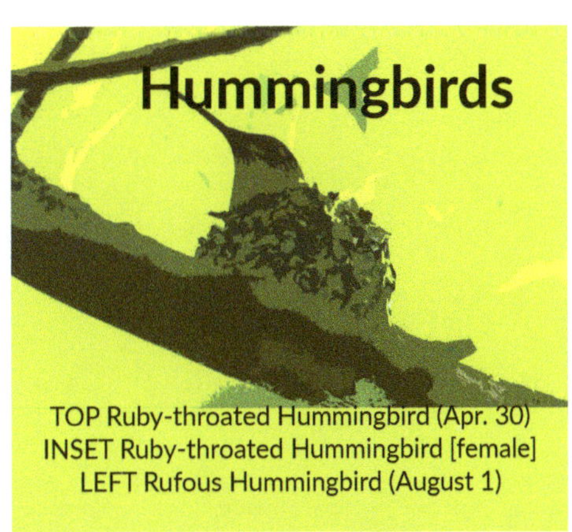

TOP Ruby-throated Hummingbird (Apr. 30)
INSET Ruby-throated Hummingbird [female]
LEFT Rufous Hummingbird (August 1)

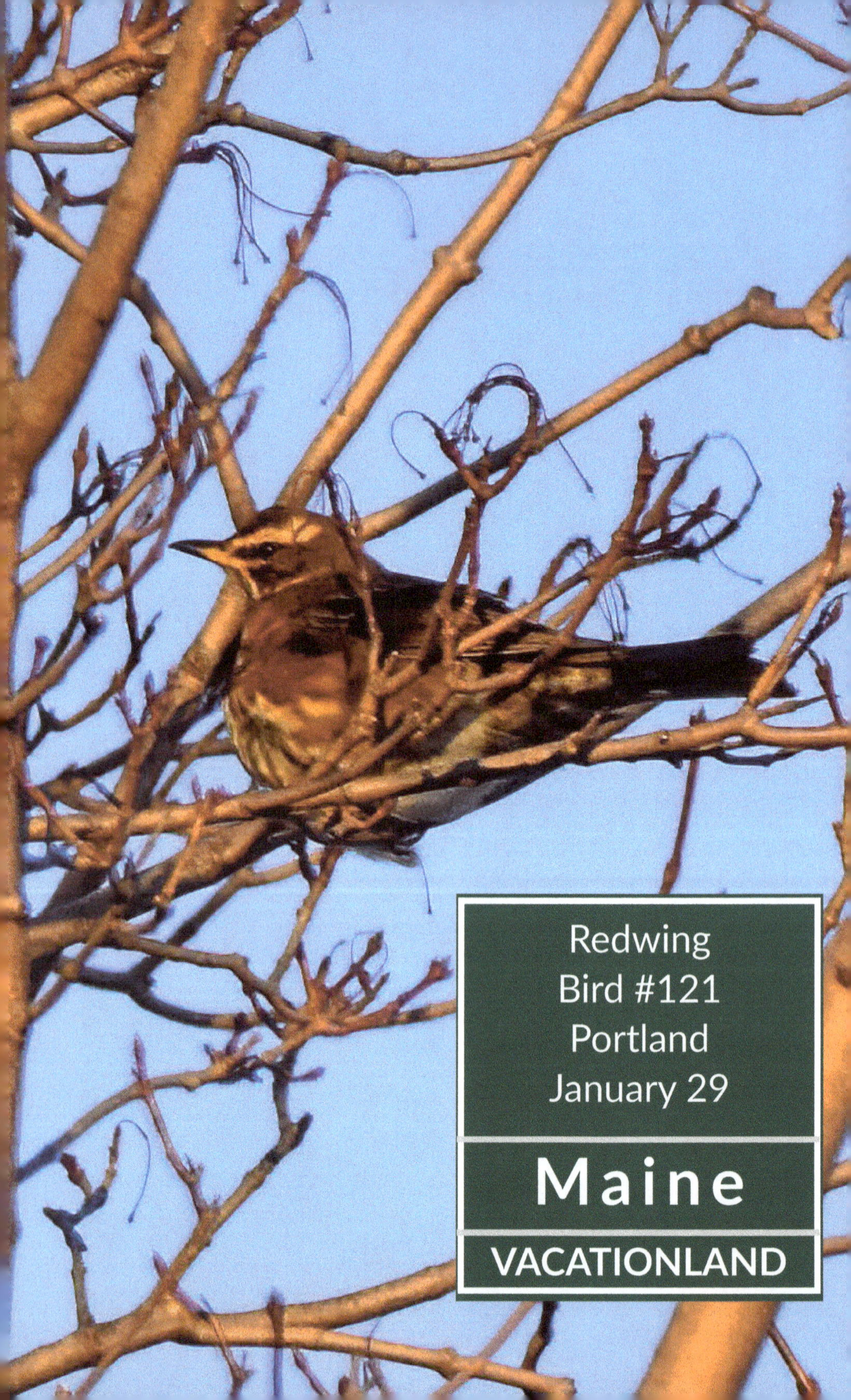

Redwing
Bird #121
Portland
January 29
Maine
VACATIONLAND

According to Woody Allen, "80% of success is showing up." I'm pretty sure he wasn't talking about birding, but the axiom carries over.

Through most of January, there was a Black-headed Grosbeak being seen at Capisic Park in Portland. I made ten trips and spent dozens of hours standing in the cold hoping for a fleeting glimpse of this Maine rarity.

On January 29, I arrived for my latest vigil around 1:00 PM and was soon joined by some of the best birders in the State, including a few young superstars. When birders flock together like this, everyone begins to tell war stories ("Remember when the Pink-footed Goose . . ."), and there is much laughter.

Eventually the cold started to seep into our bones, the stakeout became quiet, and the number of birders began to shrink. By 4:00 I was beginning to make deals with myself: "You can leave after Doug and Josh leave" or "You can leave at 4:30."

About 4:10 pm as feeling was leaving my fingers and toes, Chris Sayers, a young prodigy, ran up the hill exclaiming that a Redwing had just been seen. Suddenly all the young guys were gone, running as fast as they could. Perplexed, I thought, "A Red-winged Blackbird is rare this time of the year but nothing to get so excited about."

By the time I caught up with the youngsters (I was 62 at the time) I began to vaguely remember a European bird, similar to the American Robin, named "Redwing". The Redwing is an Eurasian species that belongs in southern Europe or even Iran at that time of the year.

The Maine Redwing was quickly located, and we watched it move through the trees with our Robins. For ten minutes we were able to view it with our binoculars and photograph it from afar. Certainly, this was the second rarest bird I saw in Maine during 2021, and the Black-headed Grosbeak (which I found a week later) no longer seemed that important.

For the next couple of weeks, Capisic Park became the birding capital of the United States with birders traveling to Portland to see this rare visitor.

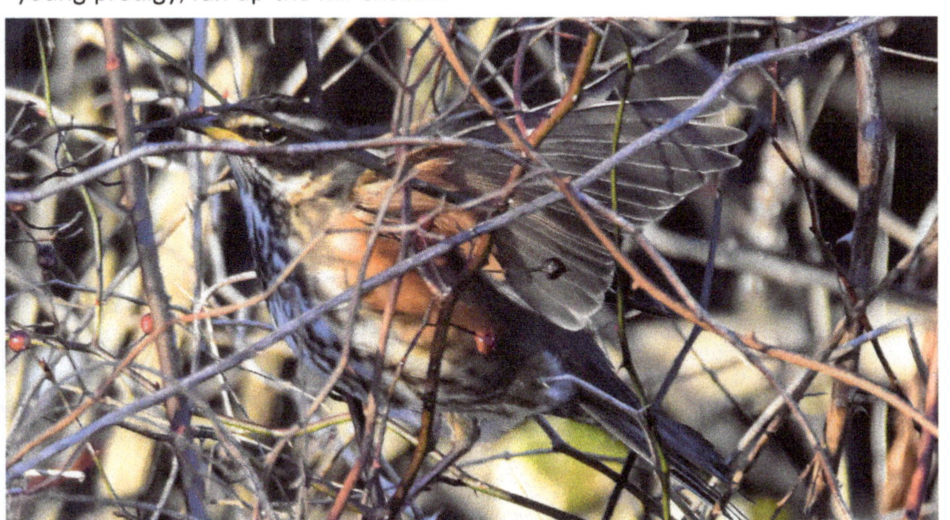

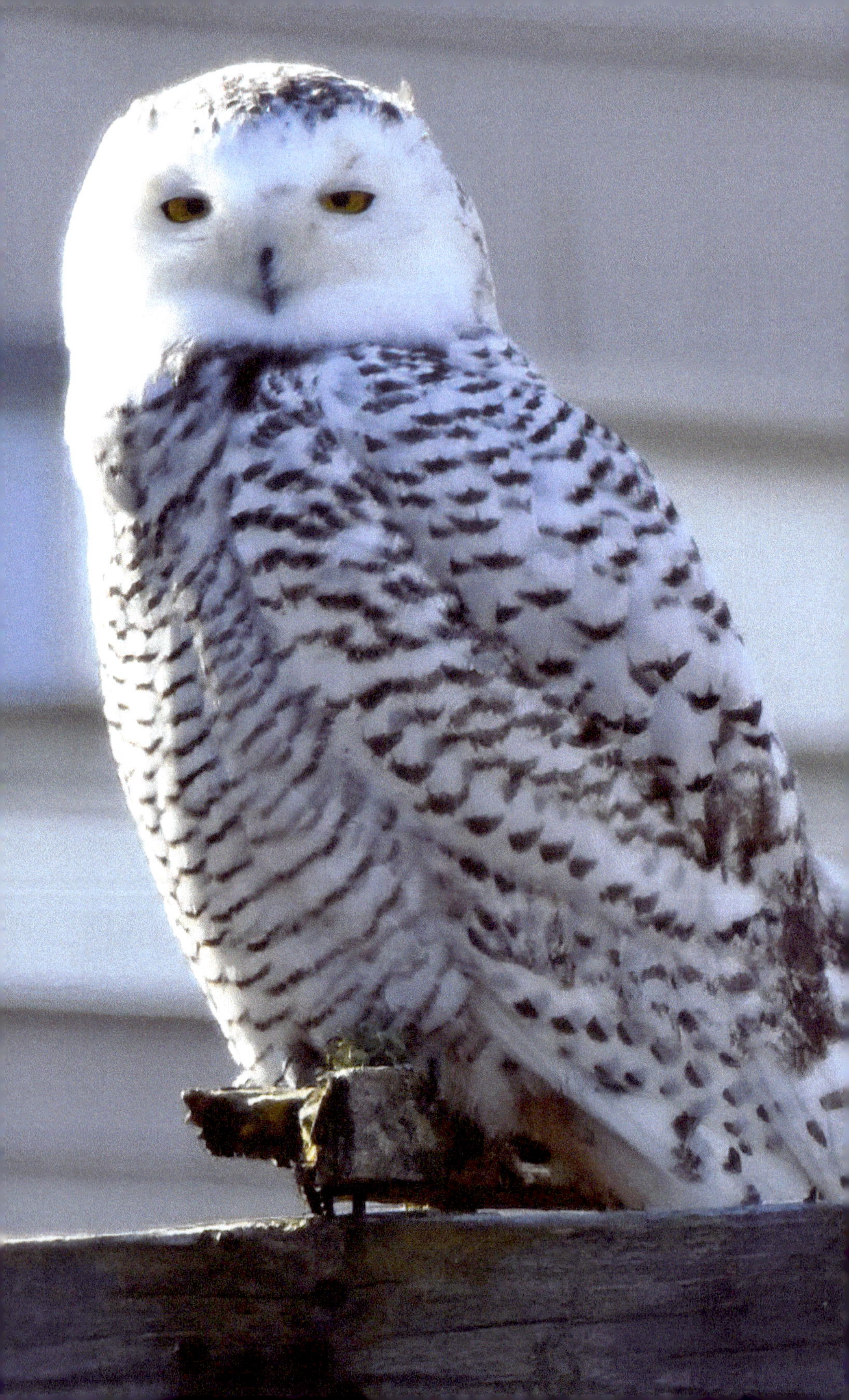

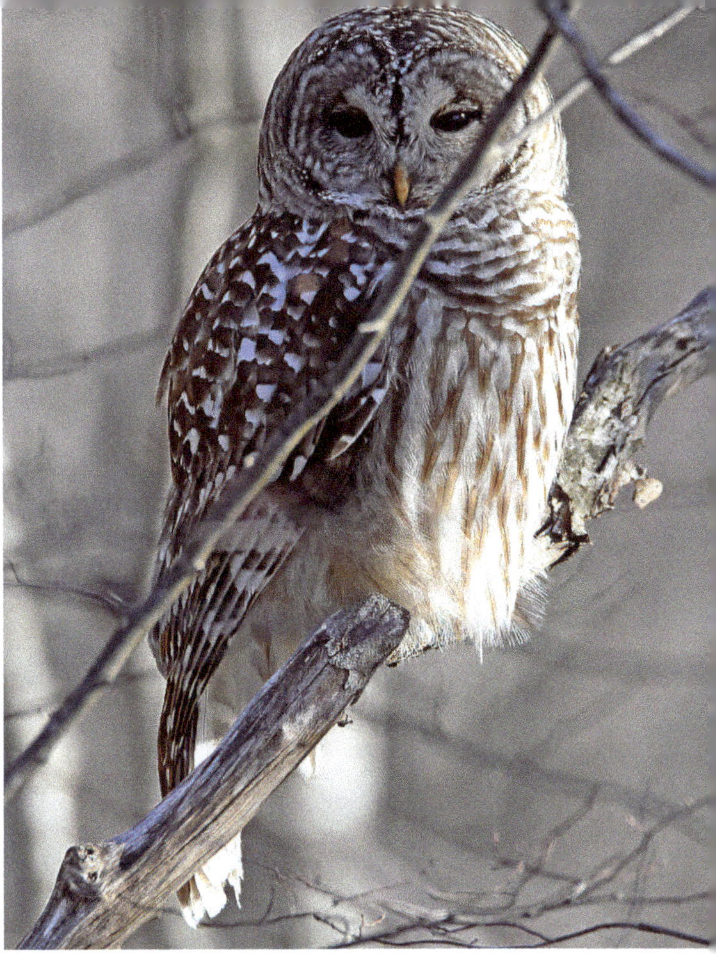

On an early March morning a fellow birder and I were standing along a wooded country road scanning a stream that was free of ice, hoping to spy the Pied-billed Grebe reported to be lurking along the edge.

I glanced across the road and noticed one of those plastic owls that folks place on their roofs or boats to scare off pigeons and gulls. I remember thinking that this was an unusual place for someone to hang an owl scarecrow. Then the plastic owl moved its head.

For eight years I've been trying to photograph a Barred Owl. Facebook and Instagram are filled with iPhone snapshots of this owl sitting on deck railings, hoods of cars and power lines. I've seen them at a distance being mobbed by crows and their haunting, song *Who cooks for you, Who cooks for you* is often heard at night during the winter (and occasionally during daylight). But seeing one up close was obviously beyond my birding abilities.

While we never found the Grebe, I was pleased to finally photograph a Barred Owl, up-close and personal.

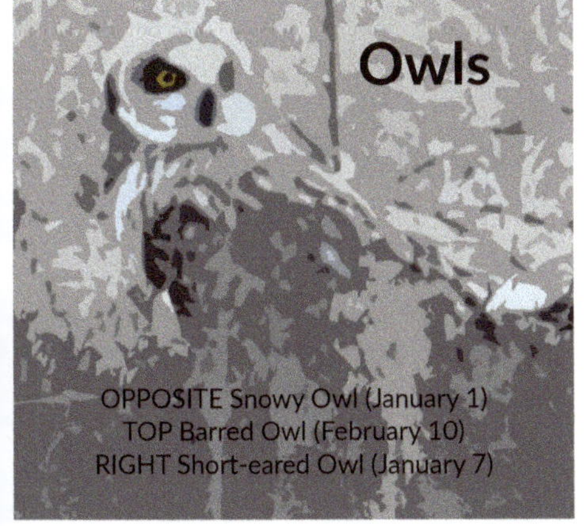

Owls

OPPOSITE Snowy Owl (January 1)
TOP Barred Owl (February 10)
RIGHT Short-eared Owl (January 7)

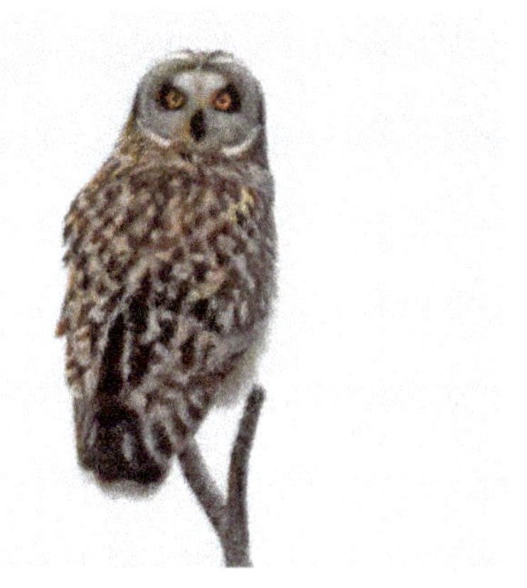

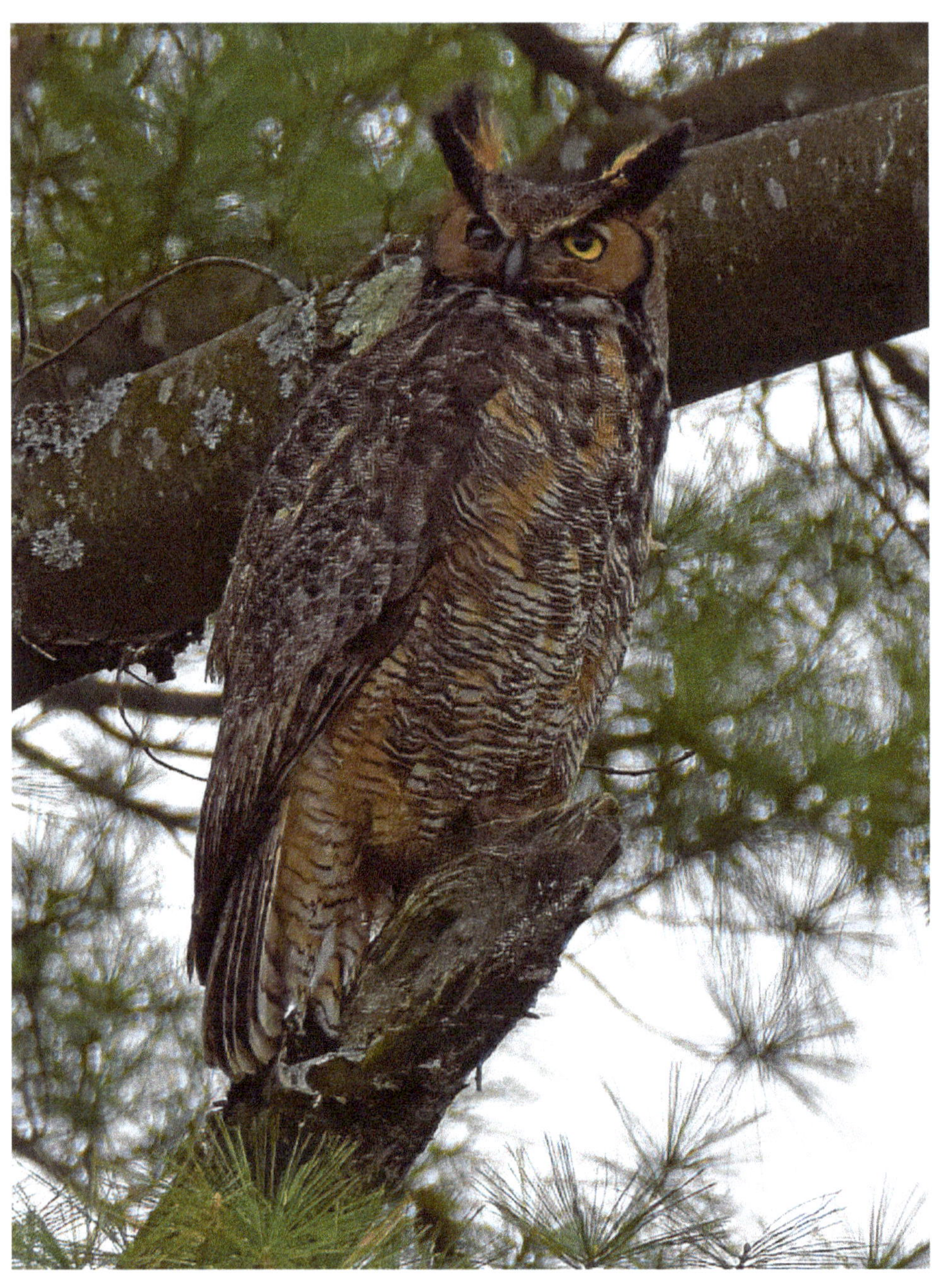

This book is filled with stories of how I found a particular bird here and a particular bird there. Sadly, there were quite a few more failed searches than successful ones.

For instance, it took two trips to Aroostook County (nine hour round trip) to get the Greater White-fronted Goose. I made ten trips to Capisic Park in Portland trying to find the Black-headed Grosbeak.

Then there was the search for the Eastern Screech Owl.

In mid-February, I heard reports of an Eastern Screech Owl singing at dusk on Peaks Island in Casco Bay.

With its stately homes and friendly folks, coupled with a working water-front, Peaks Island could have been painted by Norman Rockwell. The island is accessible by a ferry that runs from Portland every 90 minutes or so.

The Eastern Screech Owl is a common Owl throughout most of the USA, but is very rare in Maine; it's just too damn cold.

One evening, I caught the 3:15 pm ferry to Peaks Island hoping to find "Screech".

Upon arriving I noted that a 20 mph wind blowing off the ocean on a 18 degree day is COLD, VERY COLD, IN-CREDIBLY COLD!!!

While the 20 minute walk to the owl location was miserable, the directions were good, and I found its roosting tree right away.

As I gazed up hoping to see or hear the Screech Owl, I spied a Cooper's Hawk staring back at me, and he clear-ly wasn't going anywhere.

The Owl had reportedly begun trilling most evenings around 4:00 pm as the sun began to set. Well, he wasn't going

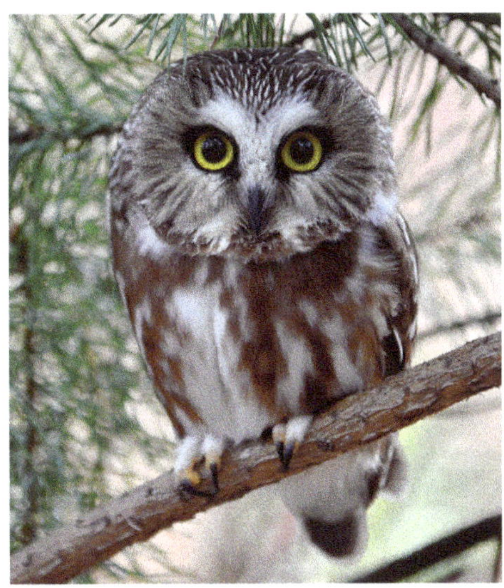

to sing with a Hawk sitting right there.

After 15 minutes my fingers were fro-zen and my head ached. I decided to cut my losses, jogged back to the Ferry and was on the 5:00 return boat.

A week later, on a warm, windless eve-ning (for February in Maine), I brought Lady Luck with me (that would be In-grid), and we found the Owl within a few minutes of stepping off the Ferry.

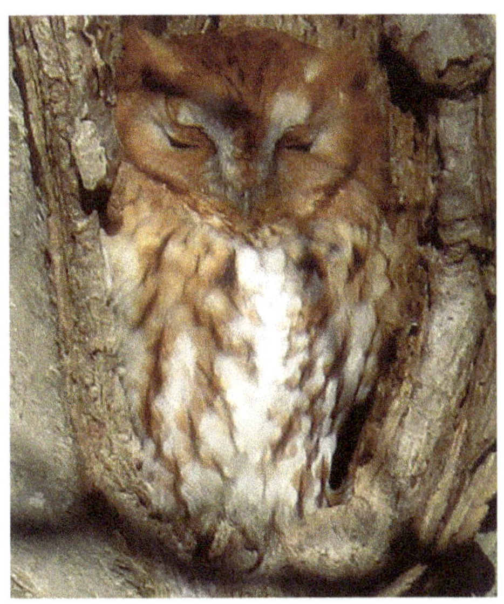

Owls (cont.)

OPPOSITE Great Horned Owl (January 1)
TOP Northern Saw-whet Owl (January 4)
RIGHT Eastern Screech-Owl (February 15)

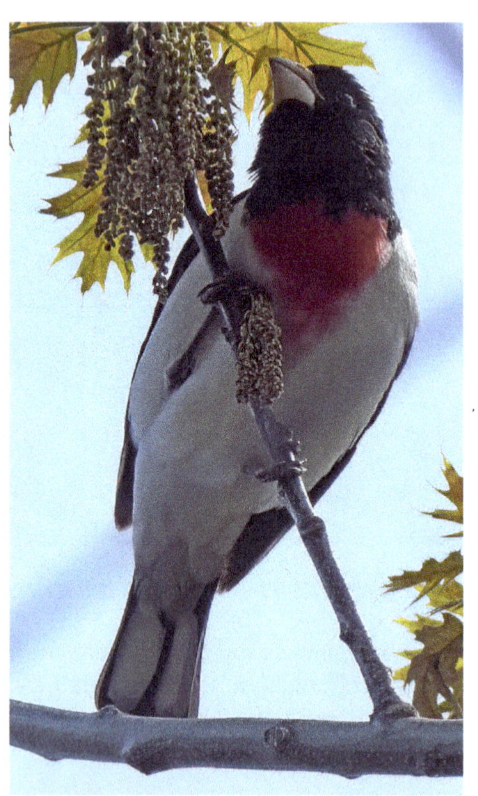

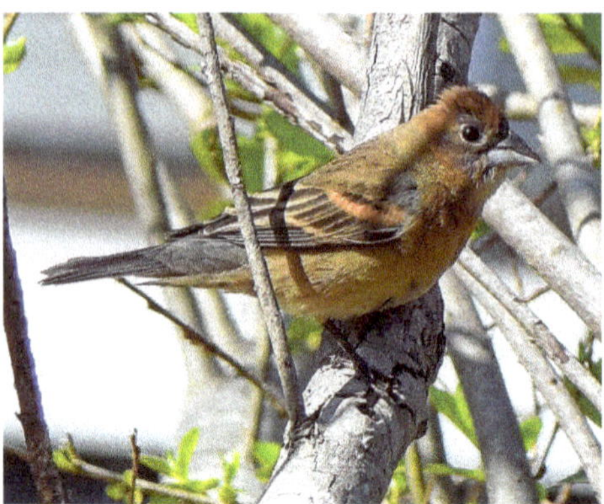

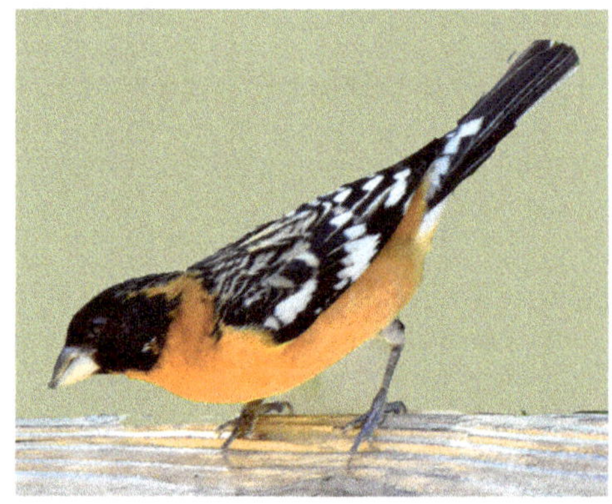

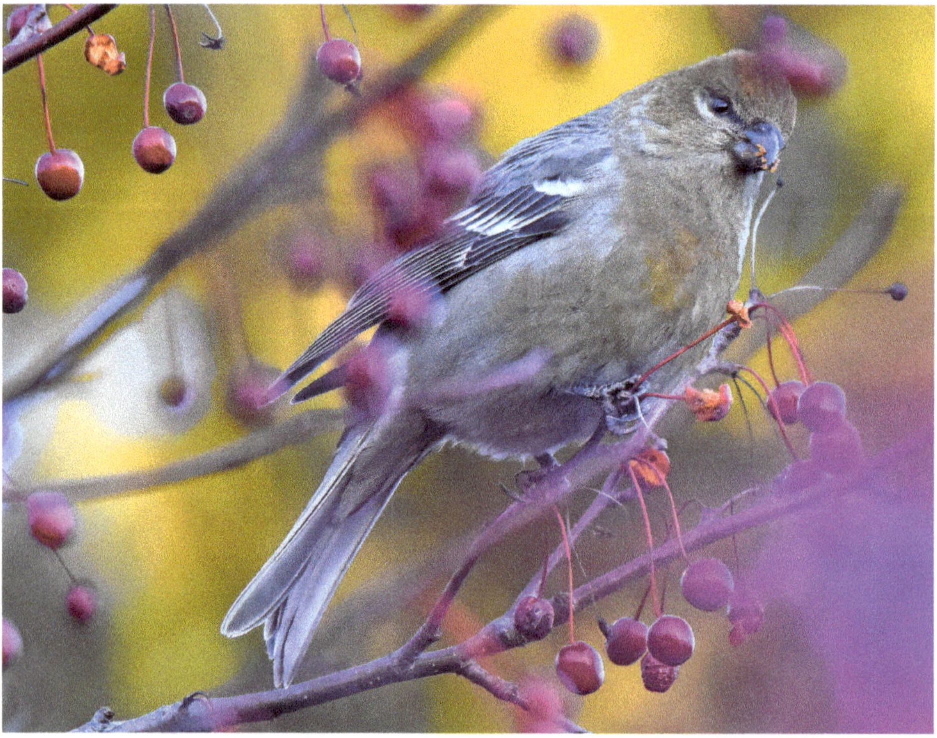

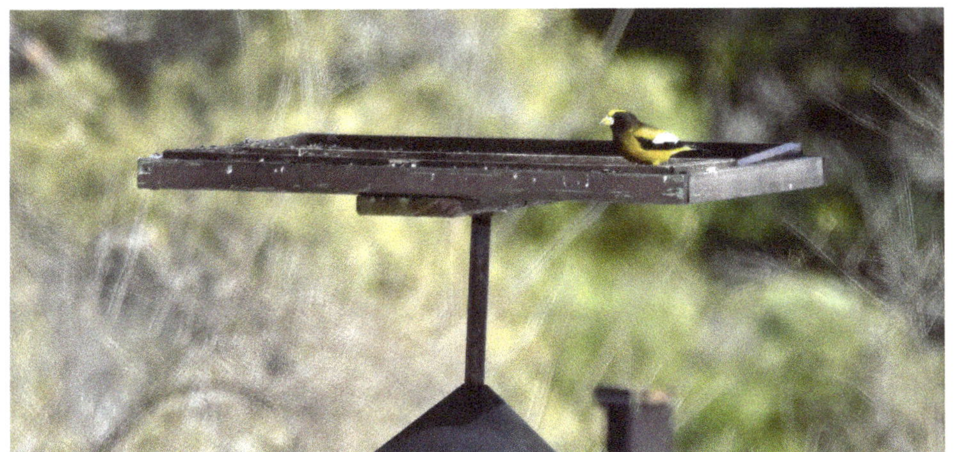

During migration season, a Maine Big Year is chaotic as we rush from place to place, from bird to bird. I say 'we', because Ingrid was with me on many of my excursions (when she wasn't teaching her 4th grade cherubs).

By late May, most of the easy birds had been checked off. However, there were so many birds moving through the state that we were constantly making decisions:

- How rare is the bird?
- Can we get it later in the year?
- How long to the bird's location?
- Will is still be there when we arrive (this flying away habit can be annoying)?

Case in point, I took the ferry out to Monhegan Island to find the Blue Grosbeak that had been hanging around the artist colony for the previous few days.

A Blue Grosbeak, whose northernmost breeding range is New Jersey, is usually seen in Maine only once or twice a year.

Upon arriving on the island, I knew I had five hours to find the bird before I had to be on the return ferry.

I searched and searched to no avail, but with just 45 minutes to go, I received a text that the Grosbeak was seen near the Island brewery, over a mile away and uphill.

I ran as fast as my less than svelte body could take me. I found the bird after a bit of searching, snapped a few photos and jogged the half-mile back to the boat landing.

I got the bird and the ferry, with three minutes to spare!!

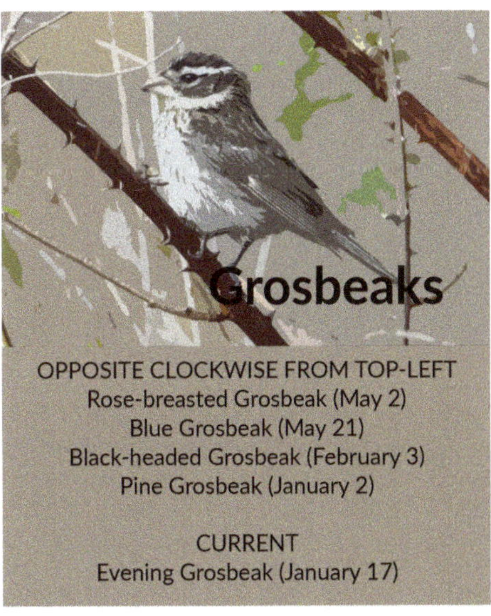

Grosbeaks

OPPOSITE CLOCKWISE FROM TOP-LEFT
Rose-breasted Grosbeak (May 2)
Blue Grosbeak (May 21)
Black-headed Grosbeak (February 3)
Pine Grosbeak (January 2)

CURRENT
Evening Grosbeak (January 17)

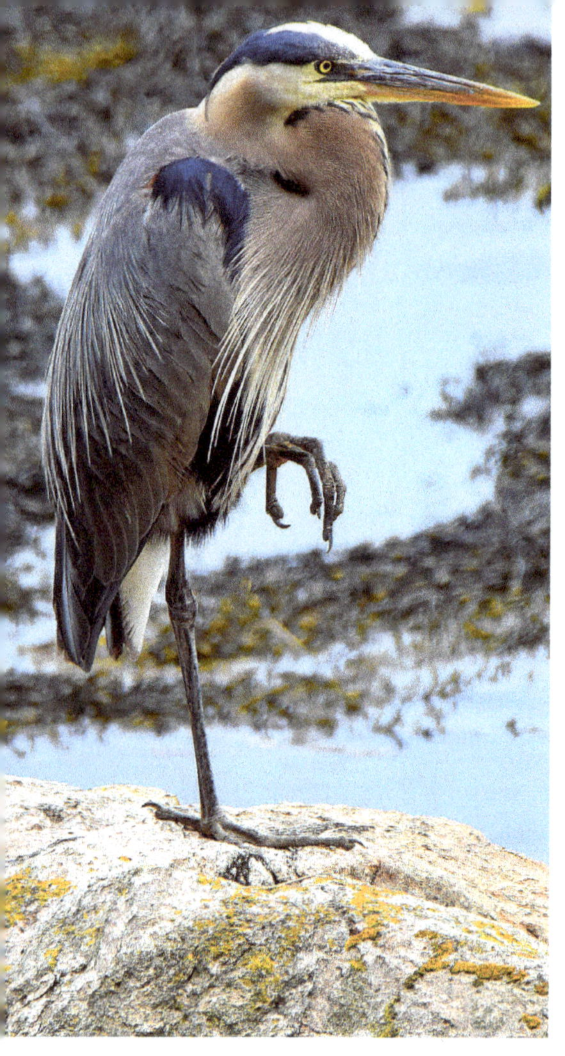

In 2000 when I moved to Wiscasset, there was a Great Blue Heron rookery a mile down the river on Berry Island. Even though I wasn't a crazy birder at that time, a regular part of our evening boat trips was cruising around the island to watch the Great Blues come in to roost for the night at the tops of the trees.

Then about 10 years ago, without warning, the rookery disappeared. Perhaps this was due to predation, maybe disease, but suddenly it was gone.

Then a couple of summers ago we found the rookery two miles up the river, on top of a railroad trestle.

Most evenings, spring through fall, one of the Herons from the rookery will land on the big rock in the river by our house and stand (usually on one leg) and wait for dinner to swim by.

Ingrid has named this bird "Herbert" and insists that every Great Blue Heron we see from one end of the State to the other is our "Herbert".

She makes me laugh every time she sees a Great Blue Heron fly over and she waves "Hi, Herbert!!!"

Great Blue Herons hold a very special place in our hearts. Ingrid's license plate is "GR8BLUE," and we have a life-sized Great Blue Heron sculpture over our front door.

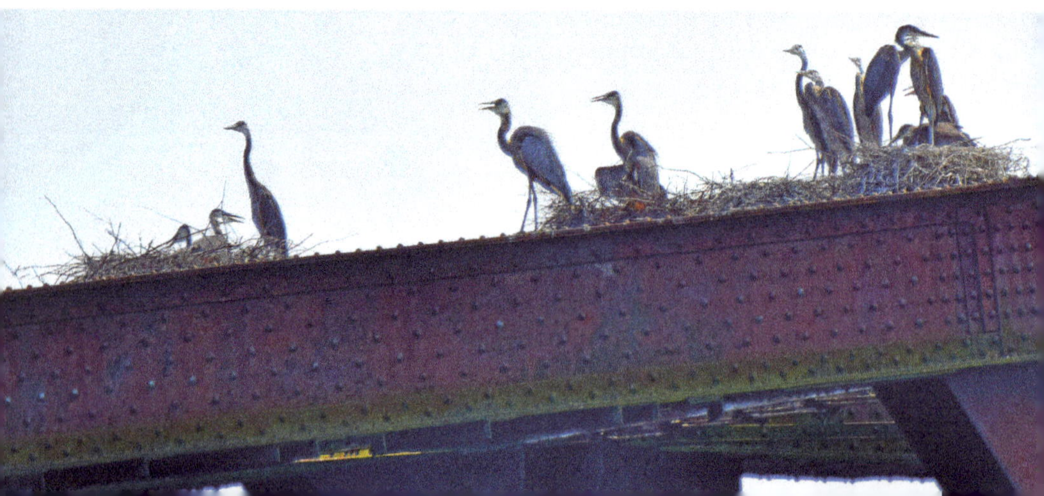

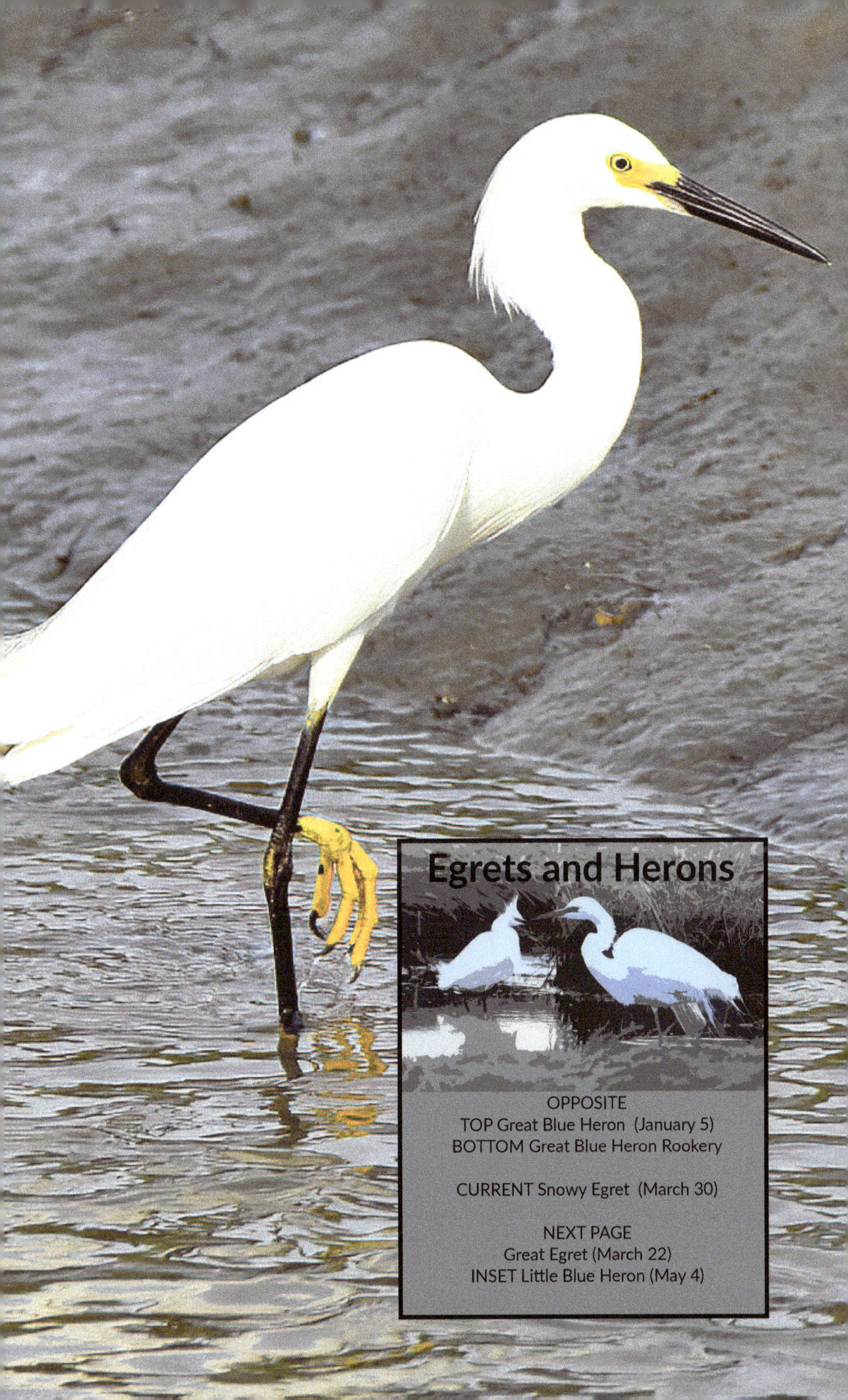

Egrets and Herons

OPPOSITE
TOP Great Blue Heron (January 5)
BOTTOM Great Blue Heron Rookery

CURRENT Snowy Egret (March 30)

NEXT PAGE
Great Egret (March 22)
INSET Little Blue Heron (May 4)

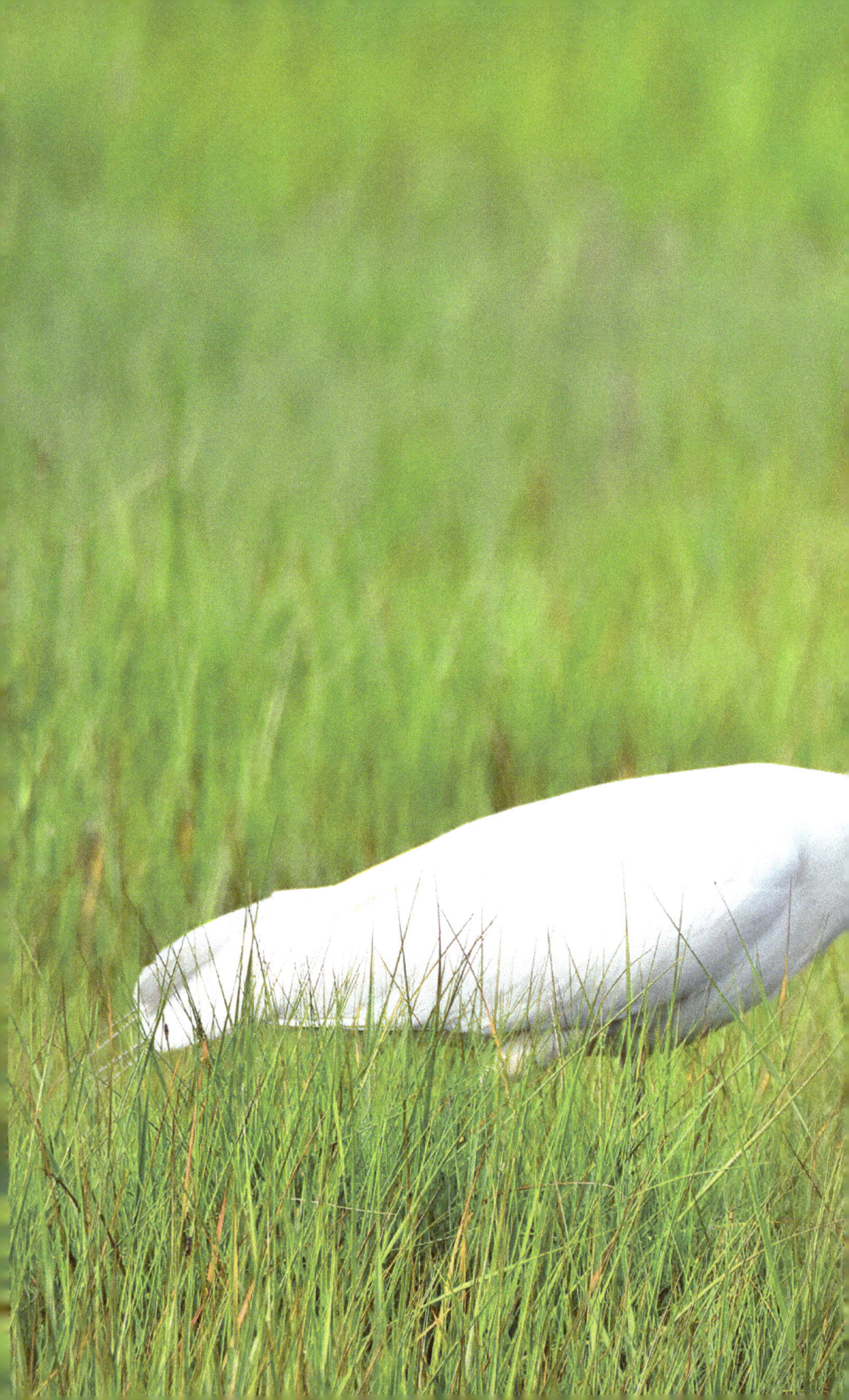

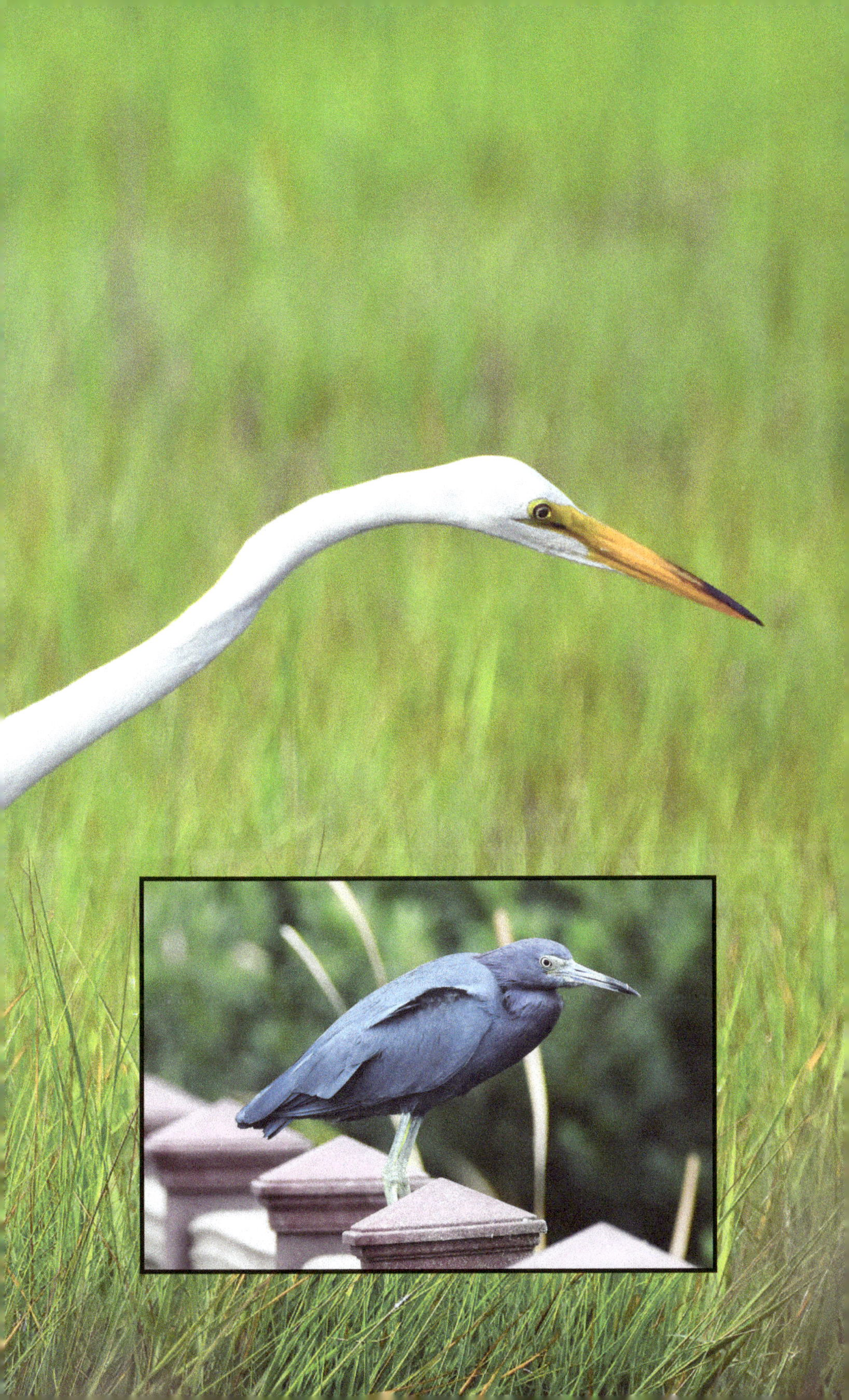

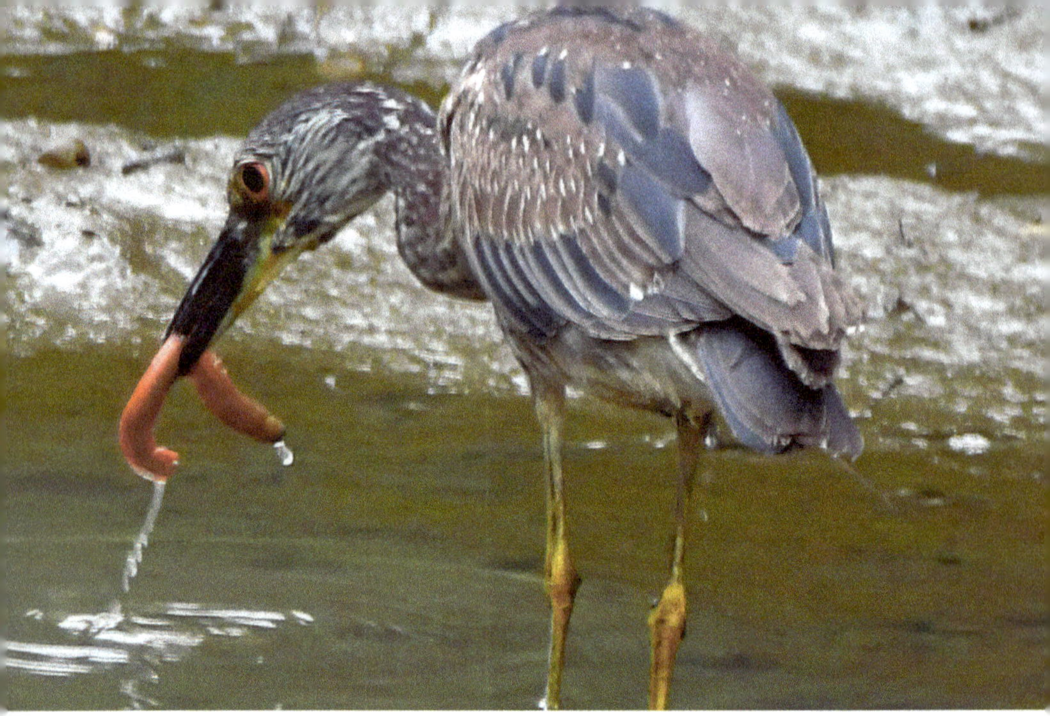

Most of us are familiar with bird migration, the annual movement of various species from their wintering grounds to their breeding territory. Generally, this means they travel north in the spring and south in the fall.

But a few perform a counter-intuitive post-breeding migration, traveling in a direction that is difficult to explain.

A case in point is the Yellow-crowned Night-Heron. The Yellow-crowned is a medium sized bird that breeds as far north as New Jersey and winters as far south as Mexico. My sister Ellen lives in Maryland and has these herons nesting in trees throughout her neighborhood.

But for some reason, in late summer a handful of juvenile Yellow-crowned Night-herons leave Ellen's backyard and travel to Maine, hundreds of miles

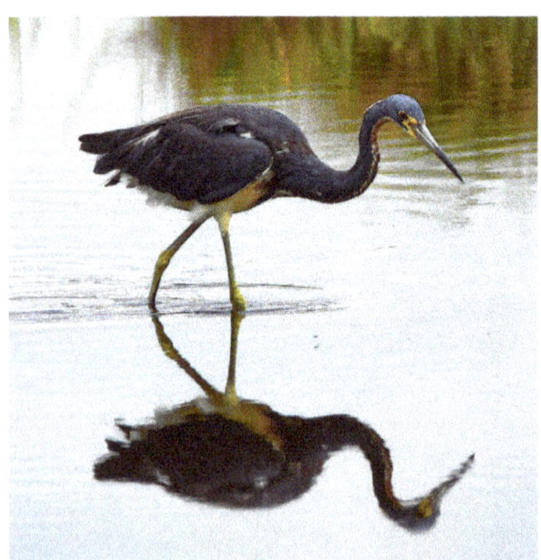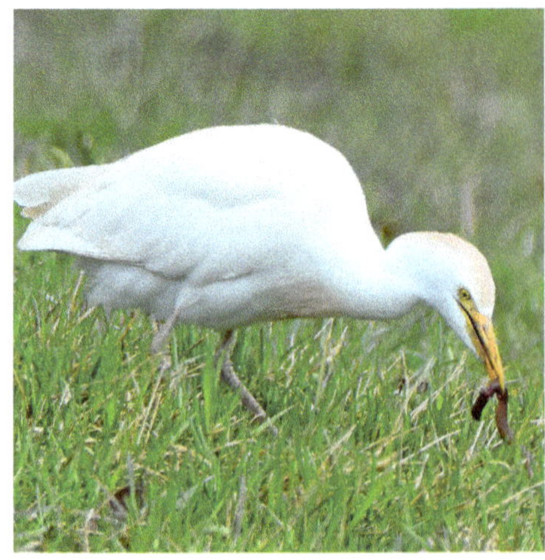

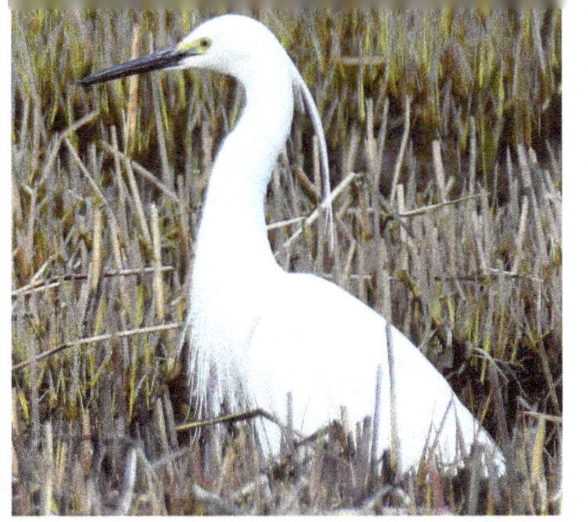

Egrets & Herons (cont.)

CLOCKWISE FROM TOP-LEFT
Yellow-crowned Night-Heron (July 26)
Little Egret (June 22)
Black-crowned Night-Heron (April 2)
Green Heron (April 30)
Cattle Egret (April 6)
Tricolored Heron (April 23)

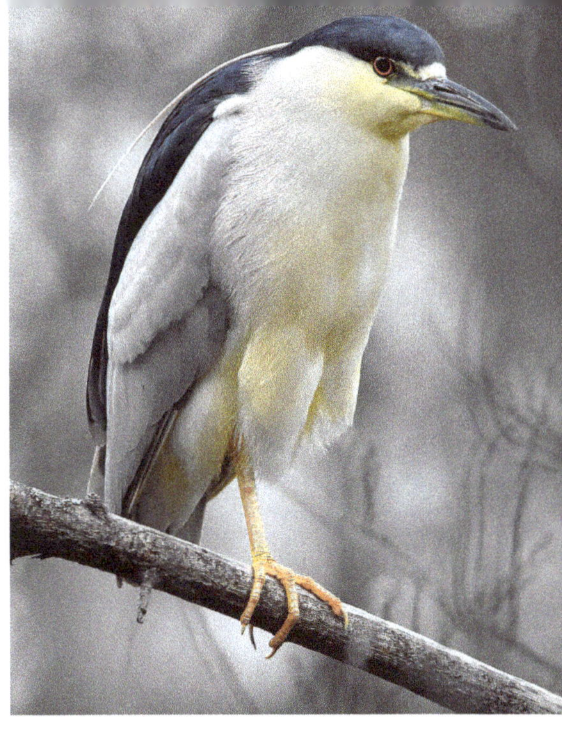

outside their range. Are they lost? Are they looking for food? Are they rebelling against over-domineering parents? Did Ellen tell them about Maine Lobster Rolls? No one knows exactly.

For most of July, Ingrid and I looked for one of these wayward birds and after more than a few wild heron chases, we found one feeding on worms in a Boothbay tidal pool.

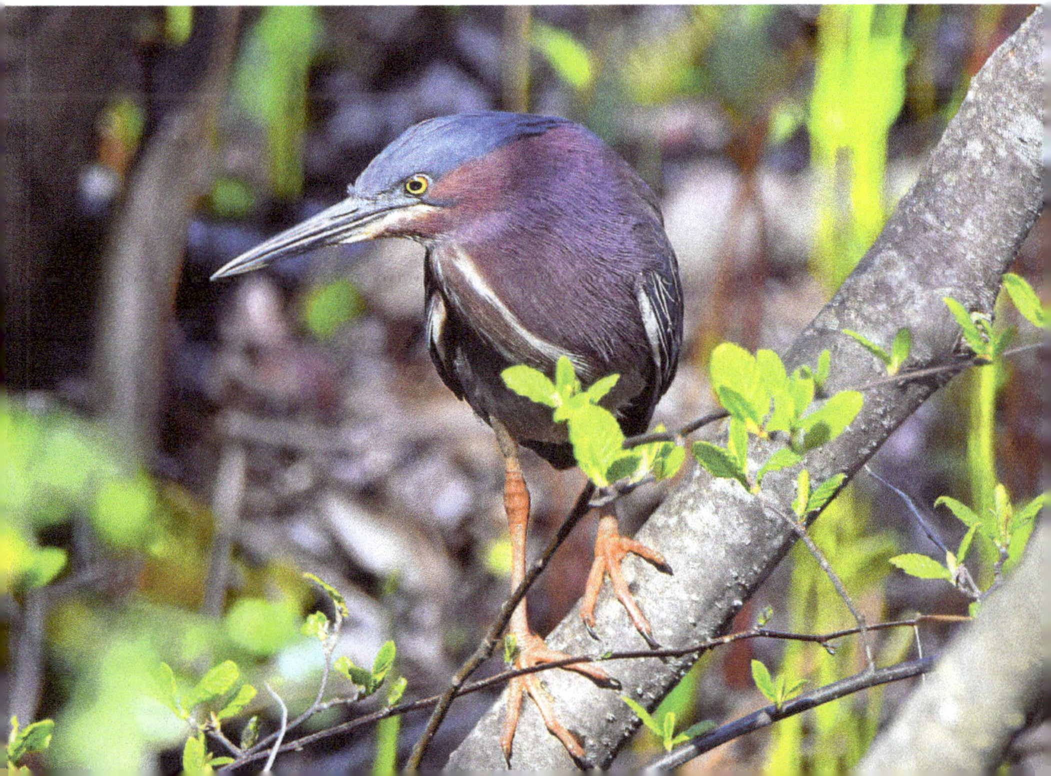

Doves

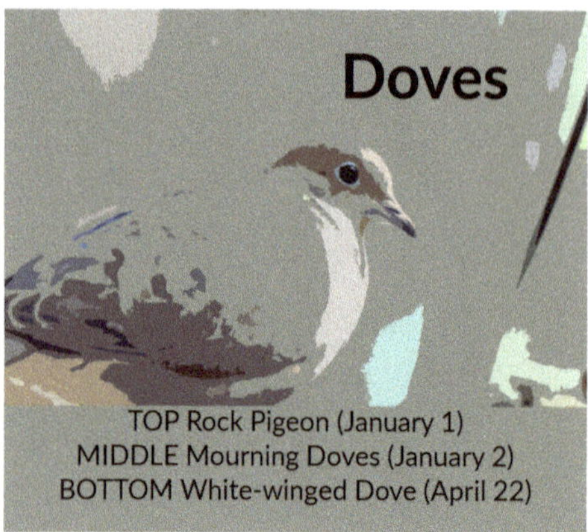

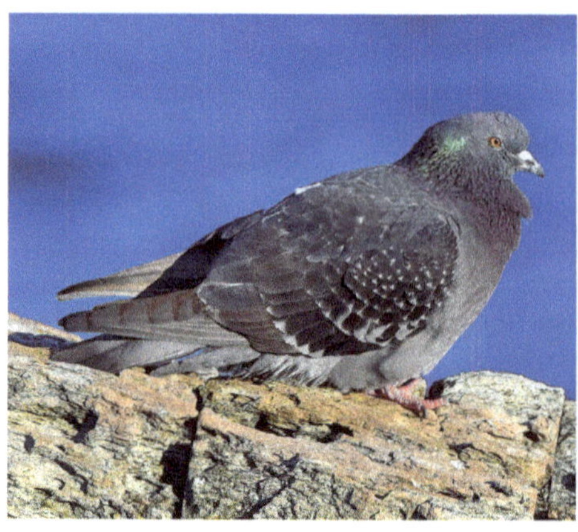

TOP Rock Pigeon (January 1)
MIDDLE Mourning Doves (January 2)
BOTTOM White-winged Dove (April 22)

The Pigeon, the ever-present resident of Maine's urban parks, bridges and buildings, is a descendant of the European domestic bird that was raised for food, messaging and racing. Birding checklists usually refer to it as a Rock Dove or Rock Pigeon.

Mourning Doves are almost as common, native to the state and found in forests, fields and at bird feeders. As a kid I was convinced that their *Who Who Who* song was that of an owl.

On April 22, a White-winged Dove showed up in a residential community in Gardiner about 1800 miles north of its normal stomping grounds in Florida.

It was a cold, gray, windy day and snowing a bit. I really didn't enjoy the two hours it took me to find this rarity. Yet, as always, it was a real thrill to see and photograph it.

Just imagine how a Florida bird enjoyed a typical Maine "spring day".

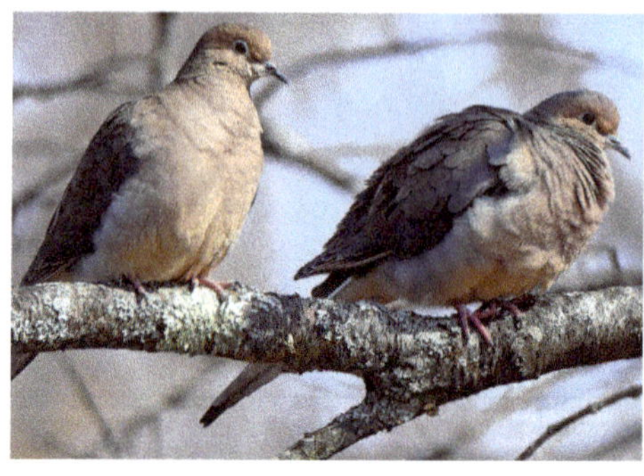

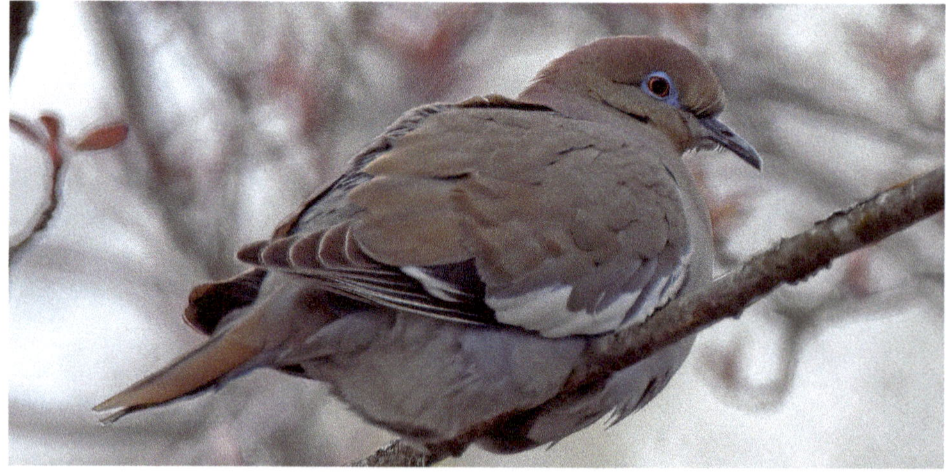

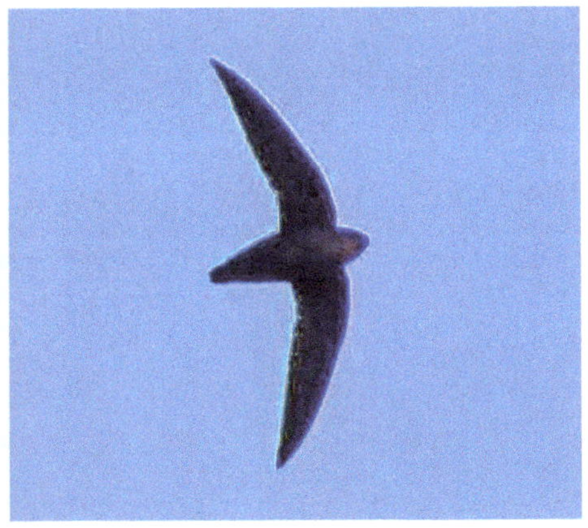

Bird #200 of my Maine Big Year was a Chimney Swift.

Basically a flying cigar, this bird spends most of its life in the air, only landing to roost in chimneys. Incapable of perching in trees like other birds, they have adapted to clinging to the insides of chimneys at night.

Before European settlement brought chimneys to North America, they nested in caves, cliff faces, and hollow trees. With the arrival of fireplaces, their population exploded. However, it is now declining as modern chimneys have caps and screens.

A long distance migrant, Chimney Swifts winter in South America and return to the Eastern USA each spring, traveling through Mexico and Texas.

I saw my first Chimney Swift of the year one afternoon over a Sewage Treatment plant in Sanford.

Later in the summer I discovered that an old chimney on the back of a dry cleaner's in Brunswick was being used by Chimney Swifts as a nightly roosting spot.

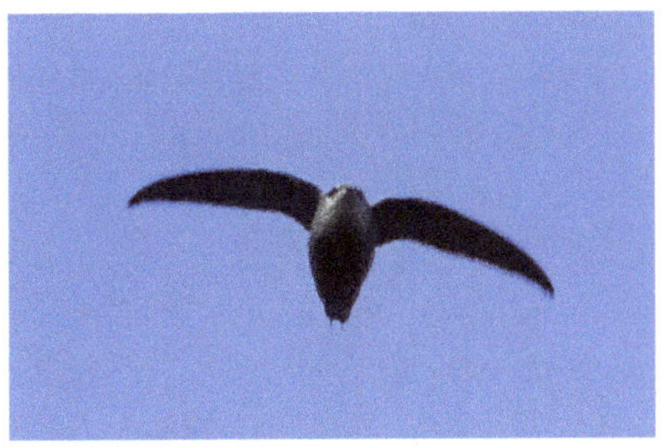

Arriving around dusk, I watched hundreds of Swifts spiral into the chimney in unison, truly an amazing sight.

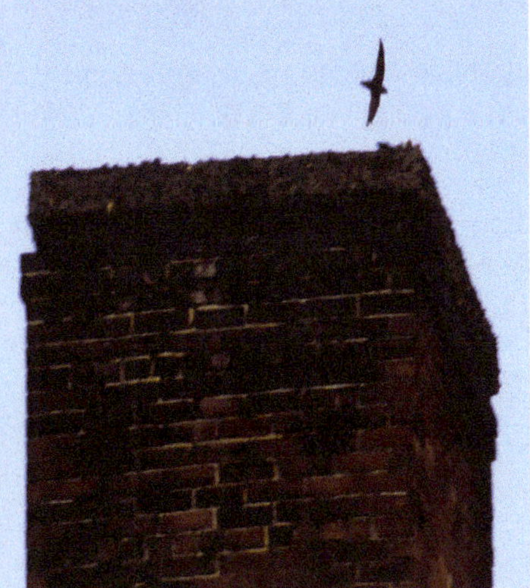

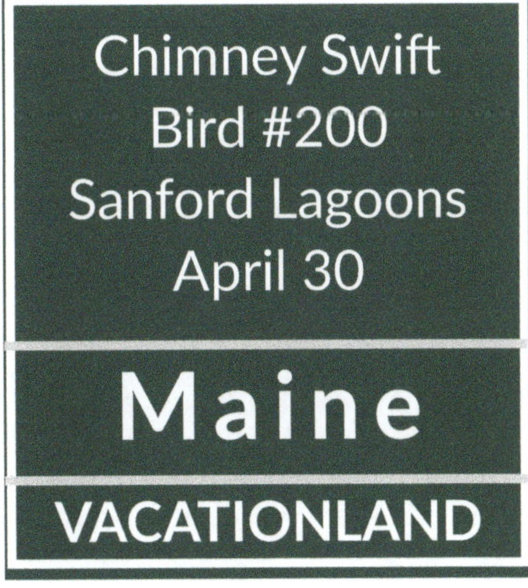

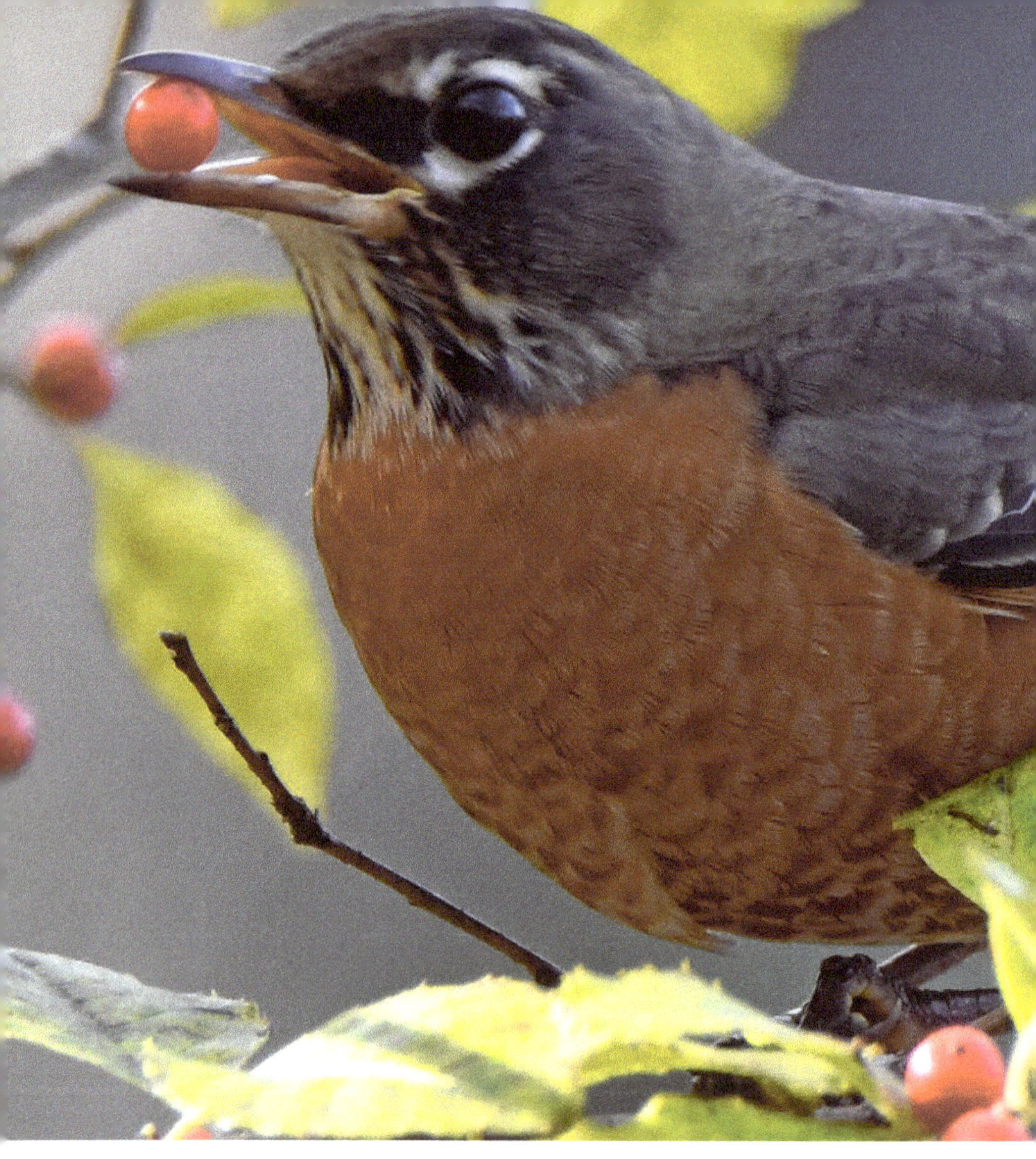

For most Mainers, Saddleback Mountain is a beautiful ski resort. For Birders, it is the summer home of the Bicknell's Thrush. To see a Bicknell's Thrush in Maine, one has to climb!!!

On a morning in early June, my alarm went off at 1:00 am (Ingrid was thrilled), and I was driving to Rangeley to climb to the top of Saddleback Mountain (4,121 feet).

Around 2:30 am, while passing through Wilton, I saw the all too familiar flashing blue lights in my rear view mirror. Once again I was being pulled over for speeding.

Time for my surefire method to get out of a ticket!!!

Police: I had you going 58 in a 35 mph zone.

Me: Oh, I'm terribly sorry. I missed the speed limit sign.

Police: Where are you going this time

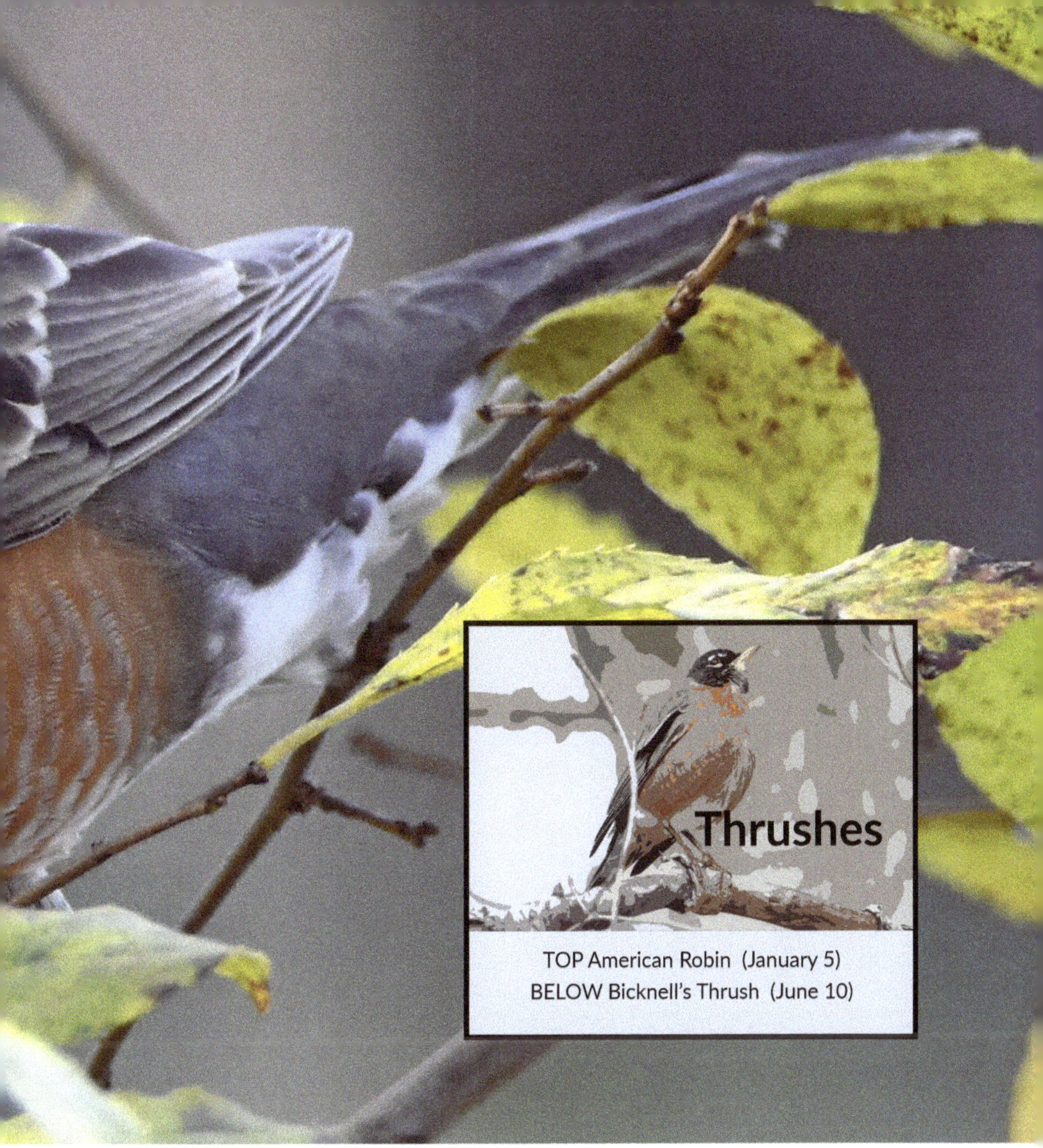

TOP American Robin (January 5)
BELOW Bicknell's Thrush (June 10)

of night?

Me (here comes my magic): I'm a birder, and I'm driving up to Saddleback to get a rare bird that is only found in Maine above the 3,000 foot mark. I want to be there at sunrise.

Police: What is the bird?

Me: It's called a Bicknell's Thrush, and it winters in Haiti and the Dominican Republic and it . . . Basically I keep talking about birds until the officer manages to interrupt me. He gives me a verbal warning and sends me on my way. This method has gotten me out of four

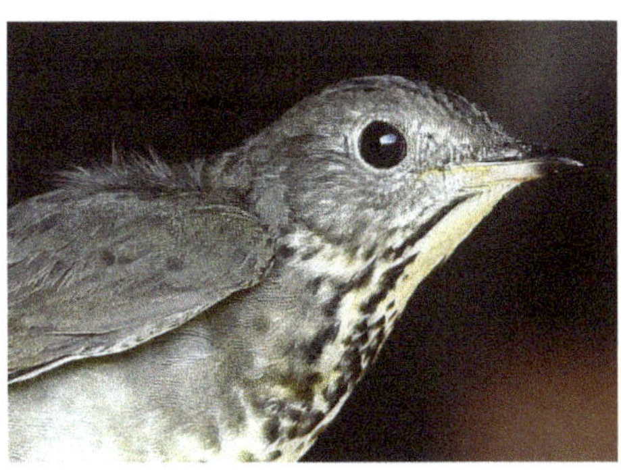

speeding tickets in the last year; they'll do anything to get me to shut up!!!!

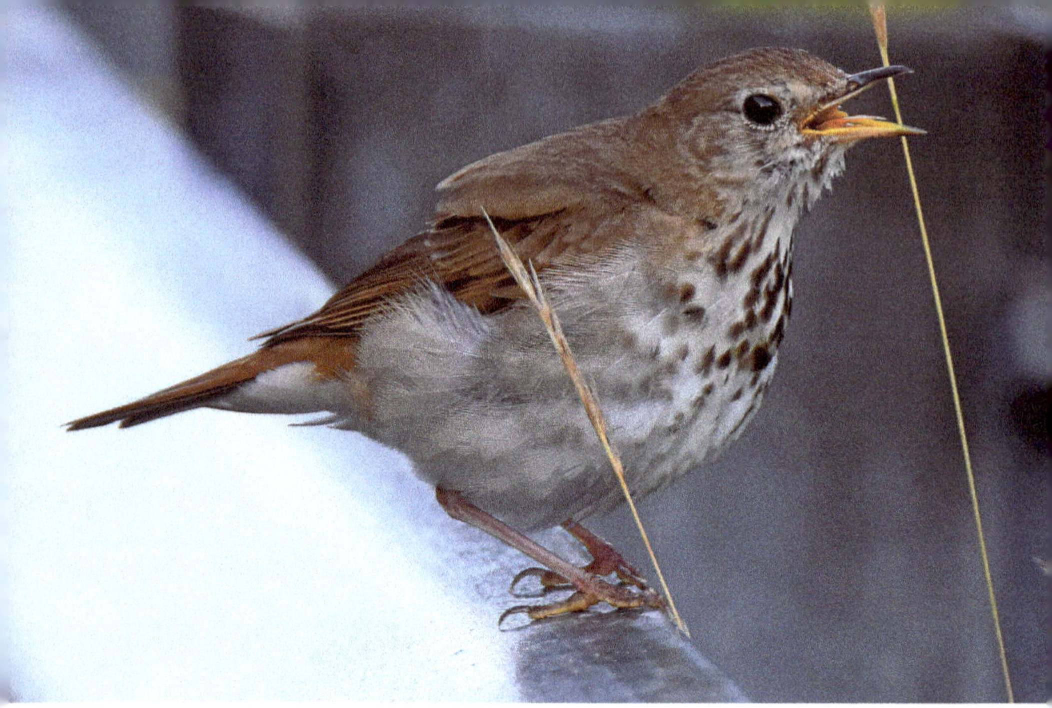

About the bird? I saw the Bicknell's singing just below the tree line.

The thrush family of birds is well represented in Maine with the easy to identify American Robin and Eastern Bluebird increasingly found all year round.

The rest are various shades of brown with spots on a white belly. They forage on the ground and lower branches, migrating in and out of the state at various times of the year and can be difficult to tell apart.

The most common of our brown thrushes is the Hermit Thrush. It is most easily identified by its brown back and red tail. The Hermit Thrush's flue-like magical call at dusk *seeeeeee frediila fridla-fridla* is familiar to all Mainers (even if we sub-consciously block it out).

Harder to find are the:

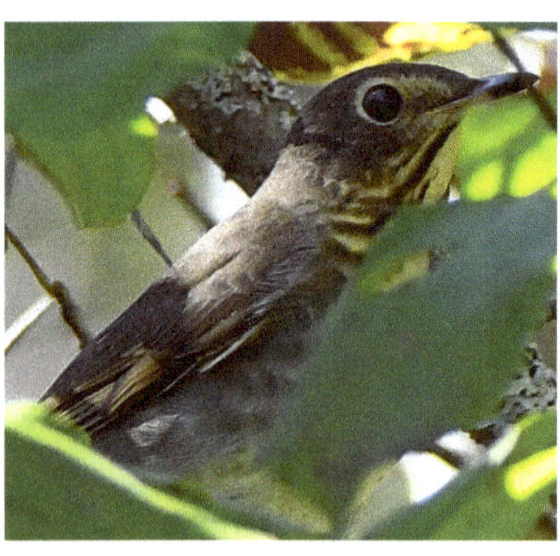

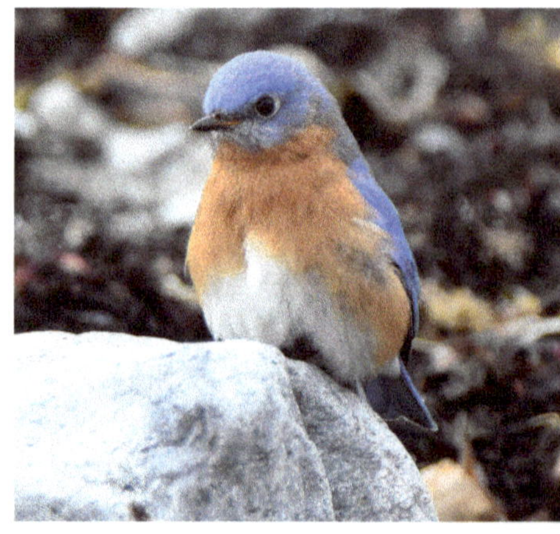

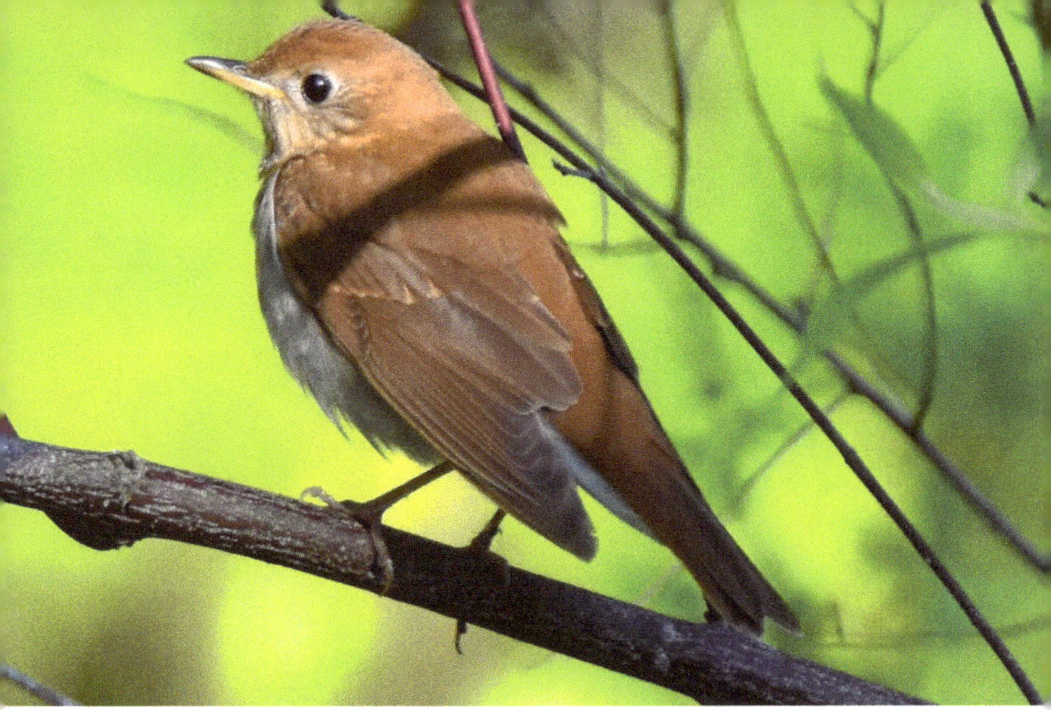

- Swainson's Thrush: Olive back with bold spectacles around the eye.
- Veery: Reddish back with very faint belly spots.
- Wood Thrush: Largest of the lot, with reddish/brown back, bold black spots and white eye-ring.

Hermit Thrushes arrive in Maine in early April, and we've seen them on New Year's Day. They don't migrate very far.

The other brown thrushes winter in South or Central America, leaving earlier in the fall and returning later in the spring.

Thrushes (cont.)

CLOCKWISE FROM TOP LEFT
Hermit Thrush (March 11)
Veery (April 18)
Redwing (January 29)
Wood Thrush (May 4)
Eastern Bluebird (January 1)
Swainson's Thrush (May 27)

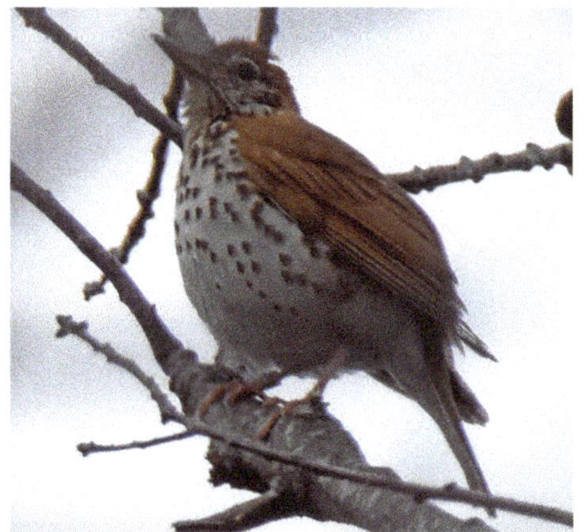

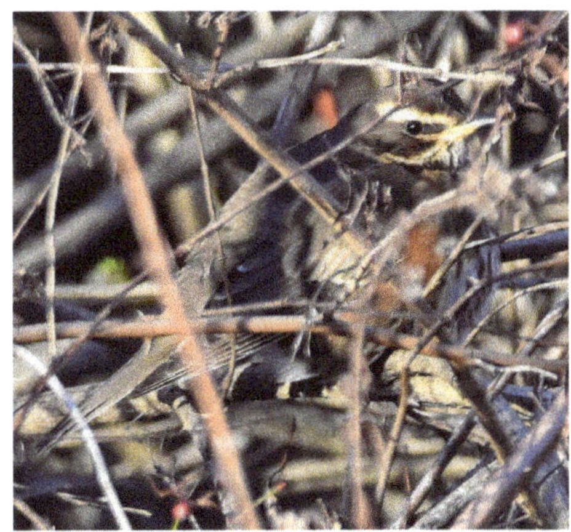

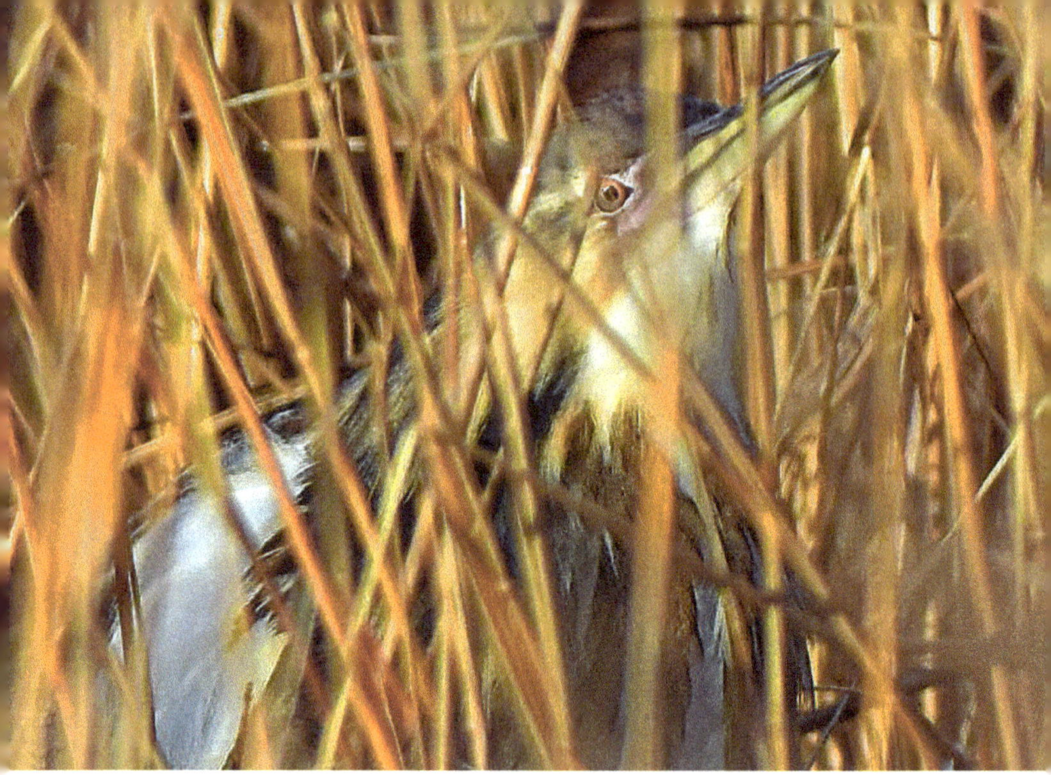

Maine is dotted with fresh and saltwater marshes filled with reeds and cattails. While the Red-winged Blackbird is certainly the most visible bird in this habitat, there are three other secretive birds lurking in the thick vegetation.

The easiest way to find them is to listen for their vocalizations in the spring and early summer. Note, I said "vocalization" because no one would seriously call this "singing".

The American Bittern makes a rhythmic gulping sound *BLOONK-Adoonk* over and over. To be honest, it really doesn't sound like a bird, more like a horse walking across a wooden bridge in a Disney cartoon.

By following the American Bittern's "song" at a marsh in Thomaston, Ingrid and I got within twenty feet of this shy and well camouflaged bird. He was watching us as closely as we were watching him.

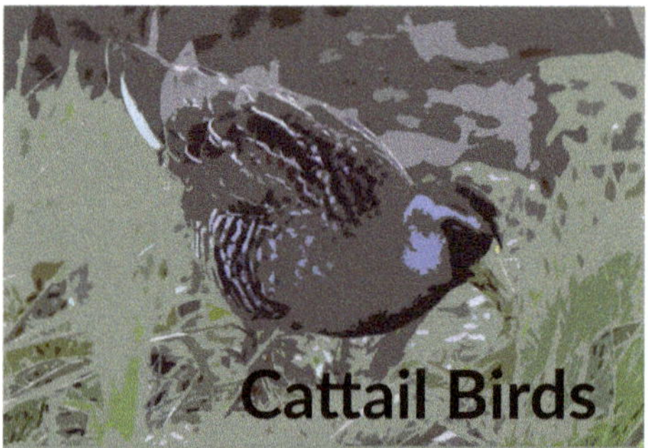

Cattail Birds

TOP American Bittern (April 12)
BOTTOM Common Gallinule (May 17)

OPPOSITE
TOP Virginia Rail (April 17)
BOTTOM Sora (April 27)

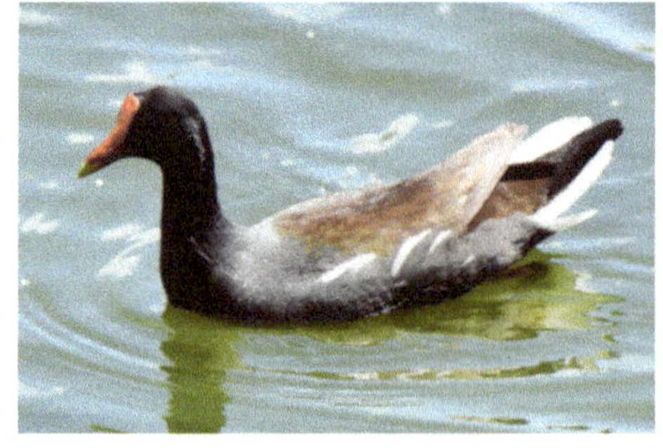

The Virginia Rail is less shy than the Bittern, often popping up in the air out of the reeds, flying for 50 feet and disappearing again.

It makes a variety of pig-like grunting sounds; a repetitive metallic *chi chi chi chi treerr*; and a squealing *kikik ik-ik*.

To photograph a Virginia Rail, one must wade into the marsh and hope the bird decides to remain in the small gaps between the cattails. If not, the bird is invisible.

Finally, there is the Sora, a hen-like bird with a long, high whinny vocalization that descends and slows at the end: *ko-WEEeee-e-e-e-e-e, ee, ee*.

To see a Sora, you have to be lucky or stand motionless for hours and hope the bird comes out.

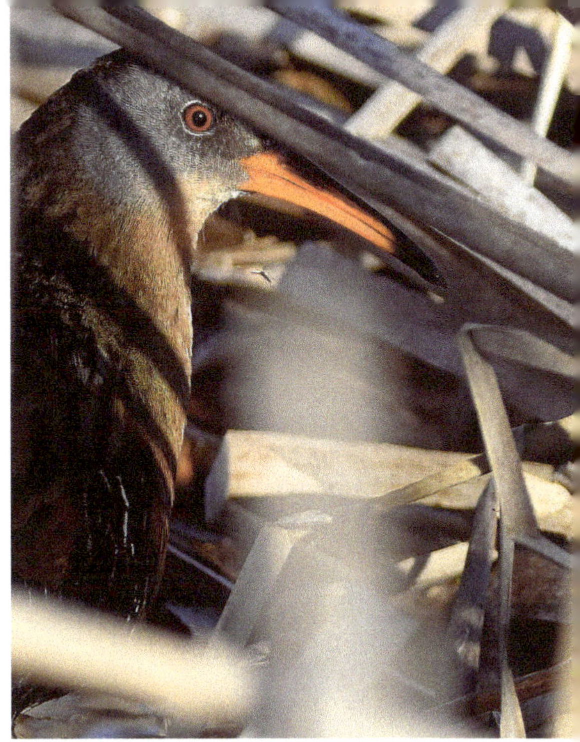

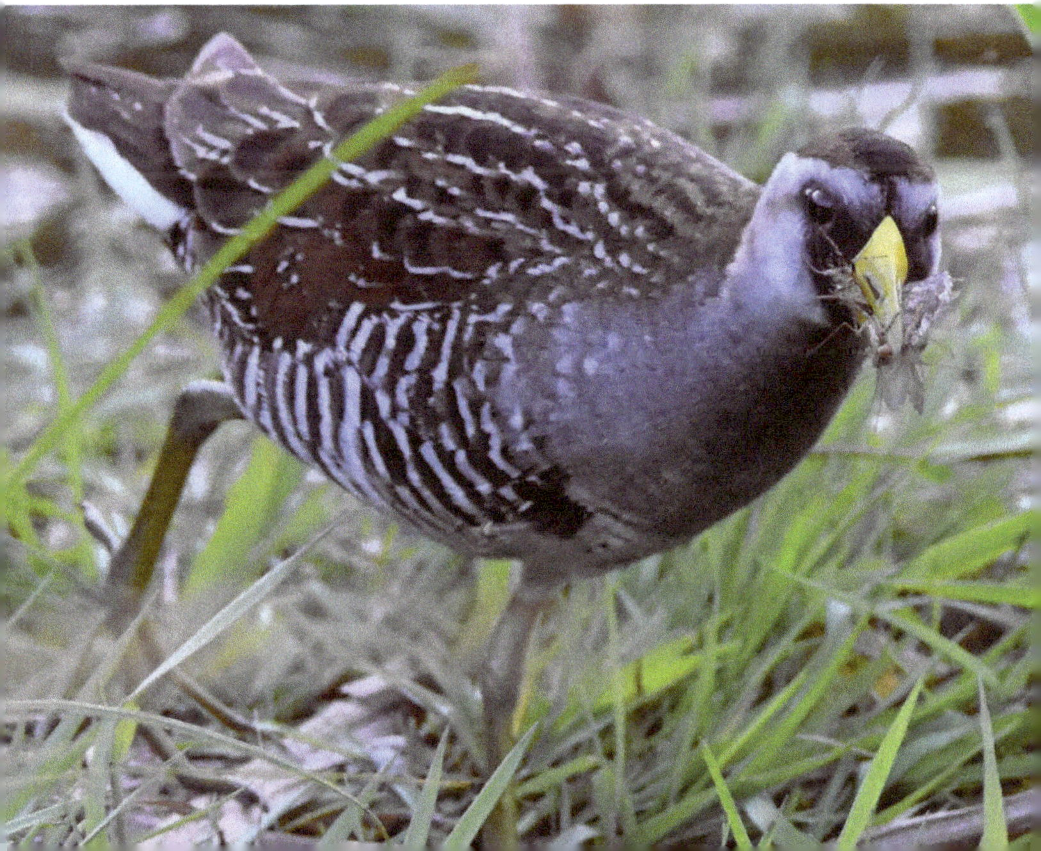

When planning my Maine Big Year, I knew my success or failure would turn on the Terns.

There are five tern species that typically breed in Maine.

The most common of these is the (you guessed it) Common Tern, which breeds on offshore islands and inland lakes. It can be found far out to sea and patrolling Maine's major rivers, arriving in early spring and departing in September. If you see a Tern in Maine, its most likely a Common Tern.

On a few off shore islands, one can find Arctic and Roseate Terns.

The Arctic is the great traveler of the animal world, migrating annually from Maine (and Canada) to the tip of Argentina and South Africa.

There are far less Roseate Terns, perhaps as few as 200 in Maine. The US Department of the Interior lists them as Endangered.

Common, Arctic and Roseate are generally referred to as medium-sized Terns.

If you see for a smaller Tern with a yellow-tipped bill, most likely at Popham Beach, you've found a Least Tern. The Least Tern nests in small depressions in the sand, making it vulnerable to dogs and careless sunbathers.

Probably the most unusual of Maine's nesting Terns is the Black Tern, a slate colored bird that is found each summer on Messalonskee Lake in Belgrade.

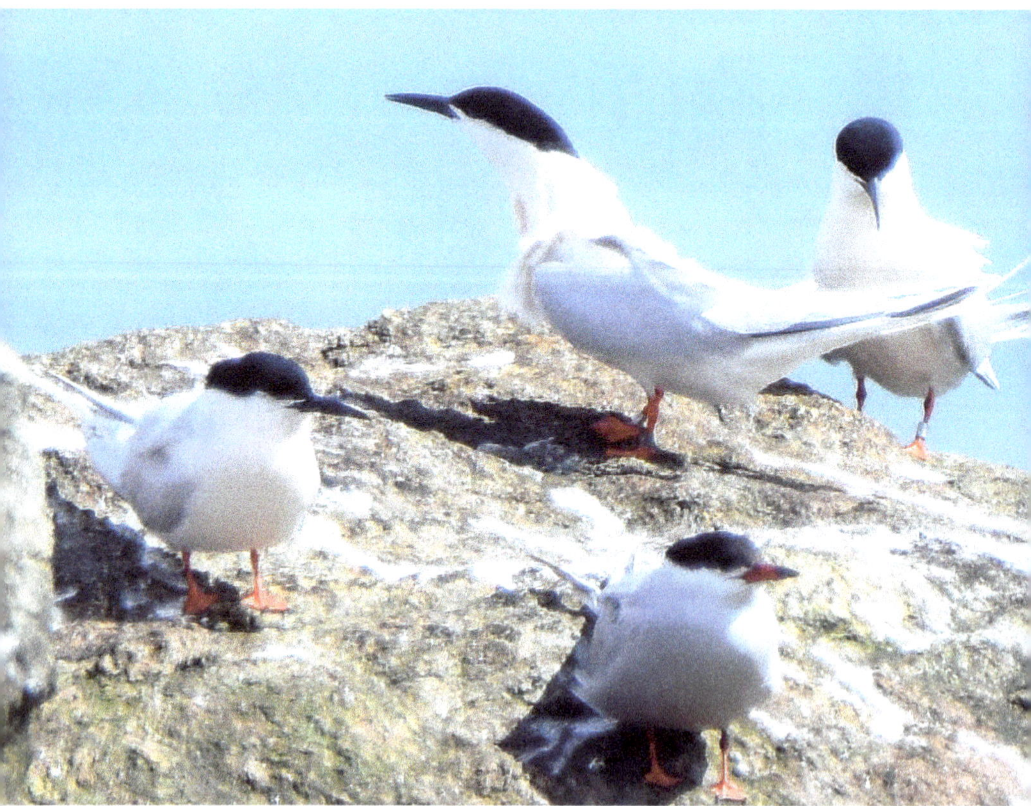

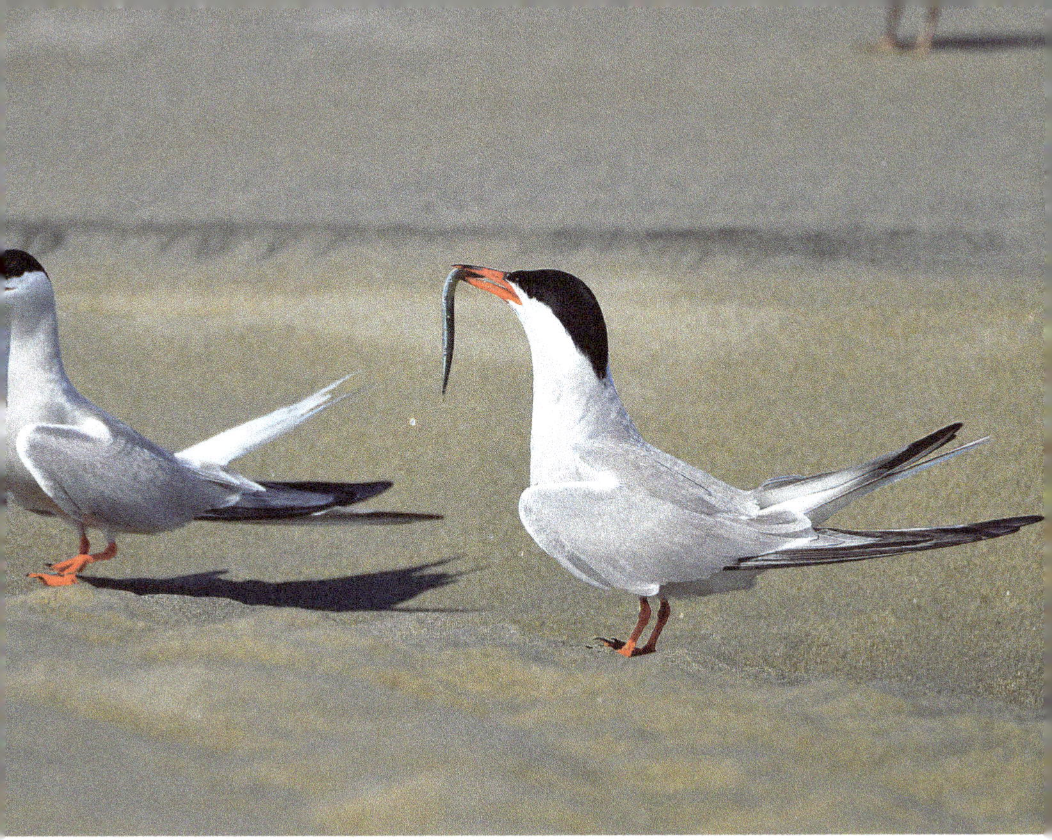

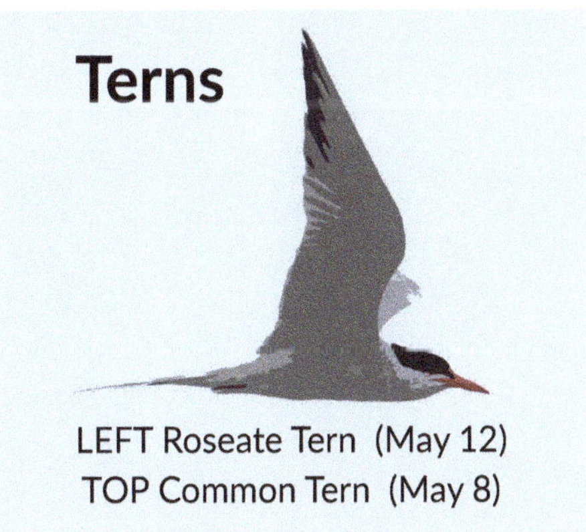

Unlike Maine's other nesting terns, it nests along fresh water lakes.

Interestingly, Black Terns turn partially white at the end of the summer as they leave for the Caribbean.

Birders come in all shapes, sizes and ages. There are old fogies (like myself), the academic ornithological types ("notice the rufous upper-wing coverts"), the matronly fanatics (made famous by Miss Jane Hathaway on the Beverly Hillbillies), and then there are the young birders.

This latter group is made up of some amazing "kids". In 2020, the top birder in Maine was Matthew Gilbert who identified 298 species, all before he got his driver's license. Thanks, Mom!!!!

There are two University of New England students: Harry Wales and Xander Vitarelli who seem to always be on a bird before I am. I'm not sure when they have a chance to study.

LEFT Roseate Tern (May 12)
TOP Common Tern (May 8)

In the summer of my Big Year, Harry did Caspian Tern research on Lake Champlain. The Caspian Tern is much bigger than Maine's nesting Terns. It has a large, almost comical orange bill.

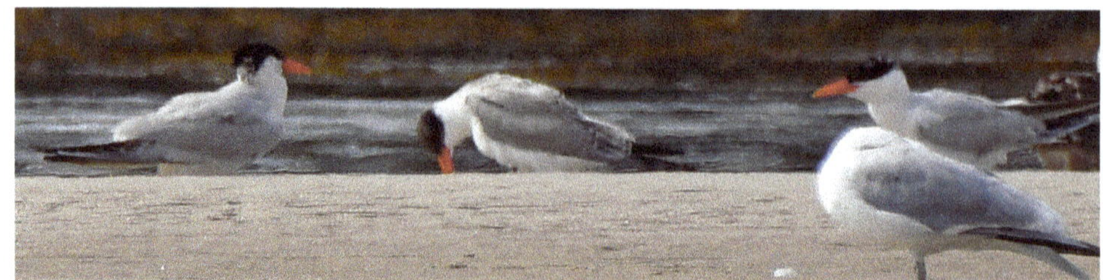

I jokingly asked Harry to bring a couple of Caspians with him when he returned to Maine. He promised to try.

Fast forward to Labor Day Weekend, I was birding on a beach in Biddeford Pool, looking for shorebirds. Across a nearby sandbar came Harry and Xander. They had just completed their first class of the semester and decided to go birding.

When I was in college and had just completed my first class of the semester, I would have been playing beer pong!!!

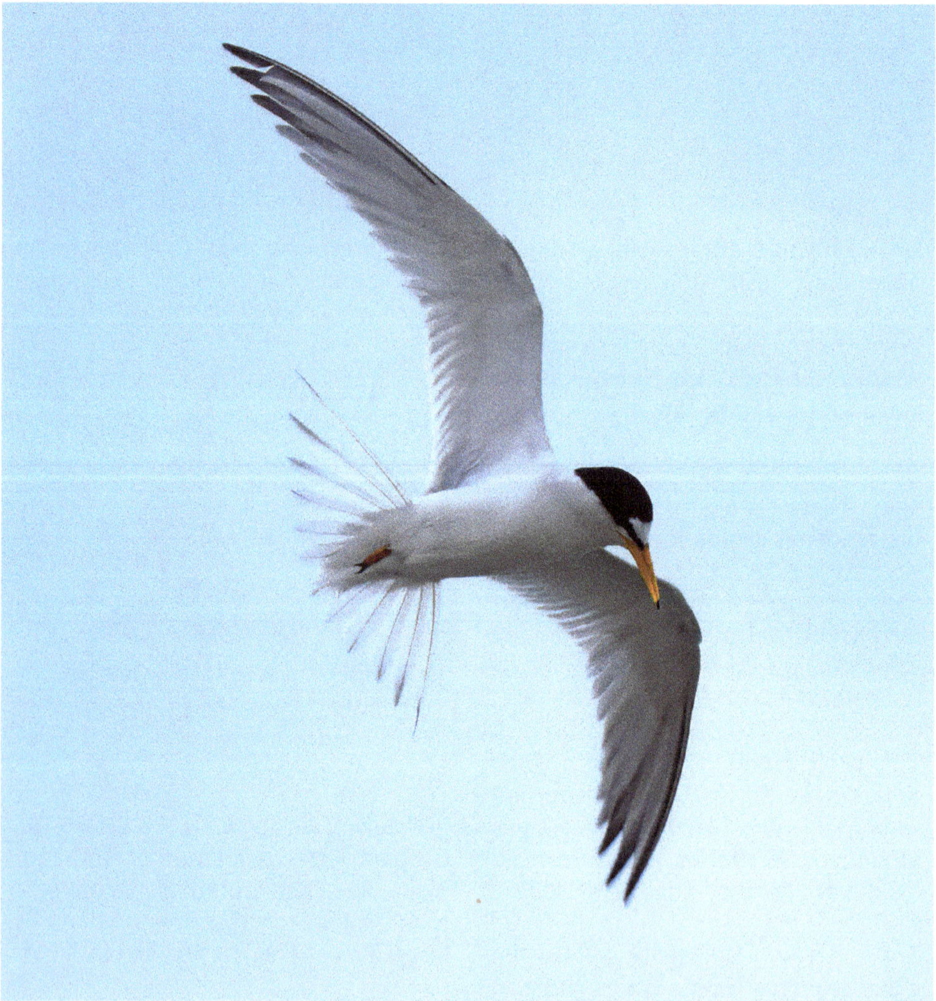

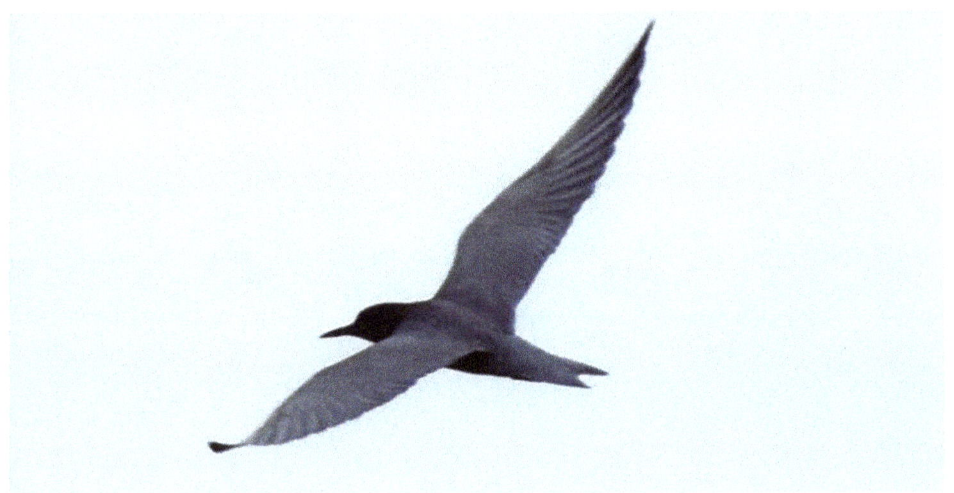

We all had fun catching up when Xander pointed at five birds flying over the water, and Harry yelled, "Those are Caspians!!!!"

How had Harry managed to bring these birds from the New York/Vermont bor-der all the way to the coast of Maine?

I didn't ask questions. I just added them to my Maine Big Year list!!!

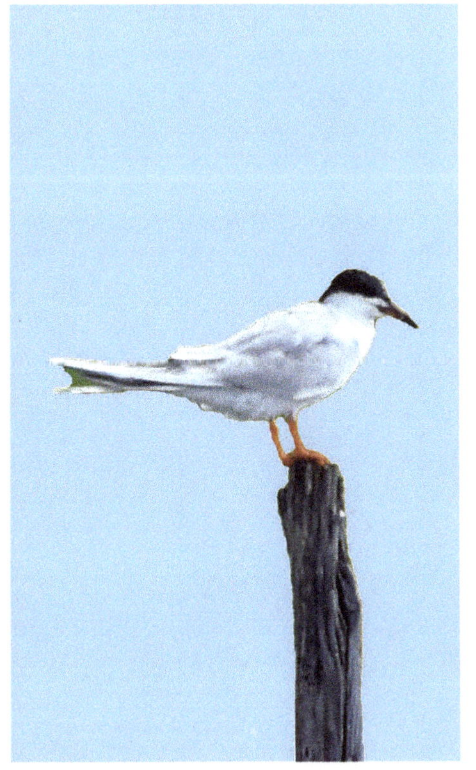

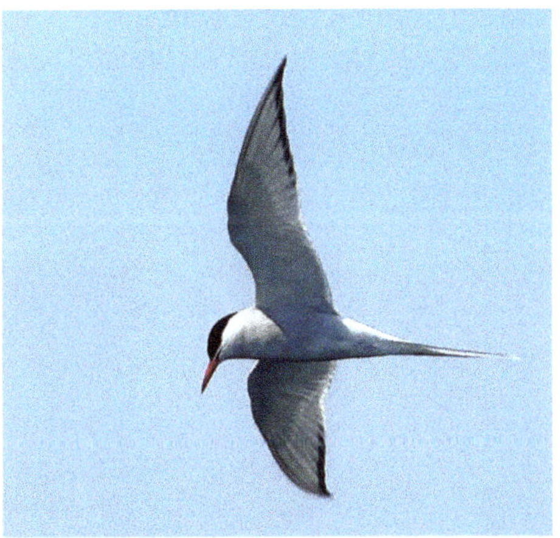

Terns (cont.)

CLOCKWISE FROM TOP-LEFT
Caspian Tern (August 25)
Black Tern (May 16)
Arctic Tern (May 8)
Forster's Tern (October 8)
Least Tern (May 9)

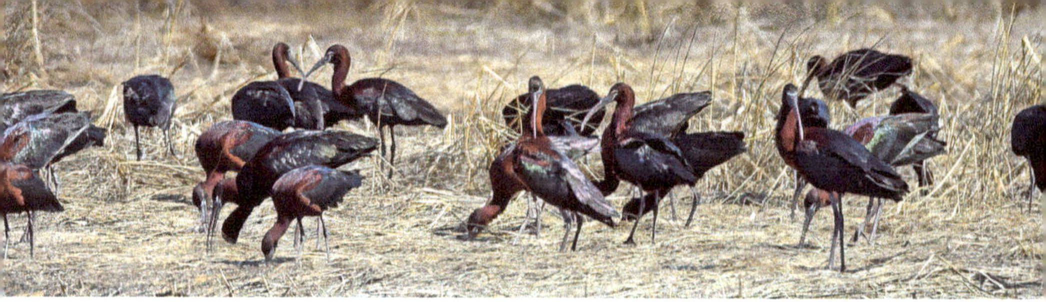

The Glossy Ibis is a common summer breeder along the southern Maine coast. If you visit Scarborough Marsh, you'll often see a dozen or more of these shimmering chestnut beauties grouped together feeding.

For the last few seasons its nearly identical cousin, a White-faced Ibis, has been hanging with the Glossies. The White-faced normally spends its summers in California, Utah and on the Great Plains.

Each spring, after this White-faced Ibis is reported, birders from all over Maine rush to the marsh. They will be trying to find that one Ibis that has pink legs and red eyes, the field marks of a White-faced Ibis, in a flock of hundreds of Glossies.

The Glossy Ibis has gray legs and a black eye. From a distance, both birds look pretty much the same.

A true birder's idea of fun is spending hours scanning a constantly moving flock of identical birds looking for the one with a red eye.

Now that's entertainment!!!!

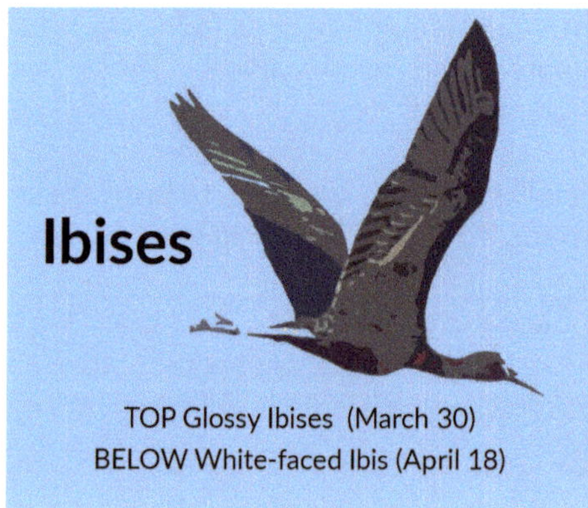

TOP Glossy Ibises (March 30)
BELOW White-faced Ibis (April 18)

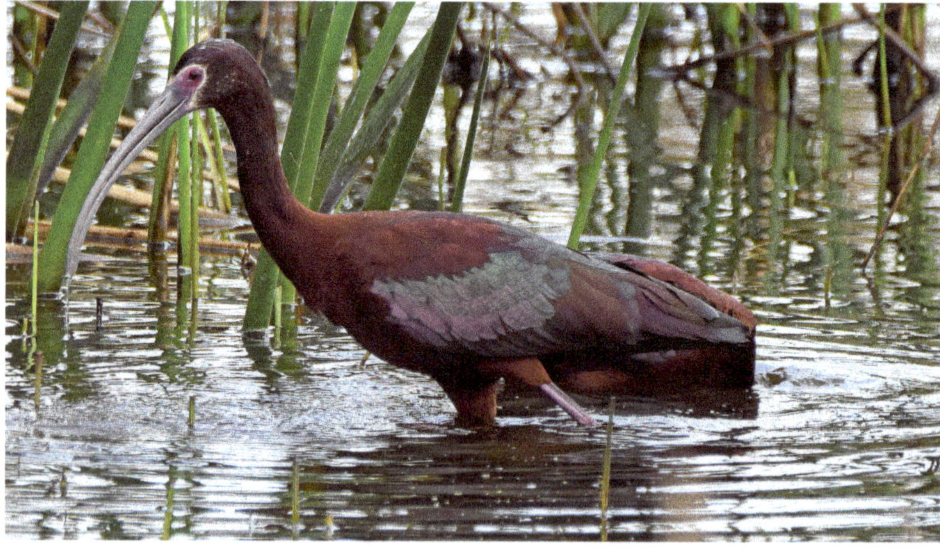

One of the fun (and not so fun) parts of a Big Year is the constant change of plans.

On a typical day, I was up before dawn with a plan on where to find a new bird to add to the year total. All that changes in a flash, often while in the car, when a new bird sighting comes in. I'll spin the car around and head in a completely new direction.

2021 was a very dry year in Maine. We didn't have much snow and during the spring, we had very little rain. But on May 5, it poured, monsoon quality rain!!! Accordingly, I decided to take a day off from birding, I needed a break.

I slept later than normal, ate a leisurely breakfast and watched a couple episodes of a series on Netflix. I took a shower, and as I was toweling off, my phone rang with a number I didn't recognize. I suspected someone was trying to sell me an extended warranty for my car, but for some reason I answered it anyway.

The caller was Louis Bevier, one of the most knowledgeable birders in America, renown on both coasts, and an individual who has been very patient with me over the years as I misidentified bird after bird after bird.

He told me there was a Ruff, a Eurasian Shorebird that is rarely seen on this side of the Atlantic, hanging out at a dairy farm drainage pond a couple of hours away.

So much for my day off.

When I was growing up, my grandparents ran a small dairy farm, and I learned where to step (that may not be mud), how to stay out of the way (that tractor may not see you) and what a storage pond contains (cows go #1 as well as #2).

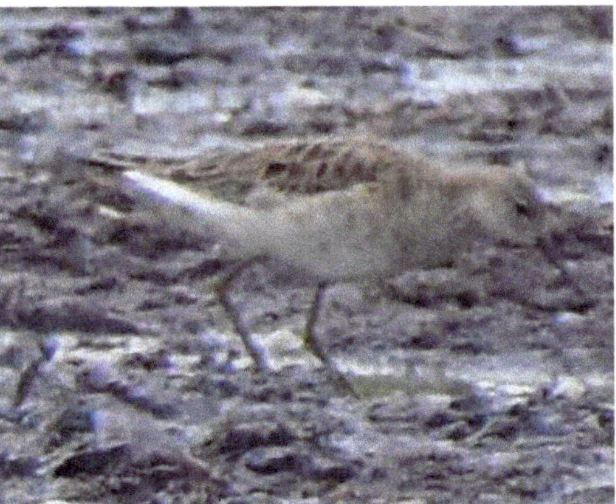

I arrived at the pond and sure enough, there was the Ruff feeding in the water(???). And speaking of water, it was still pouring.

For over a half an hour I snapped distant photos of the bird in the heavy rain. When it finally flew, my boots were gross, my camera had stopped working, I was soaking wet, and thrilled beyond belief.

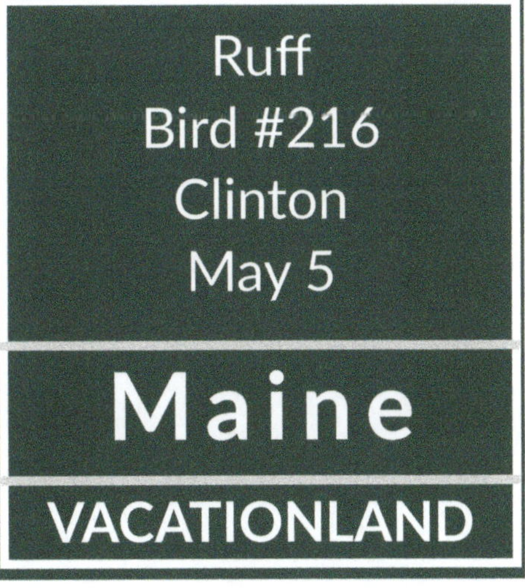

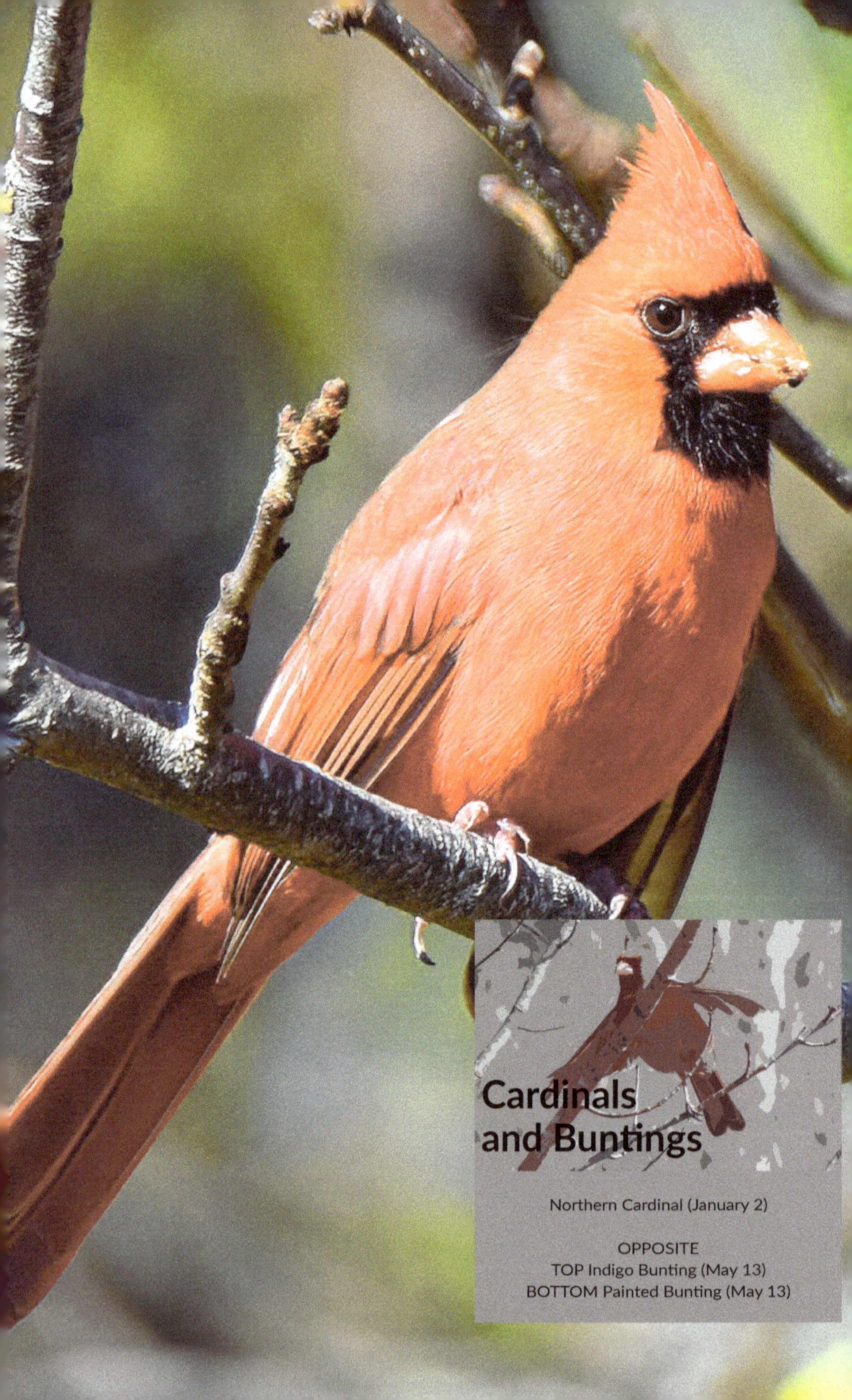

Cardinals and Buntings

Northern Cardinal (January 2)

OPPOSITE
TOP Indigo Bunting (May 13)
BOTTOM Painted Bunting (May 13)

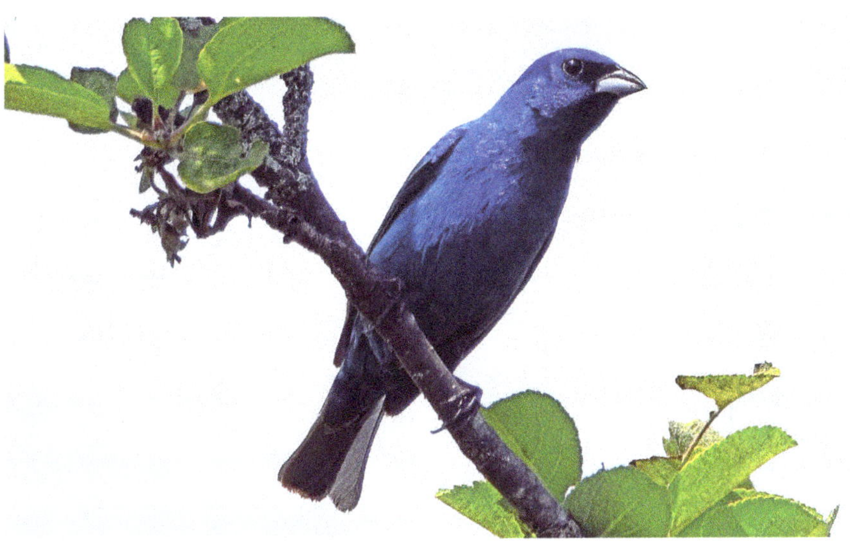

Seventy years ago, the Northern Cardinal was a rare visitor in Maine. It has since spread throughout the entire State. The bright red male and his paler, partner-for-life female have become one of the state's most prized feeder birds.

The Cardinal's distance cousin, the Indigo Bunting, is one of the most common birds in the eastern United States. However, since Maine lies at the edge of their northern range, seeing (or hearing) an Indigo Bunting in Maine is always a treat.

The Painted Bunting, a bird of the American South, that I visited at a feeder in Lubec was a once in a decade surprise!!!

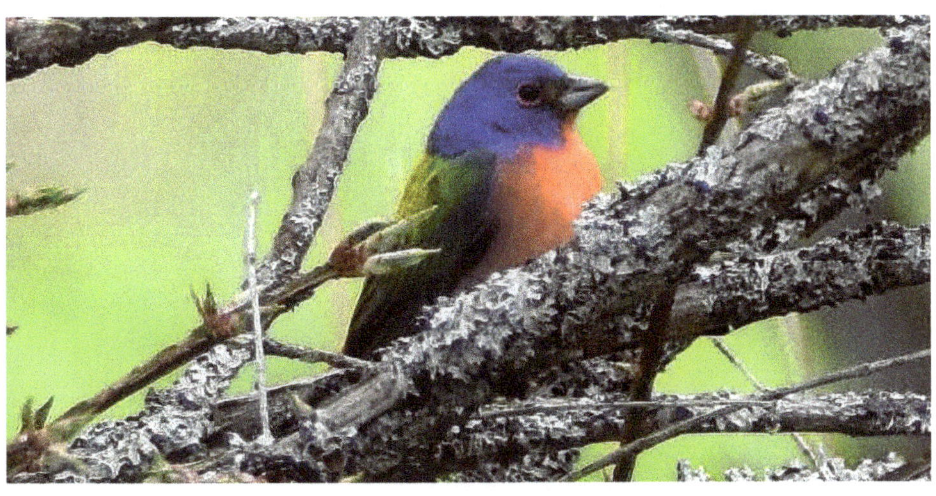

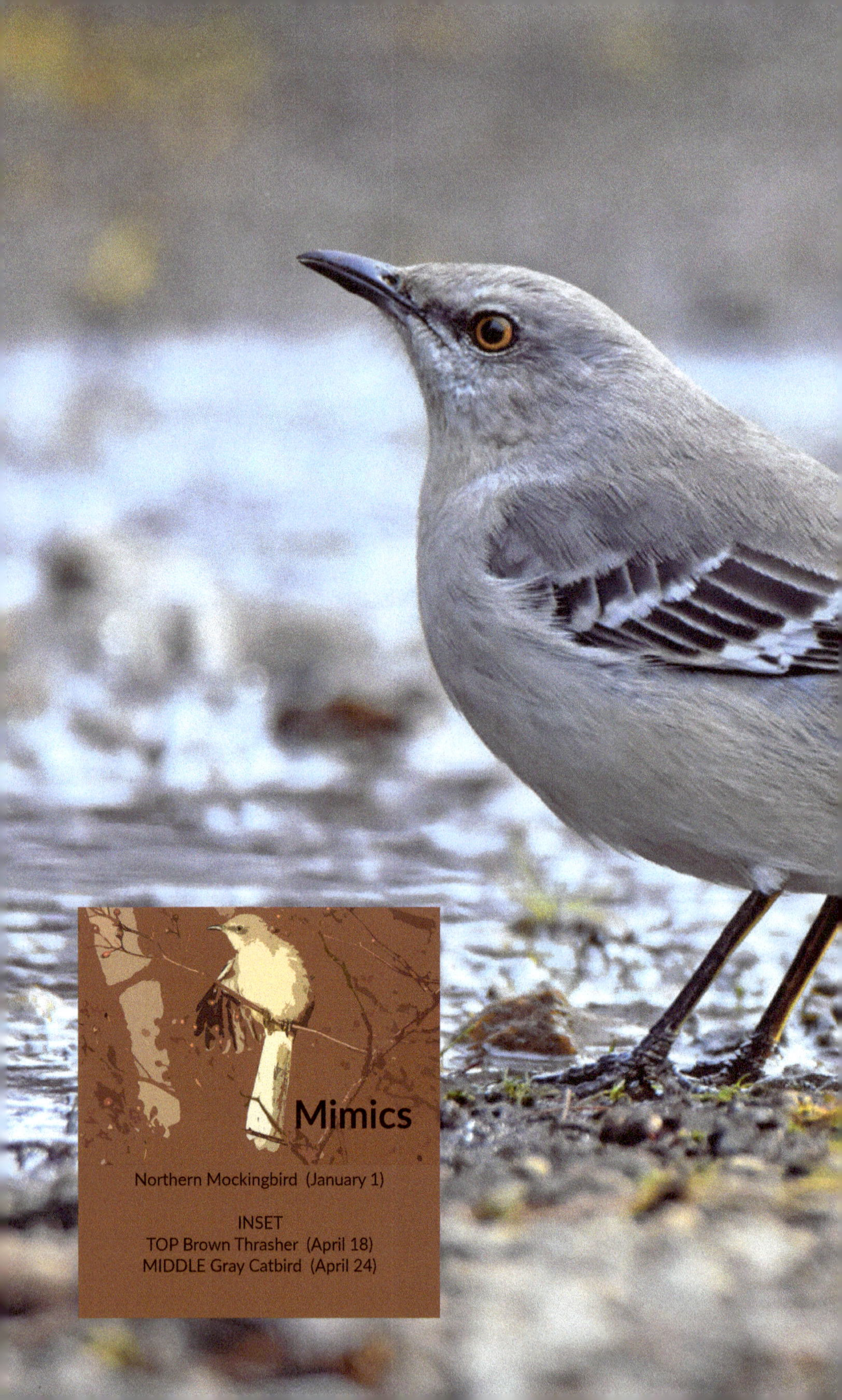

Mimics

Northern Mockingbird (January 1)

INSET
TOP Brown Thrasher (April 18)
MIDDLE Gray Catbird (April 24)

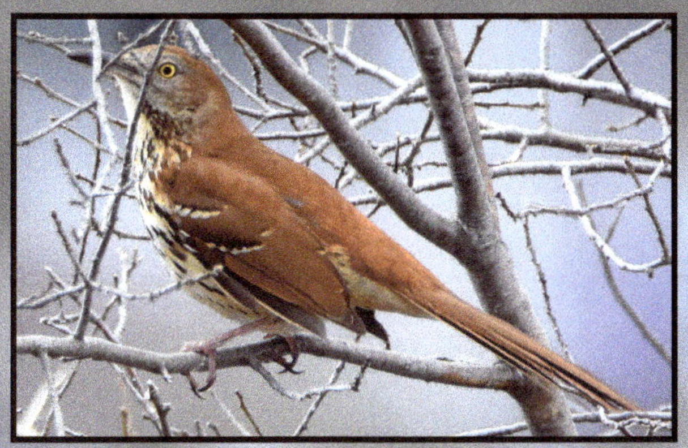

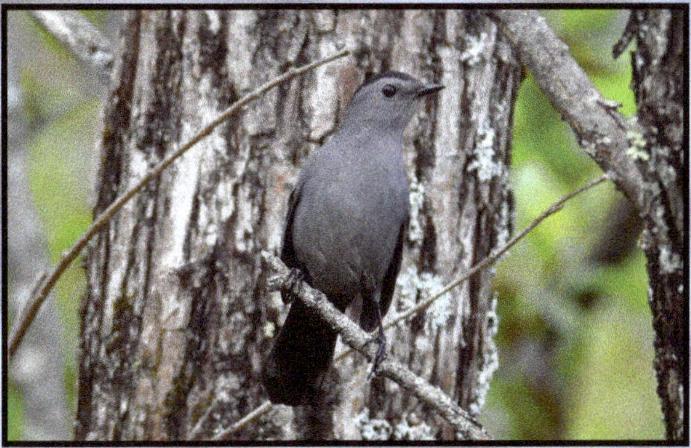

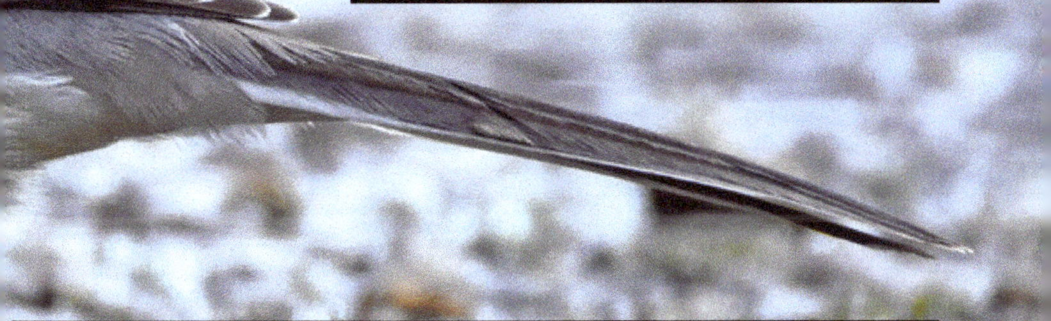

Birders use a technique in the field called "pishing" to attract small birds and get a bcttcr vicw. A pish is a small, repetitive hissing sound, similar to an alarm or scolding call that many birds make. Accustomed to mobbing larger predators, a pishing sound can attract a flock of small birds ready to chase the intruder.

While I often pish trying to flush out warblers or sparrows, many of the birds on this page, particularly the Mockingbird and Gray Catbird, will also respond. It's amazing how often I will be watching movement in a thicket and pish to bring the little birds closer, and all of a sudden a Catbird is a few feet away.

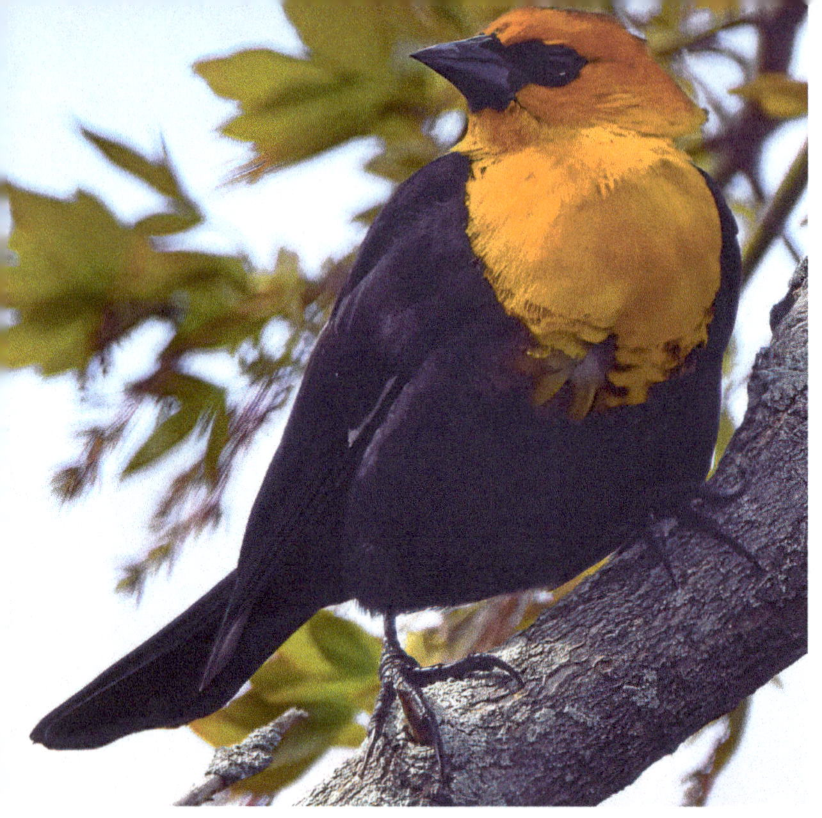

Here is where my plan kind of fell apart. I arrived in Corinna (population 2,198) with no idea where to find the bird. I slowly drove loops around a trailer park and the surrounding residential homes sweeping the area with my binoculars.

Is this a good idea?

Let's put it this way, rural Maine is well armed, and some folks might get the wrong idea about a guy with binoculars.

I used to say: "If I should die during my Maine Big Year, chances are it won't be because I fell off a mountain or got mauled by a bear. Rather it will be my habit of driving slowly around rural neighborhoods, staring into yards with my binoculars."

After 90 minutes of this nonsense, I took another tact and decided to check the cattails and woods near the lake and stream in the middle of town. Sure enough, there were hundreds of birds in the trees, all black.

I observed Red-winged Blackbirds, Common Grackles, European Starlings, Brown-headed Cowbirds and in the middle of the flock, one solitary Blackbird with a bright yellow head!!!!

On the last day of April I learned that a Yellow-headed Blackbird had been seen at a bird feeder in a mobile home park in Corinna. Yellow-headed Blackbirds belong on the other side of the Mississippi River. I had little choice but to set my alarm for 4:30 AM and head north.

Turkey Vultures are a common three season sight in Maine, and in the summer there always seems to be one or two patrolling the skies. They are one of the first migrating birds to return each spring and one of the last to leave as the weather gets cold.

It wasn't always that way. Between 1862 and 1944, there were only twelve reported sightings of Turkey Vultures in Maine. Fifty years ago, (when I was a youth) they were still rare.

Their close cousin, the Black Vulture, is a year round resident from New Jersey south to Florida and west to Texas. However, it is as rare in Maine as the Turkey Vulture was a hundred years ago.

Ingrid and I have gotten into a habit of glancing at every vulture we see, hoping to see white tips on the wings and

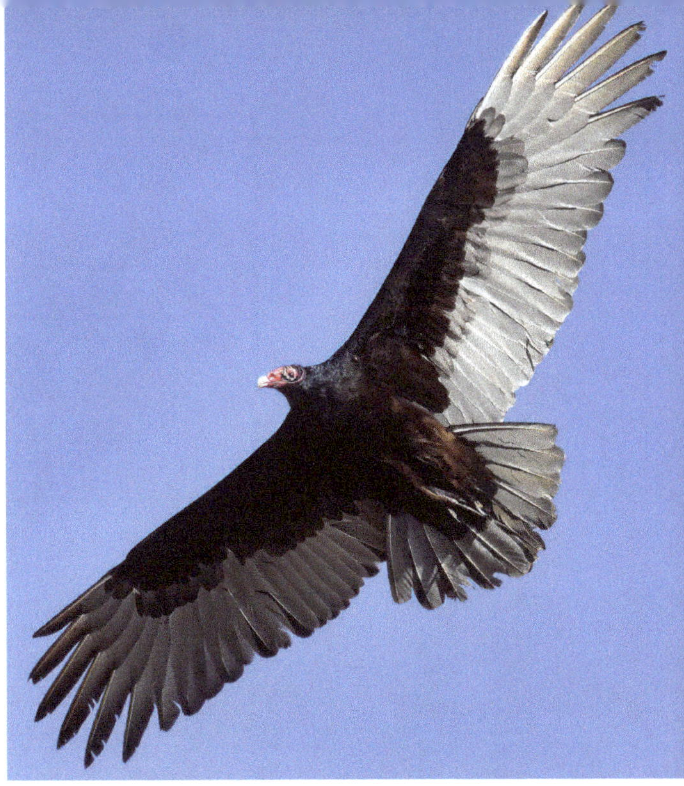

a gray head, the tell-tale sign of a Black Vulture.

On March 23, I was up early, prowling the pine trees and communication towers of Windham, looking for the Black Vulture that had been seen the day before at sunset.

We found two, and they appeared to be rubbing bills. Could these be the first breeding Black Vultures in Maine?

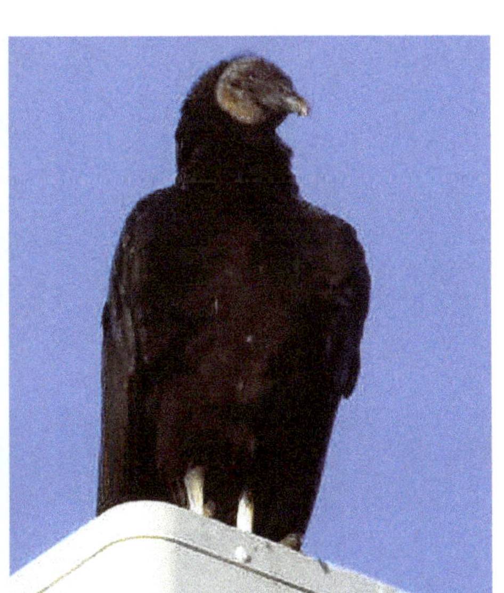

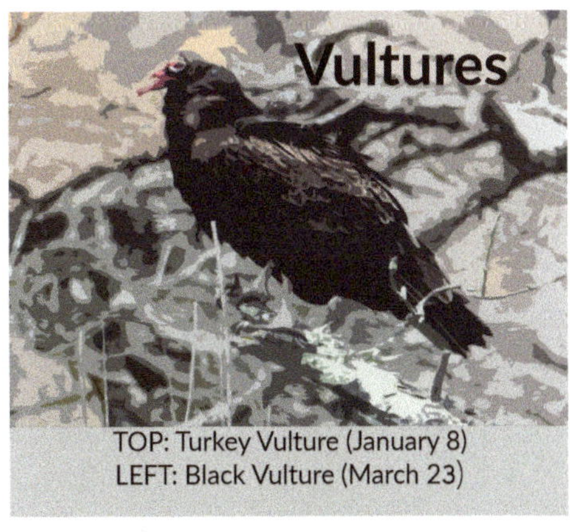

TOP: Turkey Vulture (January 8)
LEFT: Black Vulture (March 23)

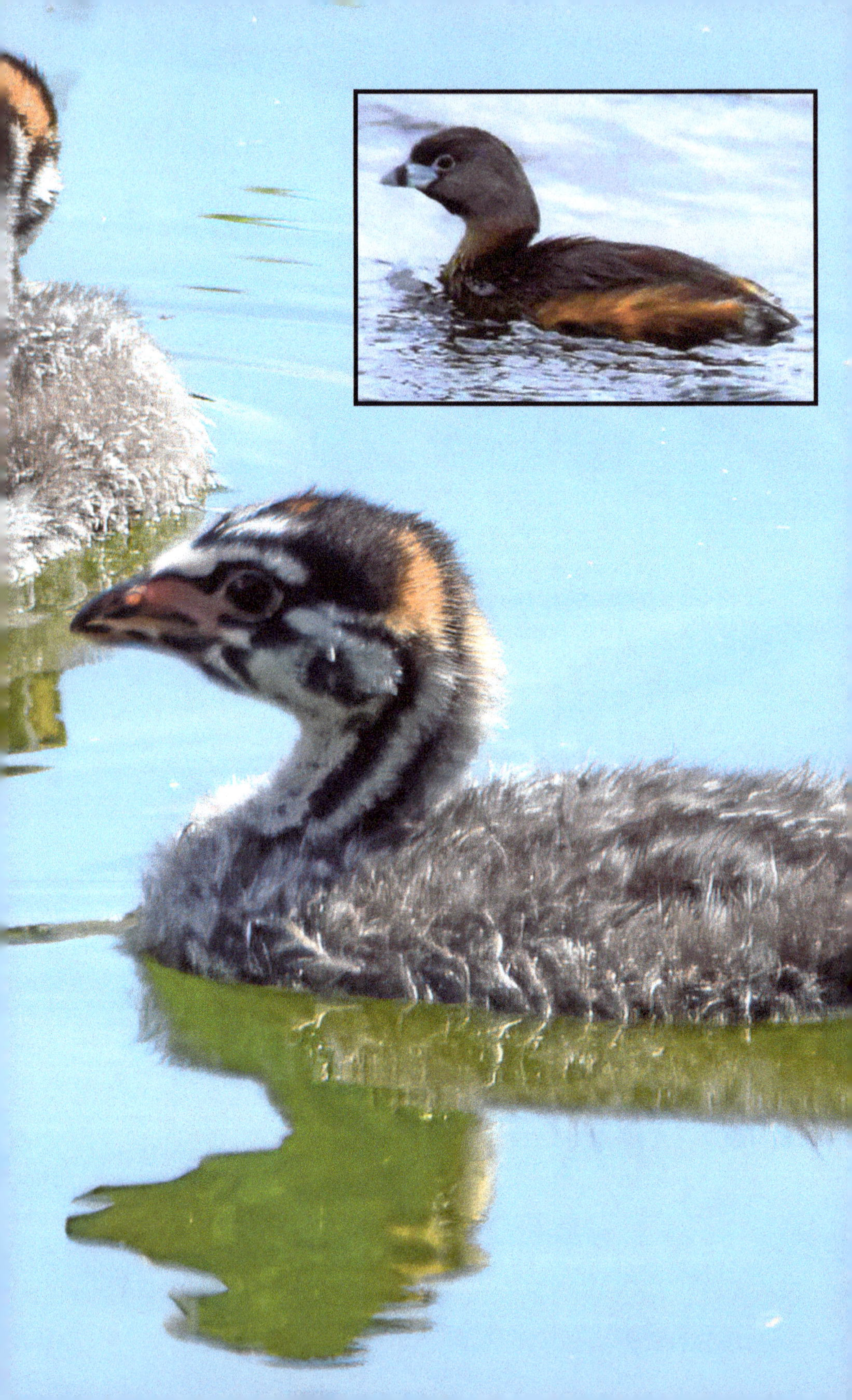

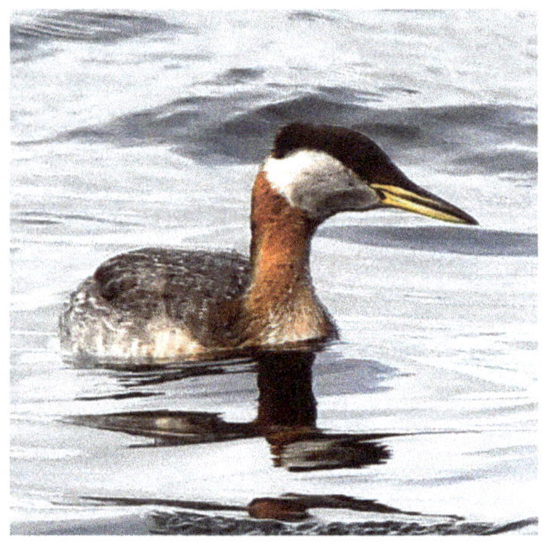

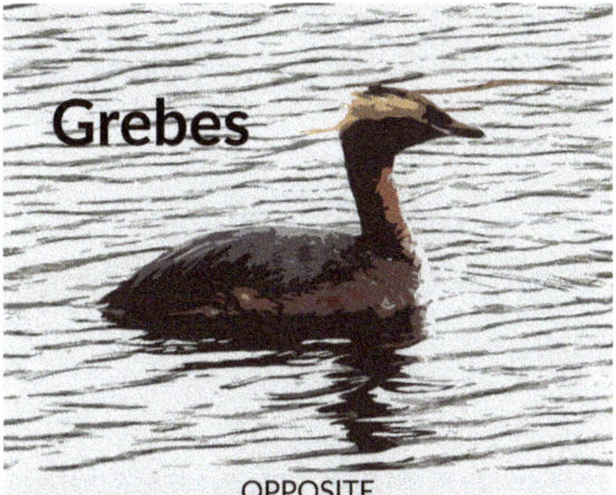

Grebes

OPPOSITE
Pied-billed Grebe Chicks
INSET Pied-billed Grebe Adult (March 15)

CURRENT
LEFT Red-necked Grebe (January 4)
BOTTOM Horned Grebe (January 1)

Grebes are water birds that repeatedly dive for crustaceans and small fish. In recent years, DNA evidence has shown that they are more closely related to Flamingos than any other species.

The tiny Pied-billed Grebe nests in Maine but winters to the south. Meanwhile, their cousins, the Red-necked Grebe and Horned Grebe, winter in Maine and breed in the Arctic.

One of the more terrifying experiences I've had birding was exploring a solitary marsh at dawn in May. A single Pied-billed Grebe started singing, and it sounded like I was in the middle of a jungle surrounded by angry chimpanzees. I'm really quite a coward.

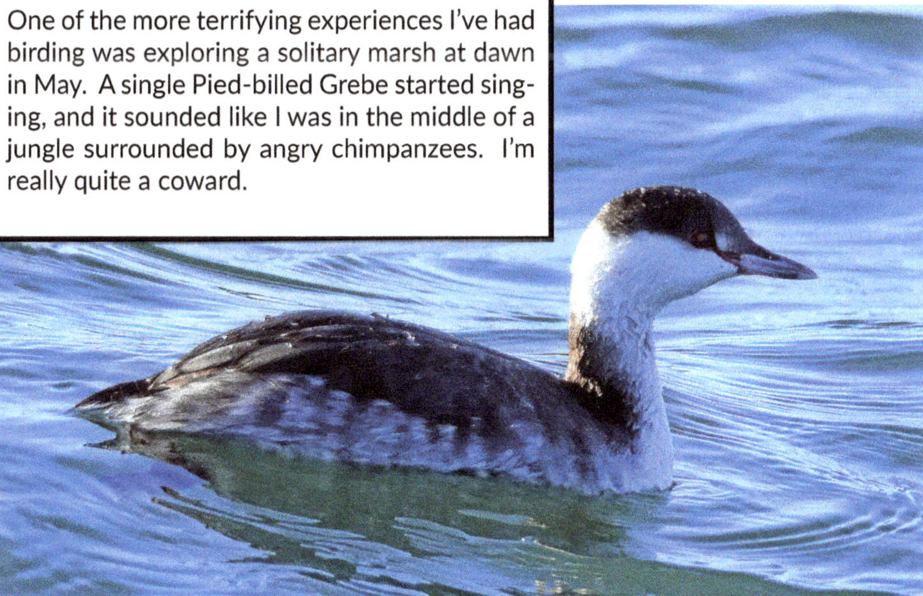

Warblers, Thrushes, Kinglets and many other bird species rely on insects for sustenance. The Flycatcher differentiates itself by catching these insects on the wing.

In summer, as many a dozen species of flycatchers can be found in the Maine woods, marshes and grasslands.

The most common of Maine's Flycatchers, the first to arrive in the spring and the last to migrate south in the fall, is the Eastern Phoebe. His repetitious *Fee-be Fee-be* song can go on for hours during mating season and sometimes all summer if the poor guy doesn't find a girlfriend.

The Alder, Willow and Least Flycatchers are often easy to find but difficult to positively identify, unless they are vocalizing. Sound is often the only way to tell the difference among these very similar looking birds

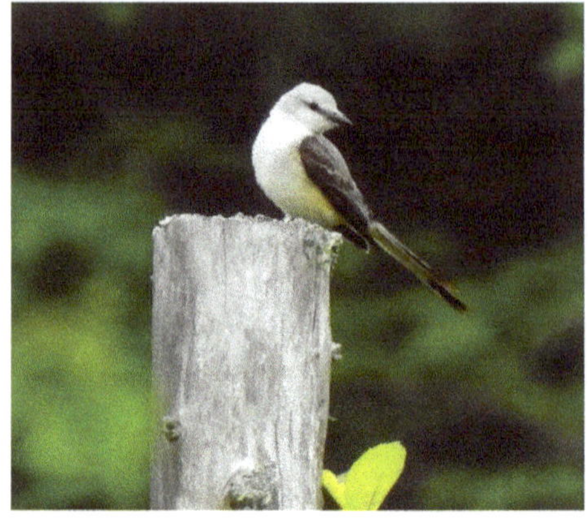

Then come the rarities:

Each summer, often in the weeks after their young have fledged, flycatchers native to Texas or California will appear in Maine and set the birding community a-flutter.

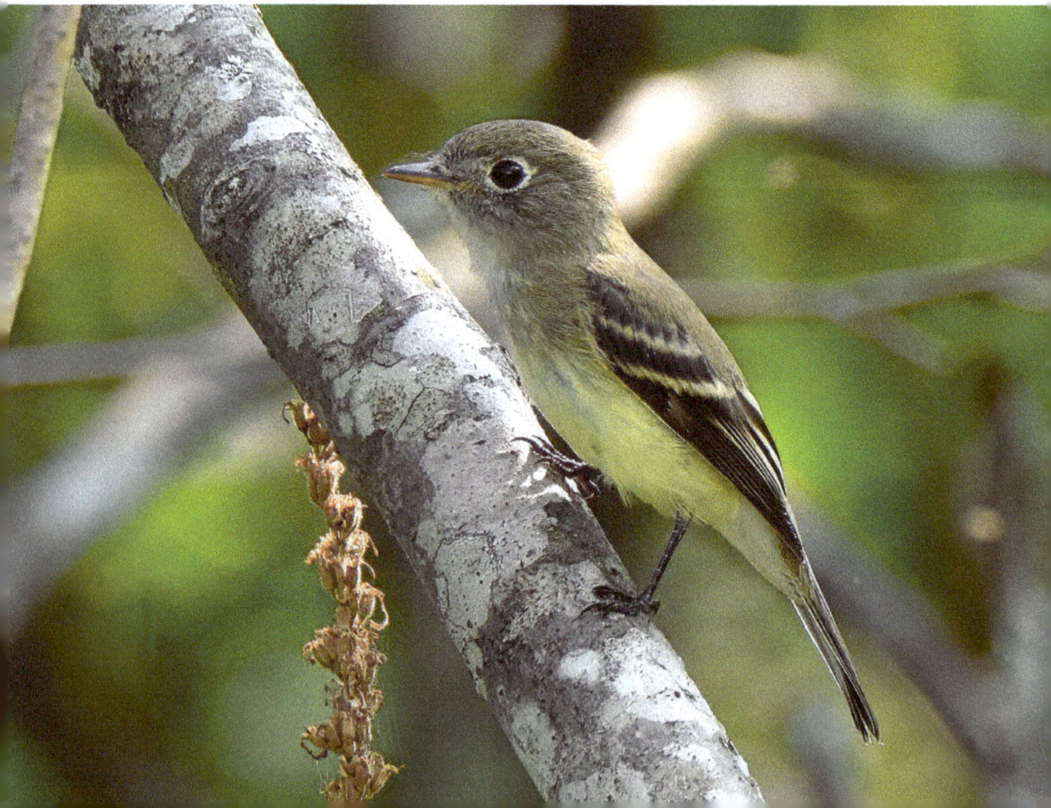

During my Maine Big Year, a Scissor-tailed Flycatcher, a bird normally found along the Gulf Coast, appeared just south of Bar Harbor and was pho-

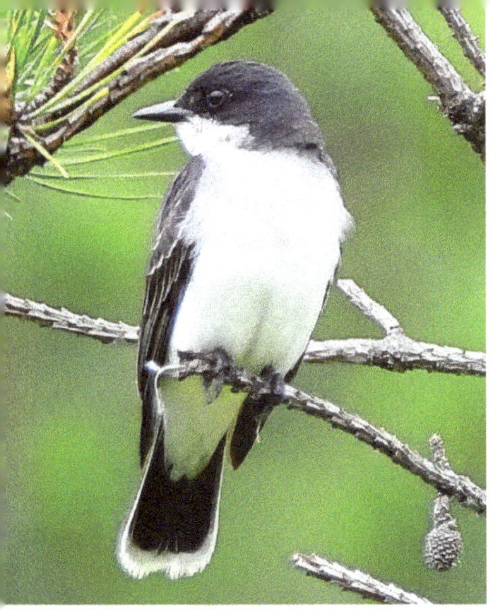

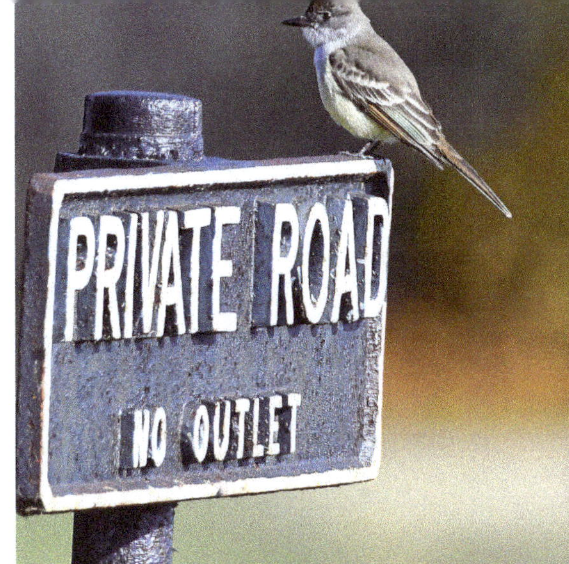

tographed for several days hunting from a cattle fence.

A Fork-tailed Flycatcher appeared on Wells Beach, a long way from its Caribbean home.

On December 3rd, a Gray Kingbird, spent weeks on a Biddeford Beach when he should have been in South America.

When it comes to Flycatchers, one never knows what will show up.

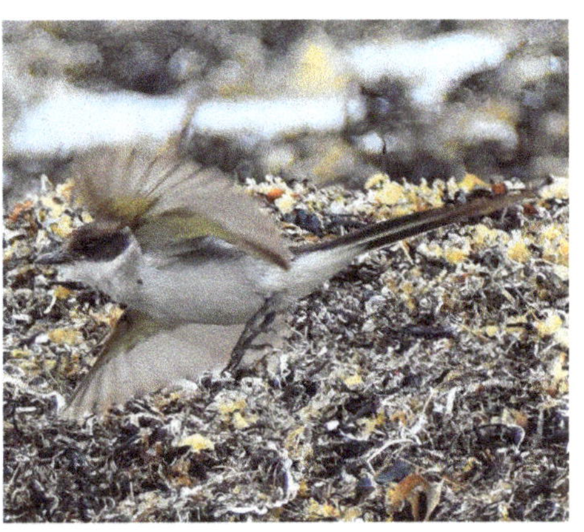

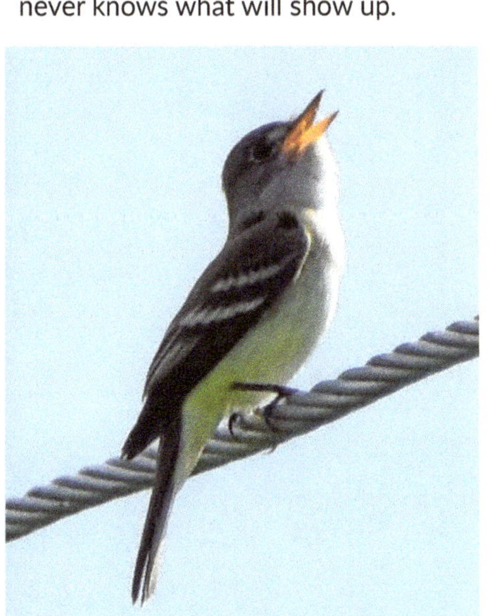

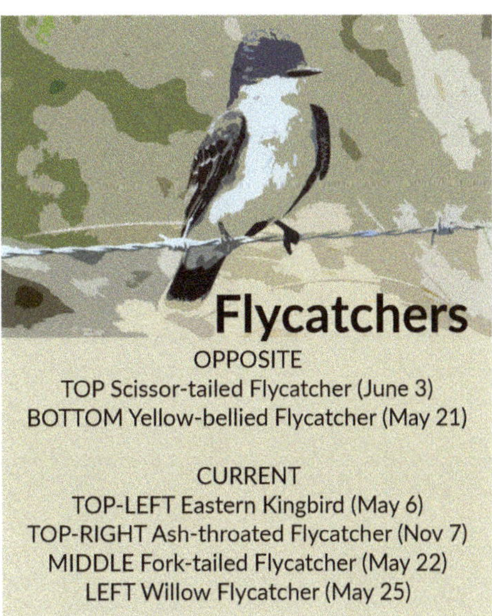

Flycatchers

OPPOSITE
TOP Scissor-tailed Flycatcher (June 3)
BOTTOM Yellow-bellied Flycatcher (May 21)

CURRENT
TOP-LEFT Eastern Kingbird (May 6)
TOP-RIGHT Ash-throated Flycatcher (Nov 7)
MIDDLE Fork-tailed Flycatcher (May 22)
LEFT Willow Flycatcher (May 25)

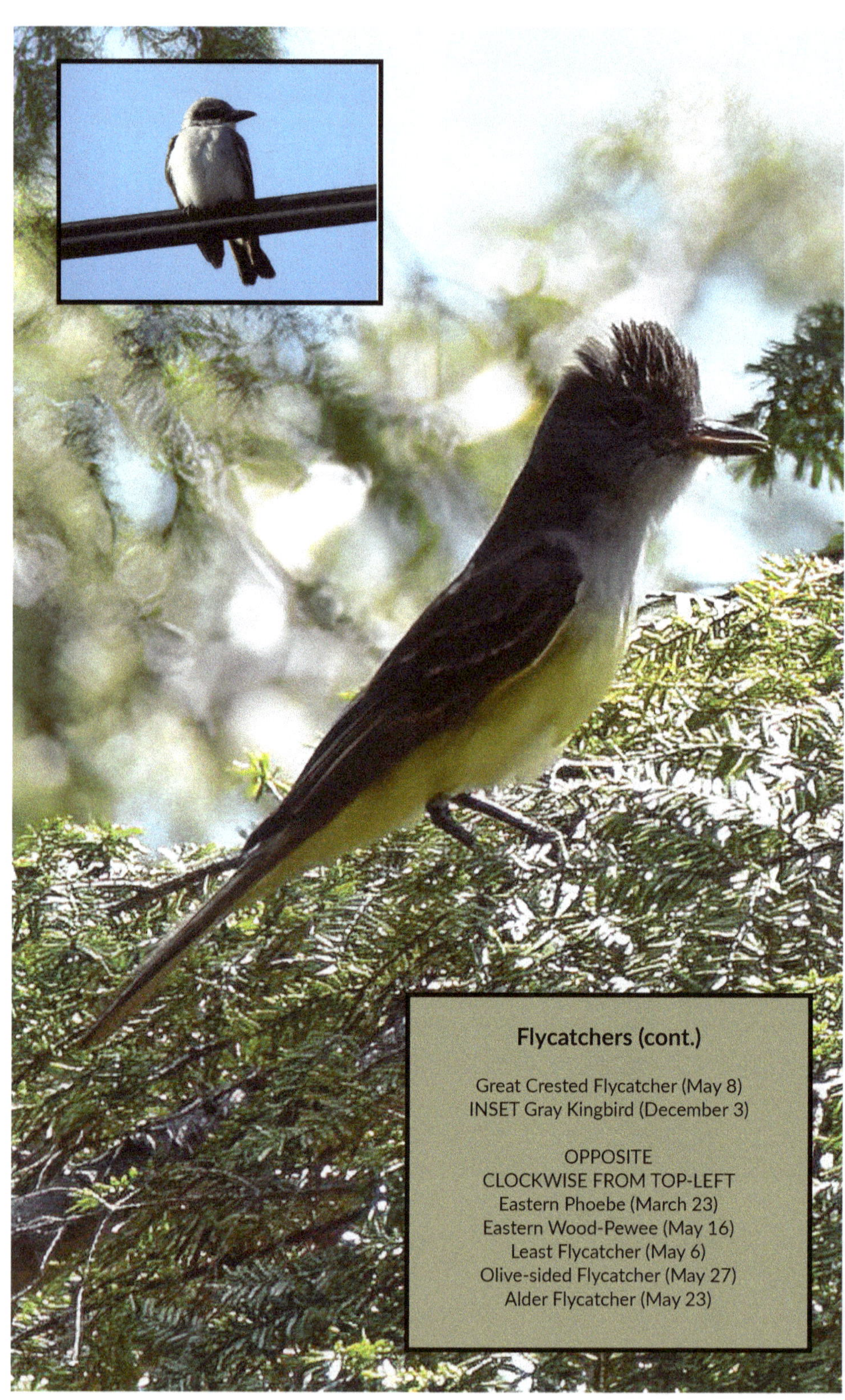

Flycatchers (cont.)

Great Crested Flycatcher (May 8)
INSET Gray Kingbird (December 3)

OPPOSITE
CLOCKWISE FROM TOP-LEFT
Eastern Phoebe (March 23)
Eastern Wood-Pewee (May 16)
Least Flycatcher (May 6)
Olive-sided Flycatcher (May 27)
Alder Flycatcher (May 23)

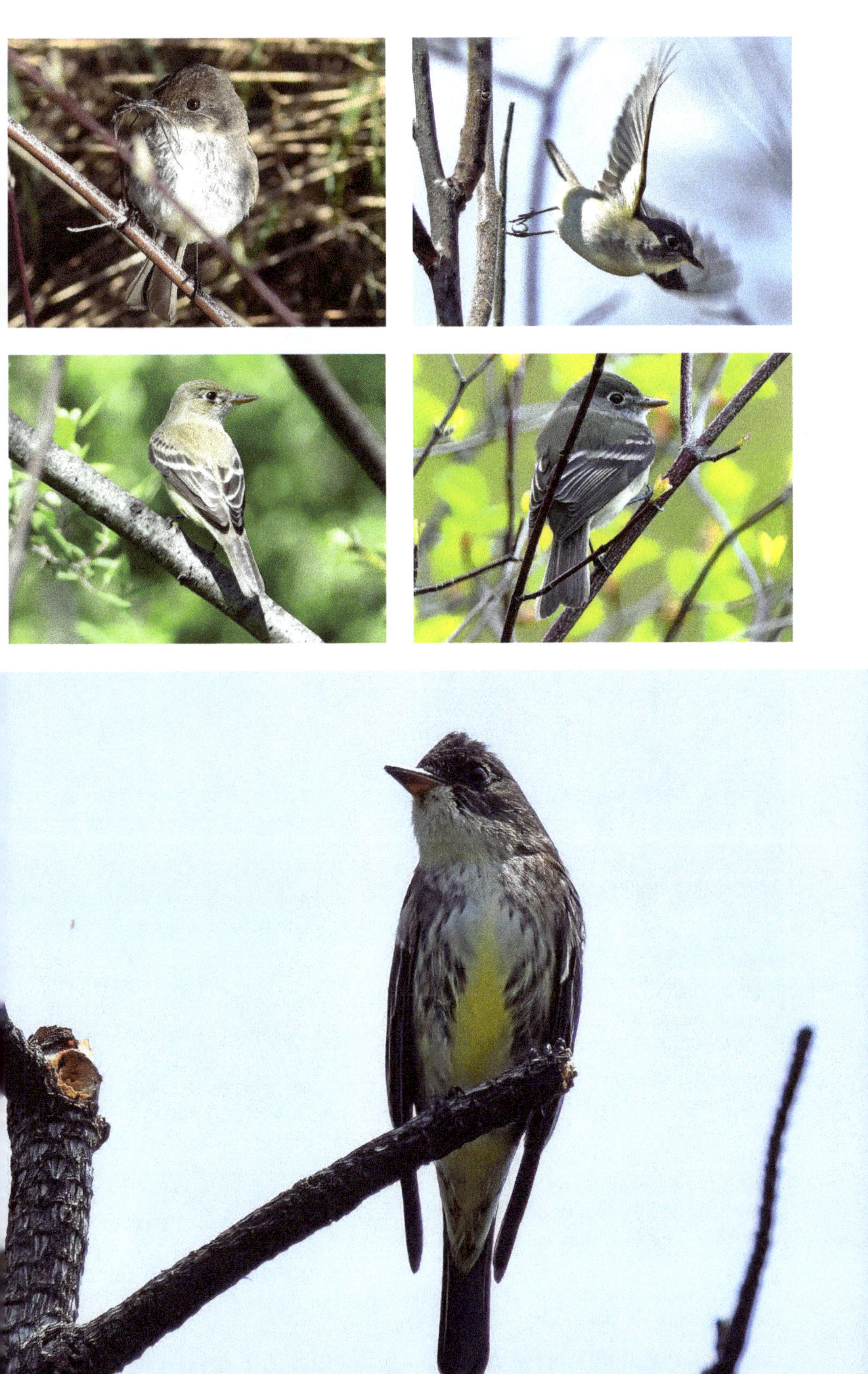

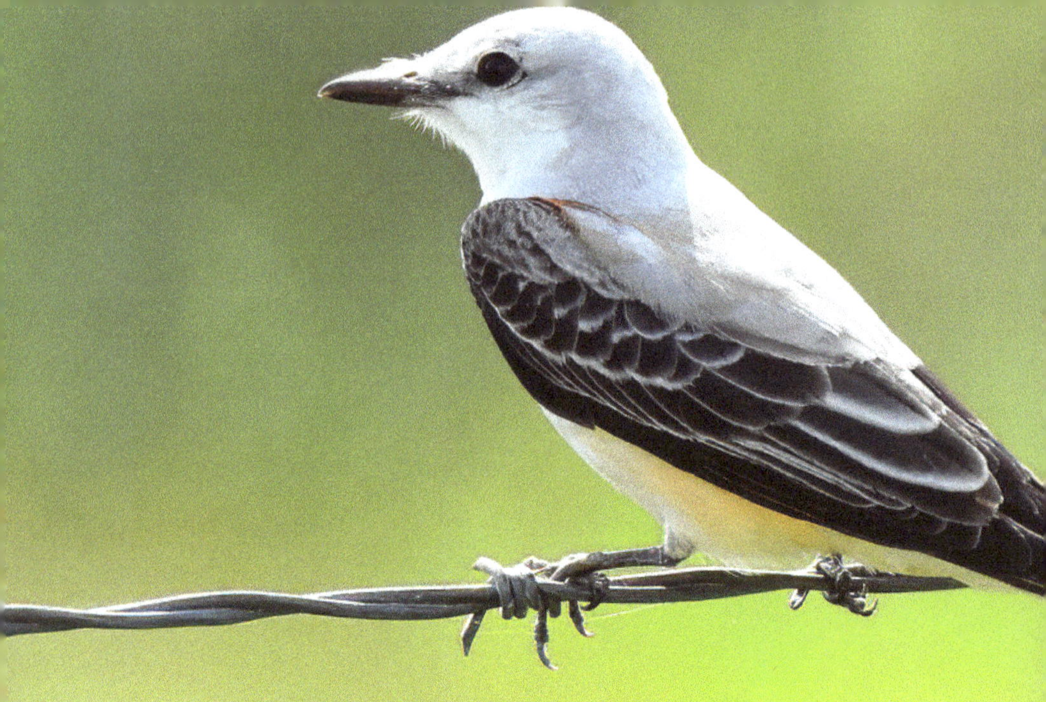

There have been a number of books (and a movie) about Big Years, and a running theme is the stress they put on relationships. Fortunately, unlike most of the spouses and partners in these books, Ingrid is also a birder and wants to get the bird as much as I do.

On June 3rd I pushed this premise to the limit. I was in Bar Harbor for a Bird-ing Festival. Ingrid took Friday off and headed north after work to join me.

We had 7:00 dinner reservations and at 5:30 I headed to the hotel to shower off a day of bug spray, grime and sweat. My phone rang. It was Ingrid calling to report a rare Scissor-tailed Flycatcher had been seen at a horse farm in Tren-ton, a mere 20 miles from our hotel. I couldn't risk it flying off over night, so I rushed to the horse farm (passing In-grid going north as I sped south).

When I arrived, Michael Good, a re-nown birder, was also there. Together

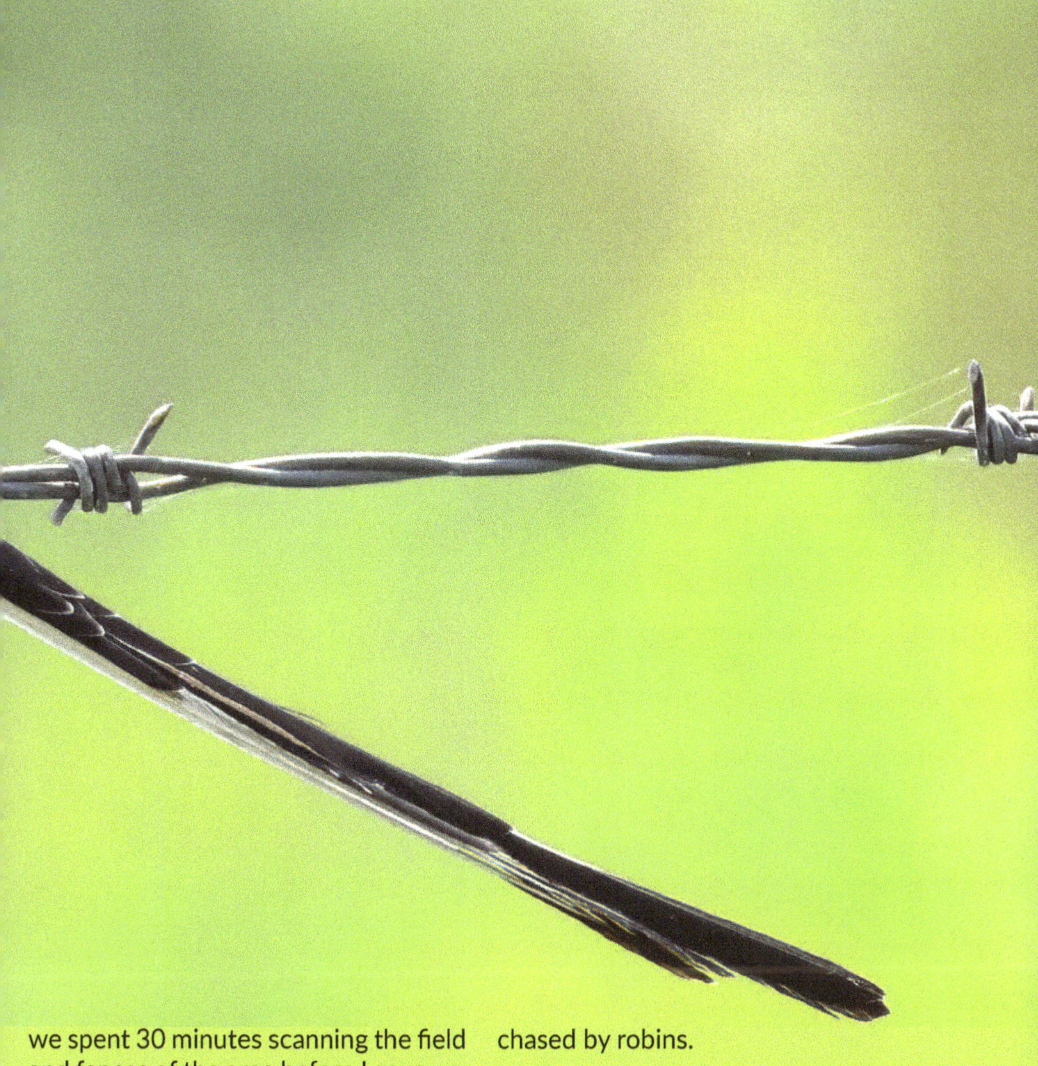

we spent 30 minutes scanning the field and fences of the area before I gave up, as I had dinner reservations.

Just as I was pulling into the hotel parking lot, my phone rang, it was Michael. He was on the bird. I called Ingrid not knowing what to do. She said, "Go get the bird, and we will figure out dinner when we you get back."

I love this woman!!!

I found the Scissor-tailed Flycatcher, a bird that belongs in Texas or Mexico, perched on a fence, occasionally being chased by robins.

Later we had a wonderful steak dinner, me smelling like Deep-Woods Off and pine pitch, but I was truly happy knowing that I was the luckiest man in the world.

The next morning, Ingrid was able to see the bird herself.

The couple that birds together stays together!!!

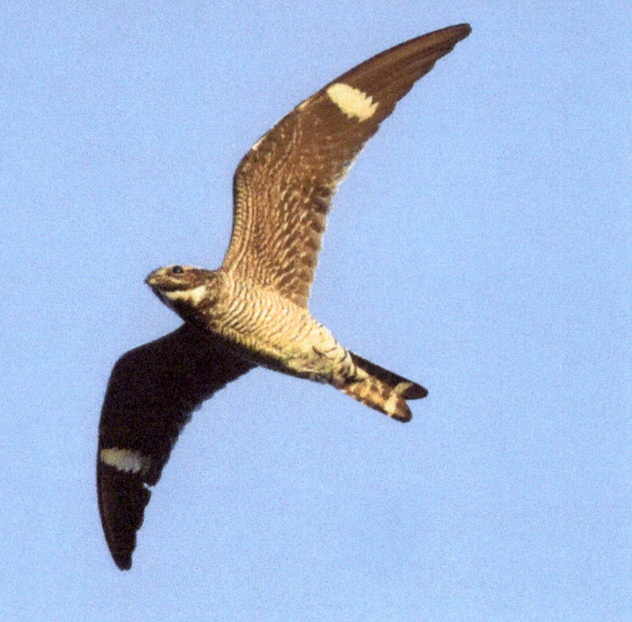

will's-widow, a nocturnal bird common to the American South, but rarely strays north of Cape Cod.

A friend had heard one at this location back in mid-May, and my date and I were hoping it was still around.

The Chuck-will's-widow and it's close relatives, the Eastern Whip-poor-will and Common Nighthawks are Nightjars, birds that hunt for insects at night. They are rarely seen but are known for their emphatic singing. Nightjars are sometimes called Goat-

With the pandemic seemingly winding down, date night had returned to America, normally dinner and a movie.

For the Whitakers, we start with dinner, then a 90 minute drive, followed by a five mile hike, down a scary road, in pitch blackness, in the middle of a forest, surrounded by mosquitoes.

Ingrid is one lucky lady!!!

This night's target bird was the Chuck-

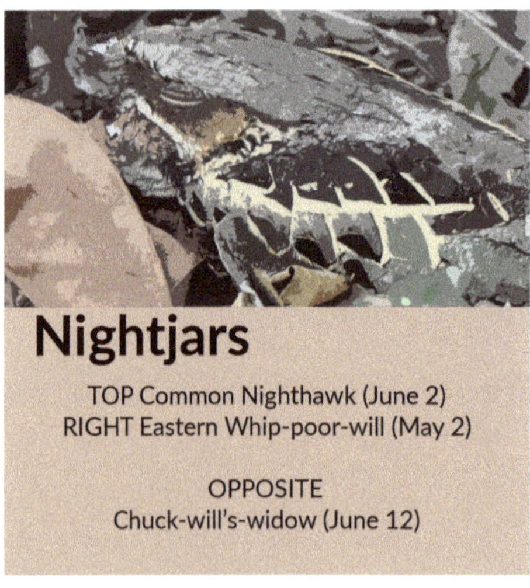

Nightjars

TOP Common Nighthawk (June 2)
RIGHT Eastern Whip-poor-will (May 2)

OPPOSITE
Chuck-will's-widow (June 12)

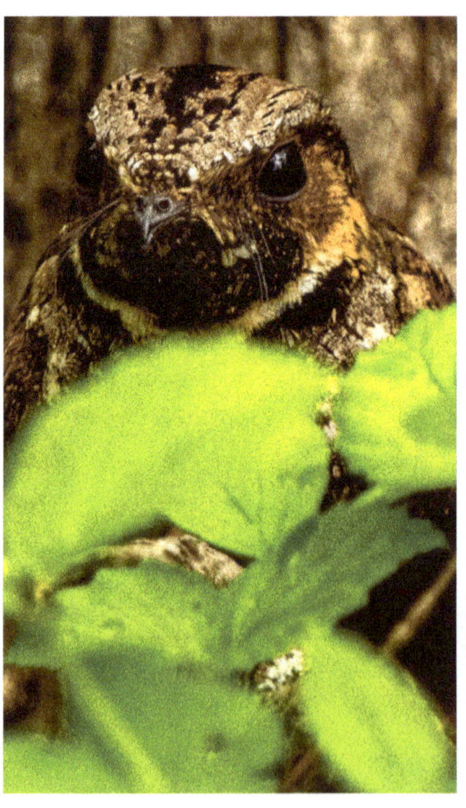

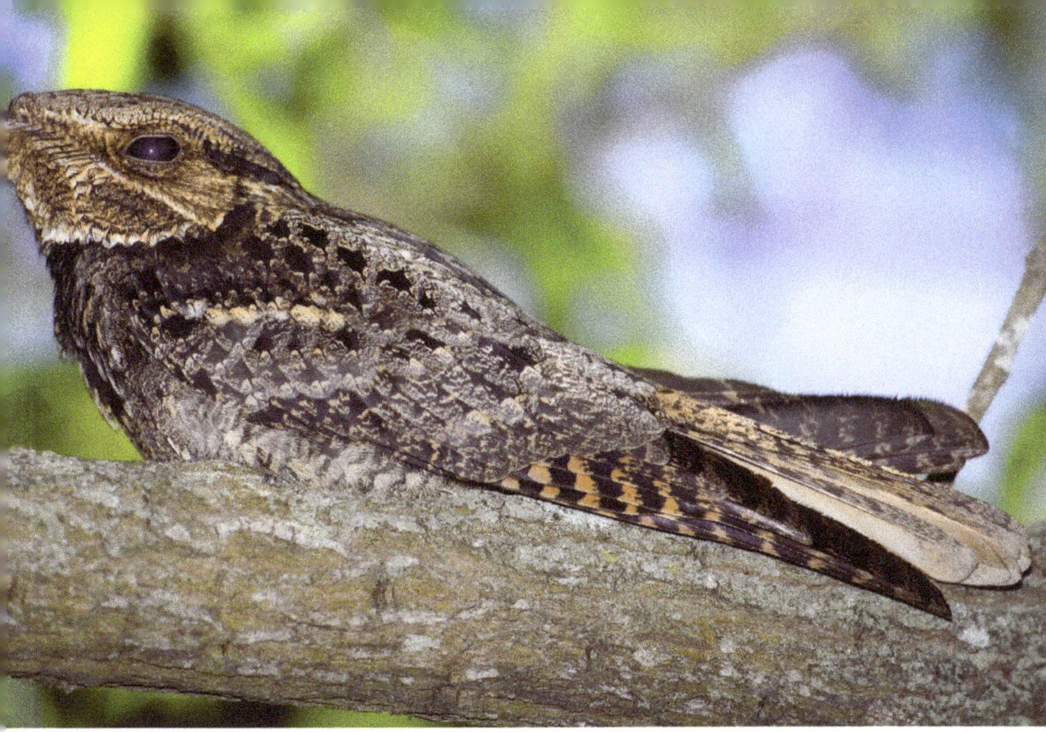

suckers due to a myth, carried over from Ancient times, that they drink the blood and milk of goats (Aristotle actually wrote about it.).

On the hike in, we saw a couple of Common Nighthawks fly over. The males began their territorial buzzing followed with a "Boom" sound produced by an acrobatic dive.

Shortly after arriving at the meadow where the Chuck-will's-widow resides, Ingrid and I both observed him moving at the far side of the field.

Just as it became really dark, "Chuck" began to sing. *CHUCK-wills-WIDOW CHUCK-wills-WIDOW CHUCK-wills-WIDOW*. Over and over and over.

In the distance an Eastern Whip-poor-will began to compete with Chuck, *WHIP-puwi-WEEW WHIP-puwi-WEEW WHIP-puwi-WEEW*.

As we began our long walk back to the car, Chuck seemed to follow us, continuing to "sing" in the trees just to our left for over a quarter mile.

We both got sightings of "Chuck", a couple of Common Nighthawks flying over and heard a Whip-poor-will at a distance.

The Goatsucker Trifecta!!!!

Chuck-will's-widow
Bird #283
Orland
June 12

Maine

VACATIONLAND

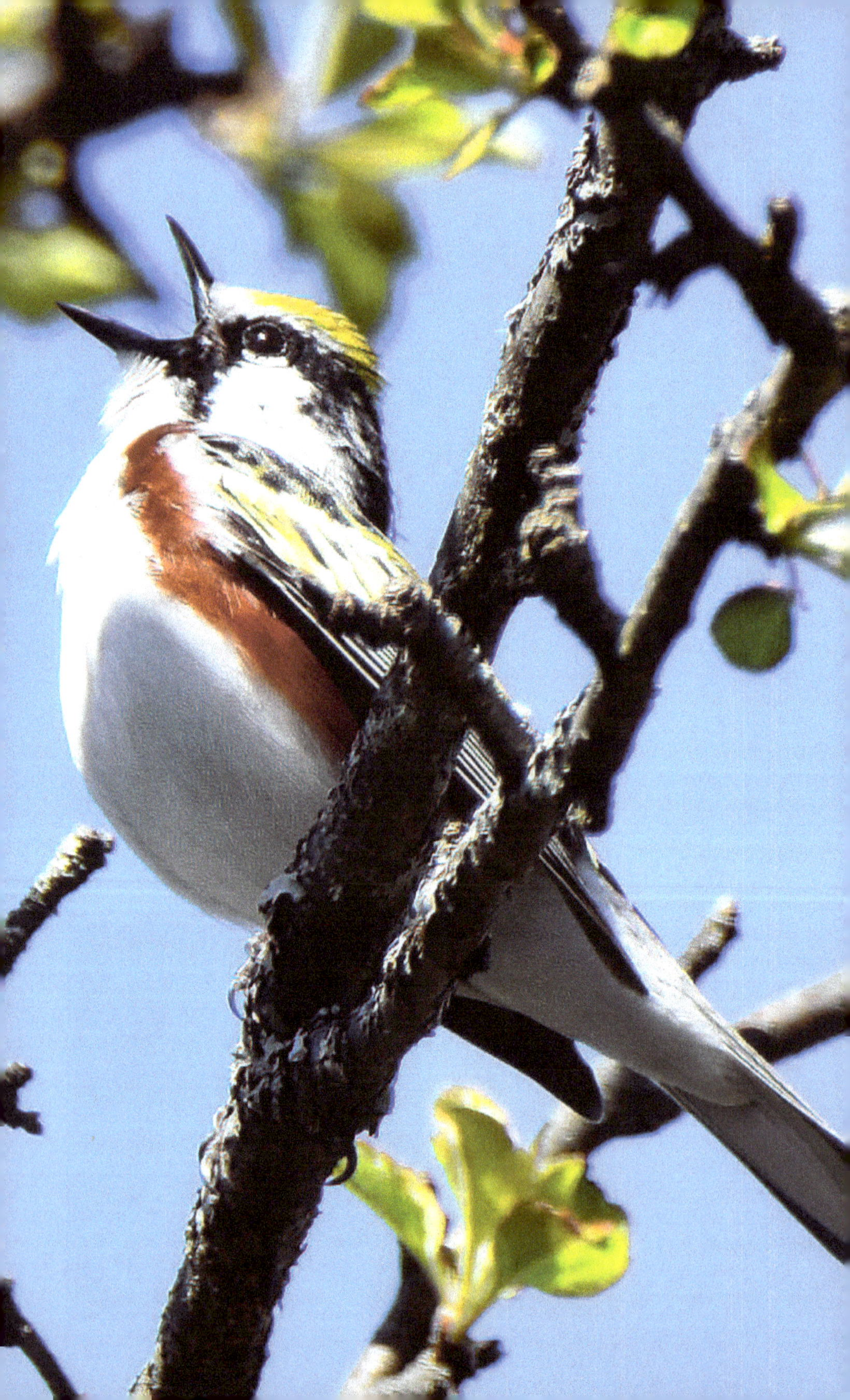

Warblers

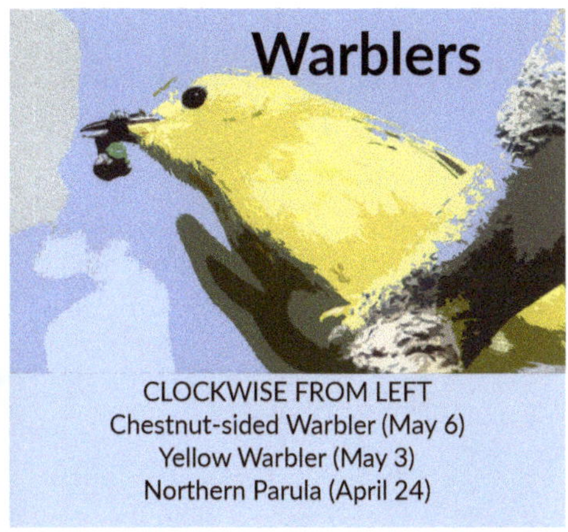

CLOCKWISE FROM LEFT
Chestnut-sided Warbler (May 6)
Yellow Warbler (May 3)
Northern Parula (April 24)

May is the best month of the year for birding in Maine. Warblers are moving from their winter homes in the Caribbean and South America. Many are heading north to the Boreal Forests of Canada and even the Arctic.

These brightly colored bug eaters are often visible at eye level, moving through bushes and trees in a whirlwind of motion.

At some of Maine's more Warbler friendly "hotspots", you'll see a dozen birders staring through binoculars at a shrub 20 feet away, calling out the birds as they appear: "Yellow-rumped" ... "Green" ... "Parula" ... "Chestnut".

Suddenly someone will see the very desirable "Blackburnian" and eleven birders will simultaneously whisper, "Where???"

After spending the morning staring up at birds in the canopy, Ingrid and I will have "warbler neck", an actual

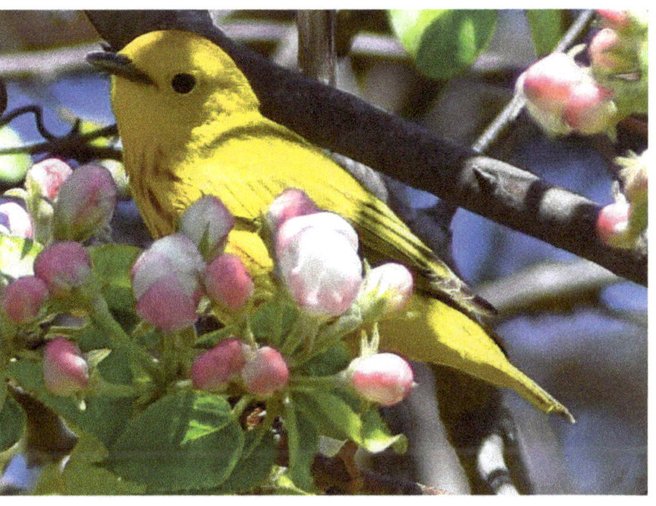

and somewhat painful condition caused by a combination of binoculars and a neck strained at 45 degrees.

When you're about to call it a day, you'll hear about a Bay-breasted Warbler sighting, slam the car door and run back into the woods.

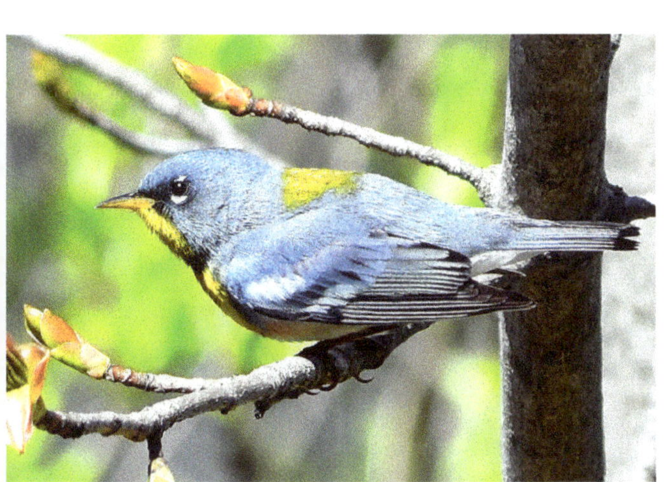

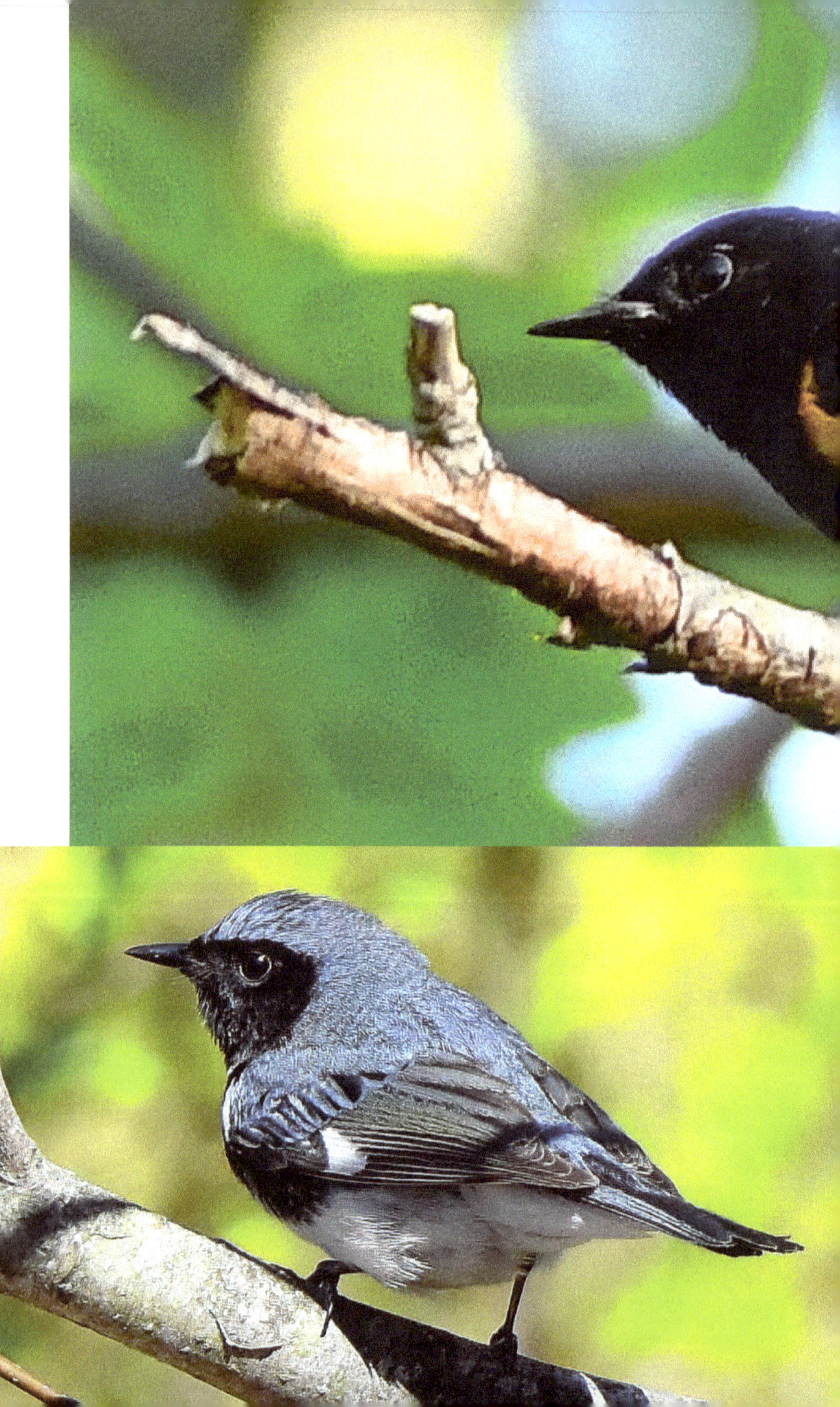

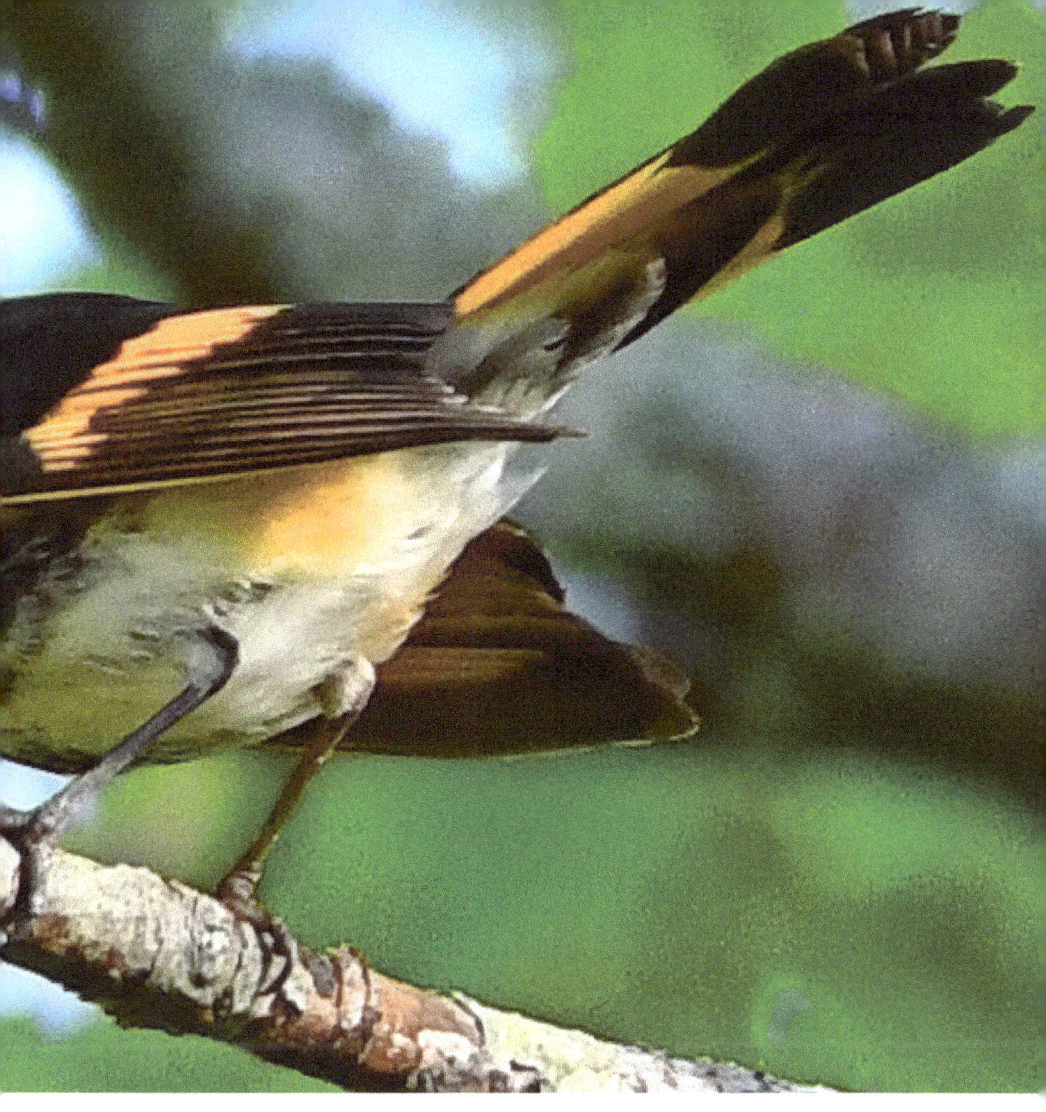

The vibrantly colored warblers moving through Maine in May return again in the fall, this time (in most cases) without their bright plumage.

In autumn it can be a real challenge to determine the species as many fall warblers look nearly identical, especially female warblers. Thus, when doing a Big Year, it is best to fill one's checklist on the migration north.

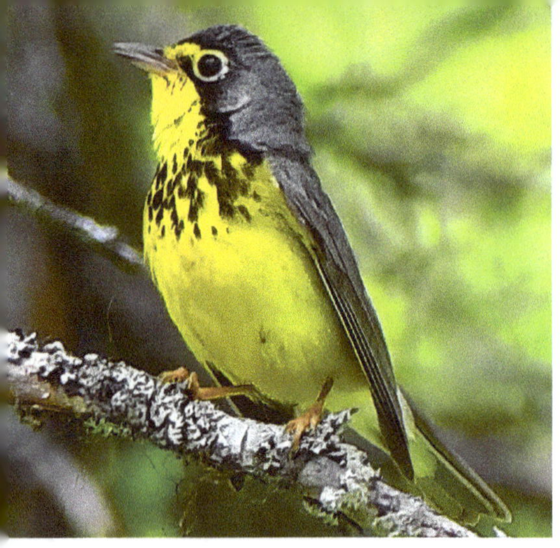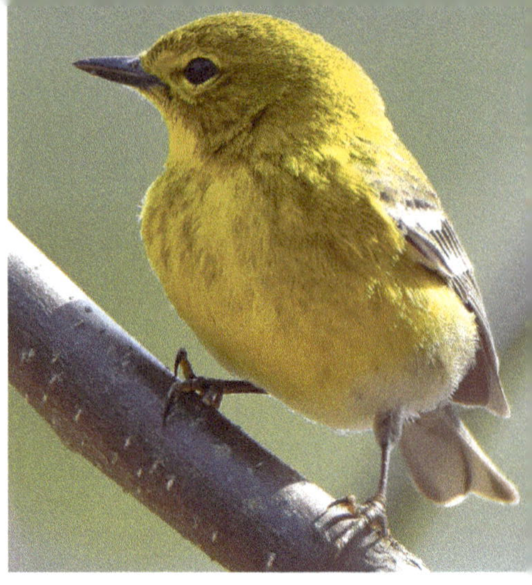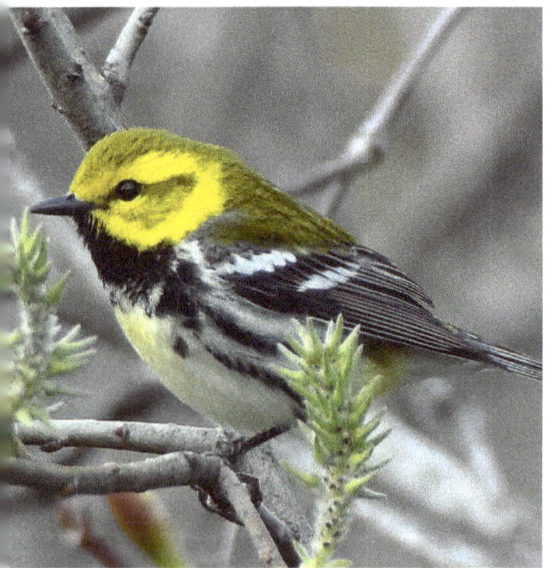

Warblers (cont.)

CLOCK-WISE FROM TOP LEFT
Canada Warbler (May 9)
Pine Warbler (March 11)
Common Yellowthroat (May 2)
Yellow-rumped Warbler (January 6)
Magnolia Warbler (May 8)
Black-throated Green Warbler (April 28)

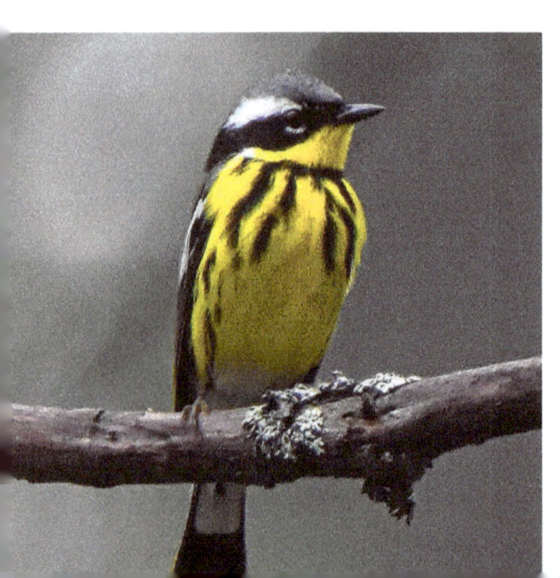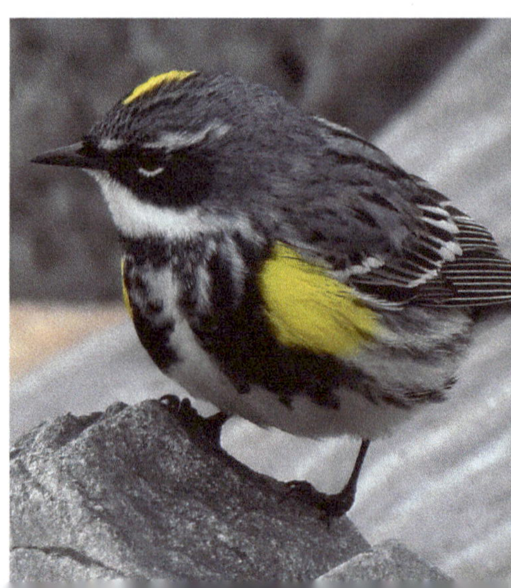

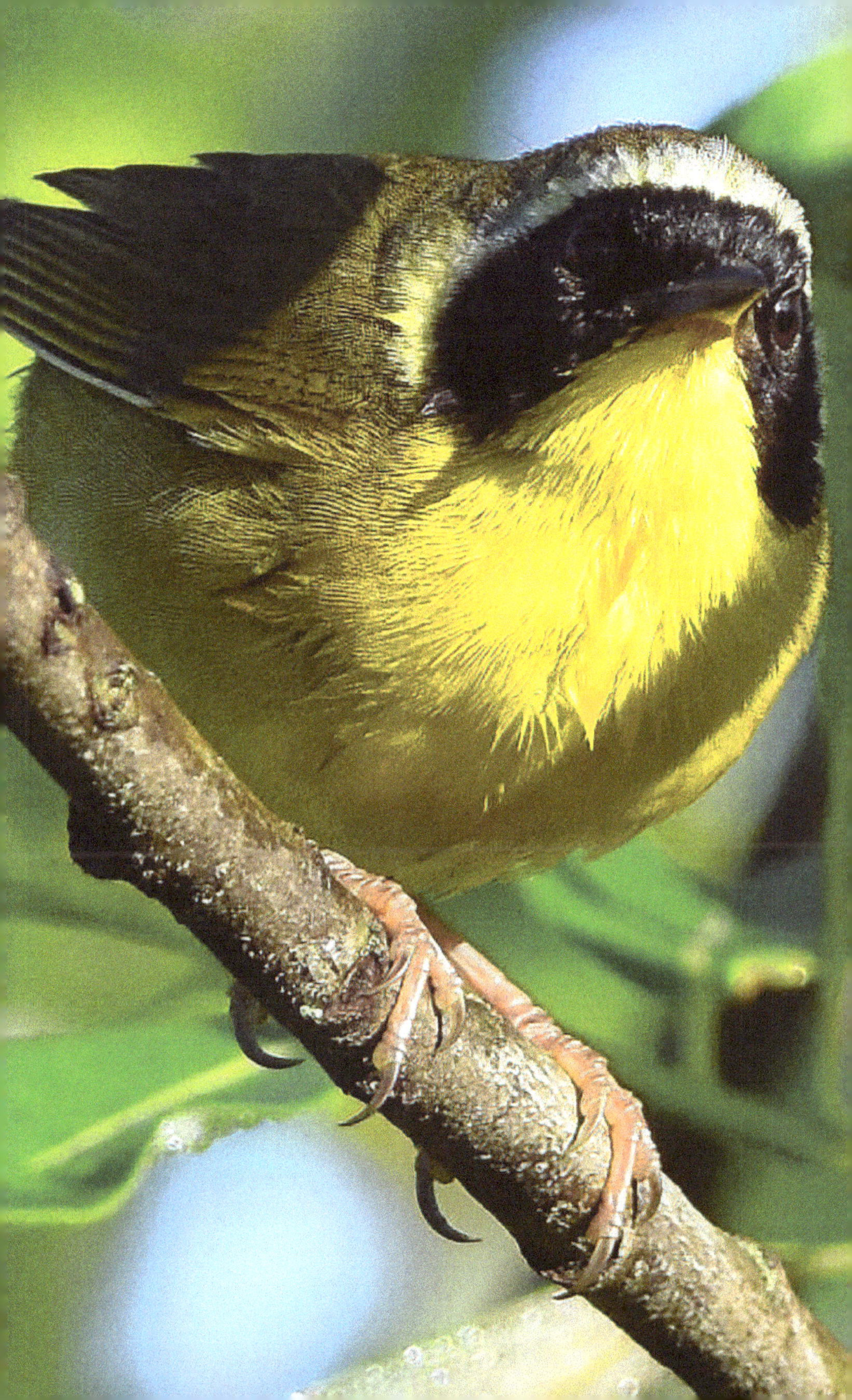

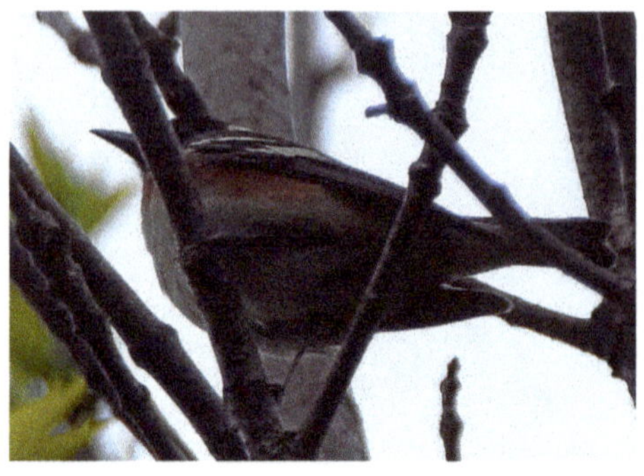

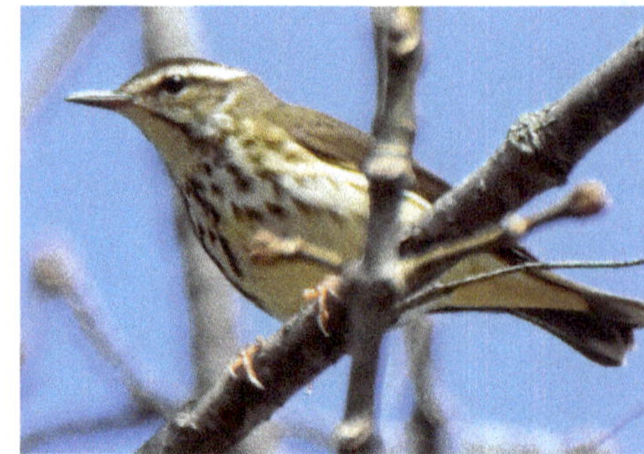

Several Christmas's ago, Ingrid gave me a book: *Birdwatching in Maine: A Site Guide* by Derek Lovitch. It discusses birding hot spots all over the state in incredible detail. Directions, time of day to go, where to park, what birds you'll find and when, rarities, bathroom availability, nearby restaurants, etc. It's a great companion when we are out birding.

While perusing *Birding in Maine*, I came upon a chapter: "The Louie Loop" which details where Louisiana Water-thrushes, a warbler species, nest in Maine. I was a little shocked because I didn't think they were found in Maine except, occasionally during migration.

One April morning, Ingrid and I drove half way across the state to a rapidly running brook off a side road in a heav-ily wooded area. Nearby were the re-mains of an ancient mill that had been built by oxen and human muscle. For a half hour we wandered through the woods, mud and pricker bushes. Just when we were about to give up, I heard three short whistles followed by a jum-ble of notes, a Louisiana Waterthrush.

Over the next 5 minutes we searched for the bird, and Ingrid finally spotted him high up in a tree singing away.

We returned to the same spot the fol-lowing year for my Maine Big Year Lou-isiana Waterthrush!!!

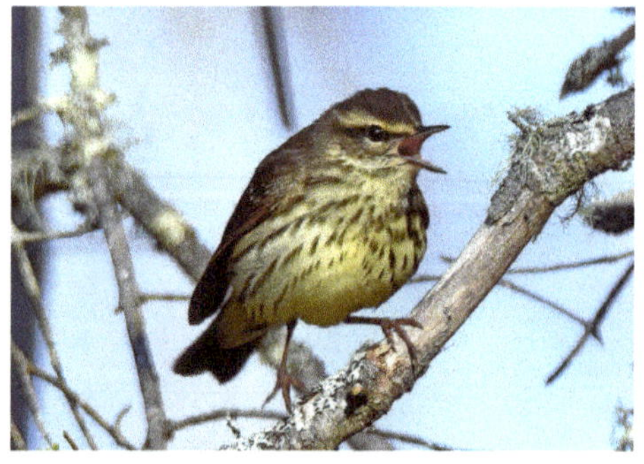

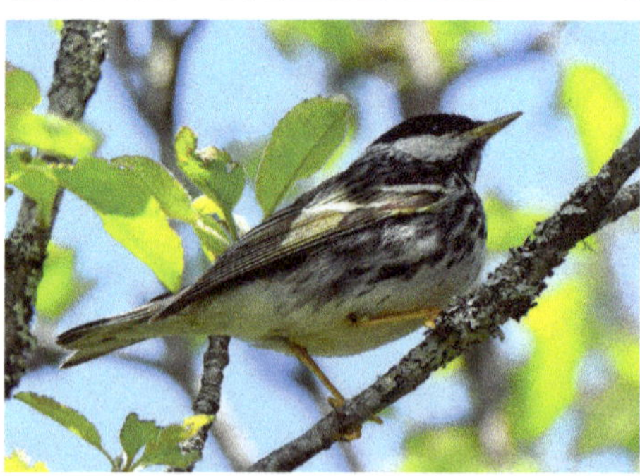

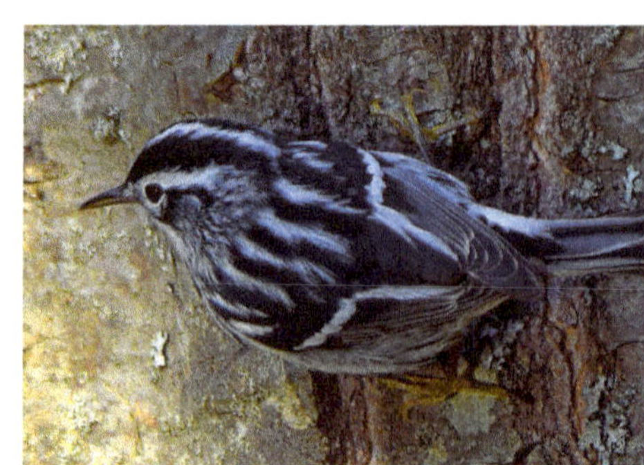

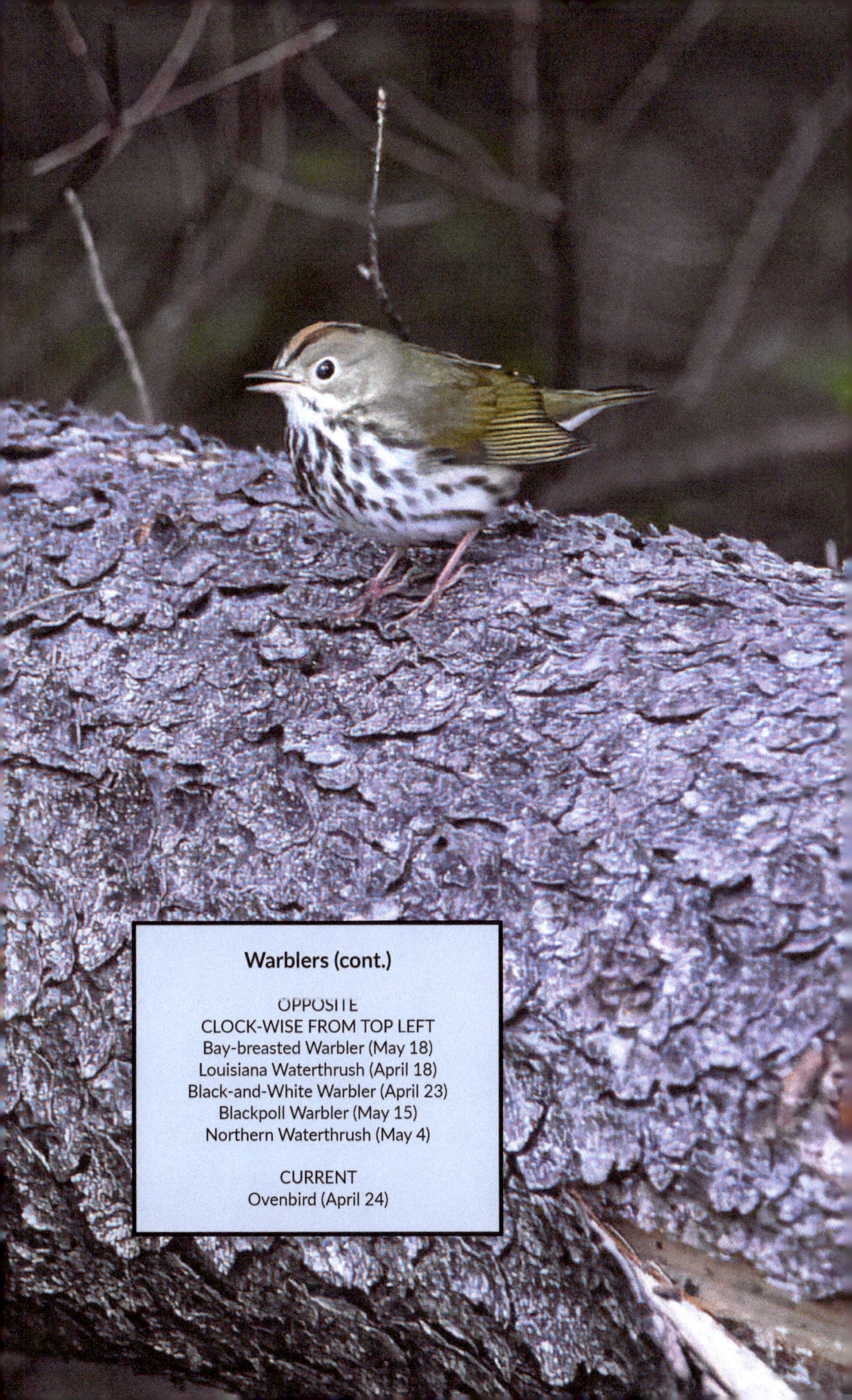

Warblers (cont.)

OPPOSITE
CLOCK-WISE FROM TOP LEFT
Bay-breasted Warbler (May 18)
Louisiana Waterthrush (April 18)
Black-and-White Warbler (April 23)
Blackpoll Warbler (May 15)
Northern Waterthrush (May 4)

CURRENT
Ovenbird (April 24)

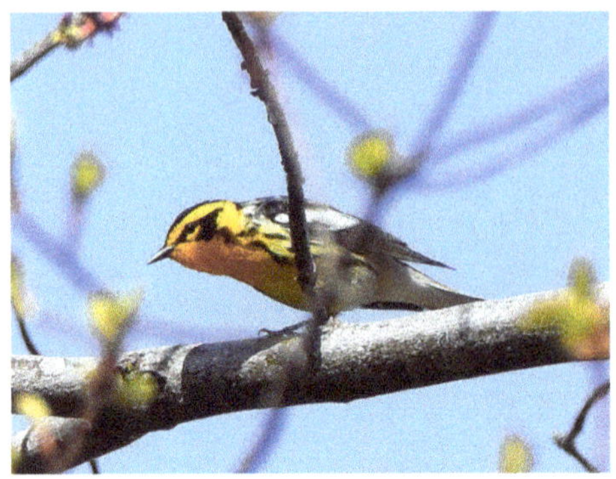

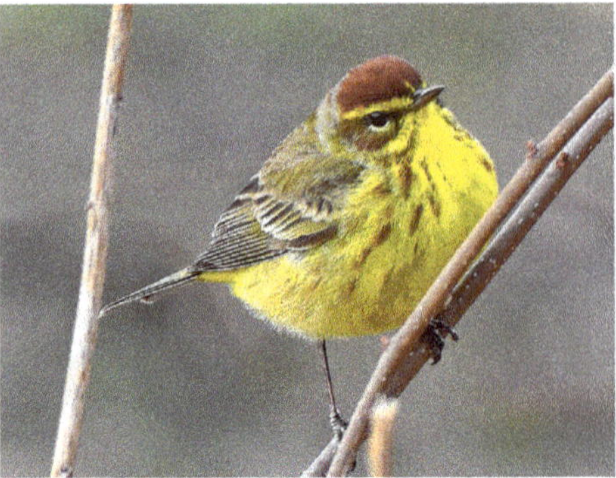

Warbler migration in Maine comes in waves.

In late April, one will see an orange/yellow bird with a red cap bobbing its tail. This is the Palm Warbler, the first scout for the onslaught to come.

Within a week, dozens of Palm Warblers will be scattered around local hot spots, with a few Pine and Yellow-rumped Warblers mixed in. This is Wave #1.

A few weeks later, the Common Yellowthroat, Black-and-white and the spectacular Yellow Warblers appear, Wave #2.

And then in mid-May, with the next wave (#3) come the really fun birds: Cape May, Blackburnian, Canada, Magnolia and Wilson's Warblers.

When you start seeing Blackpoll Warblers, Wave #4, a sense of melancholy descends as the Blackpoll's arrival means Spring Warbler migration is almost over.

Some of these birds (primarily those in wave two) remain in the state and nest for the summer. The rest continue into Canada. We remind ourselves that we'll see them all again, in the fall, heading south.

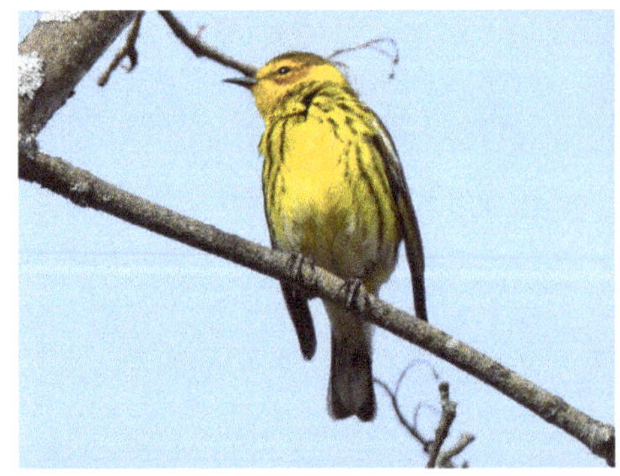

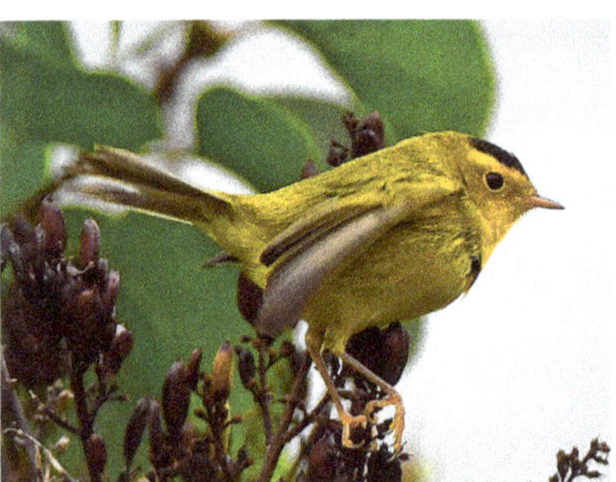

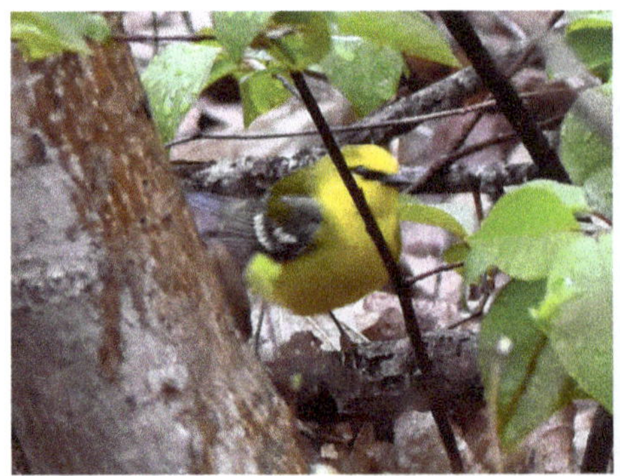

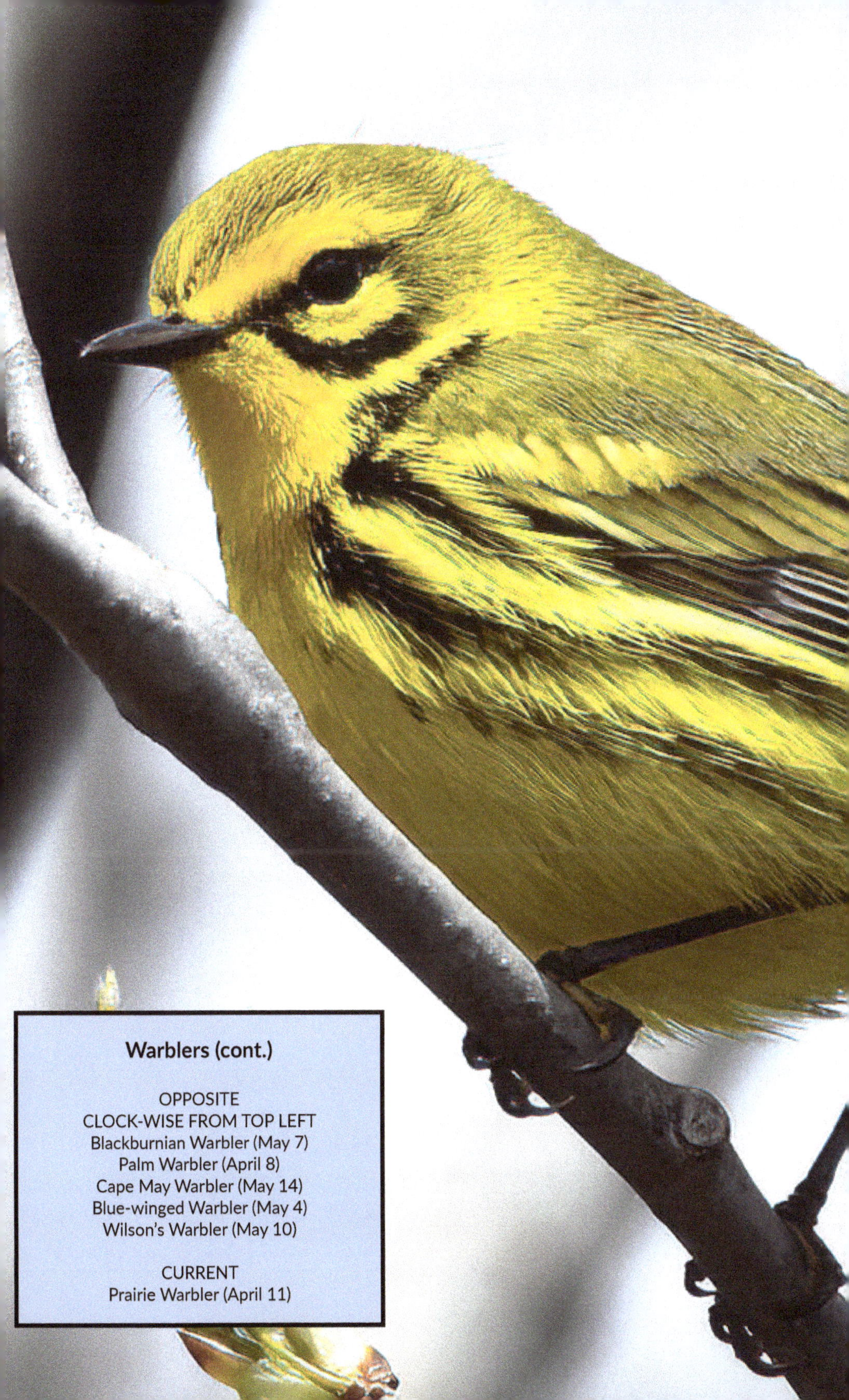

Warblers (cont.)

OPPOSITE
CLOCK-WISE FROM TOP LEFT
Blackburnian Warbler (May 7)
Palm Warbler (April 8)
Cape May Warbler (May 14)
Blue-winged Warbler (May 4)
Wilson's Warbler (May 10)

CURRENT
Prairie Warbler (April 11)

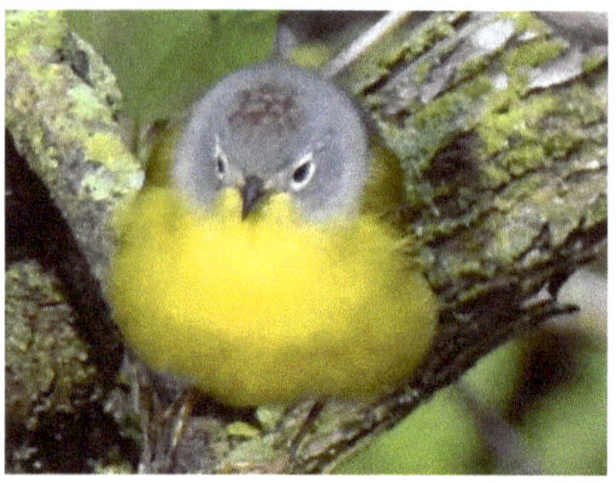

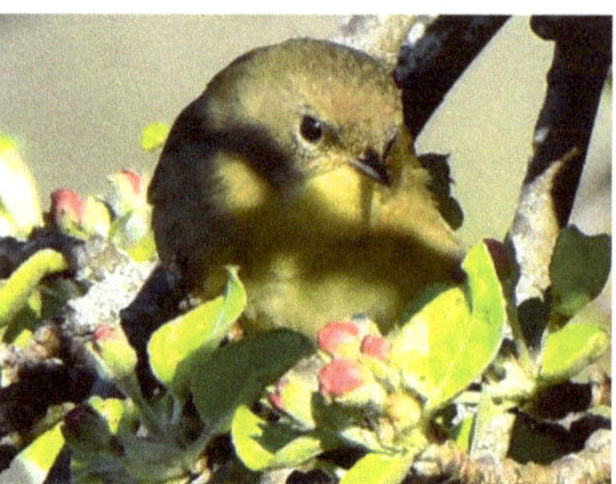

Warblers are bug eaters, feeding primarily on caterpillars plucked from foliage.

Thousands of years of evolution have taught Warblers to time their migration and breeding to the insect blooms that occur as trees and flowers explode into life for the short northern growing season.

However, some hardy Warblers can winter over!

Yellow-rumped and Pine Warblers switch to seeds when the supply of insects becomes limited.

Thus, each winter Ingrid and I find a few of these warblers along the Maine coast. These are birds that are barely eking out an existence. Some discover that a residential suet feeder is a great way to supplement their diet.

Several years ago when Maine had an unexpected cold spell in late April delaying the caterpillar bloom, bird feeders throughout the state were covered with hungry Yellow-rumped Warblers and a few Pine Warblers.

These two species are truly adaptable birds.

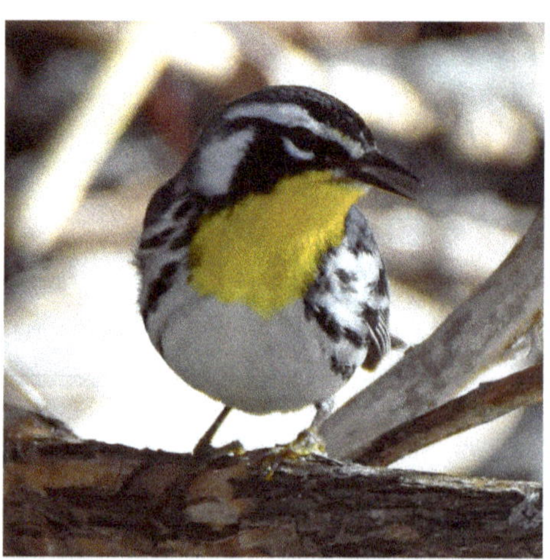

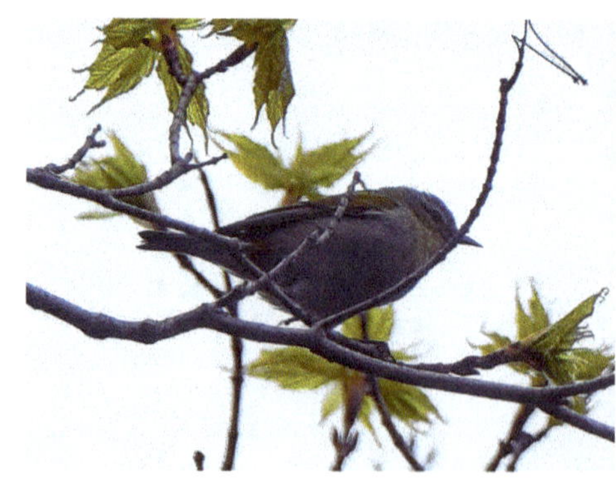

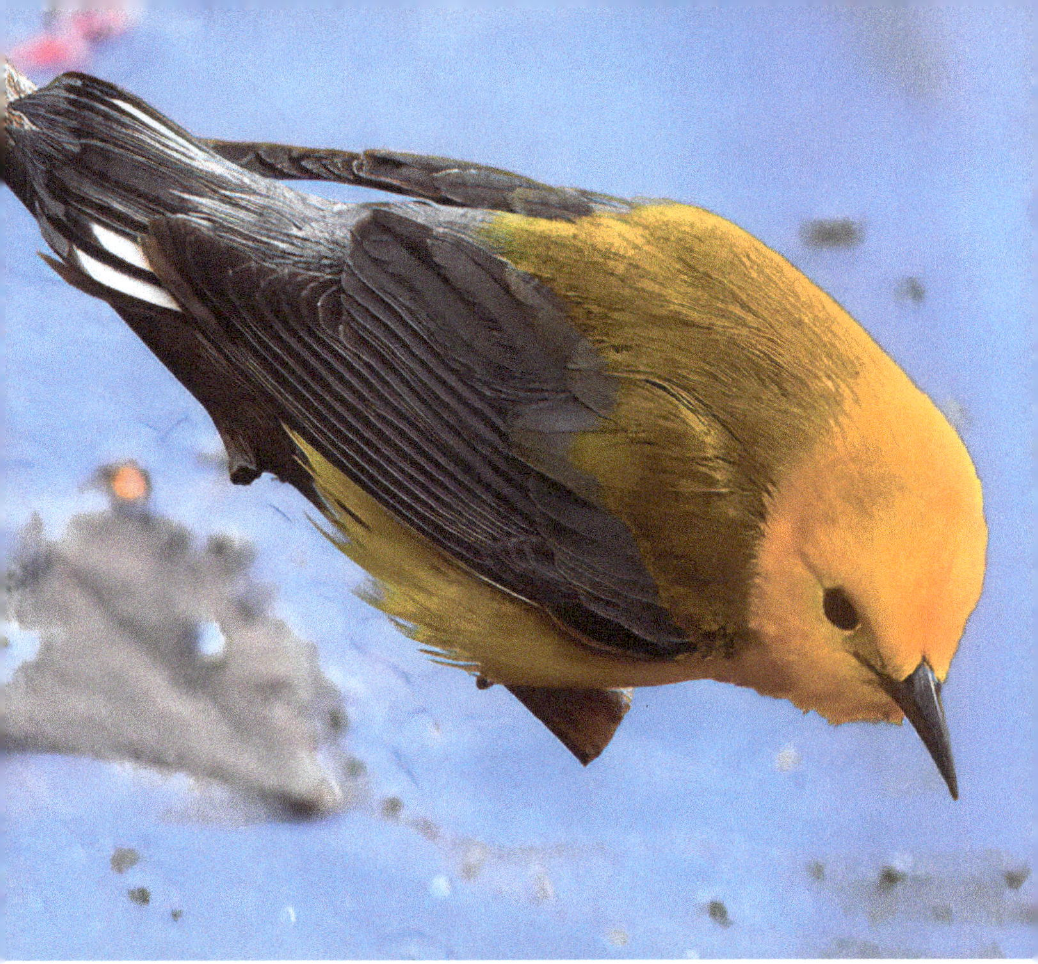

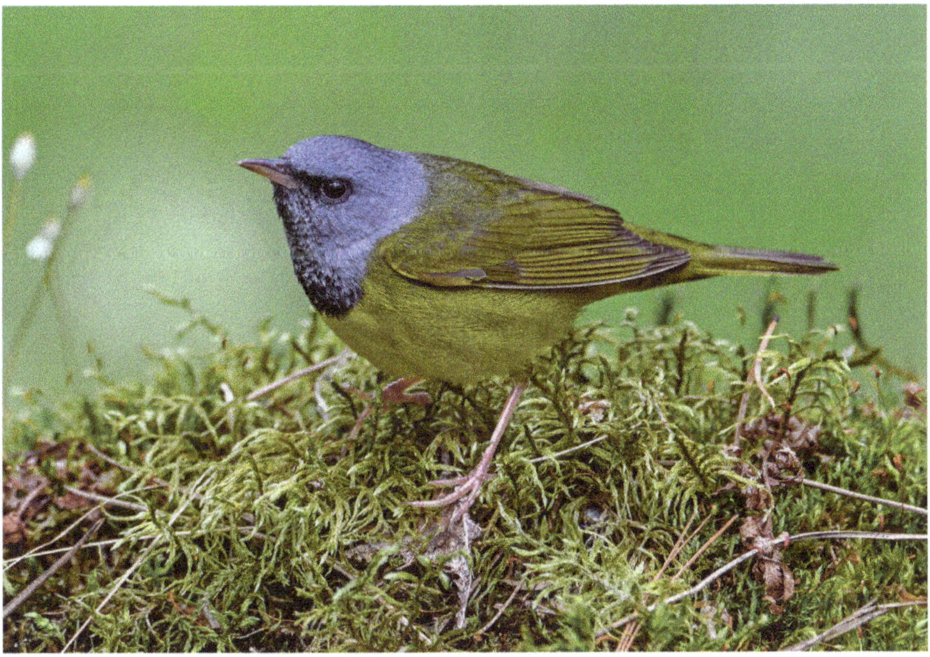

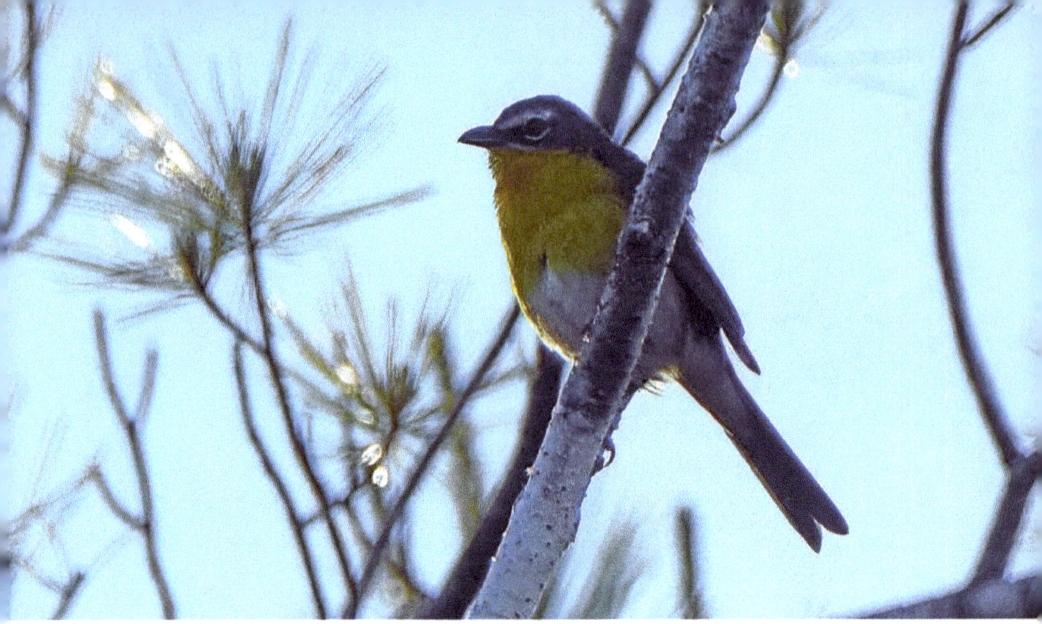

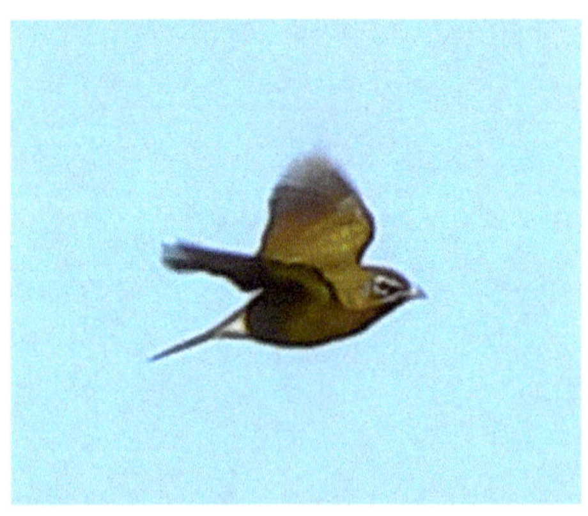

If you take a boat out into the ocean beyond the sight of land, the emptiness is breathtaking. In September, I ventured out on a Bar Harbor whale watch. About two hours into the trip, the captain stopped the boat to look around. Nothing but still water in all directions.

It was then that I noticed a tiny yellow bird flying toward the boat. This wasn't the expected giant seabird with a six foot wingspan. It looked like a warbler, a bird that eats caterpillars out of birch trees. What was it doing twenty miles out at sea?

Circling the boat once before heading on its way, this mystery bird was a Yellow-breasted Chat, a warbler-like bird that is rarely found north of New Jersey and generally feeding in shrubbery.

It was mind boggling how and why this tiny bird was flying around the Gulf of Maine.

Once considered a warbler, but now in a family of birds all to itself, several Chats showed up in the state during my Maine Big Year: once in Thomaston, again on Monhegan Island and on this particular day, far out to sea flying around our whale watch boat.

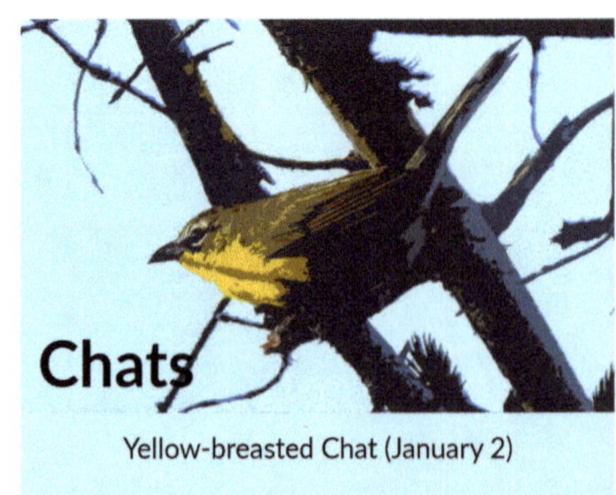

Yellow-breasted Chat (January 2)

If you pass a marsh along the U.S. Coastline you're familiar with the Snowy Egret, a graceful two foot tall bird with black bill and legs, yellow feet, and beautiful white feathers. Flocks are common, and Snowy Egrets are not particularly afraid of humans. In Europe and Africa, an almost identical bird prowls the coastline, the Little Egret.

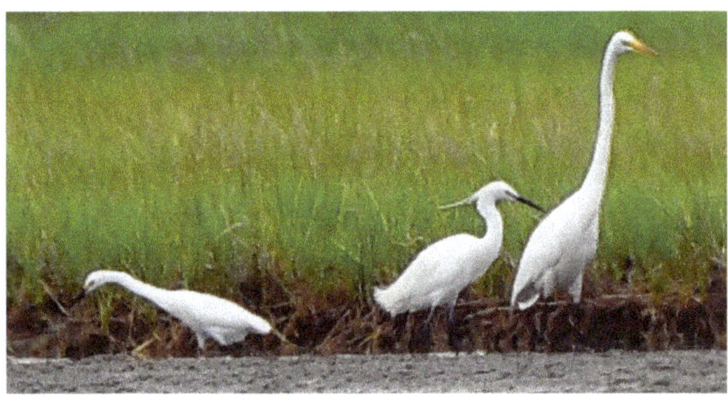

In Spring, the Little Egret has two long white plumes extending from its head to the middle of it's back. Once breeding season ends, the plumes fall off and the Little Egret looks very much like its American cousin.

Until 1954, telling the difference between a Snowy Egret and a Little Egret was not terribly important because they were separated by the vast Atlantic Ocean. In that year a Little Egret showed up in Nova Scotia and another in Barbados.

Since then, East Coast visits of Little Egrets have become more common, with a Little Egret annually appearing in Falmouth beginning in 2011.

This April, the Little Egret did not show up on schedule. In late May, one was briefly sighted, but I was on the other side of the State. By early June, Little Egrets were reported between Wells and Falmouth, yet the bird remained maddeningly elusive for me.

As July approached, I was getting concerned. Once the Little Egret's plumes fell off, it would become very difficult to discern it from the ubiquitous Snowy Egret.

Finally, in desperation, I planted myself in a bird blind in Falmouth, where the Little Egret had recently been seen. My plan was to sit there all day and hope the bird would come to me. I had my spotting scope, camera, water and snacks (gotta have snacks).

Five minutes into my all-day-sit I looked at my phone and saw that a local birder reported a Little Egret, 10 miles away. So, I packed up and rushed to Scarborough Marsh.

An hour later, via a long-range spotting scope, I got the long sought after Little Egret, feeding with other Egrets. One plume had partially fallen off. In another week the plumes would have been gone, and I'd never have found him.

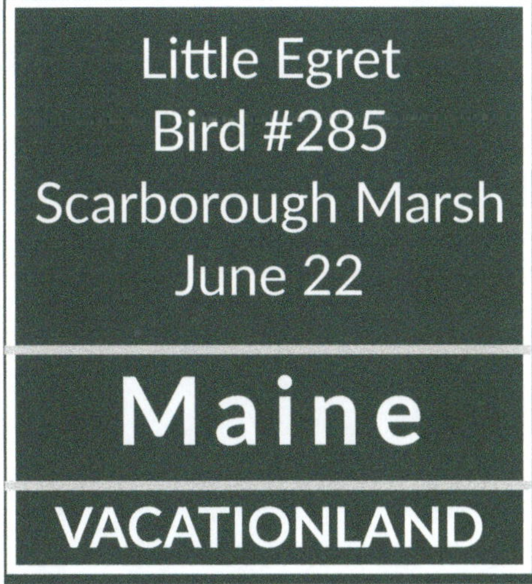

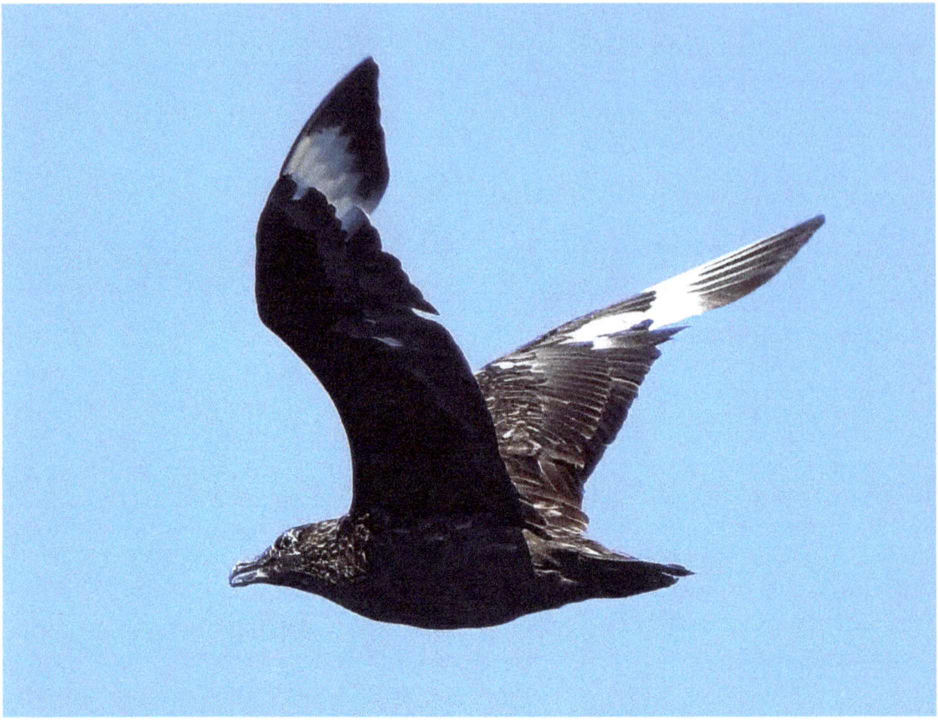

The birds of Maine extend out over the Atlantic Ocean to the Canadian Border in the north, to New Hampshire in the south and to the International Sea Border to the east.

Many species are easily accessible during sightseeing trips to Monhegan, Eastern Egg Rock, Machias Seal and the Casco Bay Islands. Puffin Cruises out of Portland and Bar Harbors are a

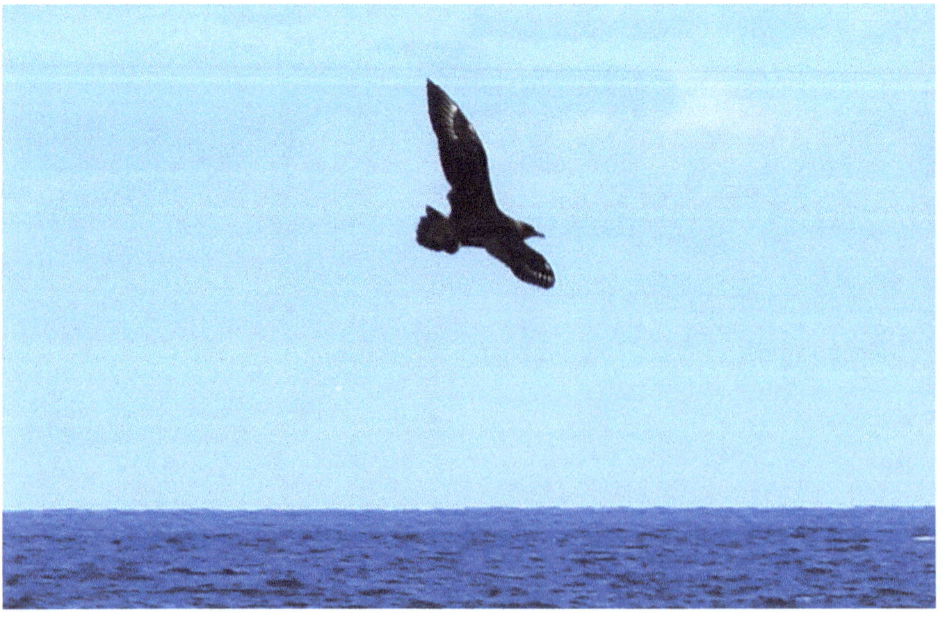

great way to see Puffins, Razorbills and Murres.

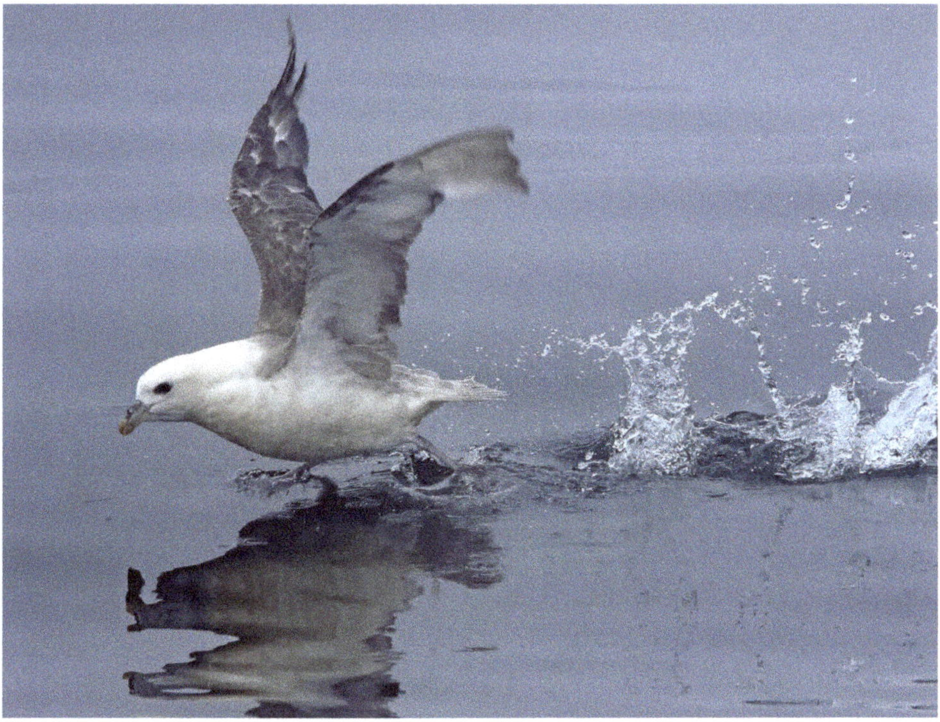

But there are birds that live even further out to sea. To see these pelagic species, one has to do a Deep Sea or dedicated Pelagic trip (or have a friend with a big boat).

Many of these birds look different from anything we see on shore. For instance, the Tubenose birds have tube-like structures that cover their nostrils, as clearly observed on the Northern Fulmar on this page. Maine's Tubenose birds include the Northern Fulmar, and the Great, Sooty, Manx and Cory's Shearwaters.

The Skuas (Great and South Polar) and Jaegers (Parasitic and Pomarine) are aggressive species preying on other seabirds, stealing their food or their lives.

The diminutive Storm-Petrels (Wilson's and Leach's) are tiny black and white birds that seemingly walk on water.

Every Pelagic trip is an adventure. Fog and rough seas can make for very poor birding, but under the right conditions, it's amazing how many fascinating birds are out there.

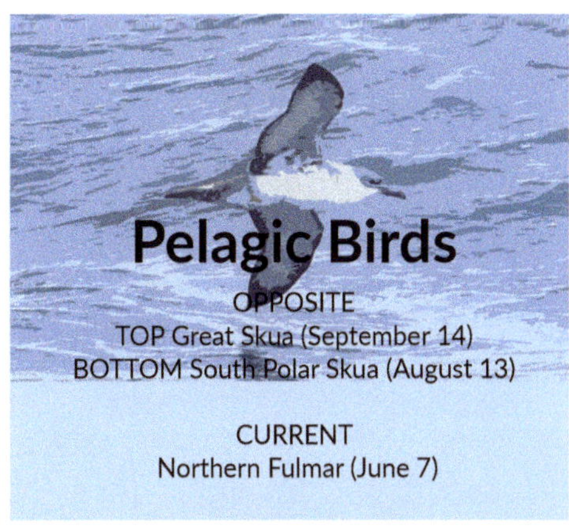

OPPOSITE
TOP Great Skua (September 14)
BOTTOM South Polar Skua (August 13)

CURRENT
Northern Fulmar (June 7)

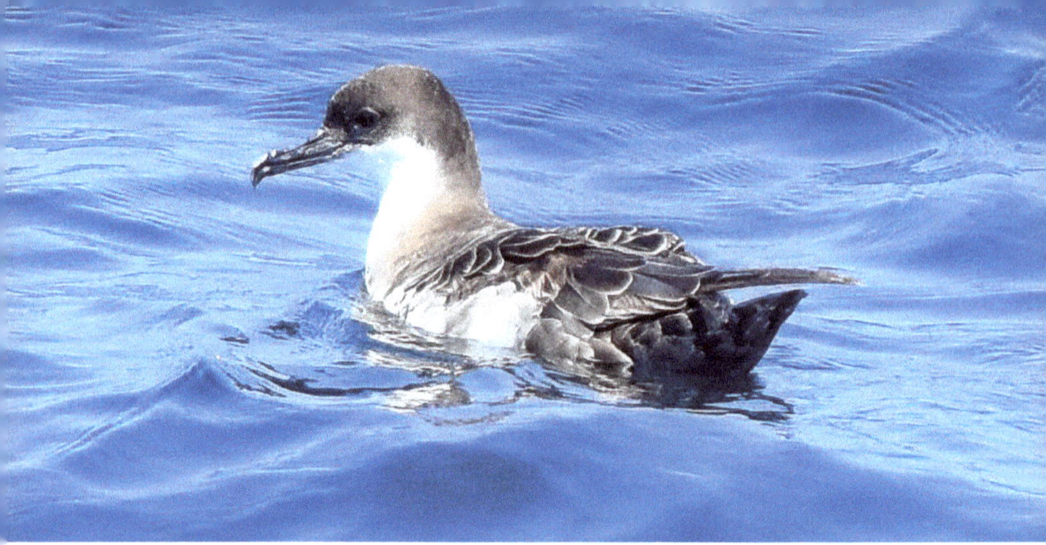

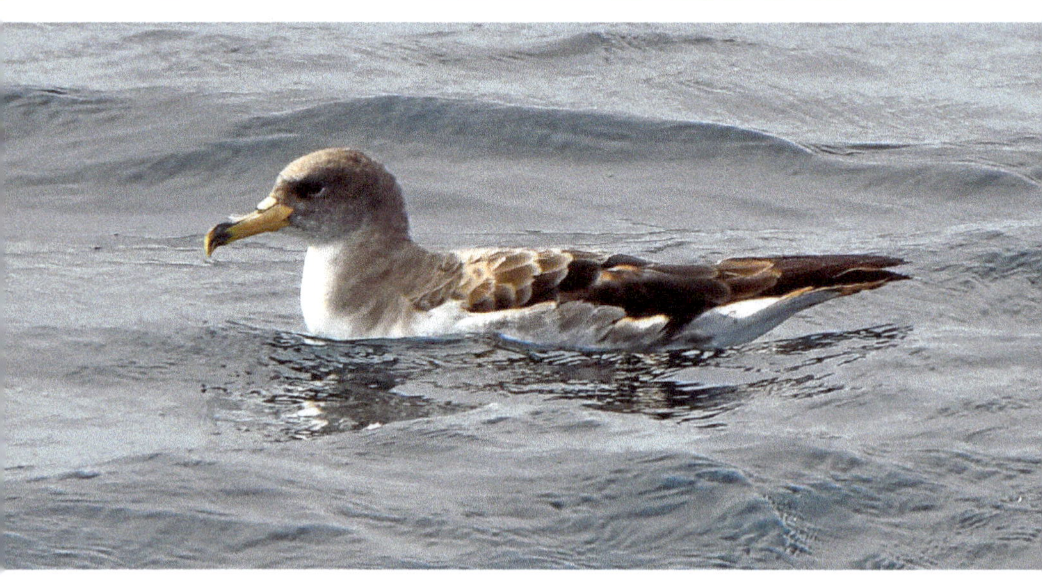

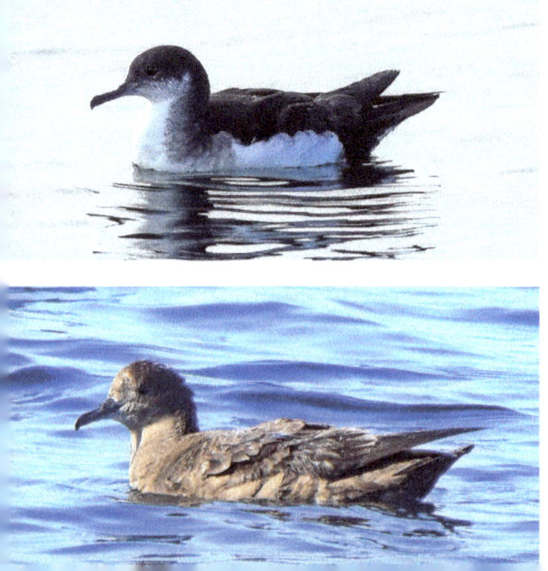

Pelagic Birds (cont.)

TOP TO BOTTOM
Great Shearwater (June 7)
Cory's Shearwater (July 23)
Manx Shearwater (July 23)
Sooty Shearwater (July 16)

OPPOSITE
CLOCKWISE FROM TOP
Northern Gannet (January 13)
Parasitic Yeager (September 1)
Wilson's Storm-Petrel (June 7)
Leach's Storm-Petrel(June 21)
Pomarine Yeager (August 18)

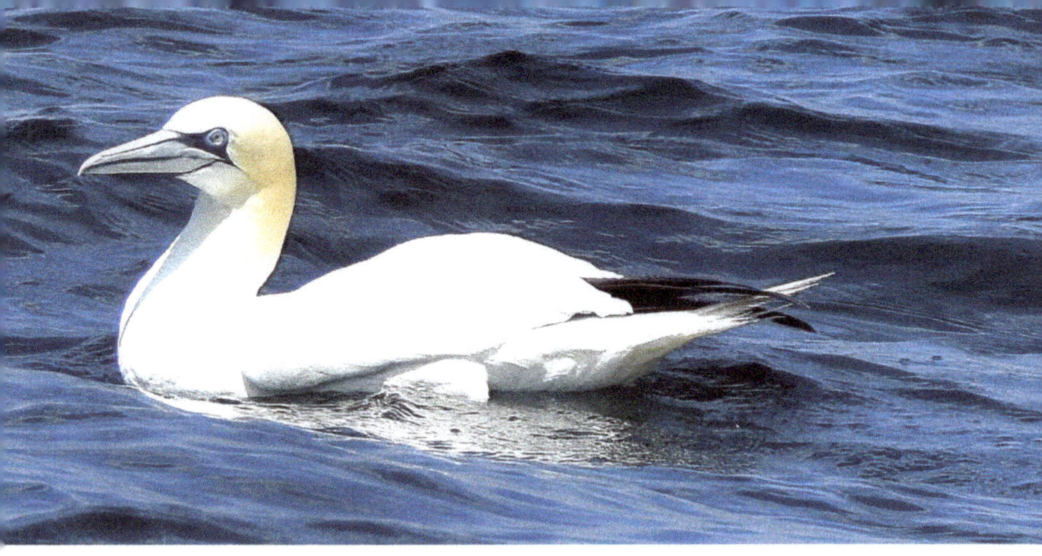

In my humble opinion, Shearwaters are one of the more remarkable birds in the world. The name "Shearwater" refers to their propensity for flying very close to the water - seemingly cutting or "shearing" the tops of the waves.

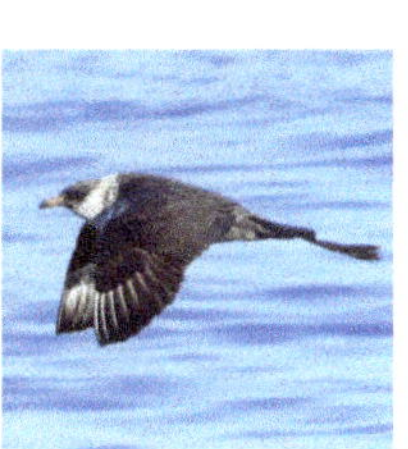

These long-winged seabirds spend their entire lives on or above the world's oceans, only coming to land to breed, nest and raise their young.

Shearwaters are some of the world's longest migrants, traveling of miles each year in search of food.

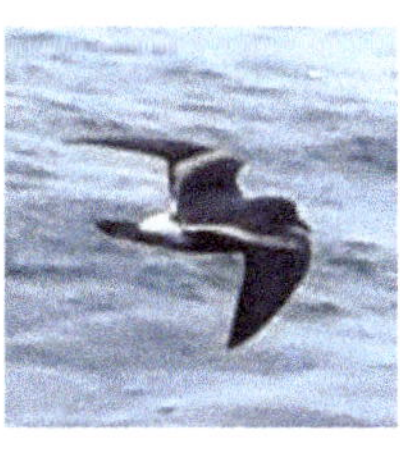

For instance, the Great Shearwater breeds during our winter on the volcanic island of Tristan da Cunha. Located in the southern Atlantic, Tristan da Cunha is the most remote human occupied island on the planet (thousands of miles from the Southern Tip of Africa and South America). Incredibly, these birds travel to the Gulf of Maine to feed during our summer.

Then there is the Sooty Shearwater (breeding on the Falkland Islands and Tasmania) and the Cory's Shearwater (the Azores off Portugal). The Manx breeds off the coast of Newfoundland and possibly on some islands off the coast of Maine.

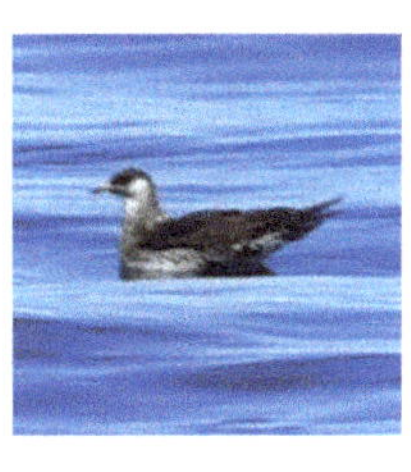

These fascinating birds can smell food miles away.

The Wilson's Storm-Petrel is considered the most common sea bird in the world, and on some pelagic trips we have seen several hundred in a day.

Wilson's forage for krill just above the waves, often appearing to

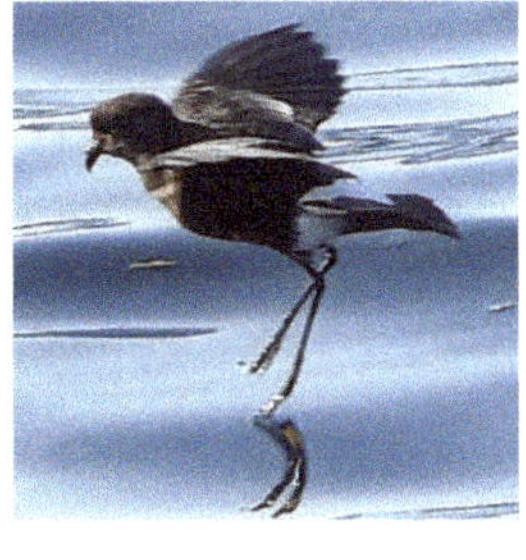

be walking on water with their distinctive yellow webbed feet.

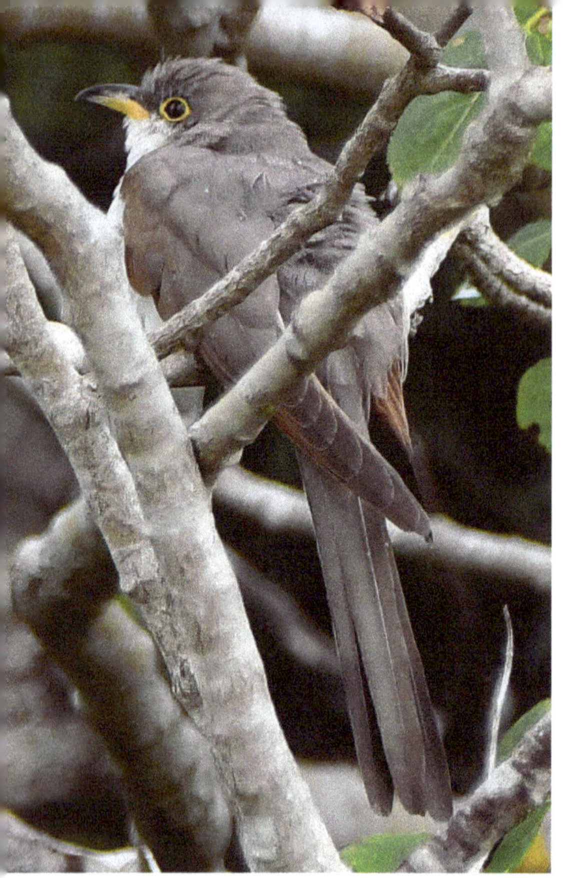

Their cousin the Yellow-billed Cuckoo is even more rare. Southern Maine represents the northern boundary of their summer range.

The Yellow-billed's song is much more guttural than the Black-billed's, almost a clicking sound and instantly identifiable.

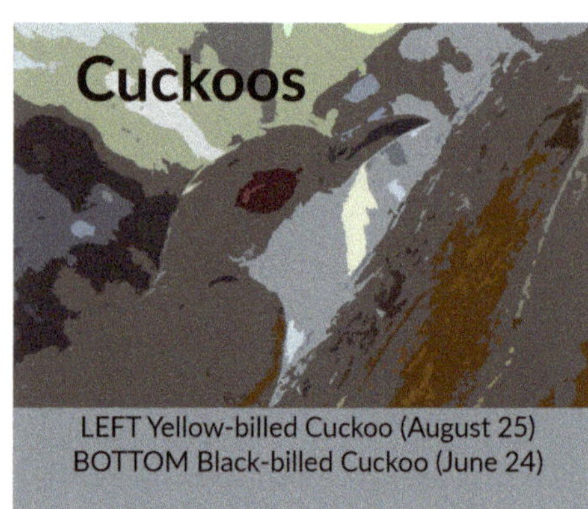

LEFT Yellow-billed Cuckoo (August 25)
BOTTOM Black-billed Cuckoo (June 24)

Before I got into birding, I associated Cuckoos with the mechanical chime in the clock my dad brought home from Germany in the 1950s. Little did I know that the Black-billed Cuckoo was a relatively common, albeit secretive, bird nesting in the Maine woods.

In the spring, when they arrive from their South American wintering grounds, the bird's almost mechanical *Cu Cu Cu Cu* song can be heard. Sighting one is much more difficult.

While they are hard to find, cuckoos can be curious. I've had them follow me through the woods, quietly relocating to see what I'm up to. Who's watching who?

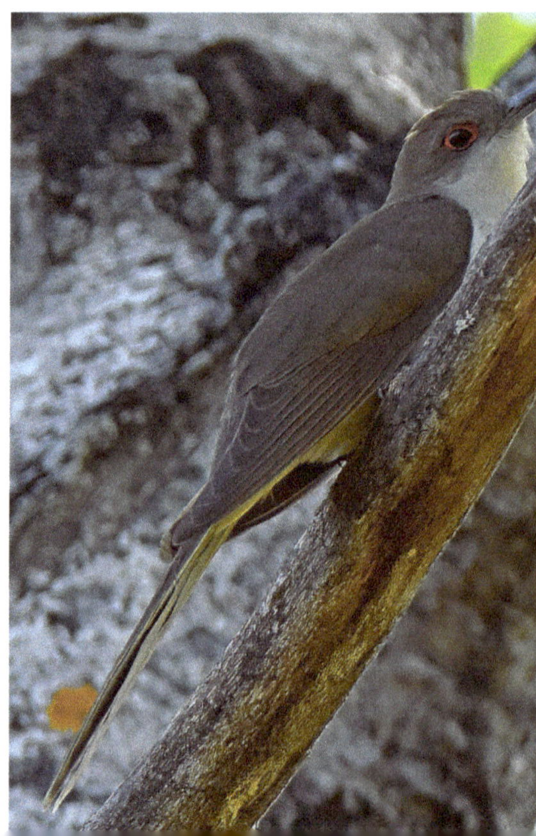

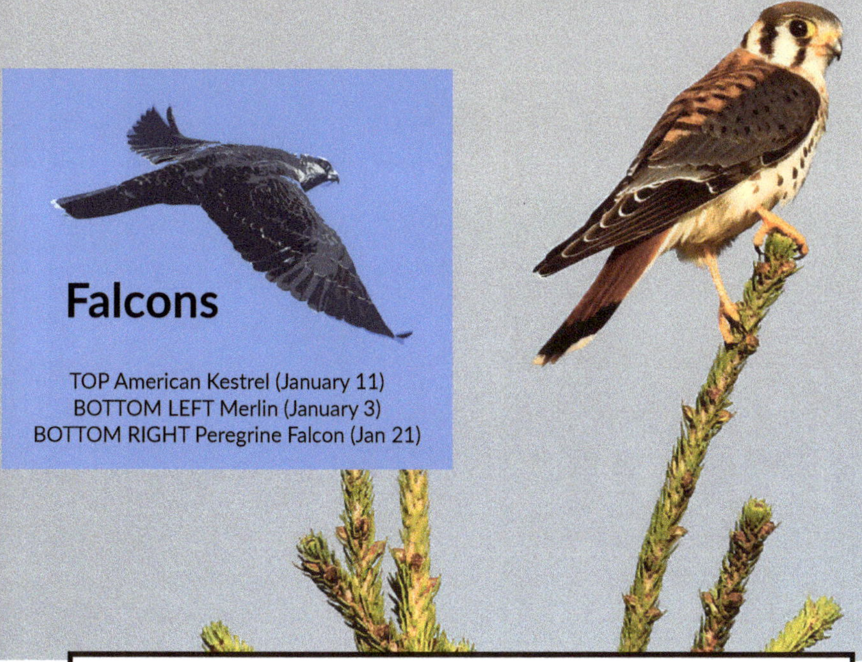

Falcons

TOP American Kestrel (January 11)
BOTTOM LEFT Merlin (January 3)
BOTTOM RIGHT Peregrine Falcon (Jan 21)

Falcons are relatively small birds of prey, striking their prey with high speed and agile attacks from above.

Once nearly extinct, the Peregrine Falcon has recovered dramatically and can now be found nesting throughout Maine, often on tall bridges and buildings.

The American Kestrel, a beautiful blue and brown raptor, nests, and breeds in Maine.

Even though Merlins breed at Maine's northern tip, their fall southbound migration is quite slow. The sheer number of Merlins moving through makes them easy to find.

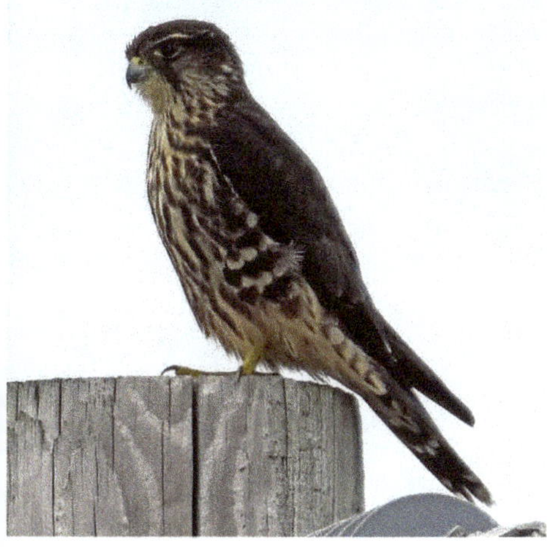

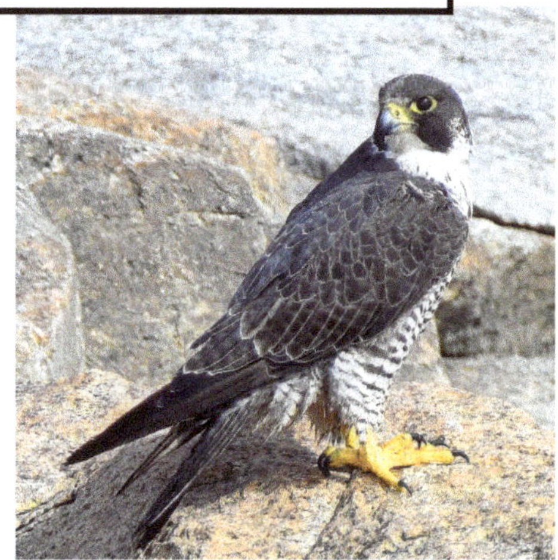

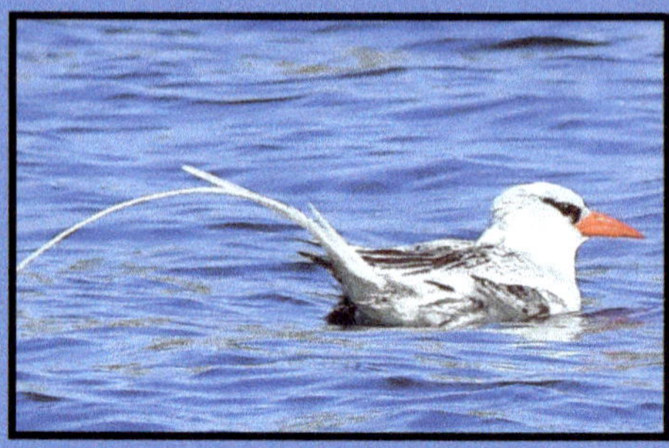

In the spring of 2005, a Red-billed Tropicbird, a stunning white bird with a bright red bill and a long streaming tail, was observed in the cold waters off the Maine coast. Thousands of miles off-course, this bird normally prowls the seas off the Lesser Antilles. It was seen off and on that summer, a male bird seemingly looking for a mate.

Incredibly, he appeared again the fol-lowing spring, settling on the rocky, remote island of Matinicus Rock. The next two summers he returned to his Matinicus home; before moving south to Seal Island in 2008. "Troppy" has returned to Seal Island, 20 miles off the Maine coast, each summer since then, thrilling birders who manage to get their binoculars on him.

Doing a Maine Big Year, I had to "get Troppy", so I hired a lobsterman to take a group of birders out to Seal Is-land.

Seal Island is also the home of thou-sands of nesting terns, Razorbills and Atlantic Puffins, and unfortunately, one mean looking Peregrine Falcon.

The Peregrine, a ferocious hunter and the fastest animal on the planet, was sitting within a few feet of the Trop-icbird's den (a slit underneath a boul-

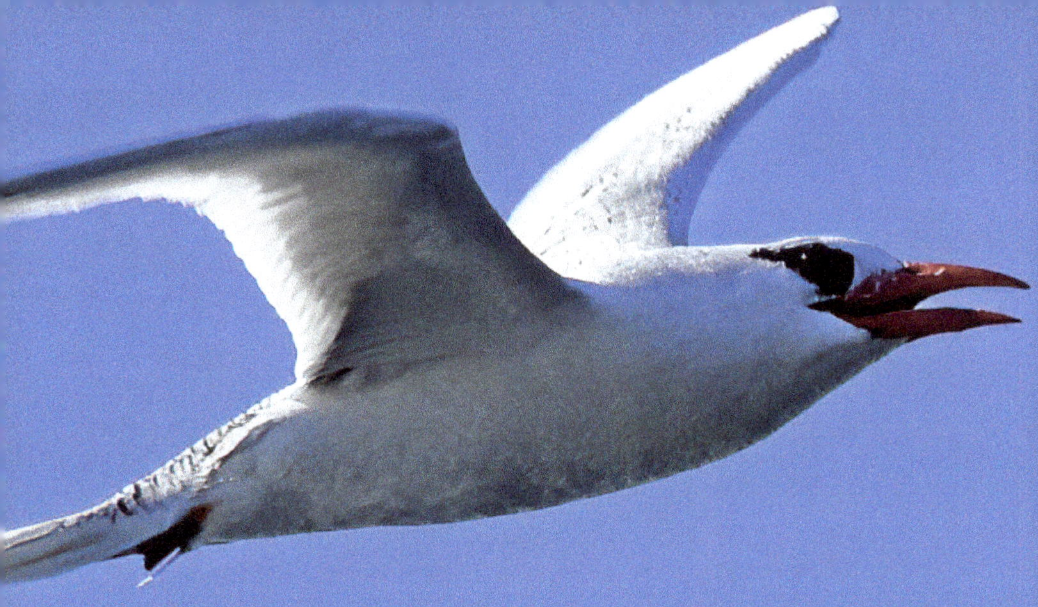

der). Though we never saw "Troppy", we had a wonderful time getting up close and personal with the Puffins. I'm not certain the Peregrine was the reason the Tropicbird never showed, but I'm sure it didn't help.

A month later Ingrid and I joined a charter of serious birders trying to see the celebrity bird.

Upon arriving, we took in the expected array of nesting birds but no Troppy. It was hot and still and slowly over the next 90 minutes, the birders became quieter and more concerned. Half the group was scanning the horizon with binoculars. The rest were staring blankly at the island.

I was sitting near the stern seeing my Maine Big Year go up in flames, Troppy was essential to get to 318. But Ingrid remained optimistic even as the afternoon wore on.

Derek Lovitch, the trip organizer was trying to calm the restless birders with stories about the Tropicbird, concentrating on Troppy's propensity to get amorous with lobster buoys when someone on the starboard side yelled, "There he is!!!"

Flying right toward us was a large white bird with a bright red bill, black mask and long white tail streamers. He flew low, directly over us as birders screamed in delight: "WOW", "Oh My Gosh", "Unbelievable".

Many of us had made multiple attempts to see Troppy, and the boat was delirious with high-fives, fist bumps and hugs.

Troppy made a couple of loops around the island and over the boat, this time with an amazing cackling call (apparently he was trying to impress the terns). He then landed in the water and proceeded to take a bath.

No one knows how old Maine's most famous bird is, but Red-billed Tropicbirds are believed to live up to 30 years. We know he must be at least 18 years old, so we may have another decade of his highly anticipated visits.

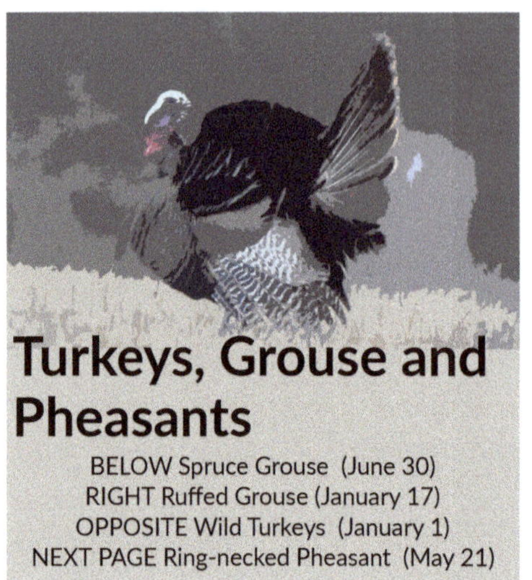

Turkeys, Grouse and Pheasants

BELOW Spruce Grouse (June 30)
RIGHT Ruffed Grouse (January 17)
OPPOSITE Wild Turkeys (January 1)
NEXT PAGE Ring-necked Pheasant (May 21)

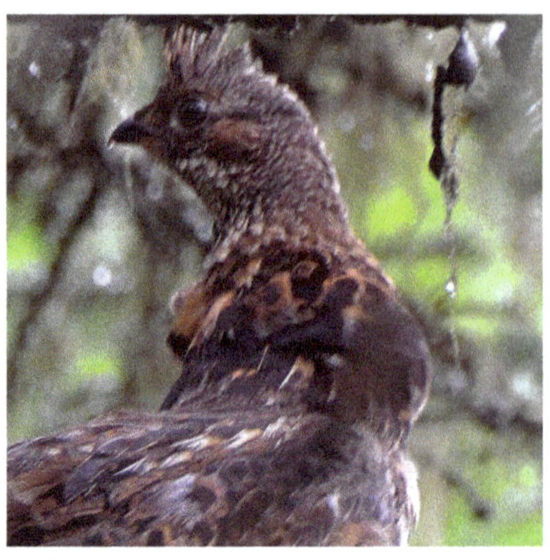

When I graduated from college in 1980, I had never seen a turkey in the wild. Forty-one years later, things have changed dramatically.

When Europeans began colonizing New England in the 1600s, ten million Wild Turkeys stretched from Southern Maine to Florida to the Rocky Mountains. As forests were cleared and the birds were hunted, turkeys virtually disappeared from Maine (and most of the northeast as well).

There were several attempts to reintroduce Wild Turkeys to the state in the 1940s and the 1960s, but they quickly failed.

Finally in 1977 and 1978, forty-one birds were trapped in Vermont and released in York County, and this time the introduced birds thrived and the population expanded exponentially.

In 1982, thirty-three of the York county birds were trapped and released in Waldo County, and in 1984 nineteen were released in Hancock County.

This reintroduction was wildly successful, as the Maine Wild Turkey population is currently estimated to be about 70,000 birds. The population continues to expand despite an annual hunting harvest of between 3,000 and 6,000 birds.

With Maine farmland returning to forest and milder winters becoming the norm (heavy snow fall keeps the population down), the number of Wild Turkeys invading private gardens and striking cars is expected to continue to increase.

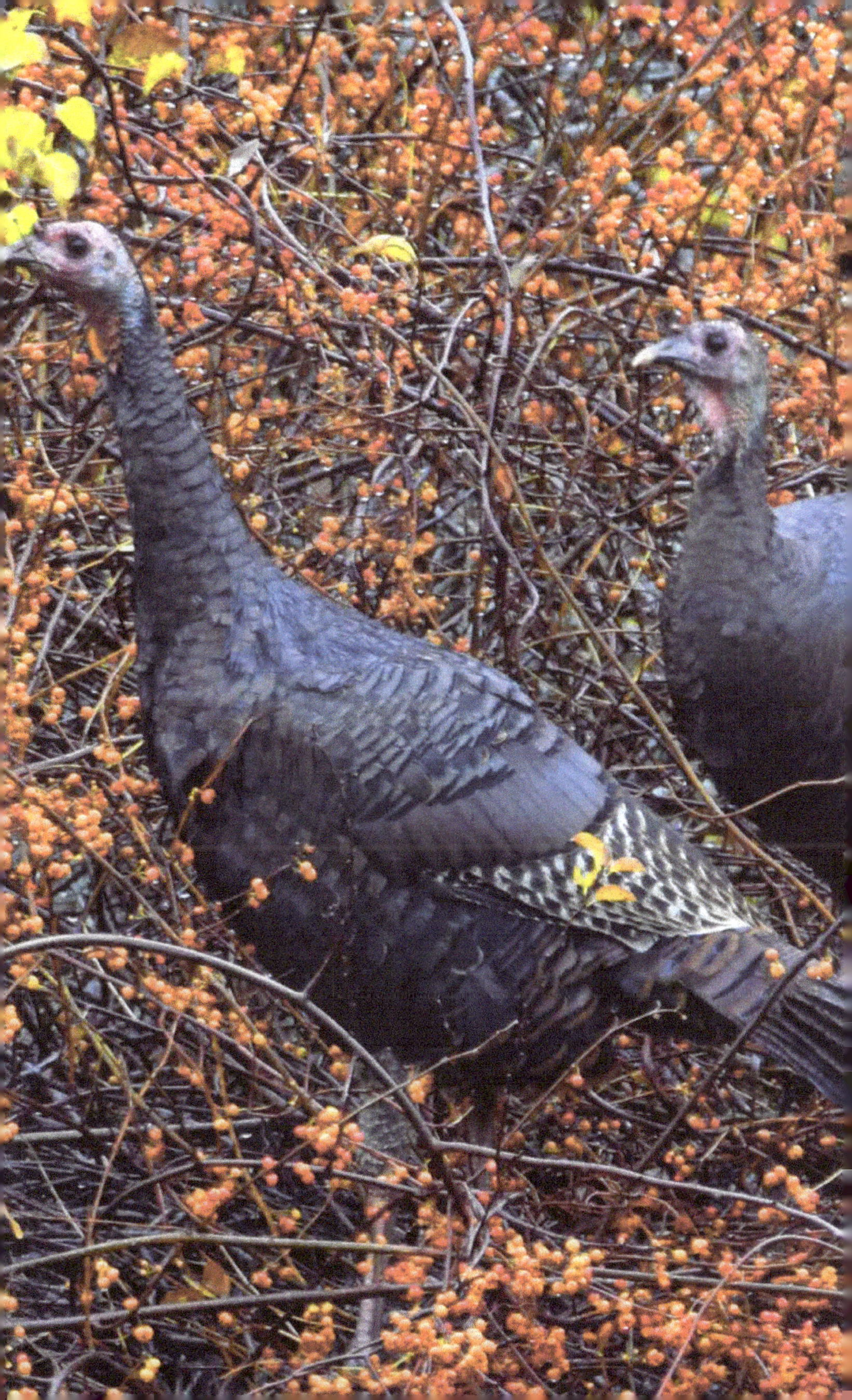

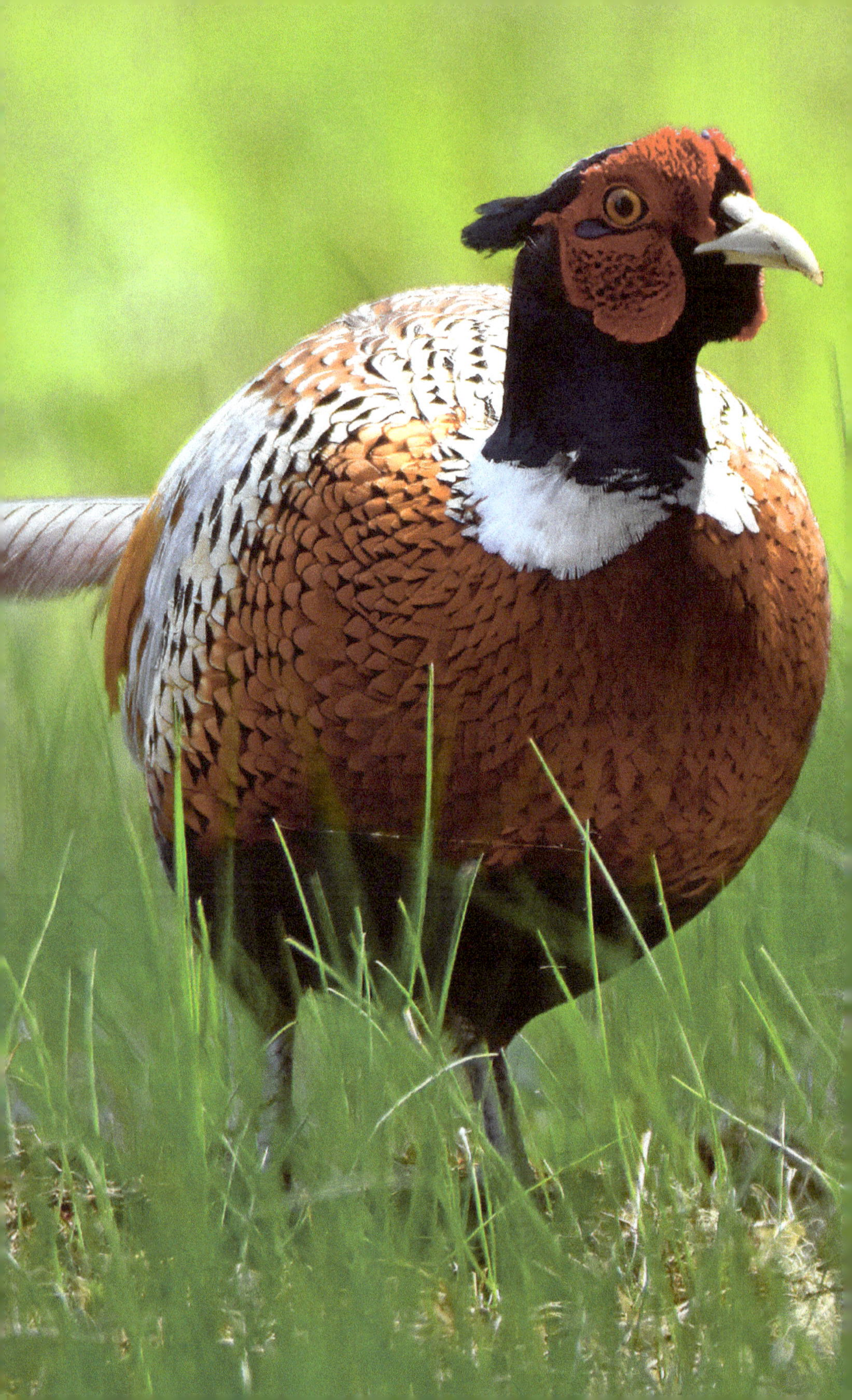

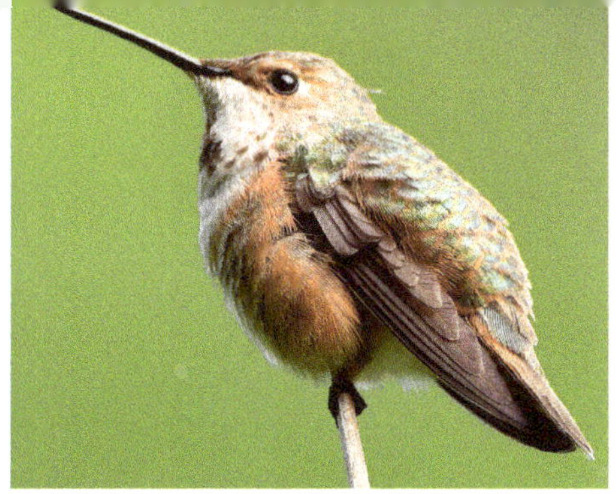

Early August is a slow time for Big Year Birding. Fall migration hasn't started yet, and it is a good time to rest and catch up on neglected projects around the house.

Ingrid was reading in bed, and I was closing things up before retiring one night, when an e-mail came in from Derek Lovitch, co-owner of Freeport Wild Bird Supply and one of the state's top birders. He had a rare hummingbird on a feeder at his home

There are 15 types of hummingbirds found in the United States, but only the Ruby-throated is regularly found in Maine, arriving in May and gone by Labor Day. To see a different hummingbird species in Maine is a big deal!!!

I ran up to the bedroom.

Me: "We're not gonna sleep late in the morning after all. We need to leave at 5:45 in the morning, a rare hummingbird has been sighted!!"

Ingrid: "Wonderful" (you really had to hear her tone to understand the true meaning of "wonderful")

We arrived the next morning at 6:30 and for the next three hours got glimpses of an orange-green hummingbird trying to approach one of the three nectar feeders scattered around the yard. Maine's summer resident Ru-

by-throated Hummingbirds were determined to keep this interloper away from "their" feeders. We watched numerous aerial dog fights between the species.

After a bit of study, birders visiting the property determined that the mystery bird was either a Rufous Hummingbird or its nearly identical cousin, the Allen's Hummingbird.

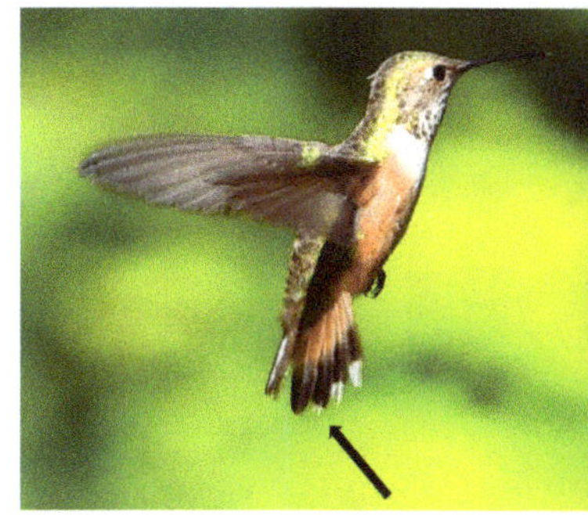

How do you tell the difference? By a careful examination of the tail feathers.

If this was a Rufous, it would be the tenth one ever reported in Maine. An Allen's would be the second one ever reported in New England.

I think we all knew it was a Rufous, but it took a number of experts several days of examining the tail feather photos to make this confirmation.

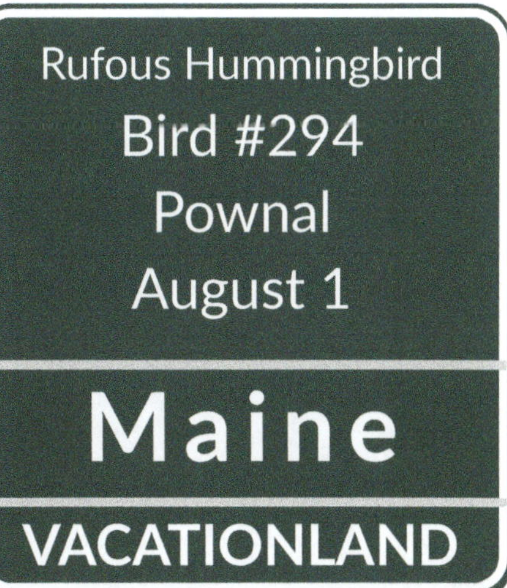

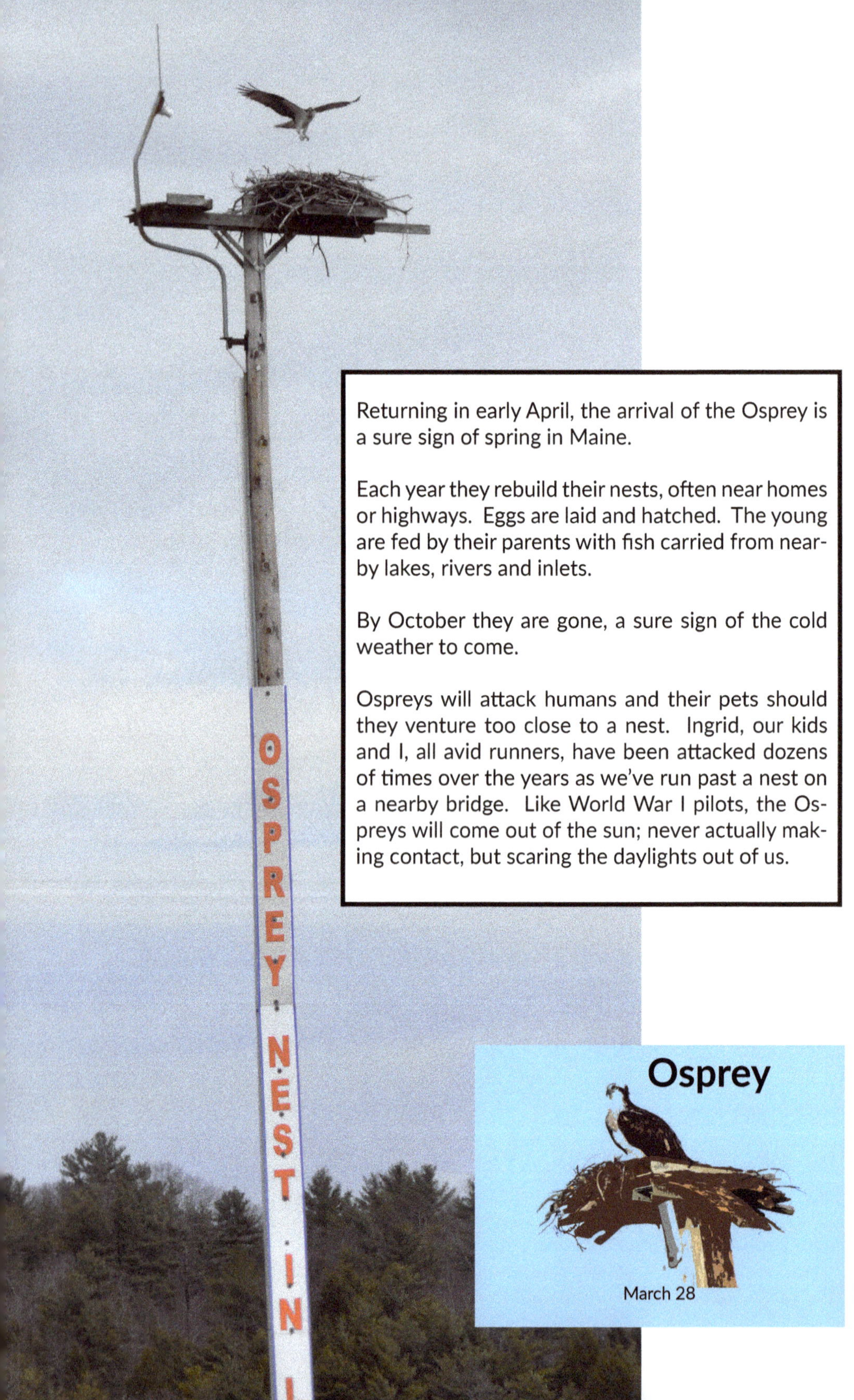

Returning in early April, the arrival of the Osprey is a sure sign of spring in Maine.

Each year they rebuild their nests, often near homes or highways. Eggs are laid and hatched. The young are fed by their parents with fish carried from nearby lakes, rivers and inlets.

By October they are gone, a sure sign of the cold weather to come.

Ospreys will attack humans and their pets should they venture too close to a nest. Ingrid, our kids and I, all avid runners, have been attacked dozens of times over the years as we've run past a nest on a nearby bridge. Like World War I pilots, the Ospreys will come out of the sun; never actually making contact, but scaring the daylights out of us.

Osprey

March 28

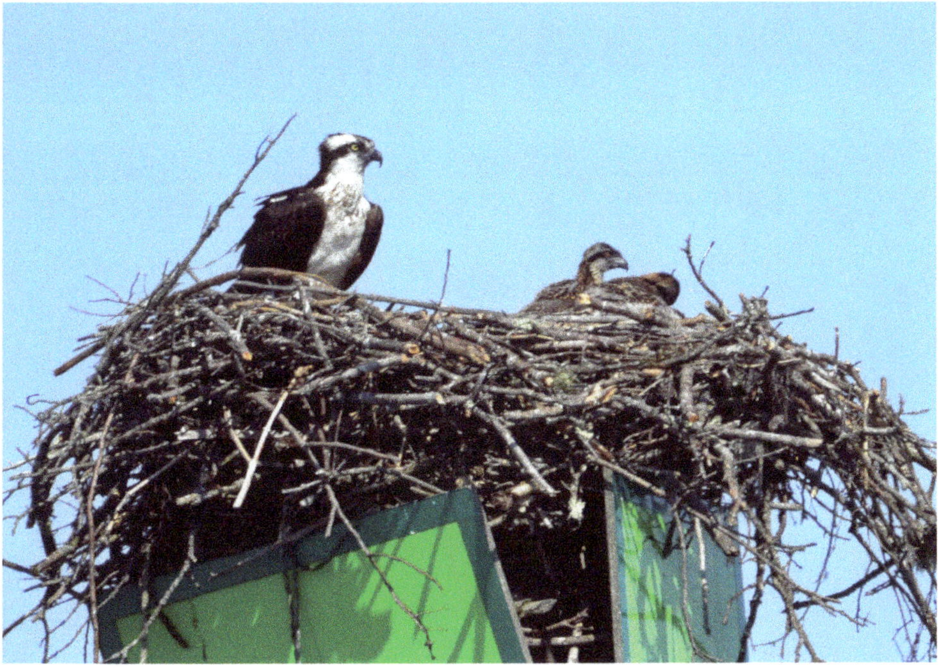

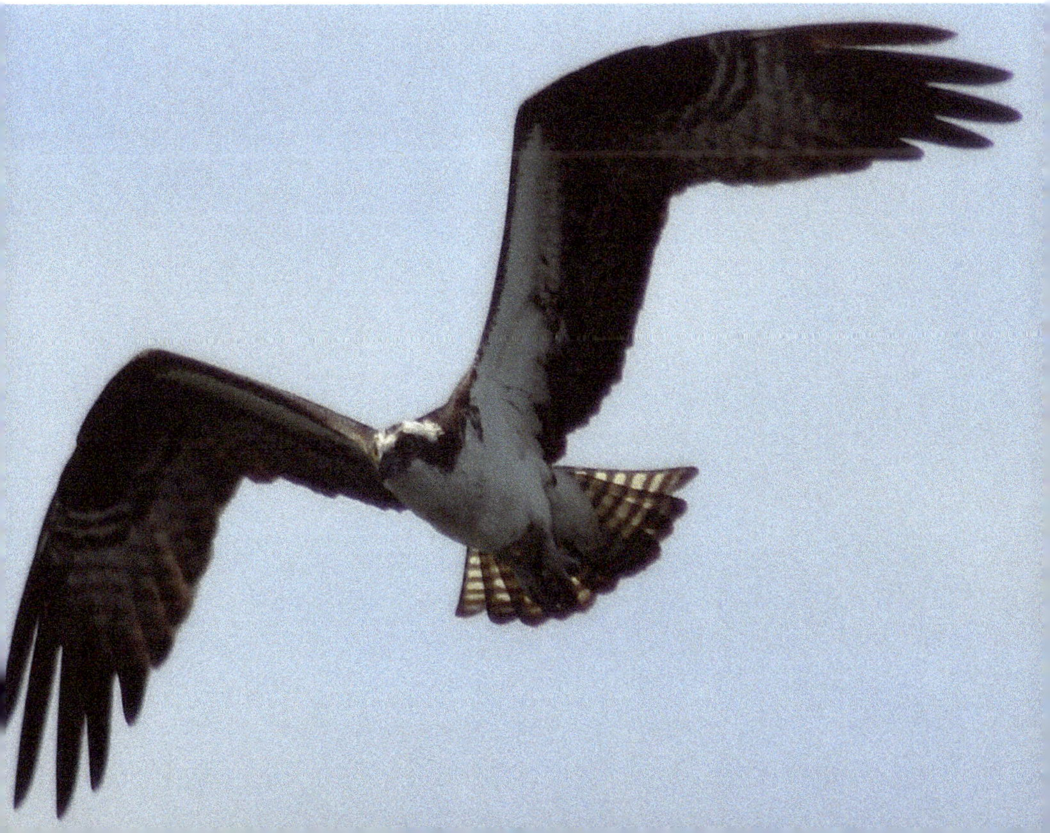

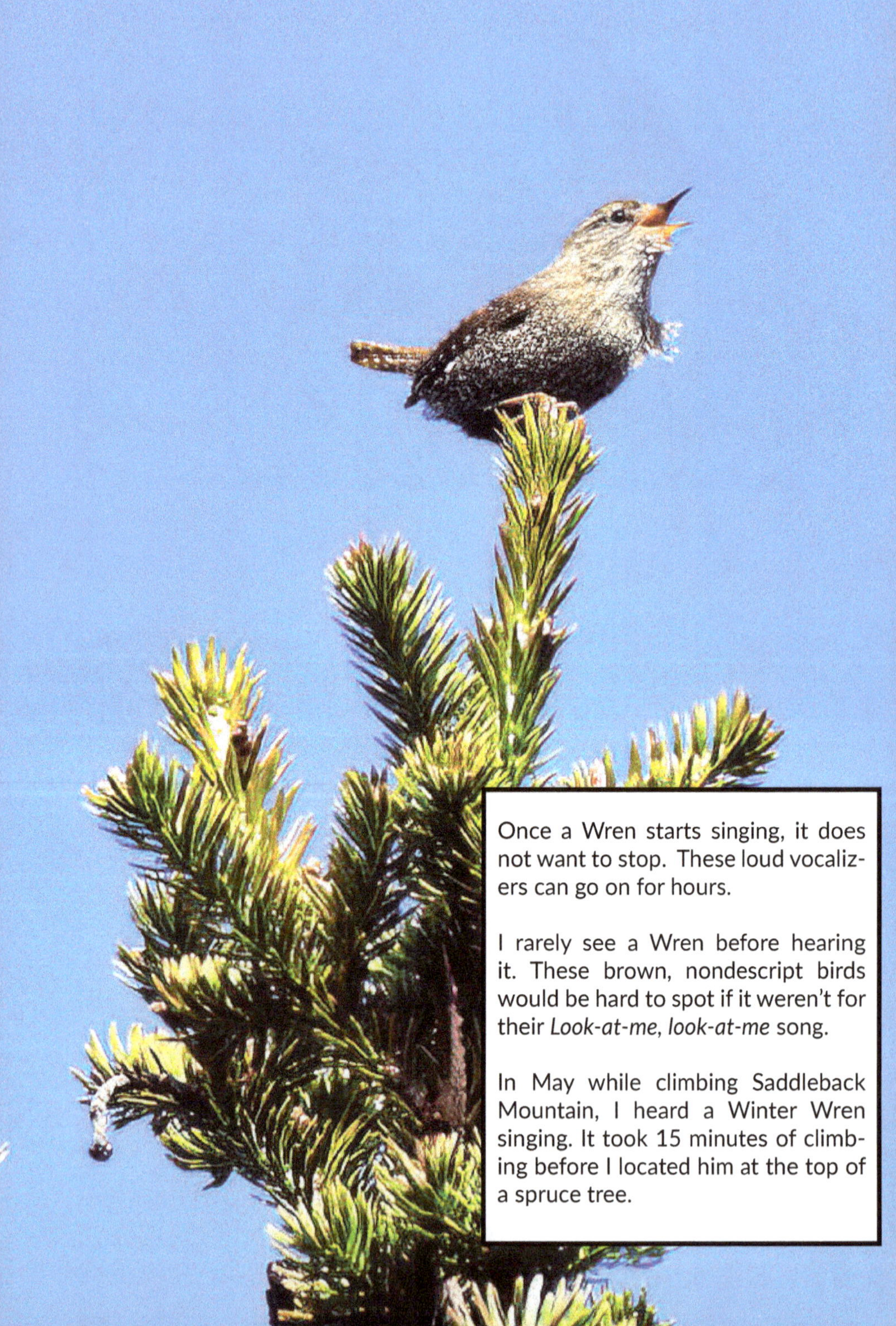

Once a Wren starts singing, it does not want to stop. These loud vocalizers can go on for hours.

I rarely see a Wren before hearing it. These brown, nondescript birds would be hard to spot if it weren't for their *Look-at-me, look-at-me* song.

In May while climbing Saddleback Mountain, I heard a Winter Wren singing. It took 15 minutes of climbing before I located him at the top of a spruce tree.

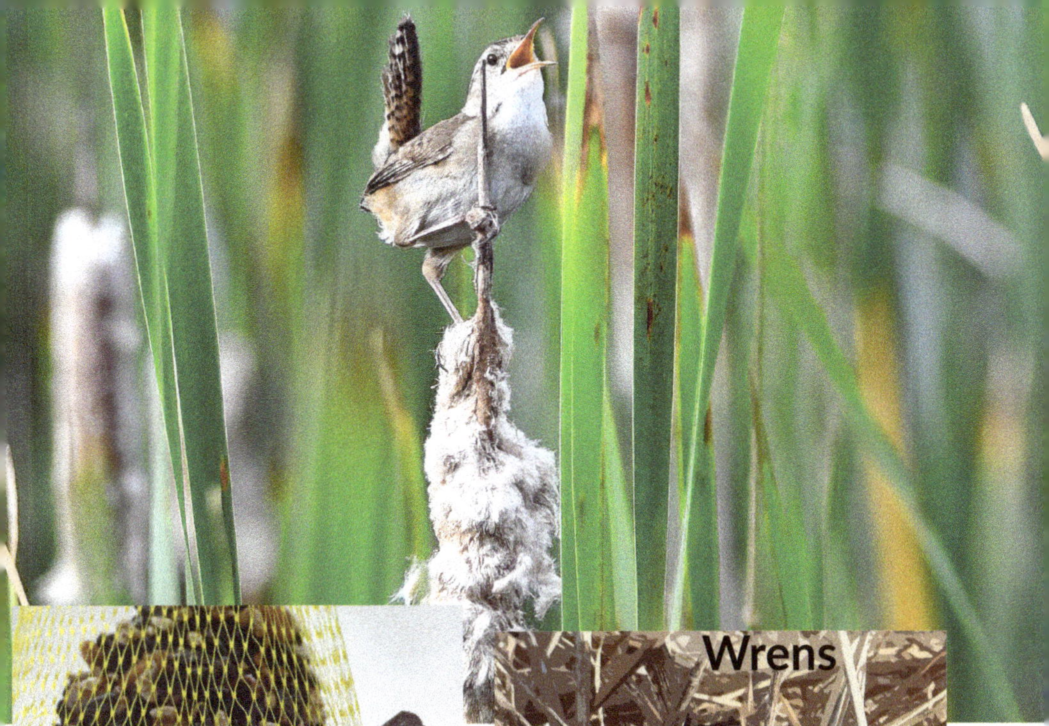

Wrens

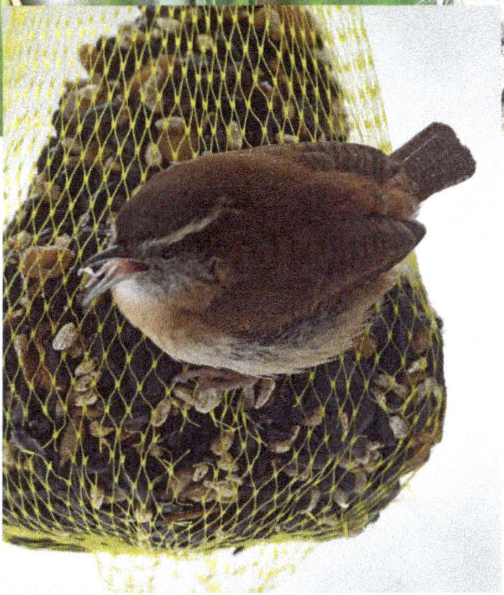

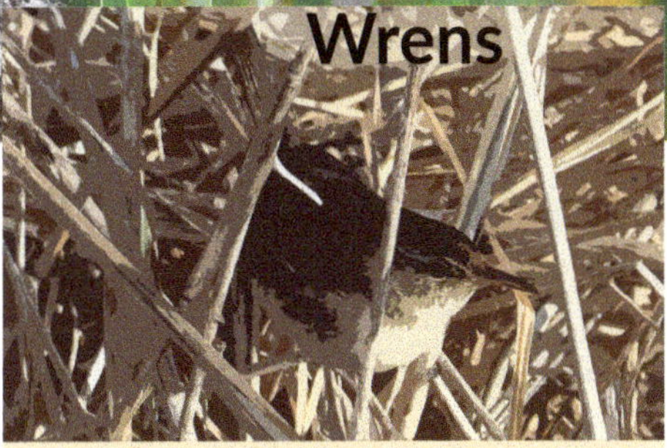

OPPOSITE
Winter Wren (April 5)

TOP Marsh Wren (April 2)
MIDDLE Carolina Wren (January 1)
BOTTOM-LEFT Rock Wren (January 4)
BOTTOM-RIGHT House Wren (April 26)

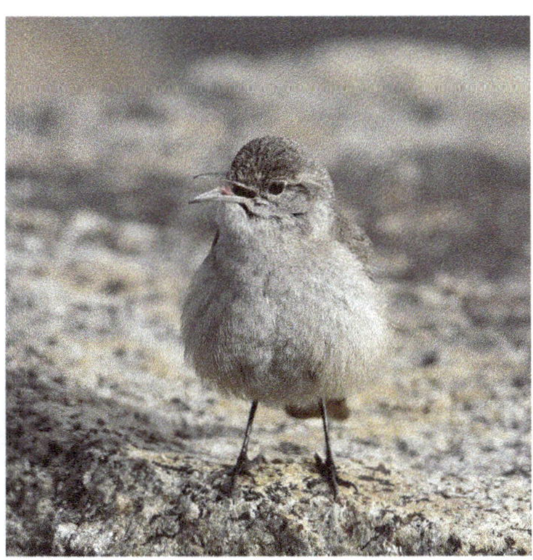

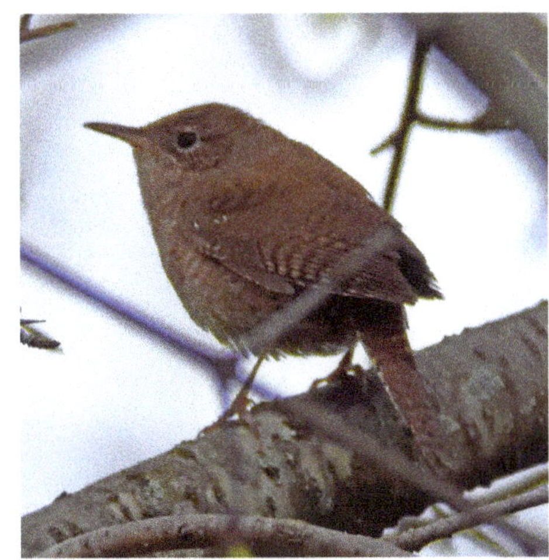

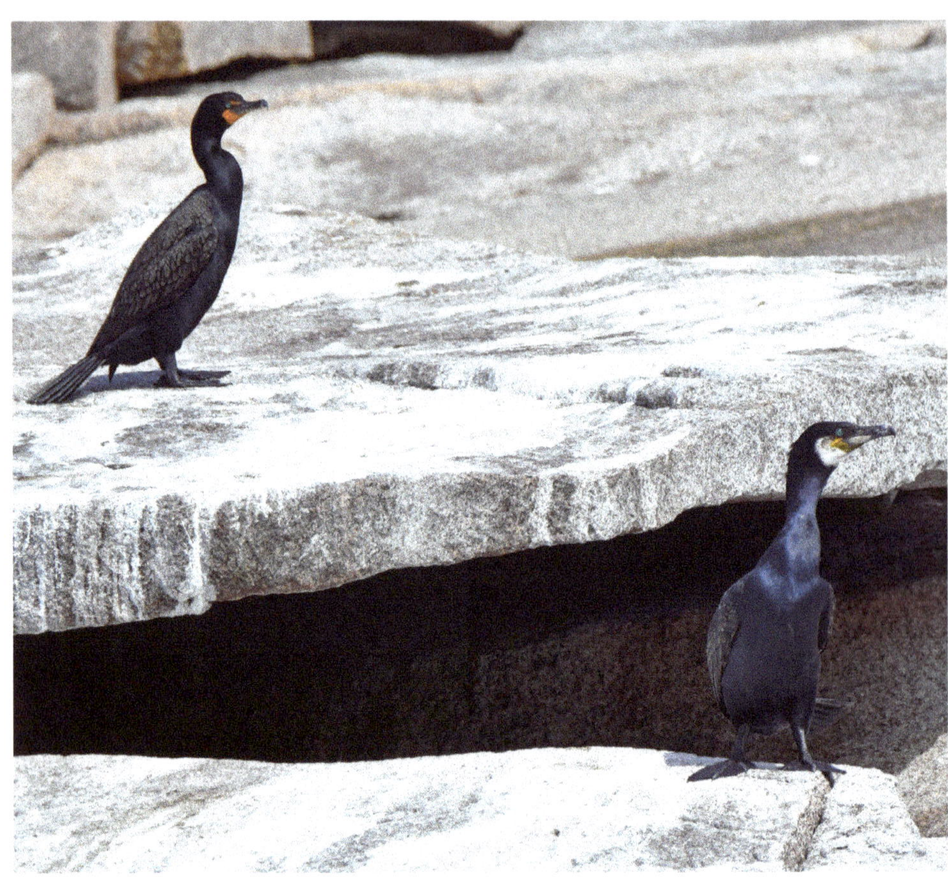

Cormorants are large black birds found along the coast and in tidal rivers where they dive for fish. In Latin, Cormorant means "sea crow." Frankly, this is an insult to crows, as cormorants can be rather smelly birds.

There are two types of cormorants found in Maine. During the summer, the Double-crested Cormorants are everywhere, generally in small groups resting on rocks or tree limbs. In the water they are amazing hunters, flying underwater to catch fish.

In the winter, the Great Cormorants come down from Canada.

With all the swimming and diving, cormorant feathers can become water-logged, a reason you'll often see them perched with their wings outstretched for a considerable amount of time. This allows their wings to dry.

LEFT Double-crested Cormorant (January 1)
RIGHT Great Cormorant (January 1)

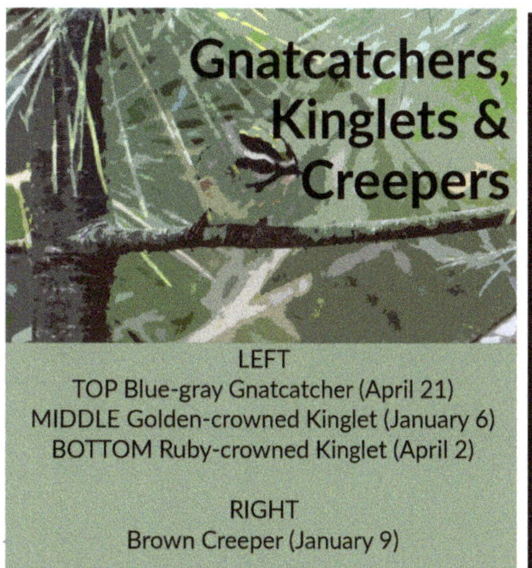

Gnatcatchers, Kinglets & Creepers

LEFT
TOP Blue-gray Gnatcatcher (April 21)
MIDDLE Golden-crowned Kinglet (January 6)
BOTTOM Ruby-crowned Kinglet (April 2)

RIGHT
Brown Creeper (January 9)

Gnatcatchers and Kinglets behave much like warblers, flitting from branch to branch in the pursuit of insects.

Southern Maine represents the northernmost range of the Blue-gray Gnatcatcher, while the Ruby-crowned Kinglet is seen in both spring and fall as it migrates through the state.

The Golden-crowned Kinglet, one of my favorite birds, is found in Maine all year round, often moving with flocks of Black-capped Chickadees.

There are theories that this bird relies on the chickadee's incessant vocalizing as a beacon to find other kinglets. Golden-crowned Kinglets need to huddle together at night to survive the harsh Maine winter.

Both of the kinglet species will show a brightly colored stripe on their foreheads during courtship or territorial displays.

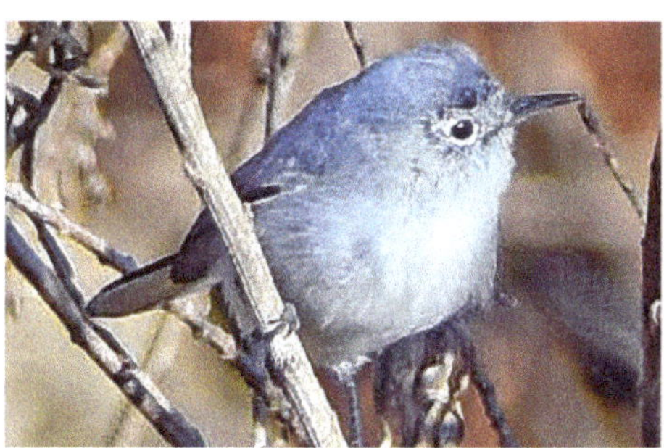

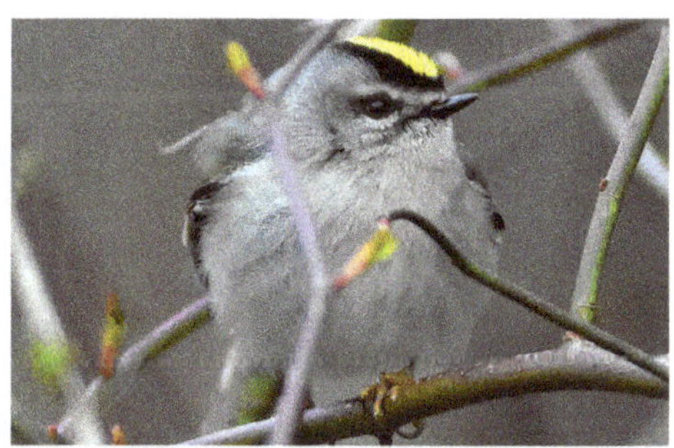

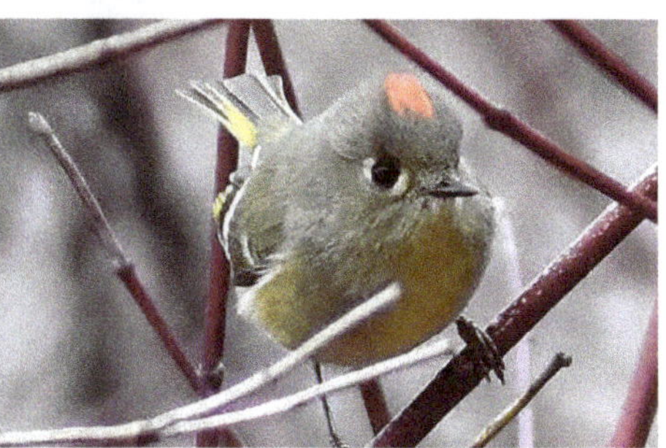

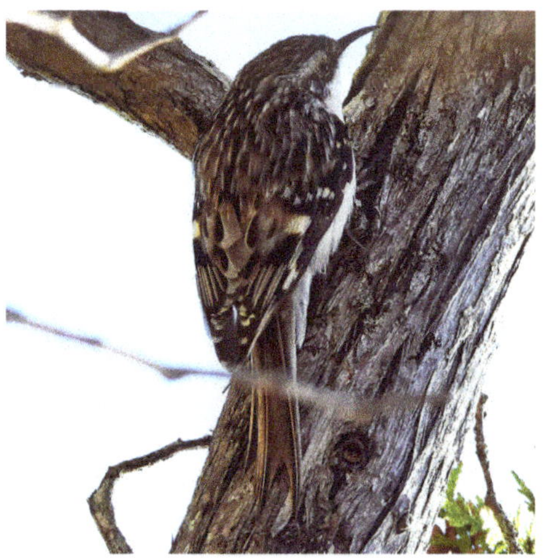

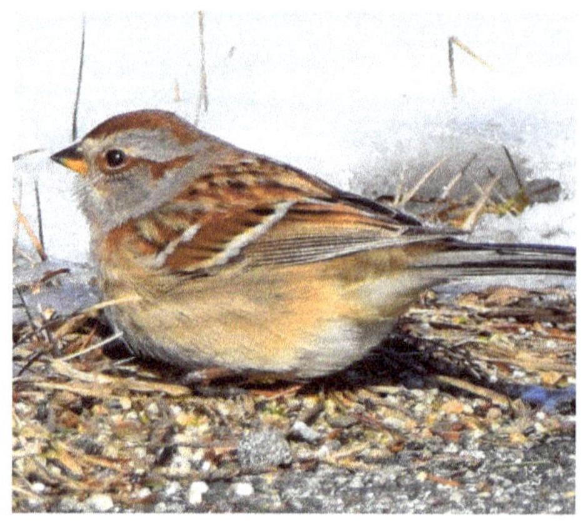

Before I became a birder, I had a general idea about the birds I saw around the house. Goldfinches, Chickadees, Crows and Blue Jays came regularly to our feeders.

And there were also these brown streaked birds called sparrows, not particularly pretty or interesting.

I was young and foolish; sparrows are great!!!

Every spring a Song Sparrow, named Belle by Ingrid, starts singing on a stump near the river behind our house. There may still be snow on the ground, but Belle's opus is an annual sign of spring. (Note to self: don't tell Ingrid that Belle is probably a male)

While the Song Sparrow is a year round resident, there are a dozen other sparrows that move in and out of the state depending on the season and habitat.

For instance, seeing an American Tree Sparrow means winter is upon us.

One of my favorite birds, the Fox Sparrow, is a harbinger of things to come. This big, rotund and reddish bird migrates through in March and early April and returns for a pass-through in November.

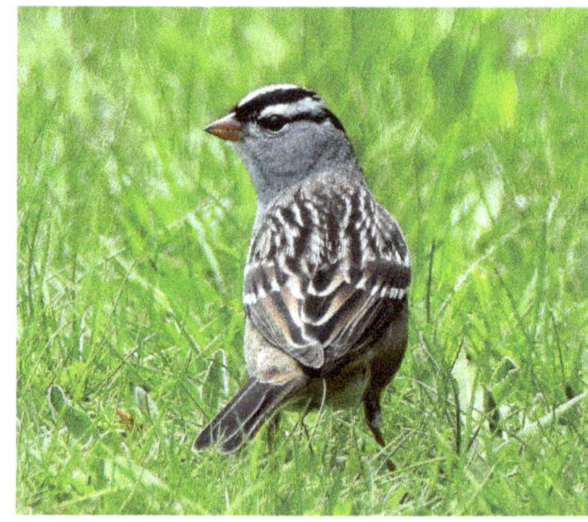

Everyone loves the White-throated Sparrow with its gaudy white, black and yellow crown and absurd white chin. When I hear its clear and unmis-

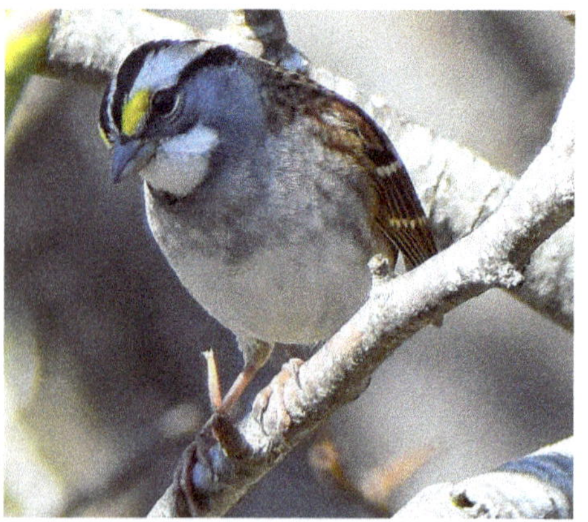

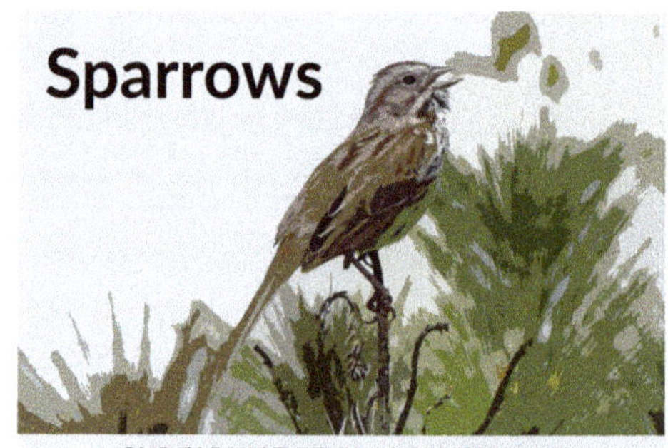

Sparrows

CLOCKWISE FROM LOWER LEFT
White-throated Sparrow (January 5)
American Tree Sparrow (January 1)
White-crowned Sparrow (May 7)

OPPOSITE
Song Sparrow (January 4)

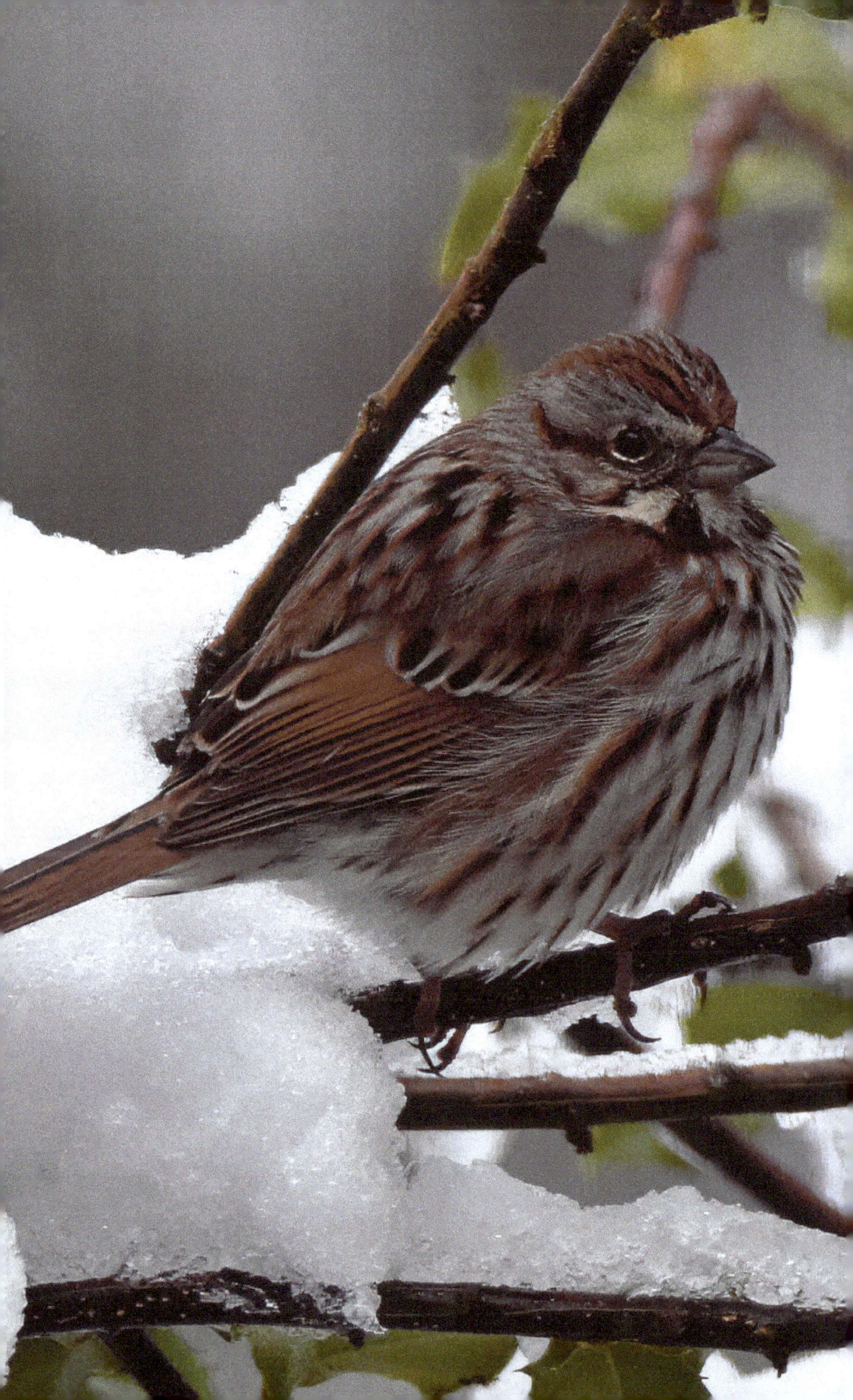

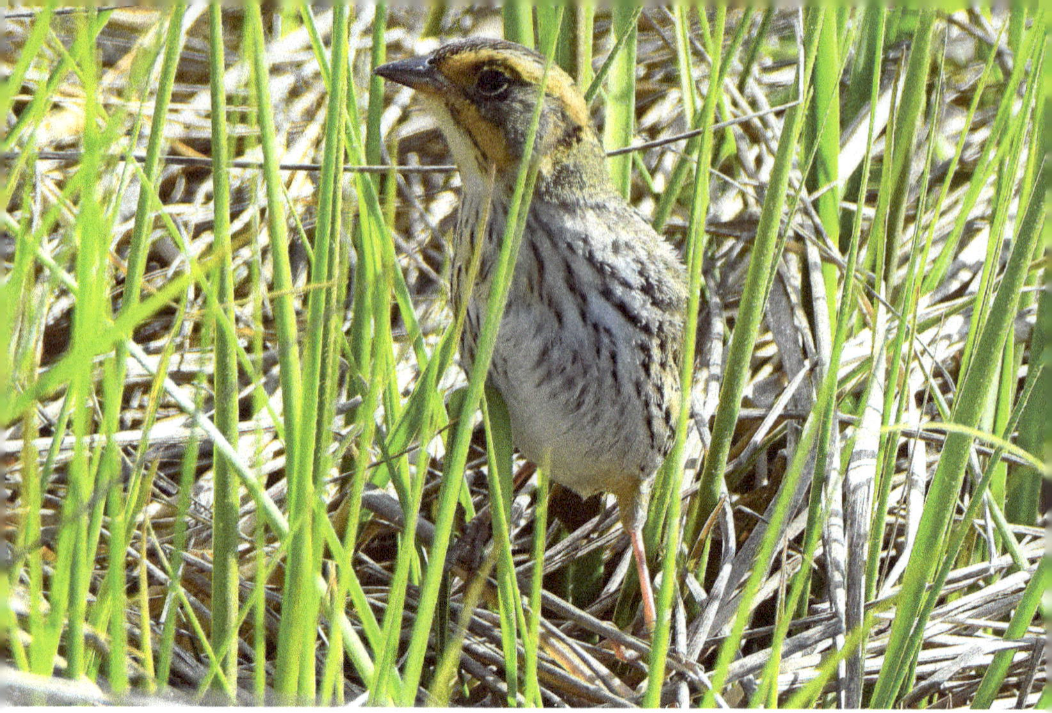

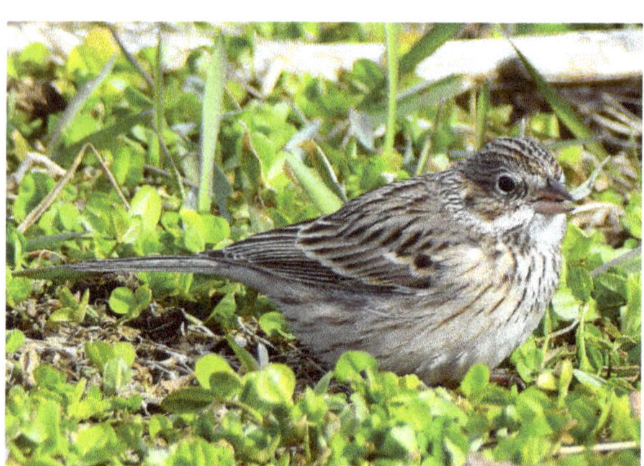

takable *Oh Sweet Canada Canada Canada* song, I smile knowing one is near.

And then there are the grassland sparrows: the Vesper, Field, Grasshopper and Clay Sparrows that rely on a few unique habitats in the state.

The nearly identical Saltmarsh and Nelson's Sparrows favor tidal grass while the aptly named Swamp Sparrow prefers, you guessed it, swamps.

Chipping Sparrows are a Maine summer bird whose long metallic trill is synonymous with hot, still summer days.

House Sparrows, an Old World sparrow, was imported into the USA in 1860 and by 1890 had spread from coast to coast. Considered a bit of a pest in the New World, it is in decline in its native Europe.

The dainty looking Lincoln's Sparrow, with its small bill and the appearance of a buzz cut, is often mistaken for the common Song Sparrow.

Sparrows (cont.)

CLOCKWISE FROM TOP LEFT
Saltmarsh Sparrow (May 15)
Fox Sparrow (January 17)
Clay-colored Sparrow (June 8)
Vesper Sparrow (April 4)

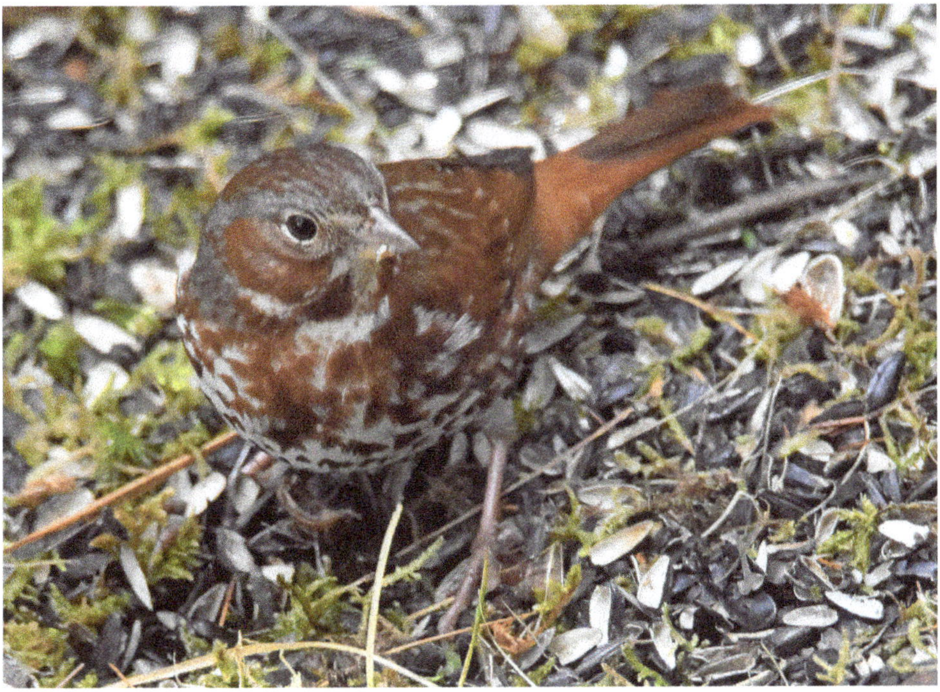

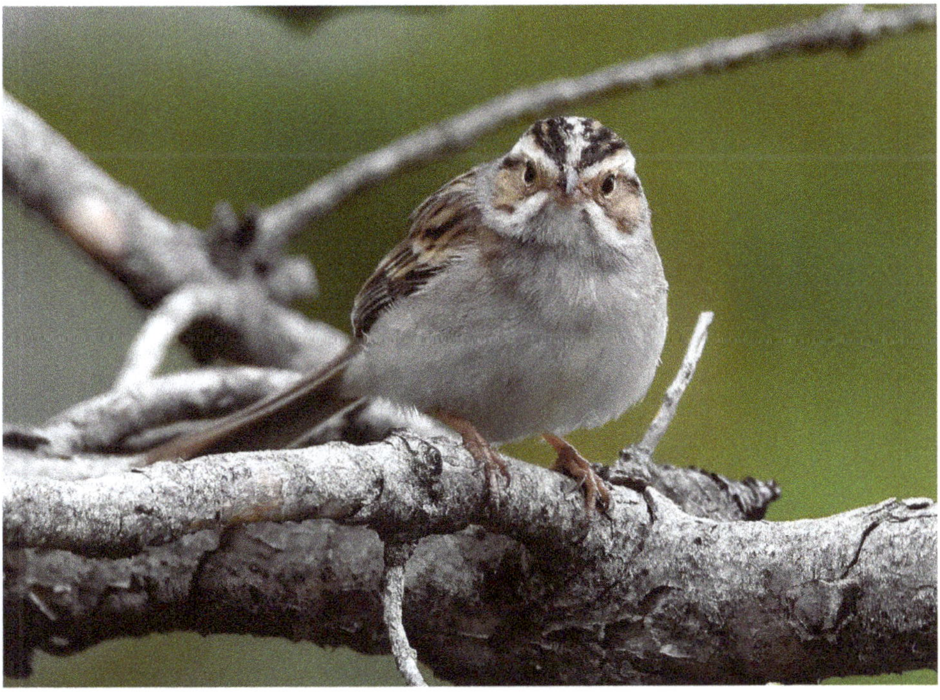

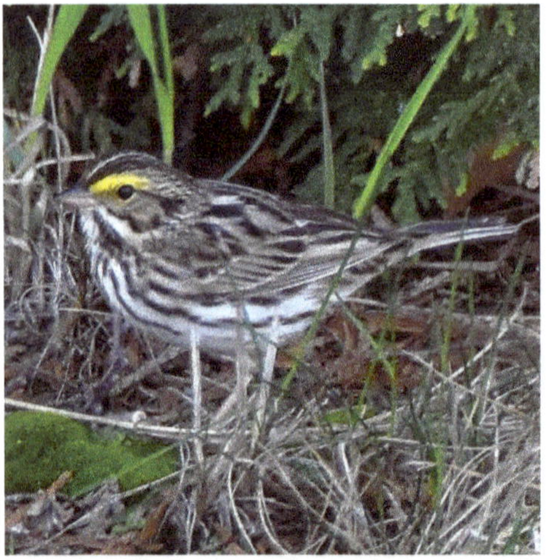

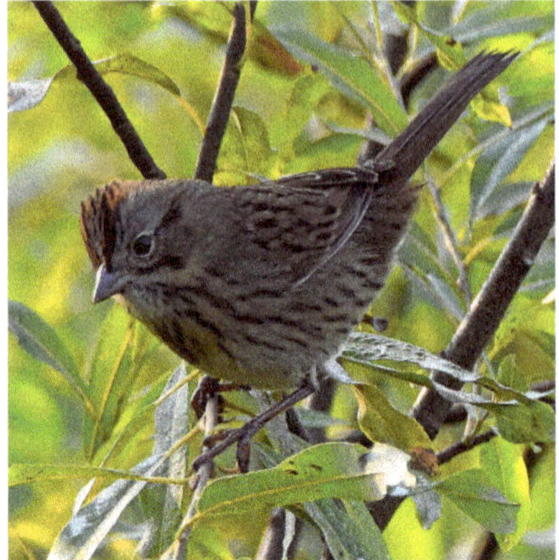

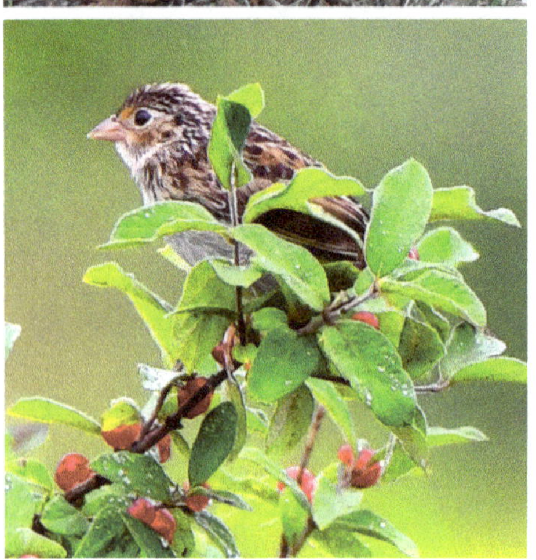

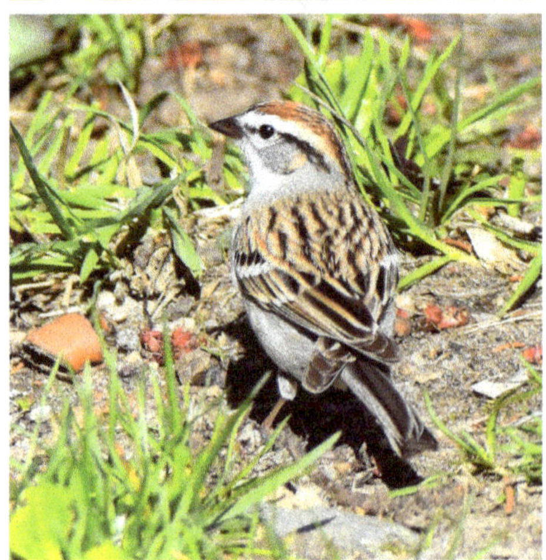

The Savannah Sparrow loves pastures and meadows and is readily identified by the bright yellow strip over the eye.

The Dark-eyed Junco is one of the most abundant birds in North America with an estimated population of 630 million individuals.

Sparrows (cont.)

LEFT TO RIGHT / TOP TO BOTTOM
Savannah Sparrow (February 1)
Lincoln's Sparrow (May 10)
Grasshopper Sparrow (May 12)
Chipping Sparrow (April 4)

OPPOSITE
LEFT TO RIGHT / TOP TO BOTTOM
Nelson's Sparrow (May 24)
Field Sparrow (March 24)
House Sparrow (January 1)
Swamp Sparrow (April 5)
Dark-eyed Junco (January 2)

FRAME
Lark Sparrow (September 3)

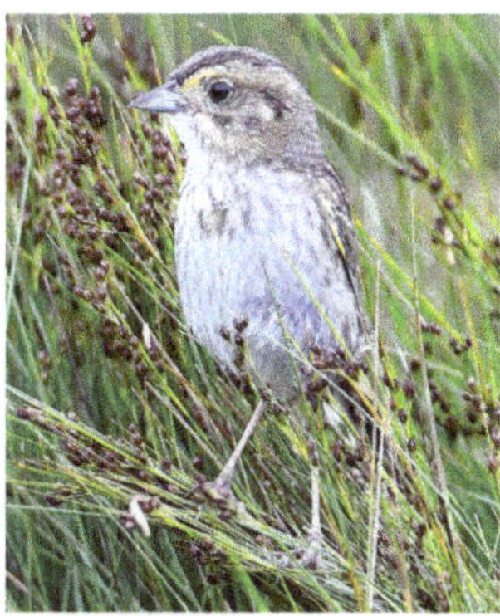
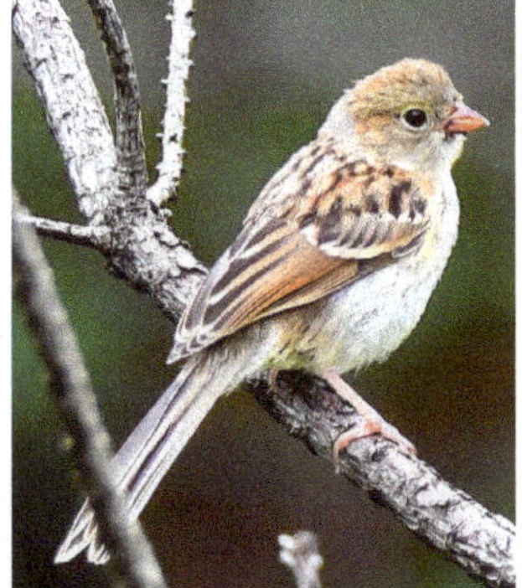
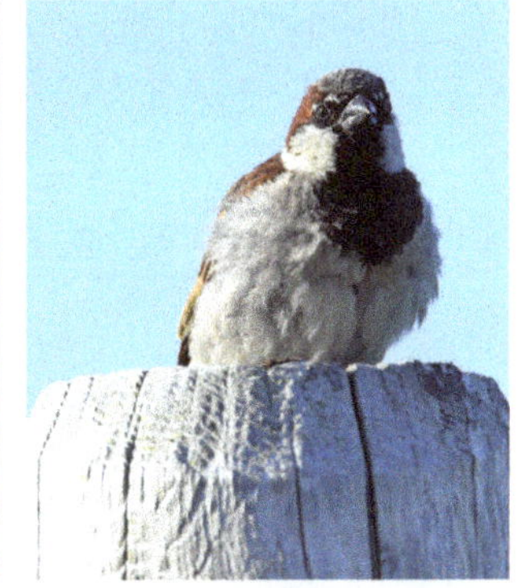
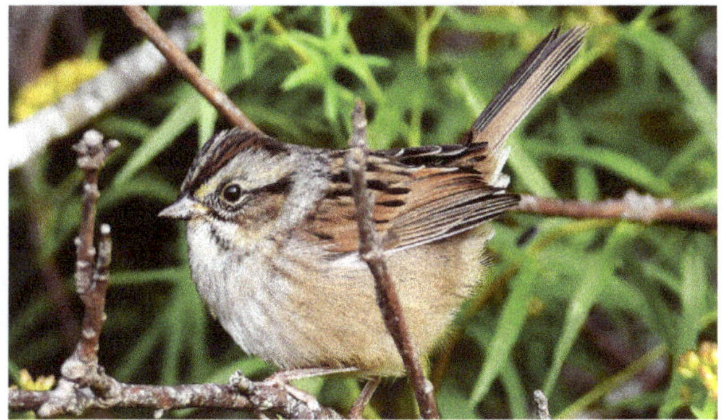
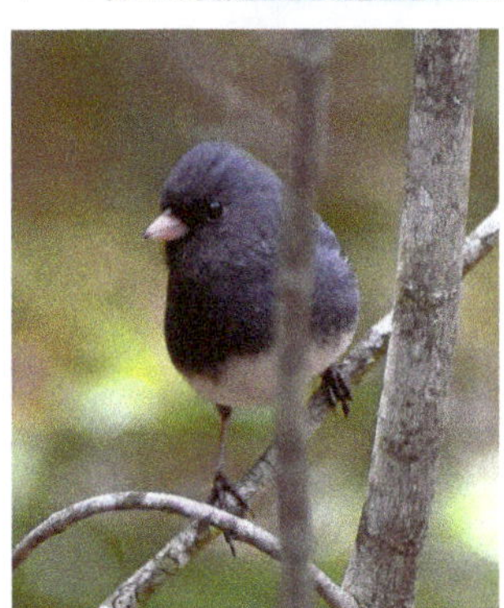

In early September, I was birding at Laudholm Farm in Wells, over two thousand acres of shore front, salt marsh, orchards, and hayfields. I covered large areas of the preserve before finding Maine Big Year Bird #306 in the damn parking lot.

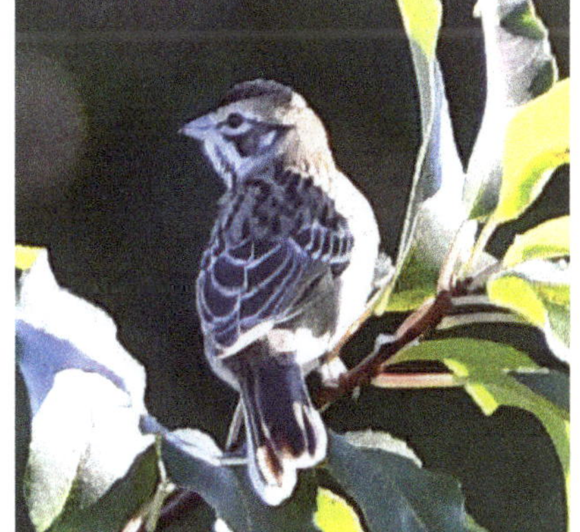

I can't tell you how often Ingrid and I spend hours trudging through "nature" looking for a particular bird, only to discover it sitting in a tree overlooking the parking lot. It happens so often that we call it the "Parking Lot Effect".

This exciting find was a Lark Sparrow, my 18th species of Sparrow in Maine this year. A bird that breeds west of the Mississippi and winters in Mexico, the Lark Sparrow is a notoriously bad navigator, and wayward Lark Sparrows show up in weird locations from Maine to Florida each fall.

Obviously, I need to spend more time in parking lots.

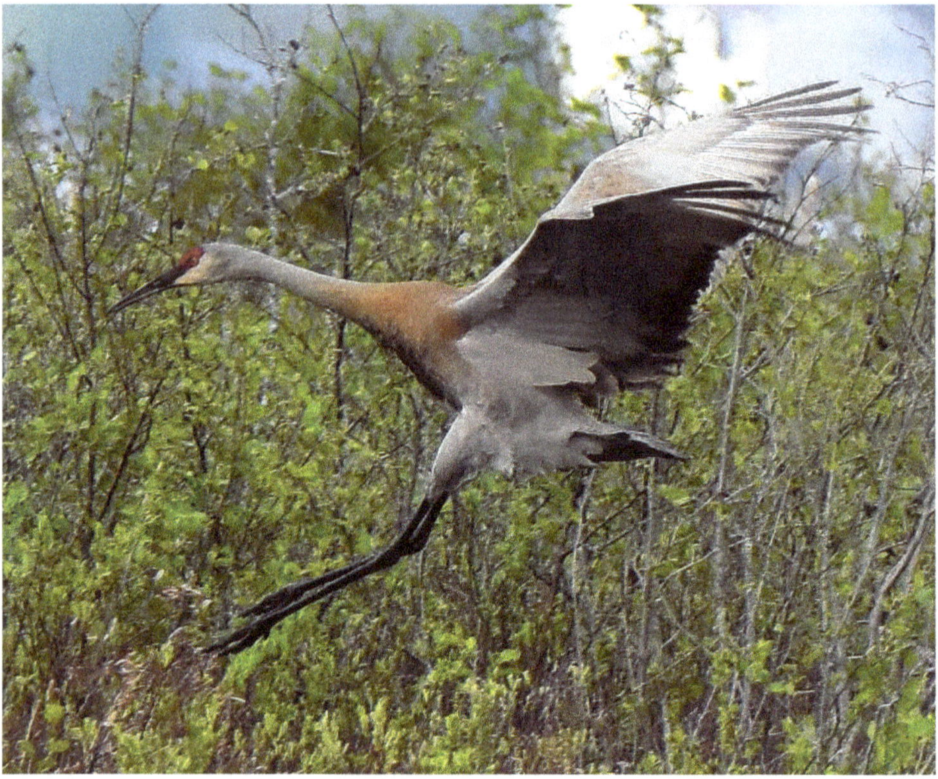

If you live along the Gulf Coast or on Great Plains, you may see thousands of Sandhill Cranes. In Maine, however, they are still a rarity, although the breeding population seems to be growing from year to year.

The best place to reliably find Sandhill Cranes in Maine is on Messalonskee Lake in Belgrade. Stand near the boat ramp from April through September, and with a little patience you'll see one or more stroll or fly by. (Note: it helps to have a spotting scope or a good pair of binoculars).

Several years back, a beloved great-aunt passed away after a wonderful and active 101 years. Ingrid and I attended the burial ceremony on a warm, late spring day in Belgrade.

In middle of the eulogy, five elegant Sand Hill Cranes flew directly over the mourners gathered around the casket.

I'm not sure anyone but Ingrid and I noticed them fly over, but it was one of those apropos moments, where something truly special occurs that makes one wonder.

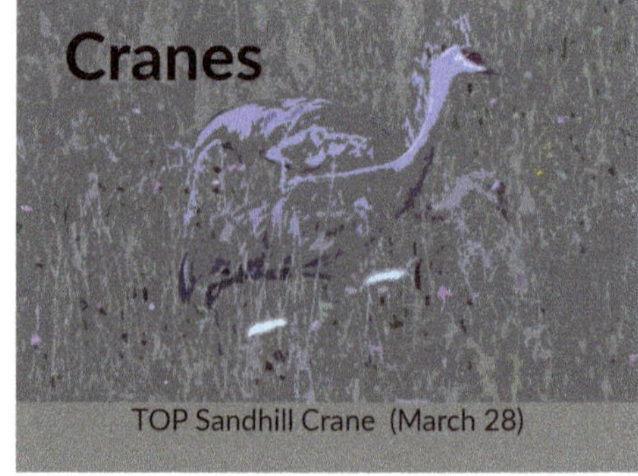

TOP Sandhill Crane (March 28)

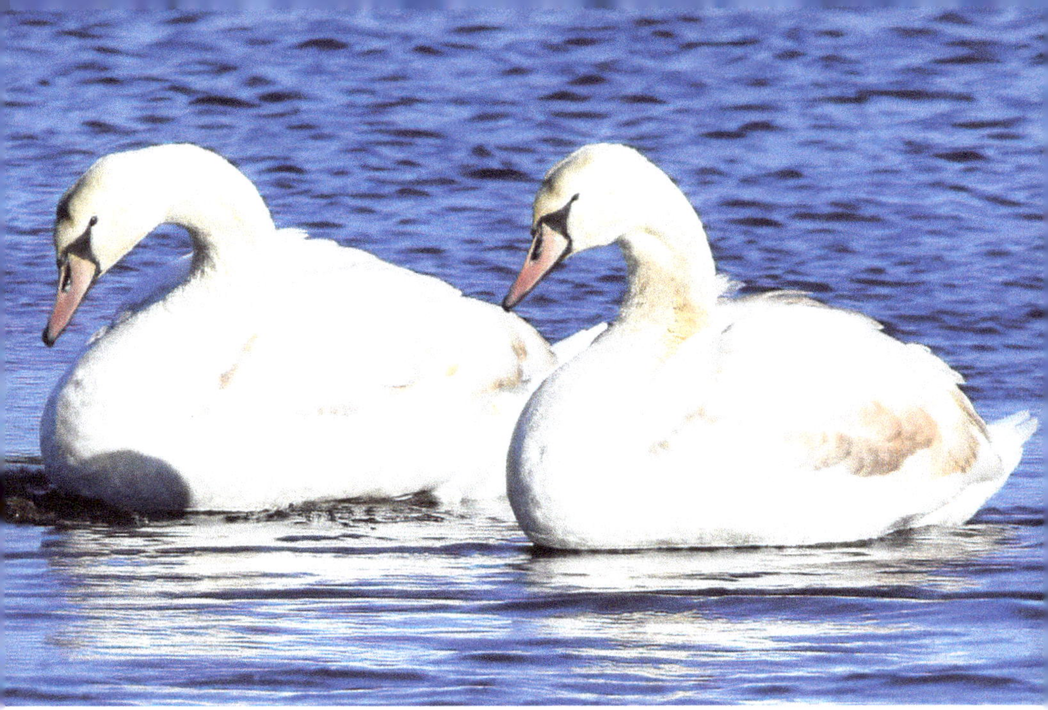

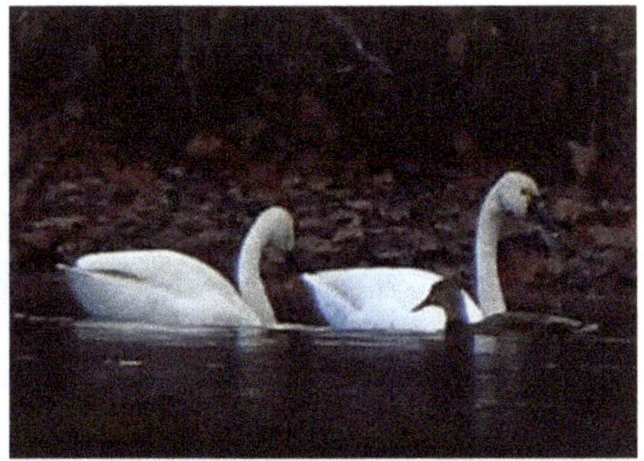

In October of 2020, three juvenile Tundra Swans landed on Little Ossipee Pond in South-central Maine. Tundra Swans are smaller cousins of the Mute Swans that are so iconic in the Northeast (think of the Boston Public Gardens).

Tundra Swans breed, as you might guess, on the Arctic tundra. Then each fall they migrate south and winter along the West Coast (Washington State to San Francisco) and the East Coast (New Jersey to Virginia).

The Little Ossipee Tundra Swans were rare visitors to Maine, and the fact that they stayed until mid-December (when the pond froze over) was VERY rare.

In mid-November 2021, two of the Little Ossipee birds showed up on the pond again, now as beautiful full-grown adults.

I'm not sure what happened to the third bird, but it's pretty remarkable that two Tundra Swans returned to Maine.

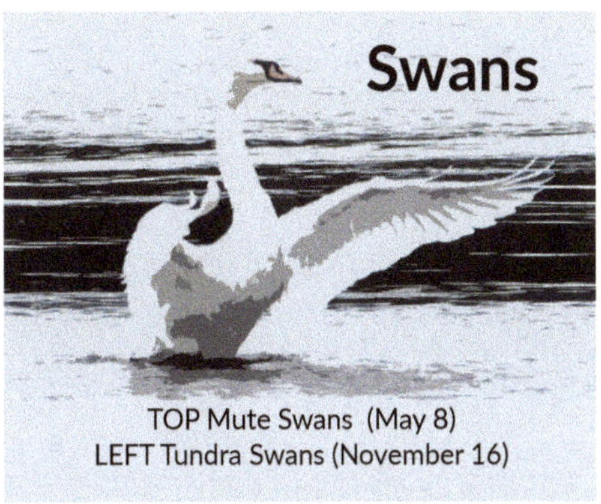

TOP Mute Swans (May 8)
LEFT Tundra Swans (November 16)

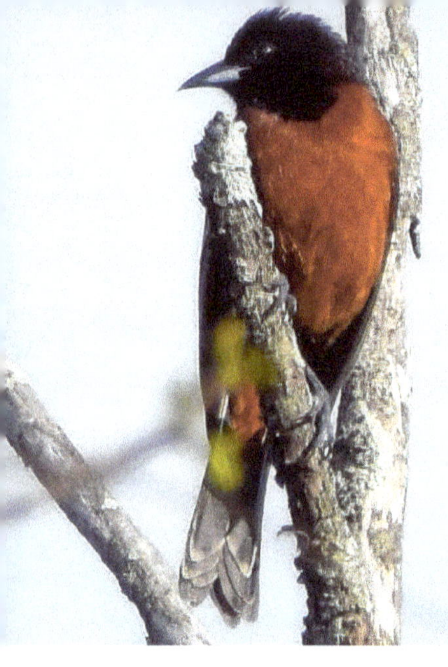

Fortunately, there is no shortage of Baltimore Orioles in Maine, and they are a common sight and sound in spring and summer.

Orchard Orioles are rarely seen in Maine, except near a small pond in the middle of Portland, at Capisic Park. There for the last six years, a pair of Orchard Orioles have nested, singing and displaying for visitors.

Orchard Orioles, both male and female, are not as bright as their Baltimore cousins.

Every spring, Ingrid and I go through bags of oranges, slicing them in halves and positioning the pieces in strategic locations around our home hoping to attract Baltimore Orioles. Some years we are very successful, and the stunning black and orange birds stay for a of couple of weeks. Other years . . . not so much.

But we often say, "If you always got the bird, it wouldn't be any fun."

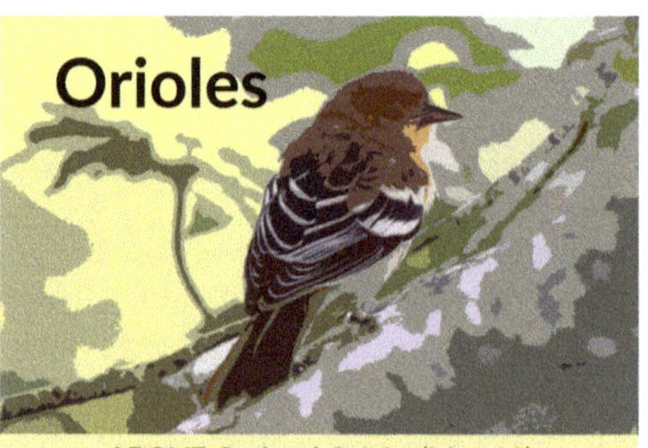

ABOVE Orchard Oriole (May 11)
BELOW Baltimore Oriole (May 8)

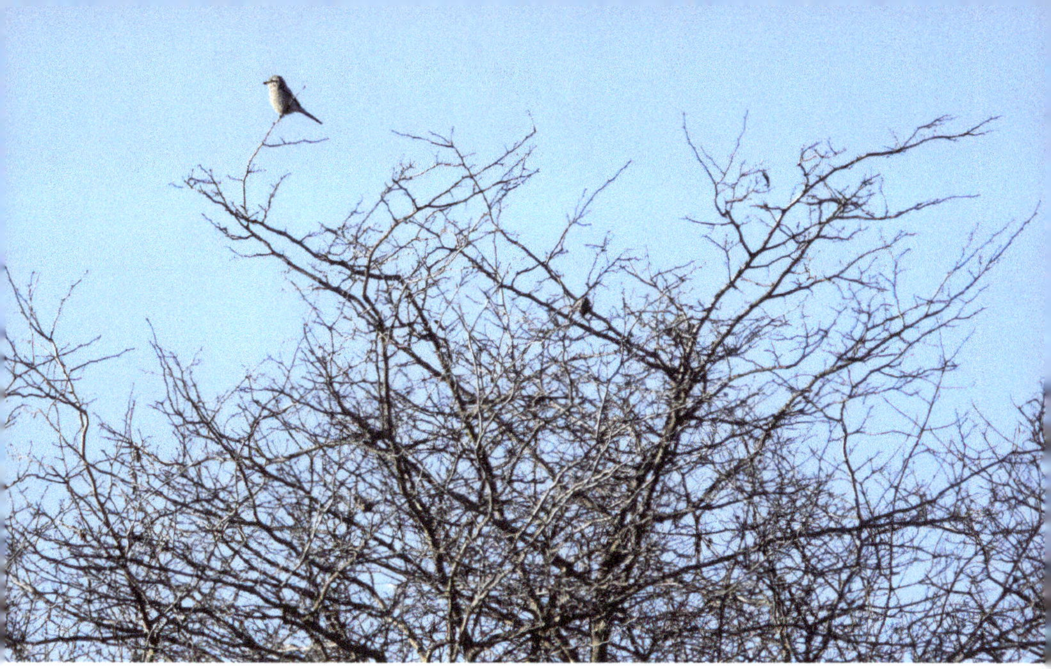

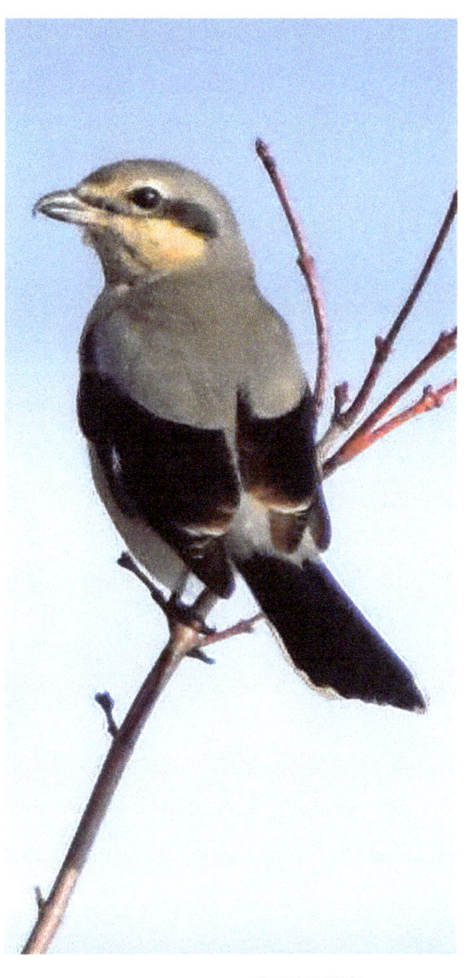

Each winter a small but imposing songbird with a black mask moves south from Canada into Maine. This is the Northern Shrike.

The Northern Shrike is a predator of other birds, rodents and insects.

You'll see one perched high on a bush or small tree. From here, it ambushes its prey, piercing it with the sharp hook on its bill.

To make this little bird even more terrifying, it will save its food for later by impaling it on a thorn or barbed wire.

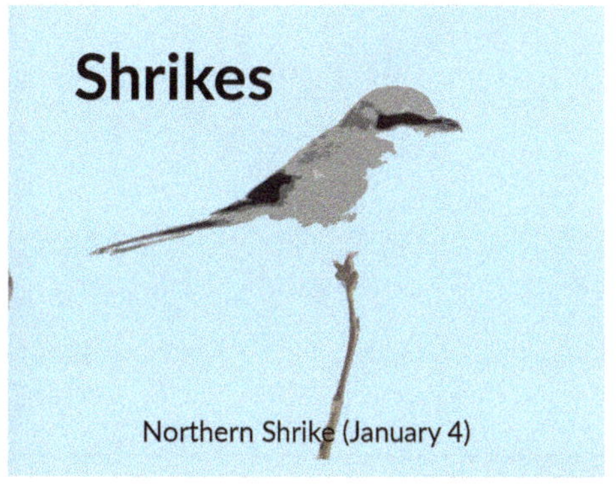

Shrikes

Northern Shrike (January 4)

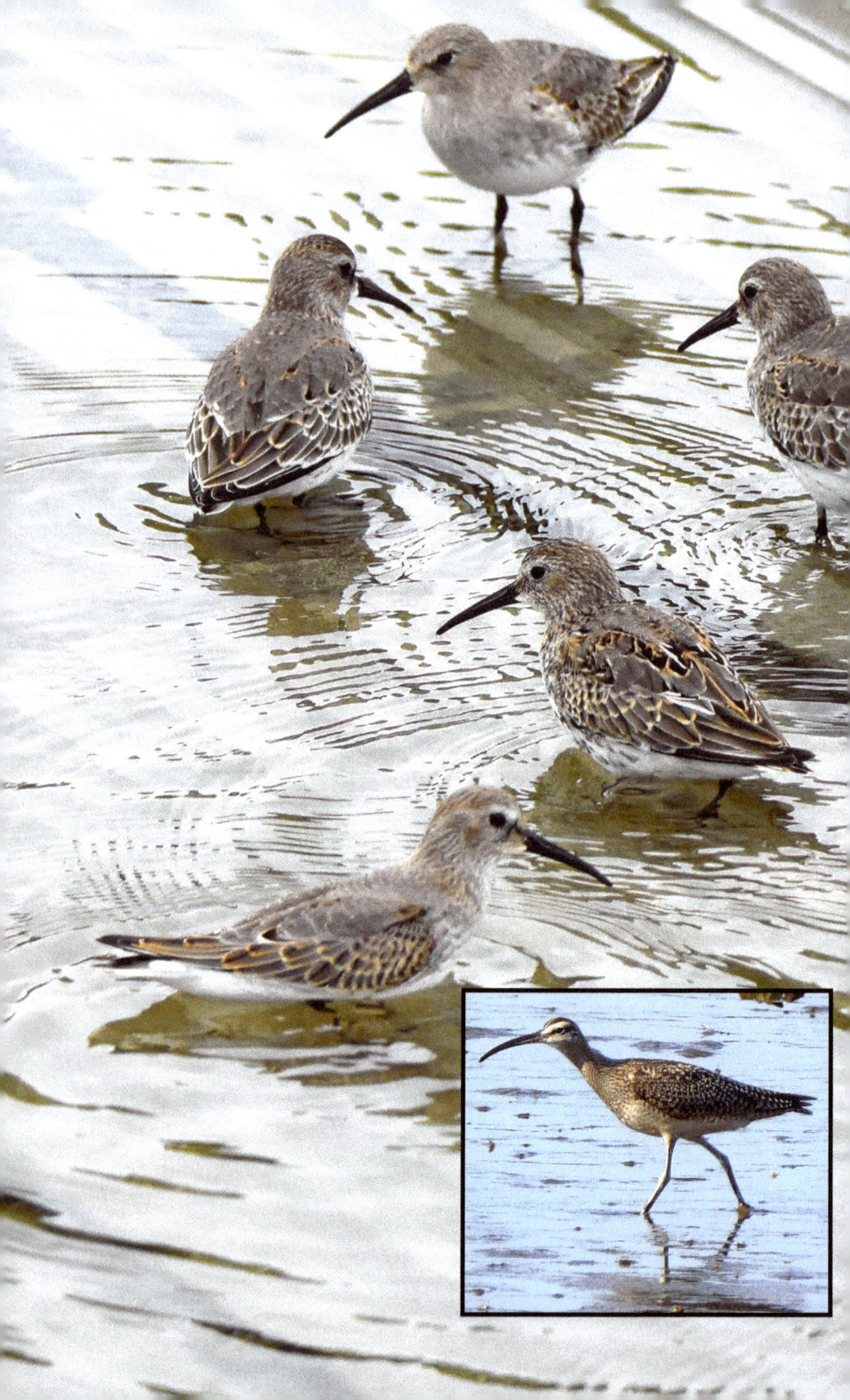

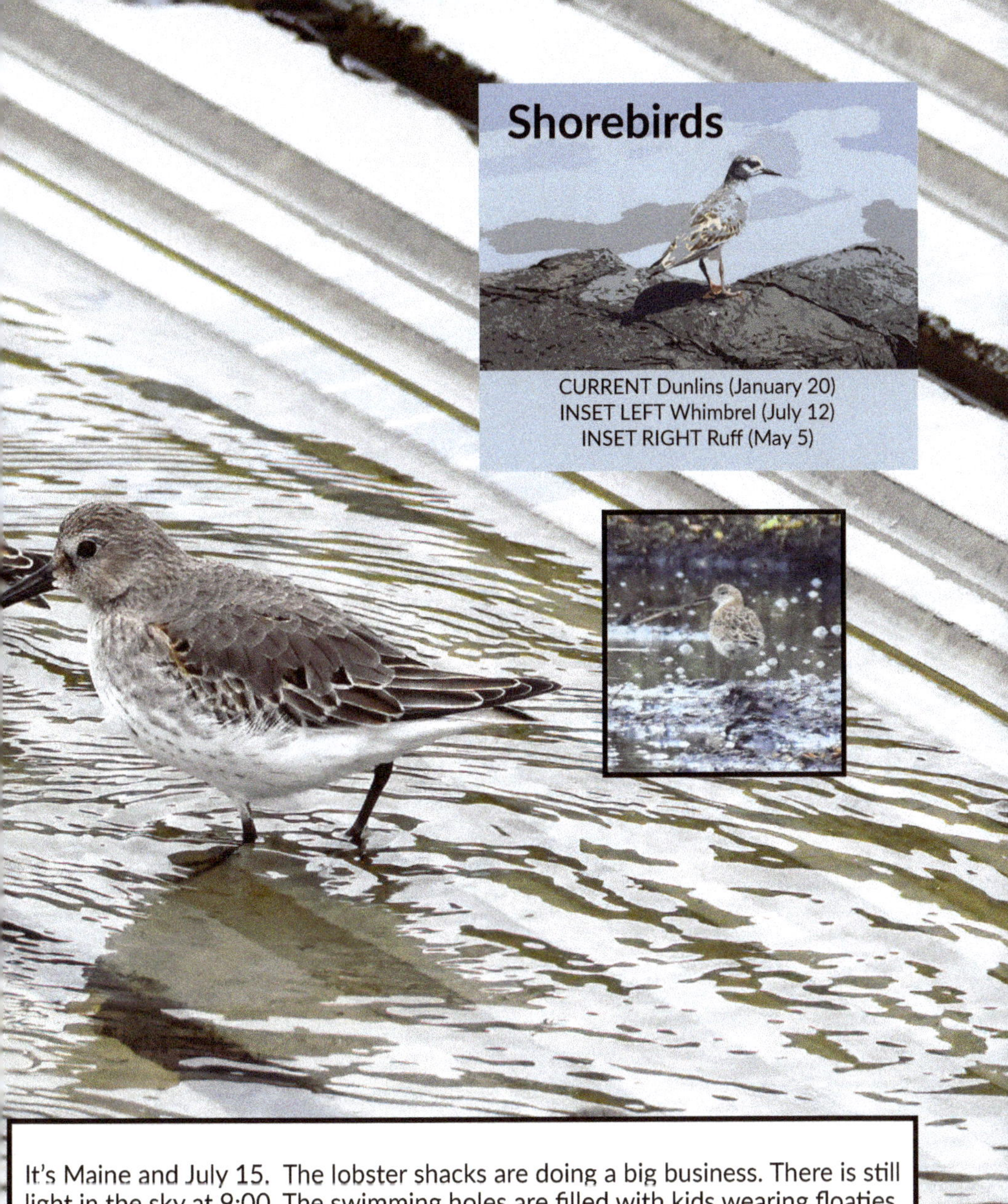

It's Maine and July 15. The lobster shacks are doing a big business. There is still light in the sky at 9:00. The swimming holes are filled with kids wearing floaties, and the beaches are crowded with sun-worshipers of all shapes and sizes.

On this mid-summer day, I set out to find a flock of Whimbrels, heading south.

That's right, the first shorebirds migrating south from their nesting grounds in the Arctic begin to appear in mid-summer and continue into October.

Shorebirds come through in waves.

Adults will often migrate a month or more ahead their fledglings, who need the time to learn to fly and fatten up for the journey.

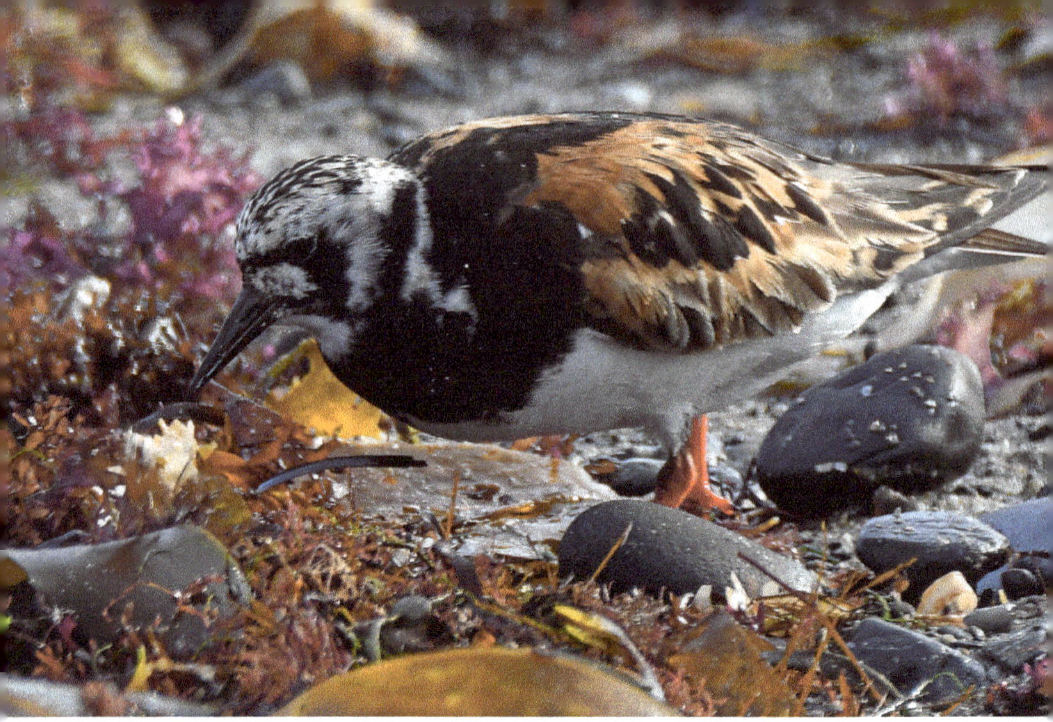

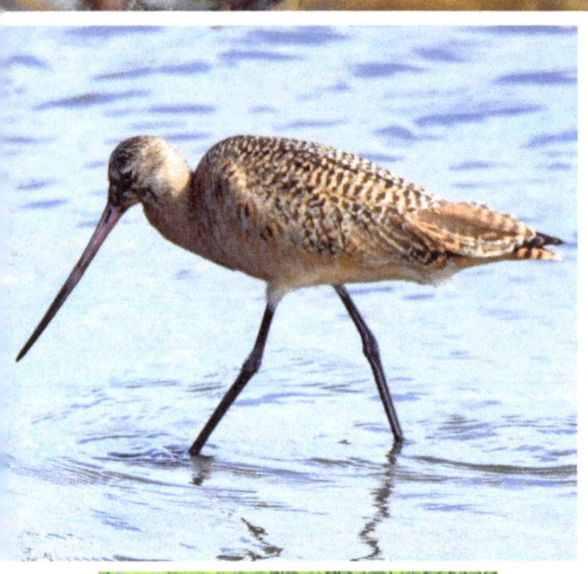

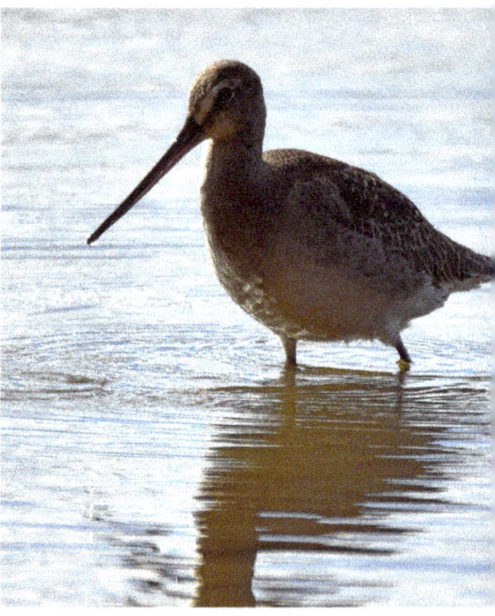

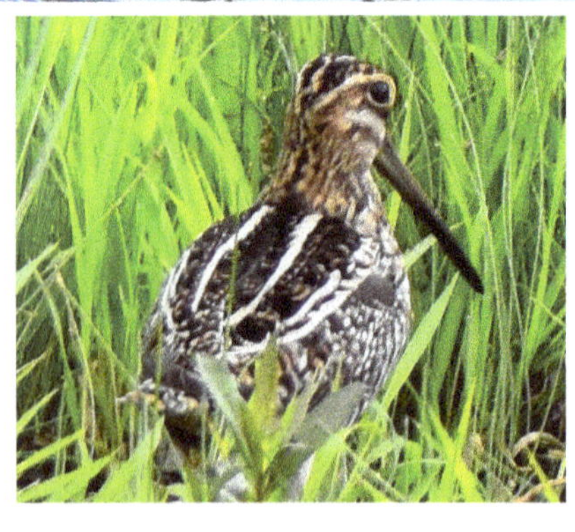

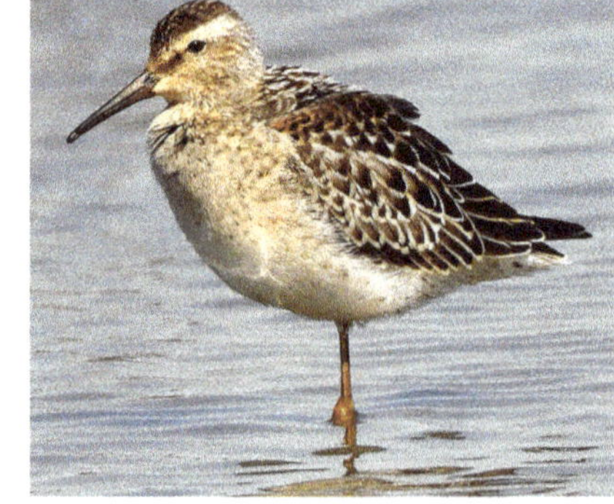

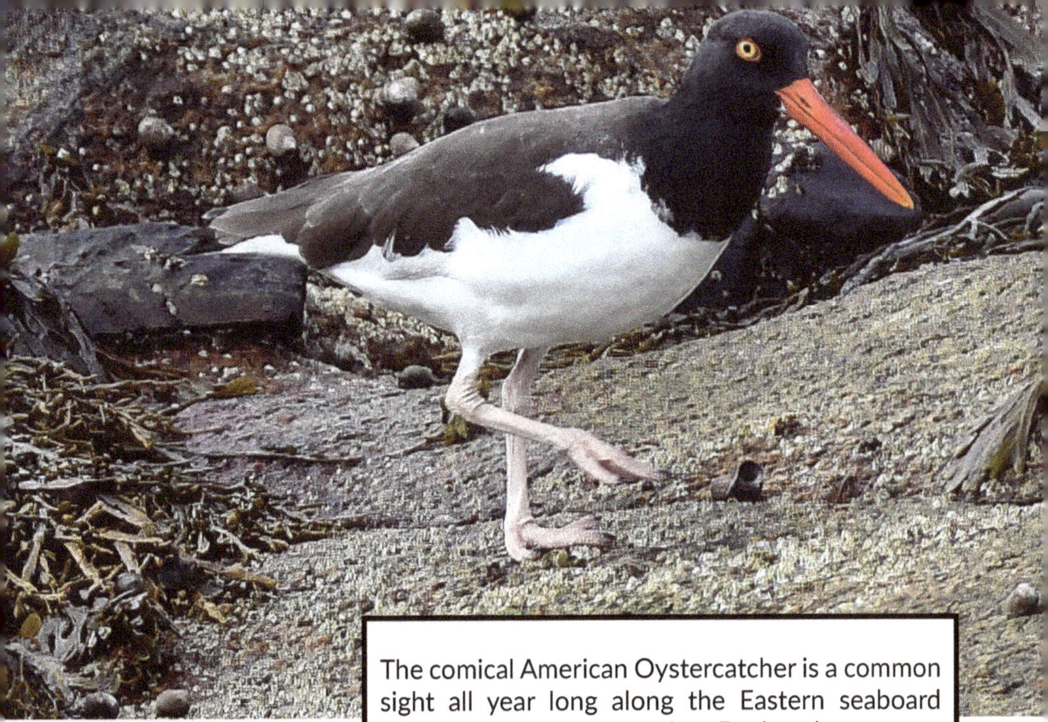

The comical American Oystercatcher is a common sight all year long along the Eastern seaboard from New Jersey to Mexico. During the summer they even nest along Long Island Sound.

To the best of my knowledge, American Oystercatchers only breed in Maine on Stratton Island, a few miles off of Old Orchard Beach.

During the summer, Ingrid and I will occasionally see an Oystercatcher browsing the water's edge at a beach or mudflat. Their carrot nose (I mean bill) always makes us laugh.

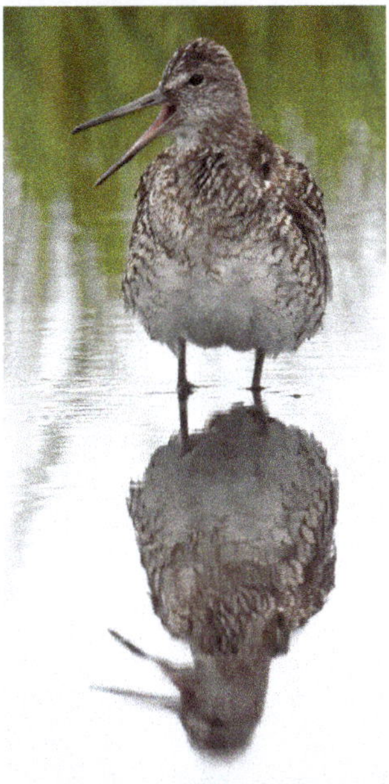

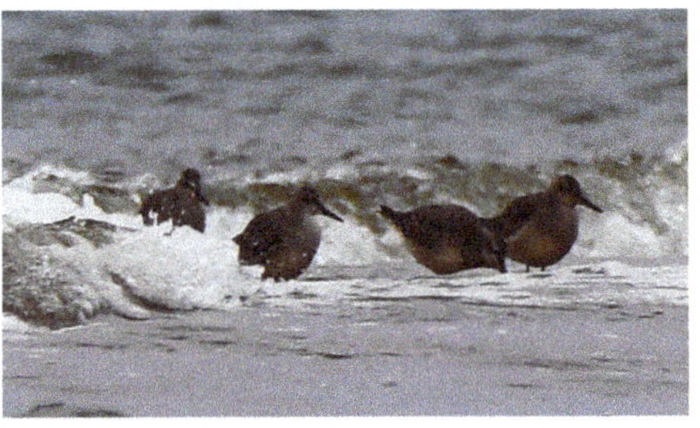

Shorebirds (cont.)

OPPOSITE
TOP Ruddy Turnstone (May 2)
MIDDLE-LEFT Marbled Godwit (Sept 19)
MIDDLE-RIGHT Hudsonian Godwit (Sept 28)
BOTTOM-LEFT Wilson's Snipe (March 24)
BOTTOM-RIGHT Stilt Sandpiper (August 10)

CURRENT
TOP American Oystercatcher (April 18)
MIDDLE Willet (April 26)
BOTTOM Red Knots (May 24)

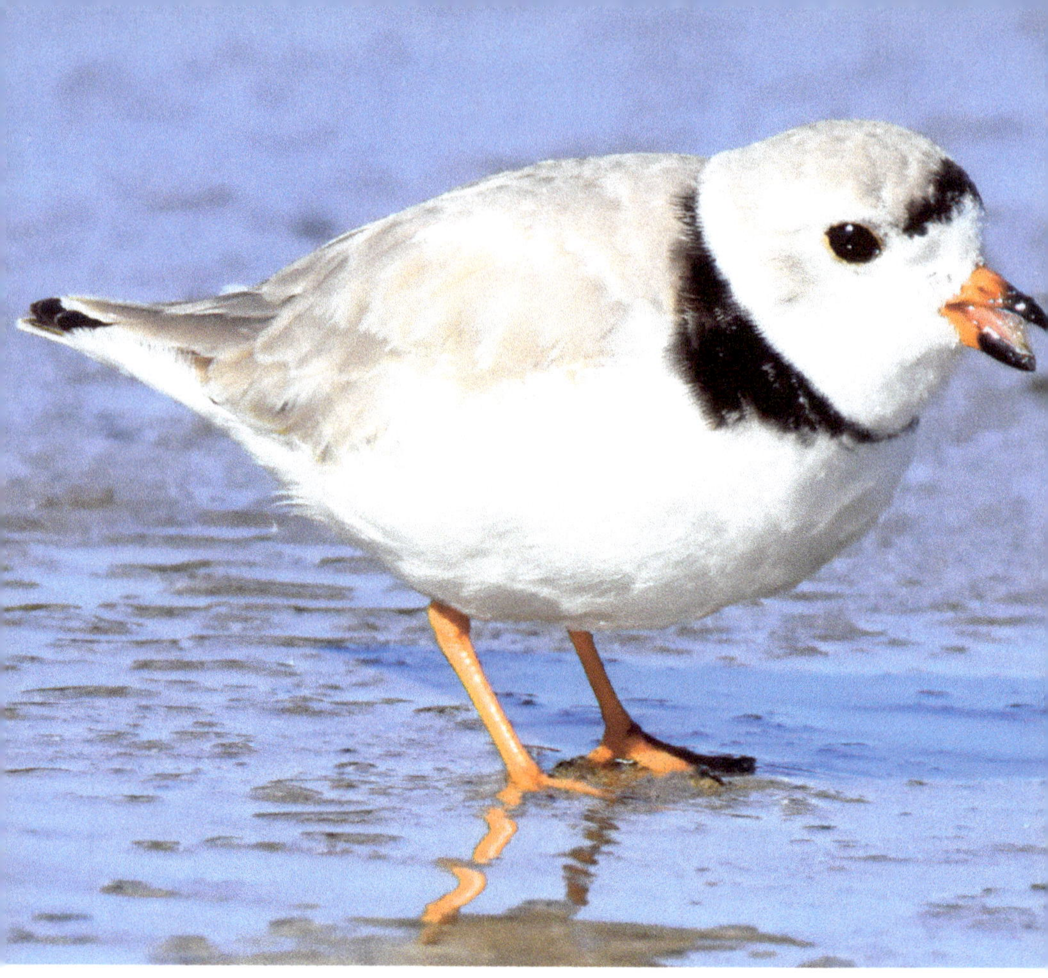

Piping Plovers are an endangered species that nests in small indentations on Maine's sandy beaches. Obviously, this makes them vulnerable to beach goers, dogs and Frisbees. Thanks to beach regulations and careful stewardship, the population has begun to rebound.

There are still challenges, however. In late March I was on the north end of Wells Beach near the dunes when I came upon a Bullmastiff playing fetch with his master. While the beach is two miles long, they decided to play where the endangered species nest each year.

Being a coward, I didn't say anything but gave the dog's owner my best withering glare, and he seemed to get the message.

A few minutes, after the dog left, I counted four, maybe five Piping Plovers.

A true sign of Spring in Maine.

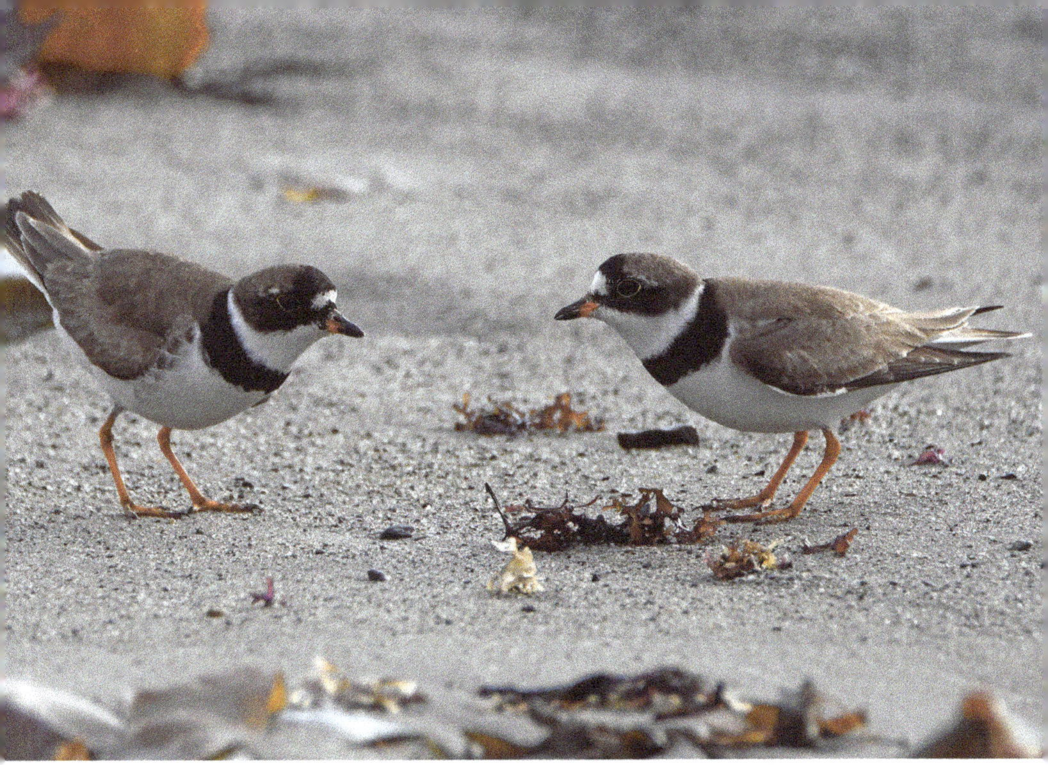

The American Golden-Plover is one of the great migrators. It flies up to 25,000 miles each year, following a circular route from the breeding grounds on the Arctic tundra of Alaska and northern Canada to southern South American grasslands and back again.

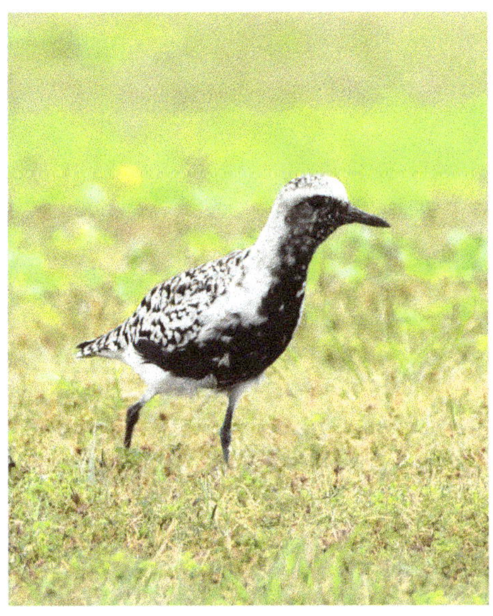

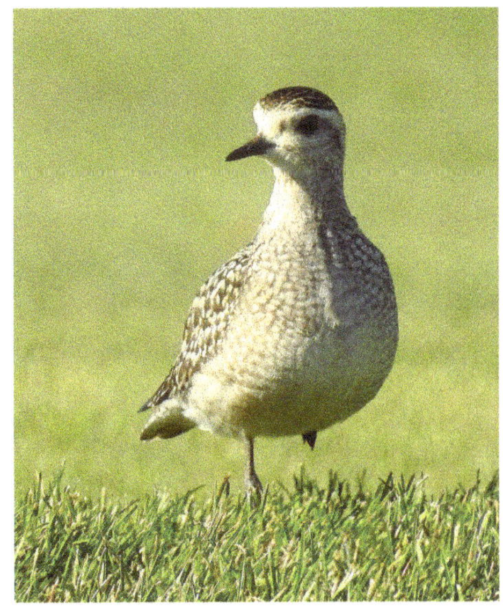

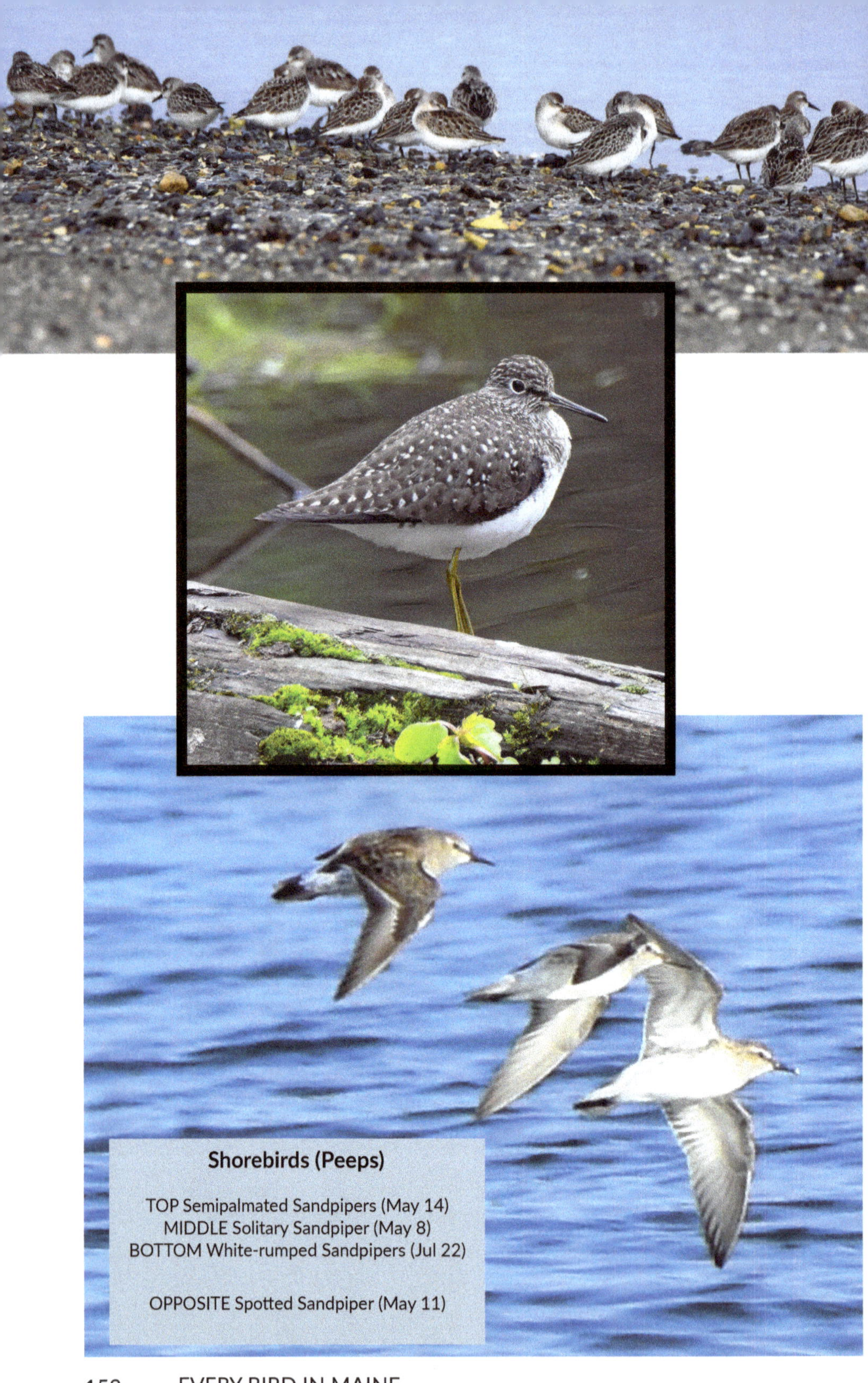

Shorebirds (Peeps)

TOP Semipalmated Sandpipers (May 14)
MIDDLE Solitary Sandpiper (May 8)
BOTTOM White-rumped Sandpipers (Jul 22)

OPPOSITE Spotted Sandpiper (May 11)

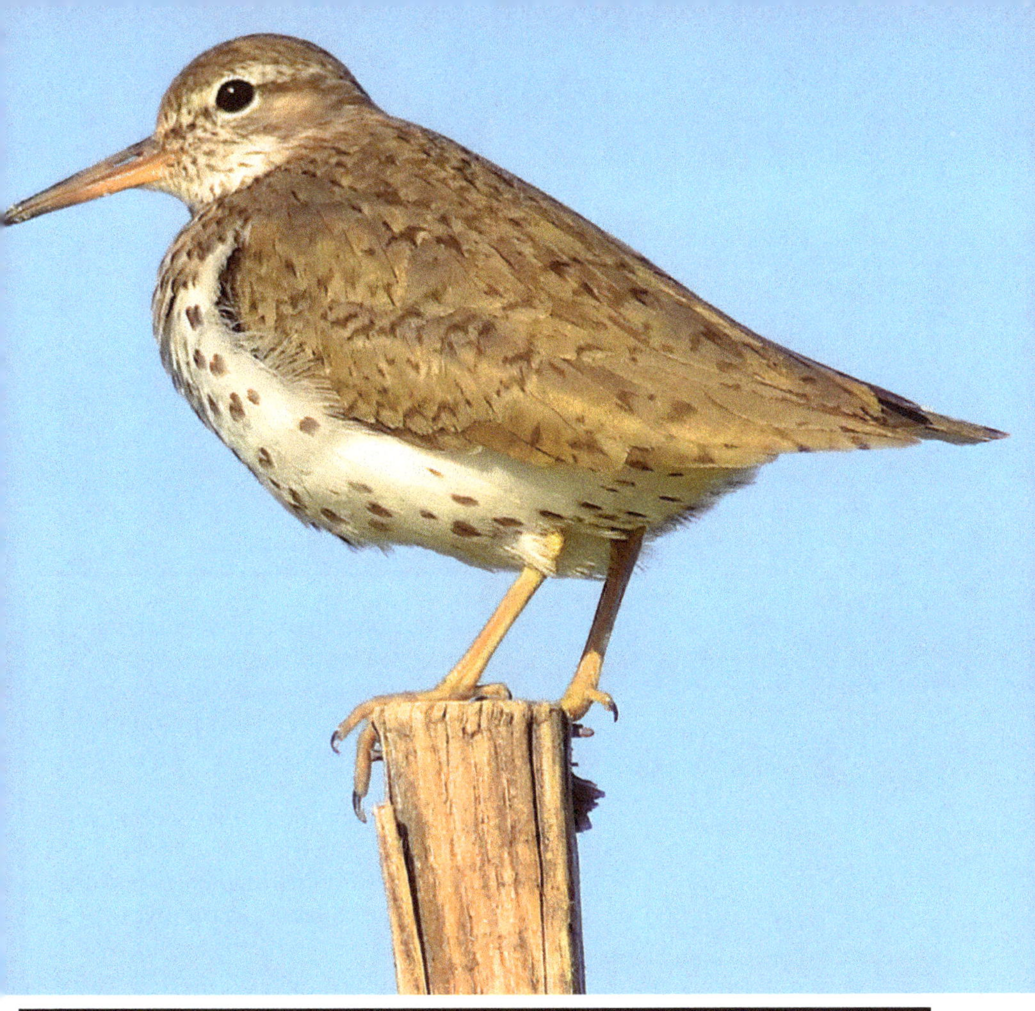

"Peeps" is a catch-all term for the tiny shorebirds found congregating on Maine beaches by the thousands during fall migration (which actually begins mid-summer).

Why the "catch-all"? There are six tiny shorebirds that look alike. Species identification requires serious study and a good pair of binoculars.

The most common of these birds is the Semipalmated Sandpiper - black legs and straight bill.

Semipalmated and White-rumped Sandpipers look much alike, except the latter is slightly larger, with wings that stretch behind the tail and a white rump that shows in flight.

The Least Sandpiper has yellow legs.

The Dunlin has a long, drooping bill.

The Western Sandpiper has a slight drooping bill and a rufous striped wing.

The Semipalmated Plover has a brown-black hood and orange legs.

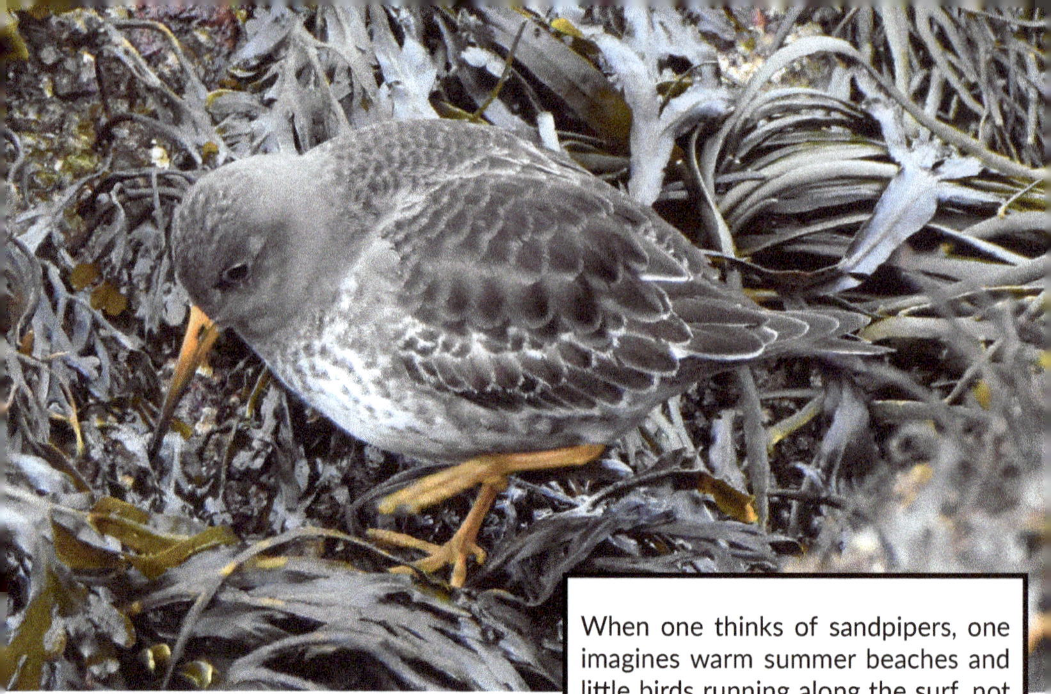

When one thinks of sandpipers, one imagines warm summer beaches and little birds running along the surf, not ice covered rocks being pounded by frosty waves.

We only see the Purple Sandpipers in Maine during the cold winter months. They feed on surf-swept rocks, often dodging the waves as they hit the outcrop. These birds rush in to feed on invertebrates pulled from crevasses and seaweed, then run back to safety before the next wave hits.

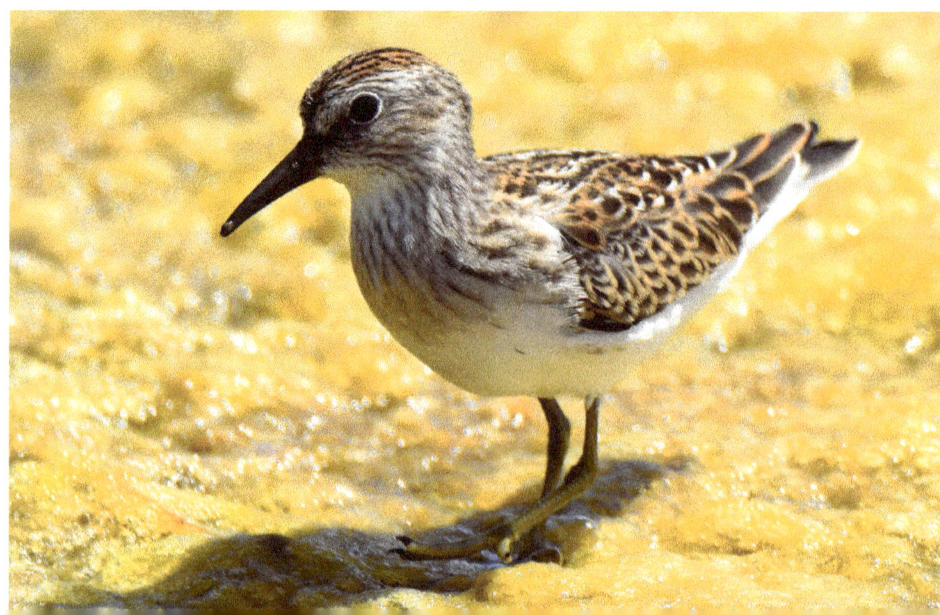

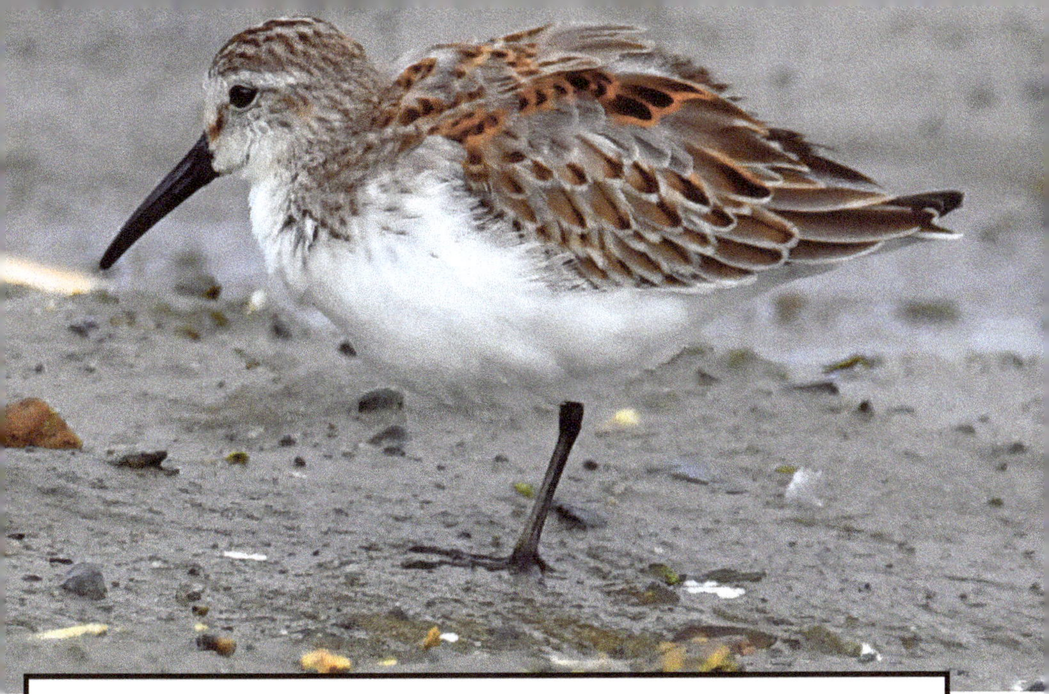

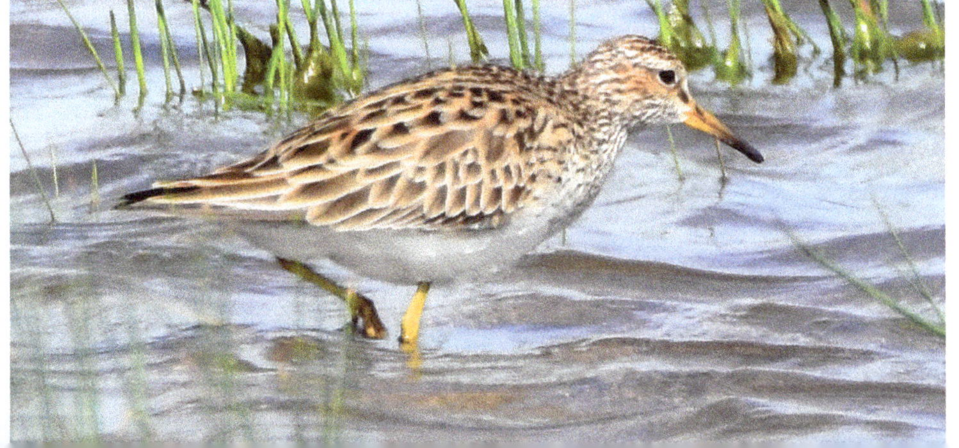

To do a successful Big Year, one has to spy all of the available bird species, and many of them hide in plain sight. For instance, in September the shore of a tide pool can be filled with several hundred Semipalmated Sandpipers and Semipalmated Plovers. Each is 5 to 6 inches tall. Some are moving; others are feeding, and periodically the whole flock will inexplicably, and in unison, leap into the air, make a circuit around the beach and land 50 feet from where they started.

Found in the maelstrom one day was a single Western Sandpiper, a species that is differentiated from the Semipalmated Sandpiper by a slightly thinner down-turned bill, white eyebrow and rusty scapular (i.e. shoulder pad).

I got my "Western" on Pine Point Beach in Scarborough. A couple of other birders had asked me to help them find a Baird's Sandpiper, and I stumbled upon the Western Sandpiper while scanning the multitude of birds running up and down the beach.

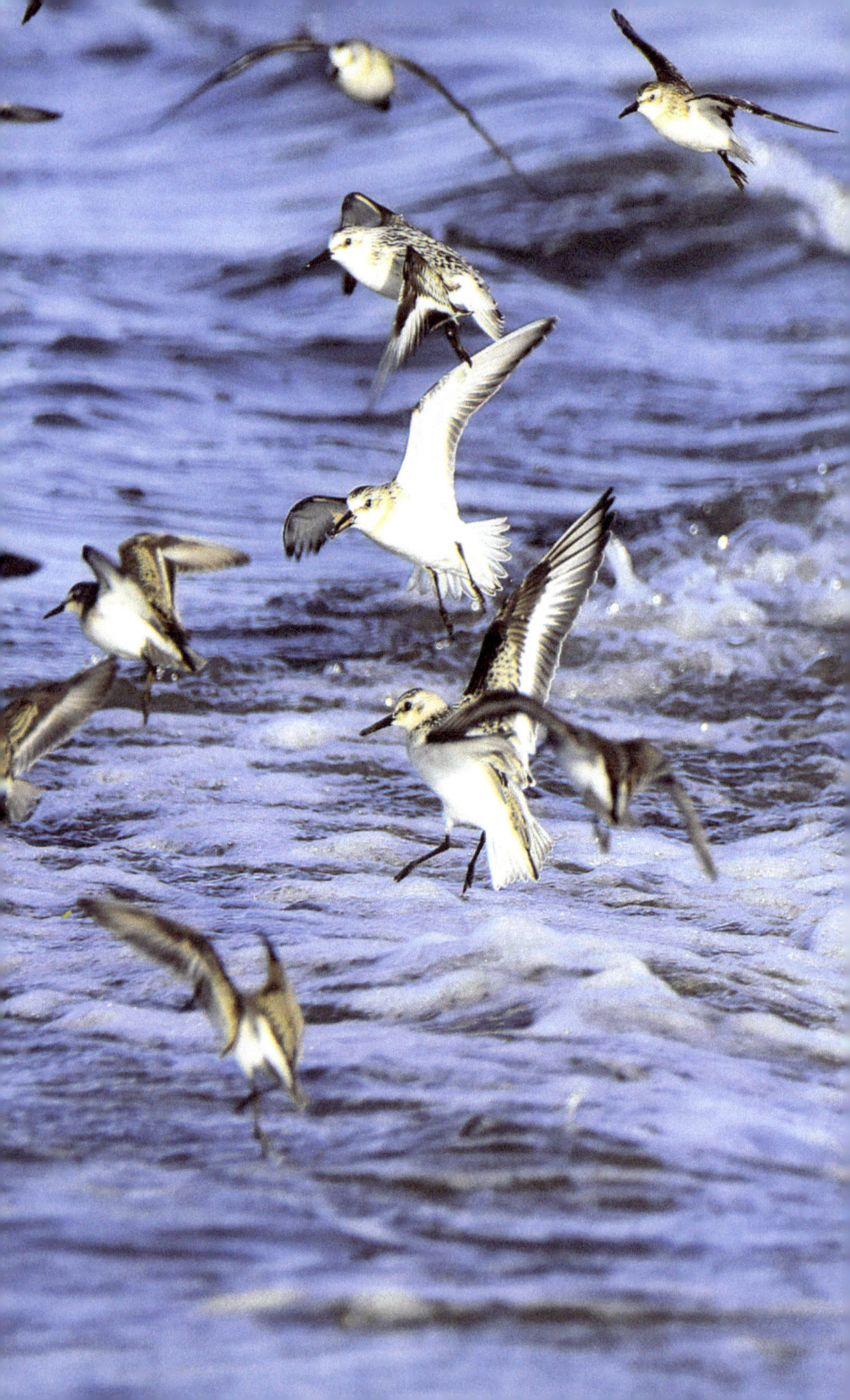

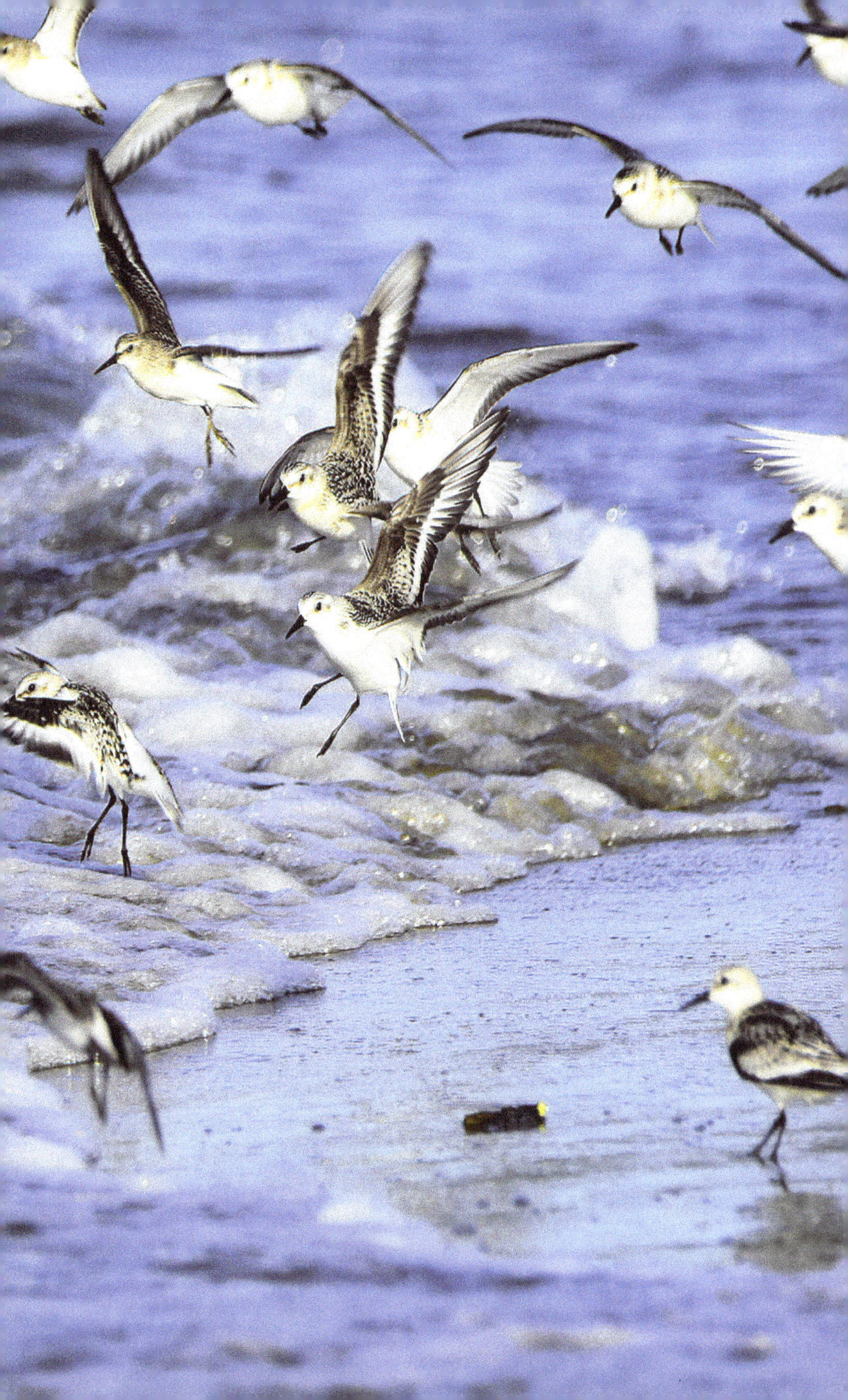

Mid-March each year, I wait for a warm evening and around dusk head over to the Zak Preserve in Boothbay. I'm seeking the American Woodcock display, a mating ritual like no other.

A few minutes after sunset, Timber Doodles (my favorite Woodcock nickname) move out of the woods into the meadow, using a comical up and down dance.

The male will begin calling with an electronic *Bzeep* song. Then the suitors spring hundreds of feet into the air and spin down to the ground using their wings to make a whistling sound.

With luck, a nearby female will be impressed!!!

Shorebirds (Grasspipers)

BELOW American Woodcock(March 10)
BOTTOM Baird's Sandpiper (August 12)

OPPOSITE
TOP Buff-breasted Sandpiper (August 28)
MIDDLE Killdeer (March 6)
BOTTOM Upland Sandpiper (April 27)

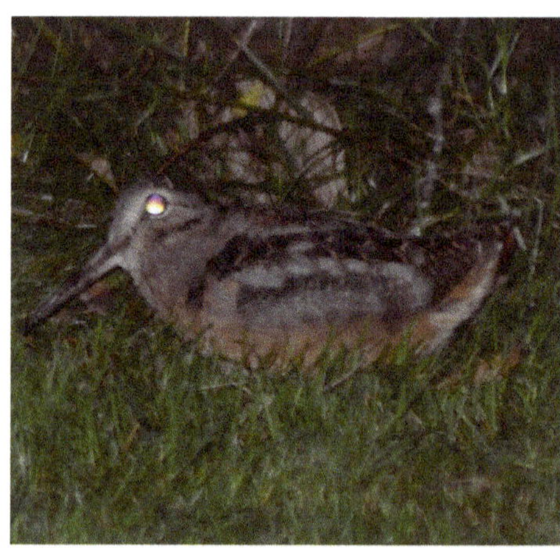

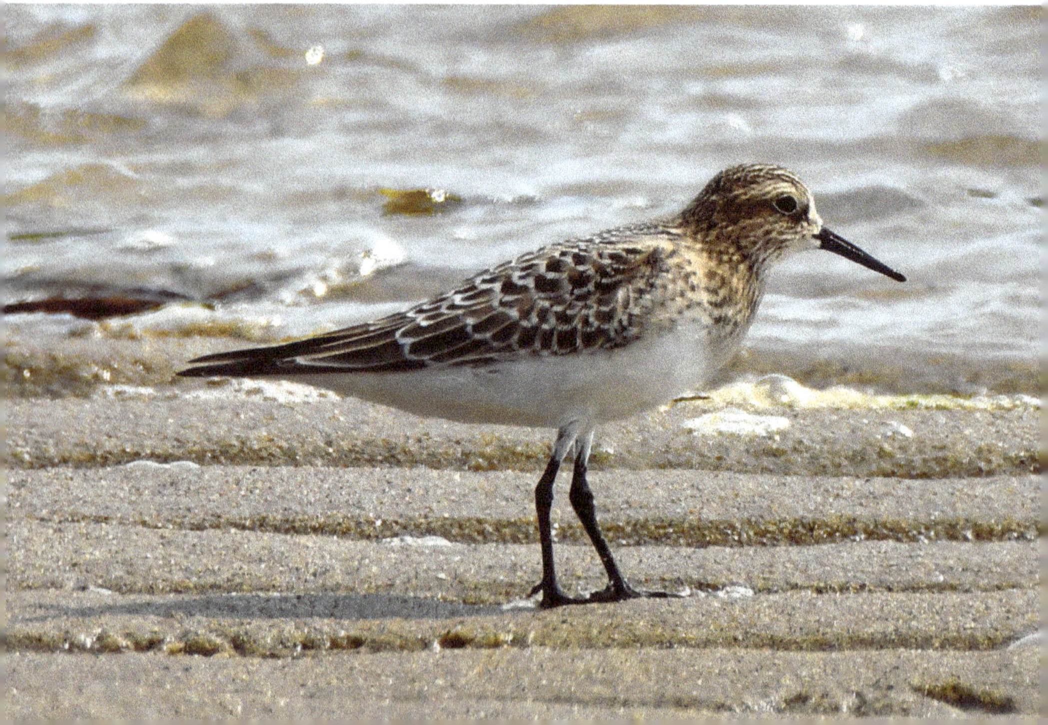

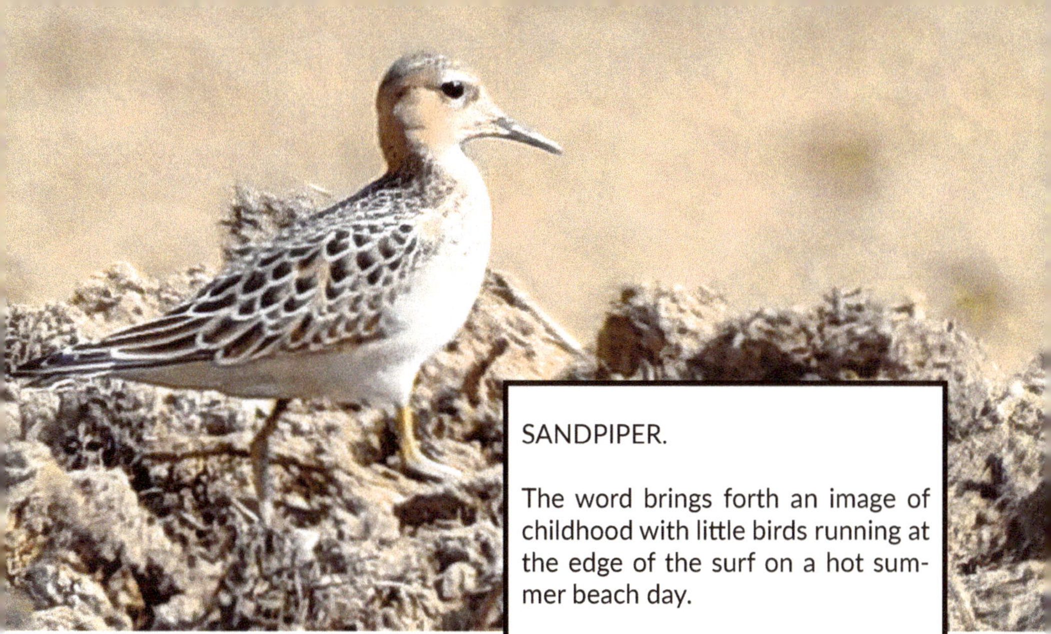

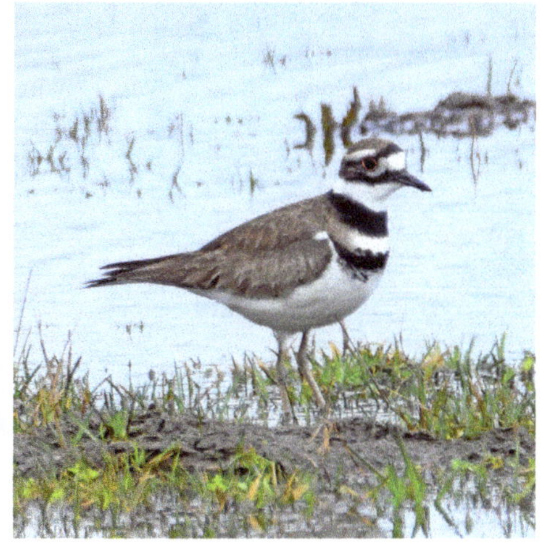

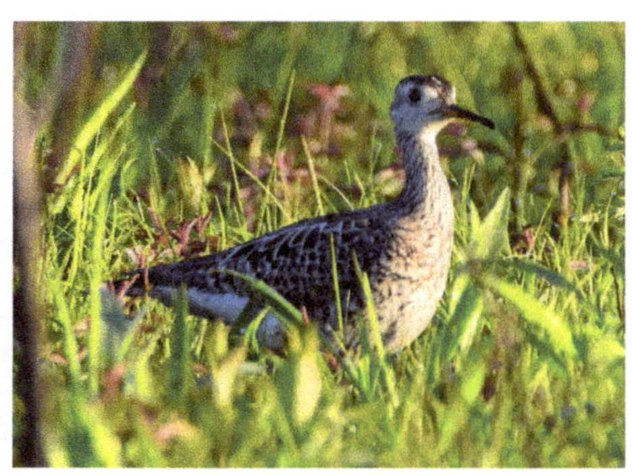

SANDPIPER.

The word brings forth an image of childhood with little birds running at the edge of the surf on a hot summer beach day.

That image is pretty accurate, as each summer thousands of sandpipers and plovers migrate through Maine, stopping to feed on coastal beaches.

There are other Sandpipers, the "grass-pipers", shorebirds that prefer a nicely manicured golf course to the beach.

For Maine Birders, the most challenging of the grass-pipers is the Buff-breasted Sandpiper. A "Buffy" nests in the northern realms of the Arctic and winters in Argentina. They generally migrate through the Mid-western states and provinces.

This tiny, two ounce bird travels from the North Pole to the tip of South America and then back again, every year.

Annually, one or two "Buffies" gets lost during fall migration and ends up on a ball or sod field in Maine.

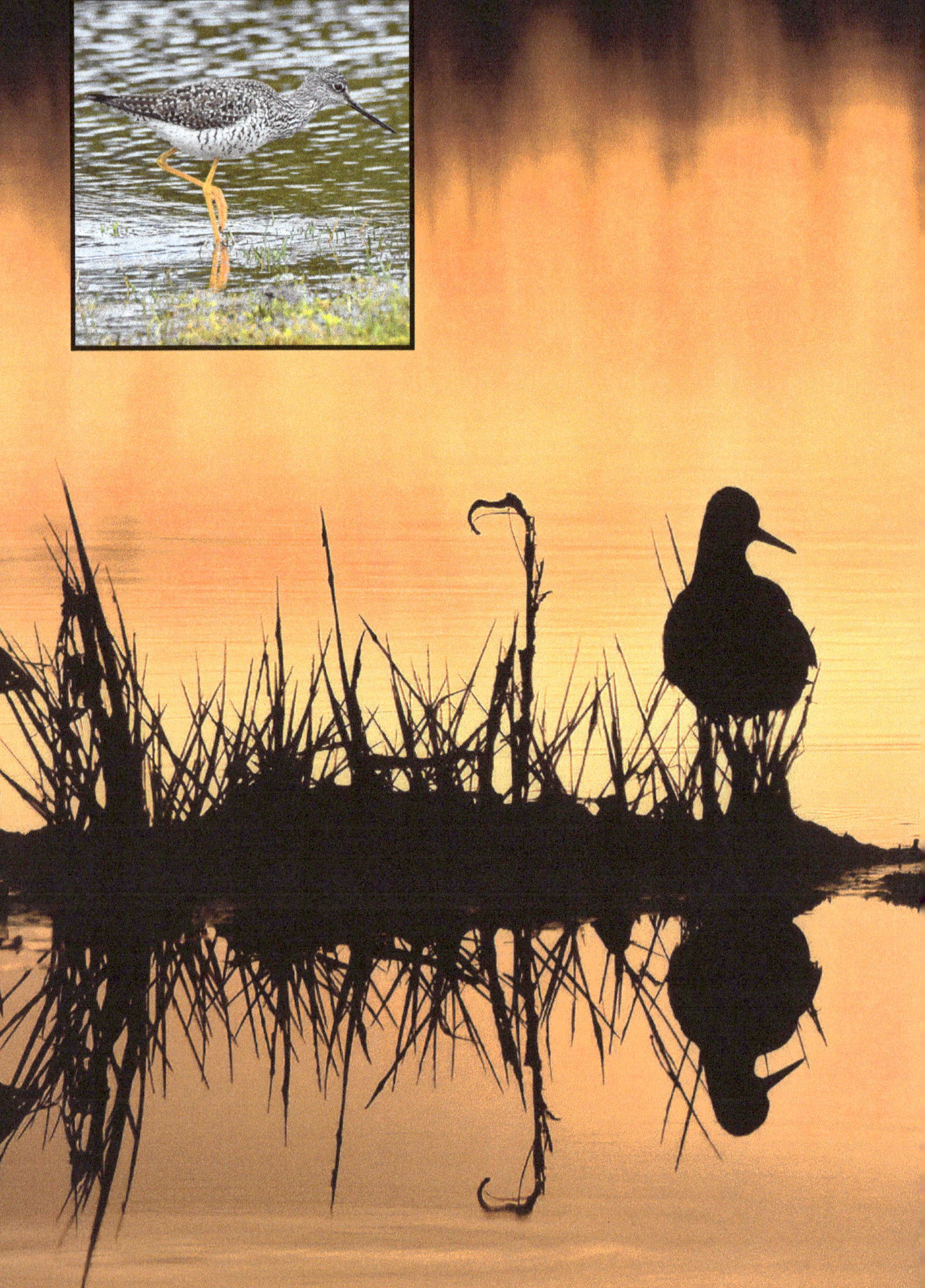

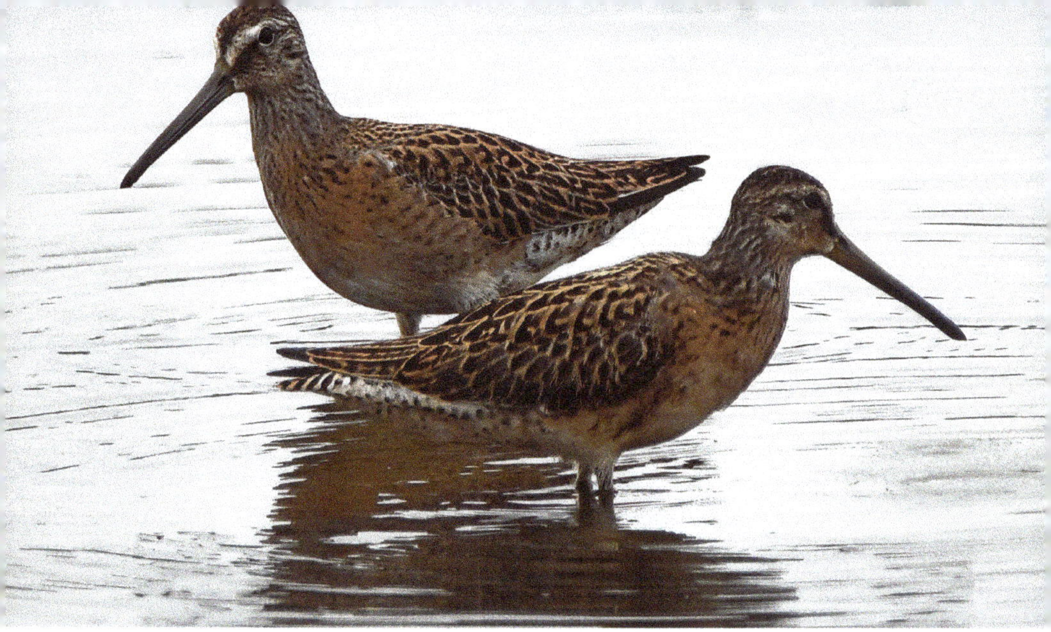

One of the most common fall shore-birds along the Maine coast can be found in the hundreds foraging in the mud, maneuvering its bill with the up and down motion of a sewing machine.

What would you name this bird and its enormous six inch long bill?

If you said "Short-billed Dowitcher", you'd be right. But clearly, this name is ridiculous.

Which brings me to my biggest pet-peeve, problematic bird names!!!

- The Red-bellied Woodpecker's red belly is virtually impossible to see unless you are holding the bird in your hand.
- The Connecticut Warbler is very rarely seen in Connecticut (The same is true about the Nashville and Tennessee Warblers).
- The Palm Warbler does not have anything to do with Palm Trees.

And there is a Long-billed Dowitcher. Its bill is only slightly and sometimes longer than the Short-billed Dowitcher.

I could go on and on.

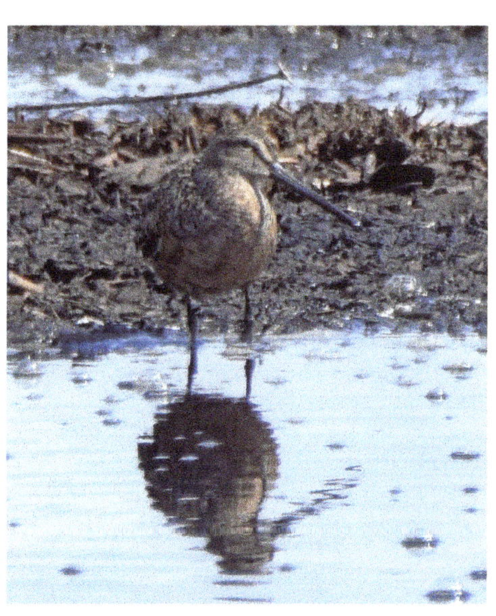

Shorebirds
(Yellowlegs & Dowitchers)

LEFT Lesser Yellowlegs (April 2)
INSET Greater Yellowlegs (April 14)
TOP Short-billed Dowitchers (May 2)
ABOVE Long-billed Dowitcher (May 11)

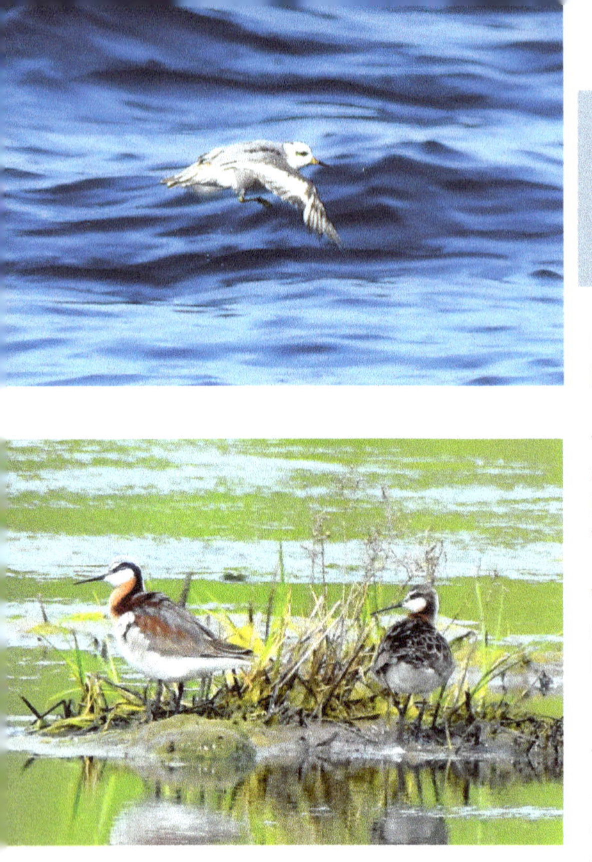

Phalaropes are slender necked shorebirds that reverse the usual sex roles. Females are larger and more colorful than their male counterparts and the aggressor in courtship. Males incubate the eggs and raise the young, while females have no involvement.

Wilson's Phalaropes normally nest near wetlands on the Great Plains, but each year a handful show up on Maine marshes.

The other Phalaropes, Red and Red-necked, are actually pelagic birds usually found feeding on seaweed masses far out to sea.

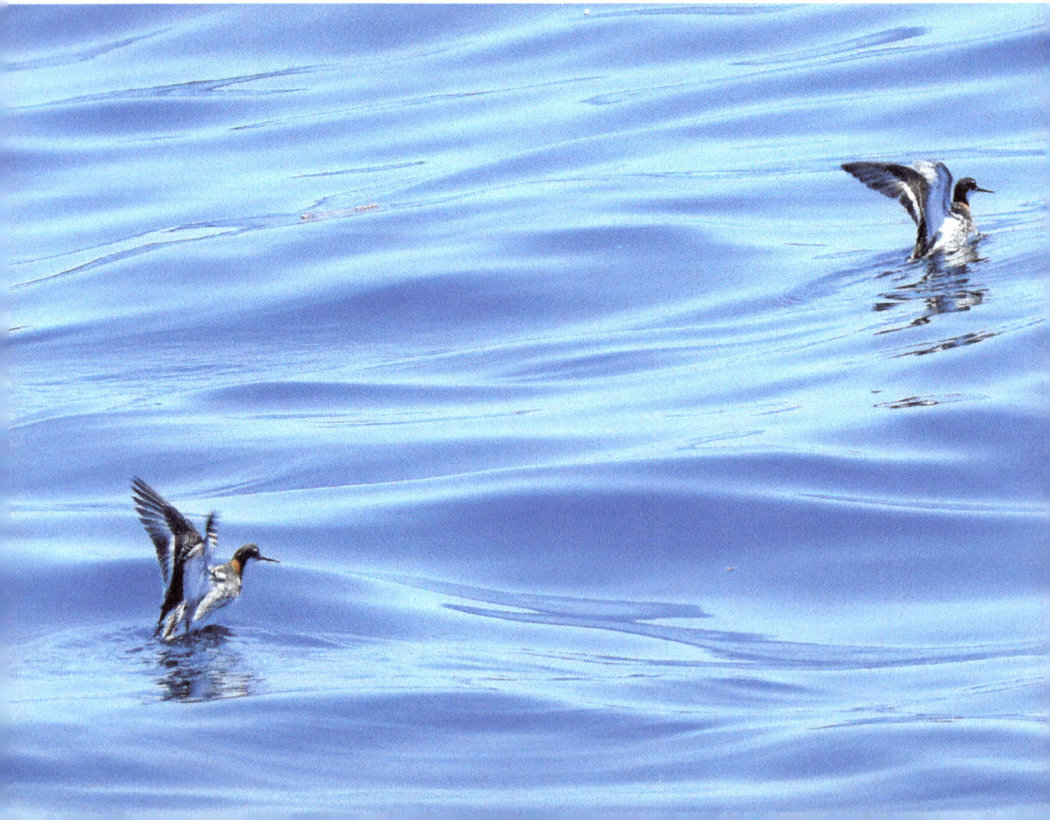

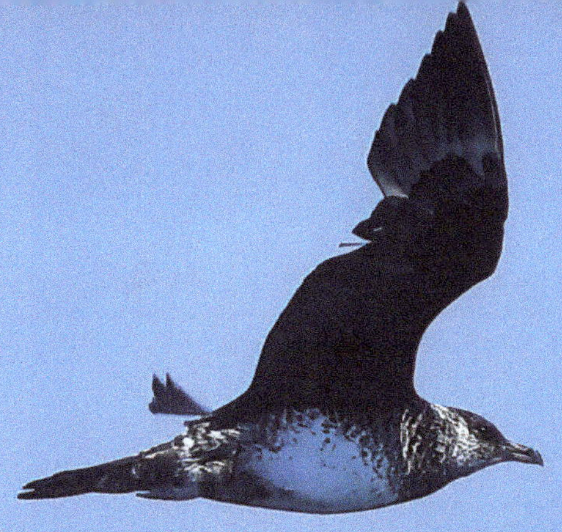

It was another Wednesday, and for Ingrid and me it was another whale watch, this time out of Boothbay Harbor. Once again, we were treated to a variety of sea birds moving around the boat. Bored tourists (it can take several hours to get to the whales) peppered us with questions:

- "What's that bird?"
- "Where do they sleep?"
- "What do they eat?"

Ingrid, being a teacher, is great and patient with her answers:

- "Great Shearwater"
- "They sleep on the water, putting one side of their brain to sleep at a time."
- "Fish, squid and krill"

I, on the other hand, tell the tourists about my Maine Big Year and for some reason, they nervously grab their children and move to the other side of the boat. Weird.

After about 90 minutes we hit a pod of Fin Whales, the second largest animal in the world (after the Blue Whale). While everyone thrilled to the behemoths moving around the boat, Ingrid and I noted the dramatic uptick in birds. The tiny Wilson's Storm-petrels were flitting about, feeding on krill, the same tiny shrimp that the whales were there for. Dozens of Great Shearwaters floated nearby and a lumbering Cory's Shearwater came close to our boat, all enjoying the feast.

Suddenly, in the distance, Ingrid noticed something chasing a Shearwater. It was a Pomarine Jaeger, the bully of the ocean. Jaegers will wait for another seabird to grab some food and then chase it unmercifully until it drops the food or regurgitates lunch. The Jaeger then settles in for a leisurely meal.

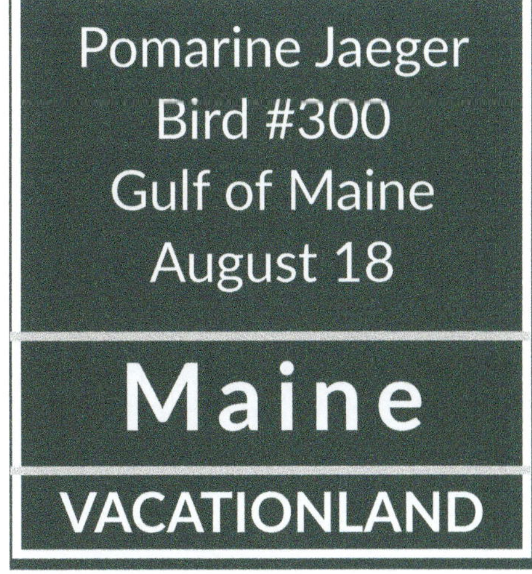

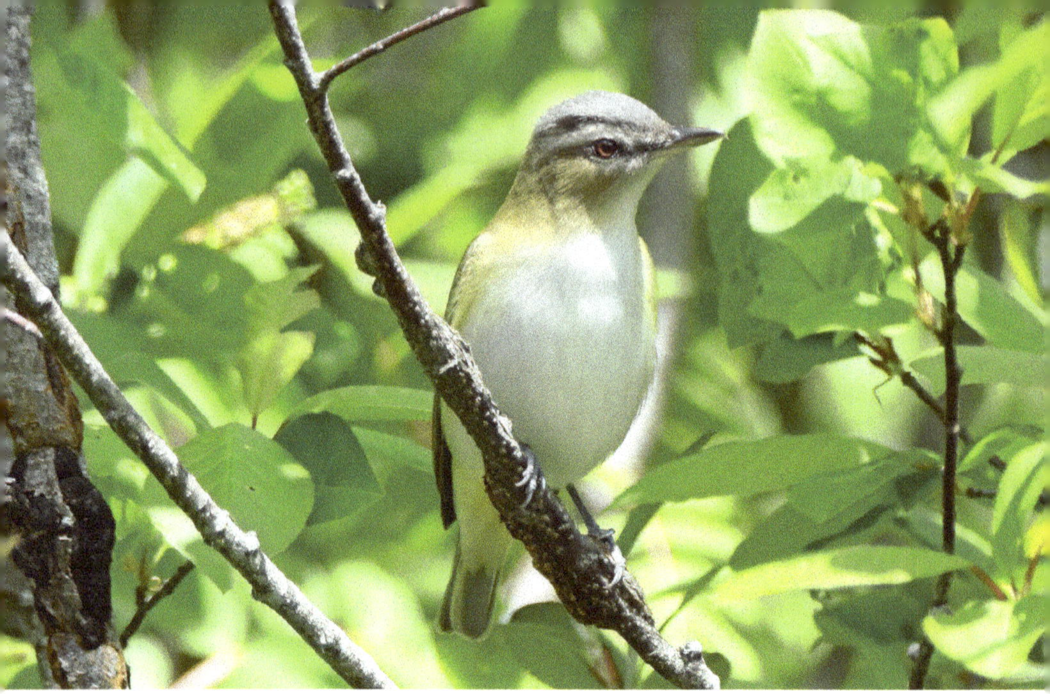

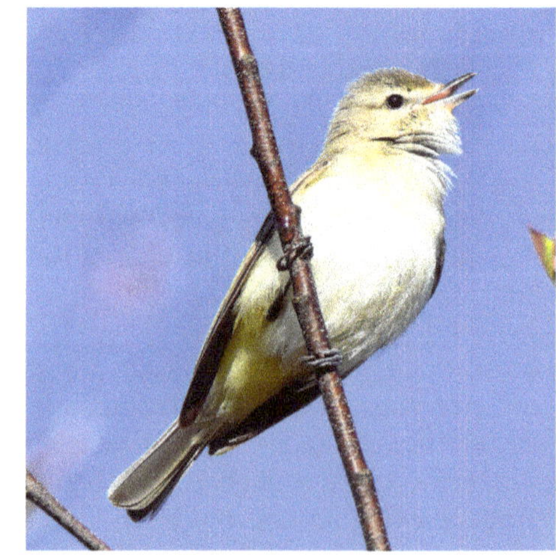

Vireos love to sing, and sing, and sing.

On a hot summer day when there isn't a breeze blowing and everything is still and oppressive, one bird will be singing over and over again, as many as 20,000 times in a day.

The Red-eyed Vireo sings constantly, a whistling phrase *Here-I-am, in-the-tree, look-up, at-the-top*. The song of this loquacious vireo can be so incessant that most of us tune it out.

The Warbling Vireo is heard primarily in the spring, and I love finding one sitting on a tree branch, ten feet up, belting out an enthusiastic rambling song repeatedly, ending each time with a high-pitched flourish.

The "white spectacled" Blue-headed Vireo sits high in trees and sings its whistle song over and over. A Blue-headed Vireo is rarely visible without a good pair of binoculars.

The less common Vireos in Maine are:

The White-eyed Vireo - white eyes and a yellow patch that curls around the eyes like spectacles.

The Yellow-throated - bright yellow and only reliably found in Maine at Brownfield Bog near Fryeburg.

And the hard to find Philadelphia Vireo, which we found sitting in an apple tree in a Cape Elizabeth cemetery.

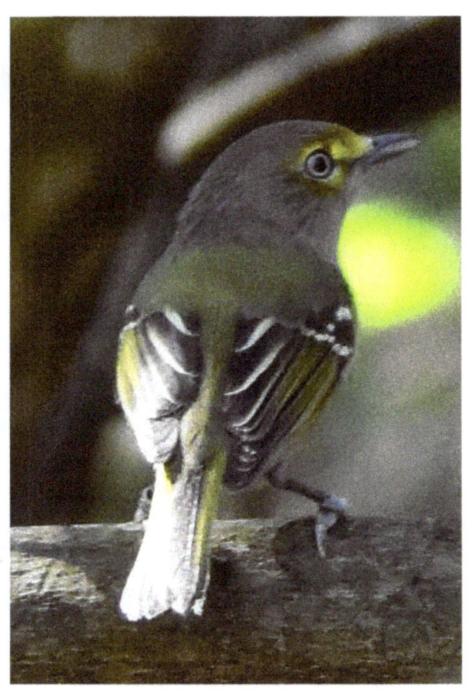

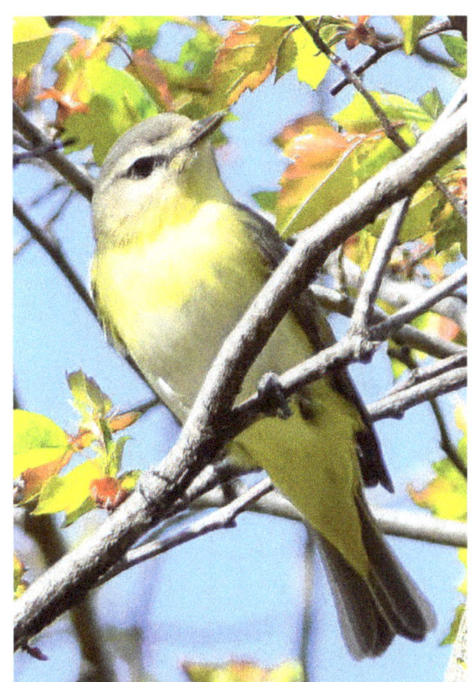

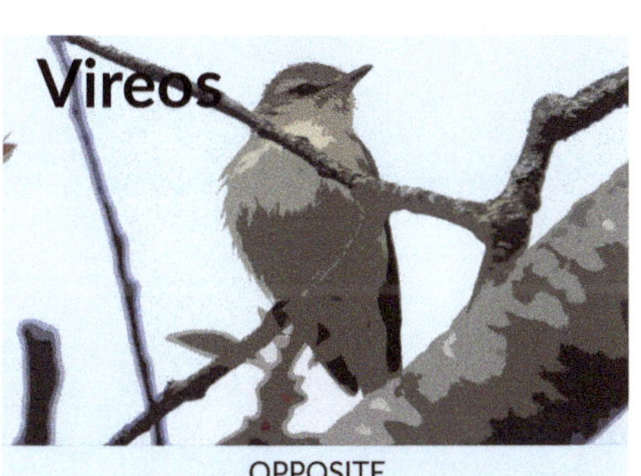

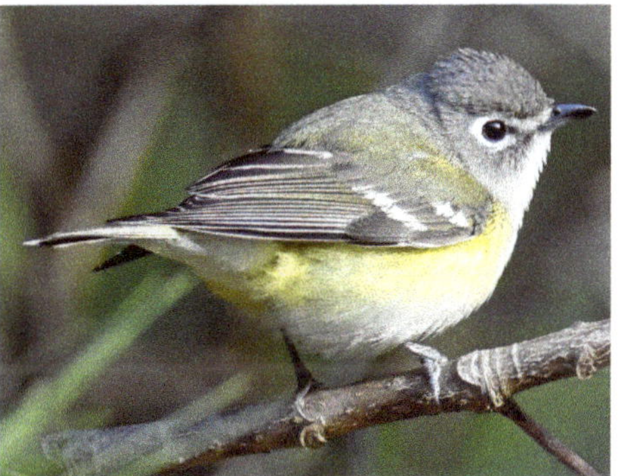

OPPOSITE
TOP Red-eyed Vireo (May 16)
BOTTOM Warbling Vireo (May 3)

CURRENT
TOP-LEFT White-eyed Vireo (May 11)
TOP-RIGHT Philadelphia Vireo (May 14)
MIDDLE Blue-headed Vireo (April 21)
RIGHT Yellow-throated Vireo (May 19)

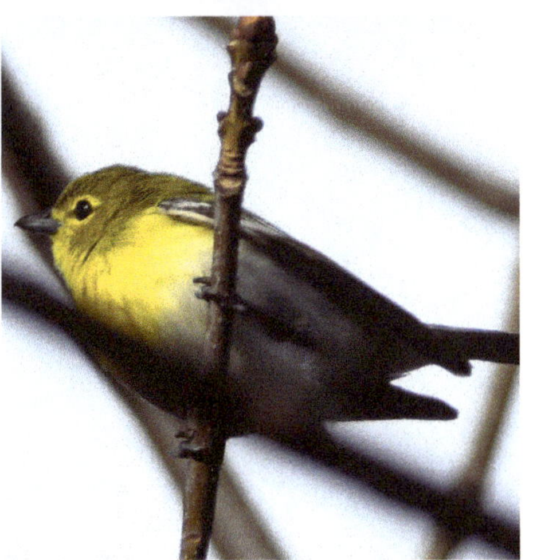

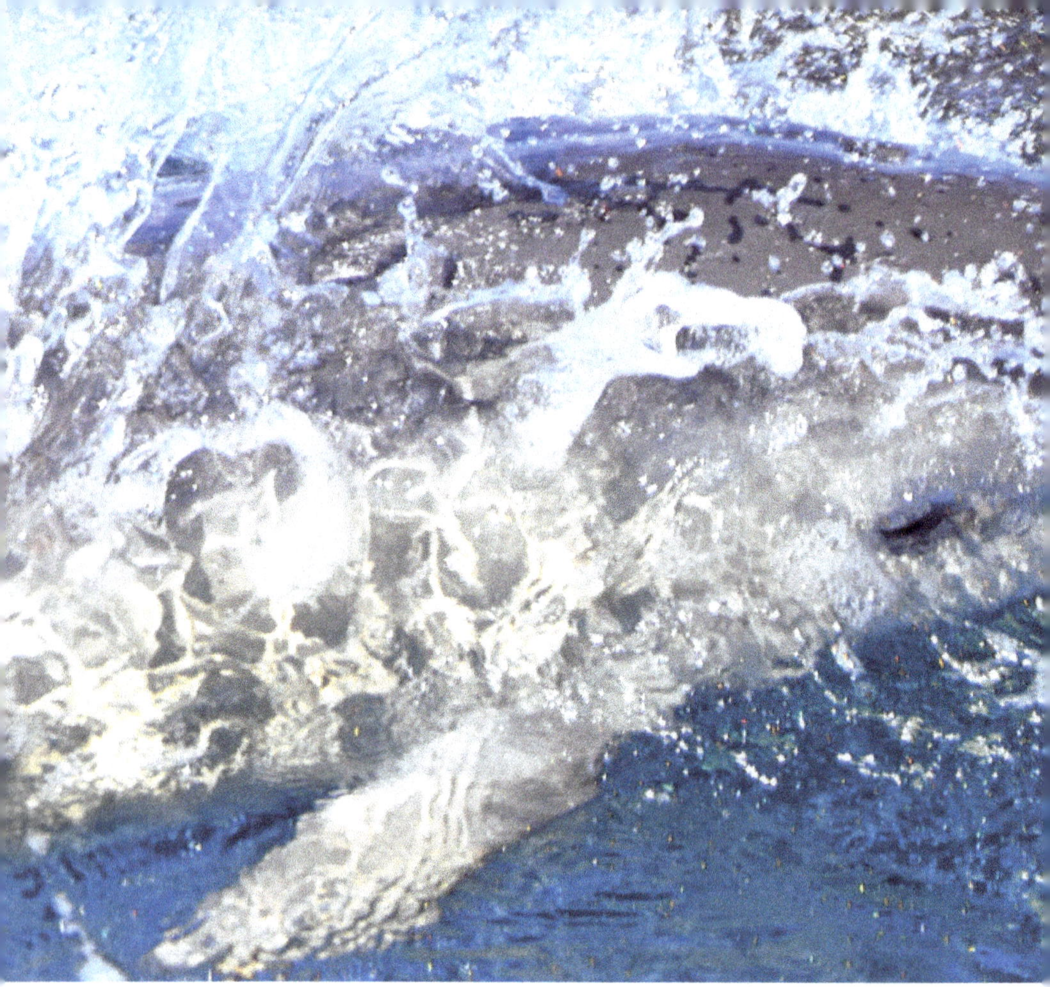

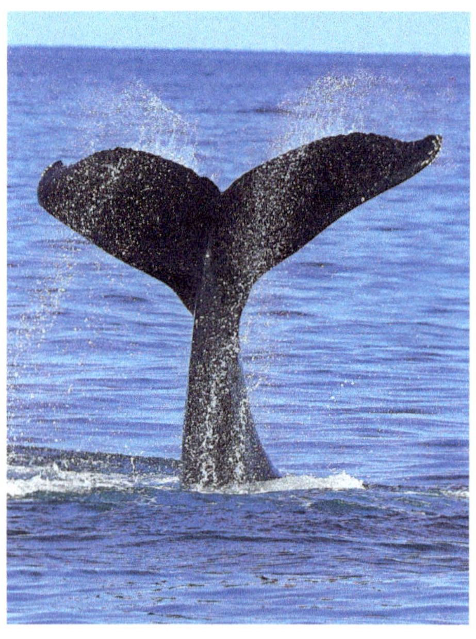

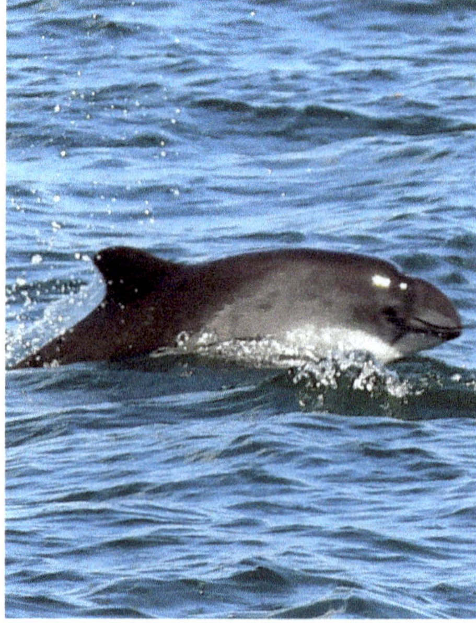

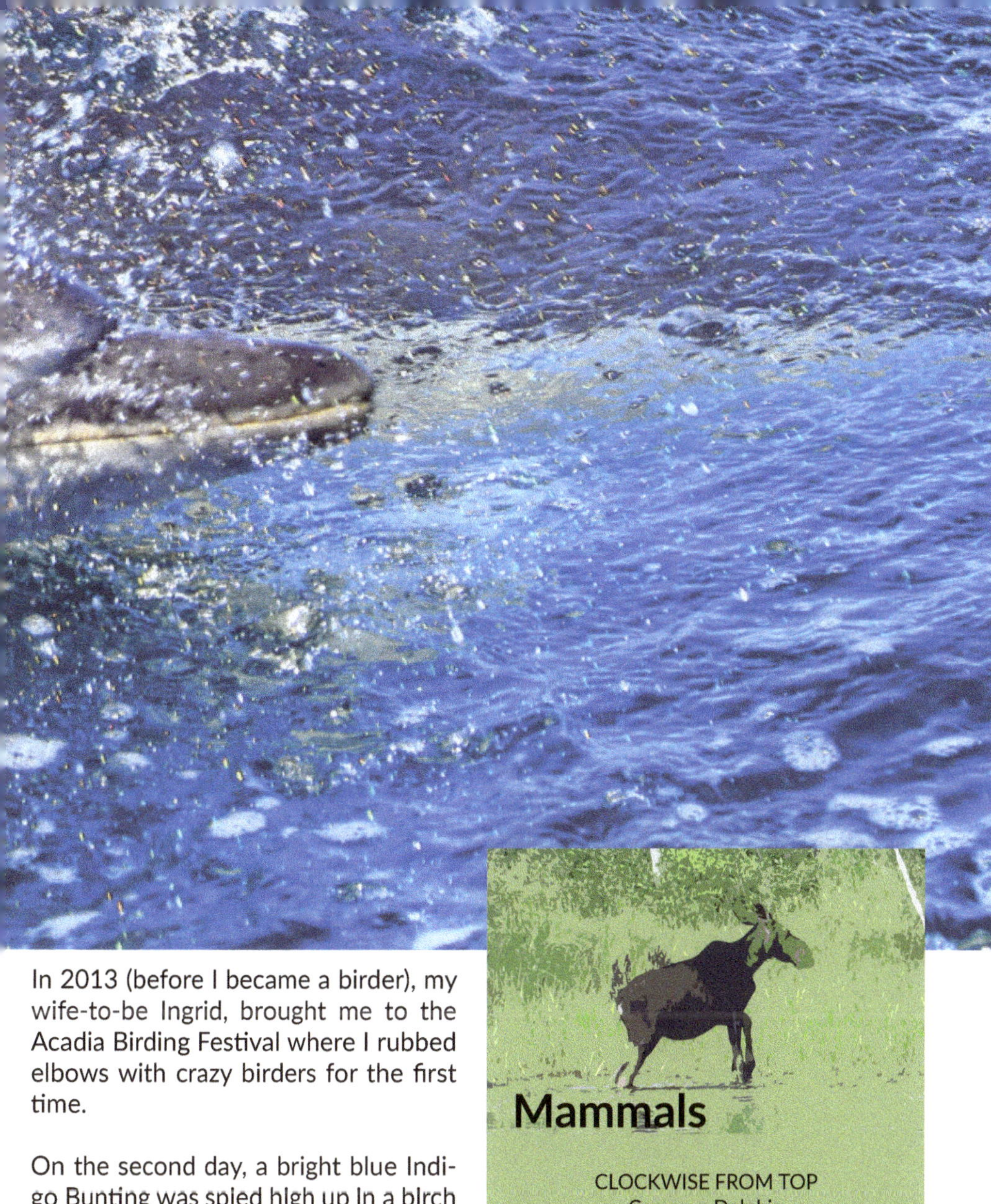

In 2013 (before I became a birder), my wife-to-be Ingrid, brought me to the Acadia Birding Festival where I rubbed elbows with crazy birders for the first time.

On the second day, a bright blue Indigo Bunting was spied high up in a birch tree. Our group froze and for the next 20 minutes *oohed-and-aahed* as the bird sang and posed.

It was then that I noticed a herd of White-tailed Deer browsing beneath the tree, not the least concerned about the birders on the hill.

I got excited about the deer and pointed them out to anyone who would listen, but I received apathetic shrugs

Mammals

CLOCKWISE FROM TOP
Common Dolphin
Harbor Porpoise
Humpback Whale

and folks went back to the bird.

A half dozen years later I still get excited about the occasional mammal I run across while looking for an elusive Indigo Bunting or the other birds of the Maine Big Year.

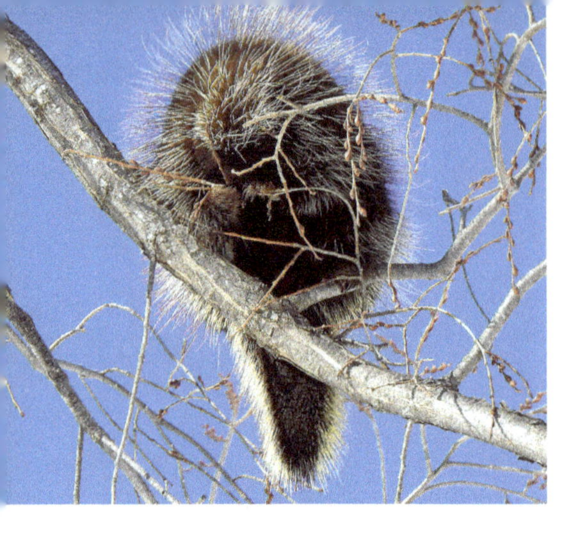
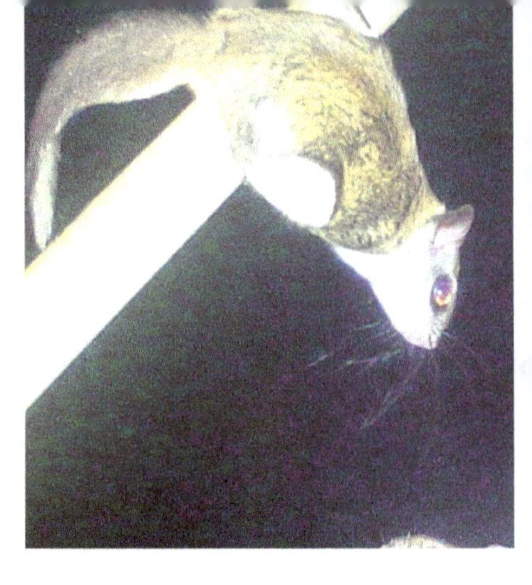
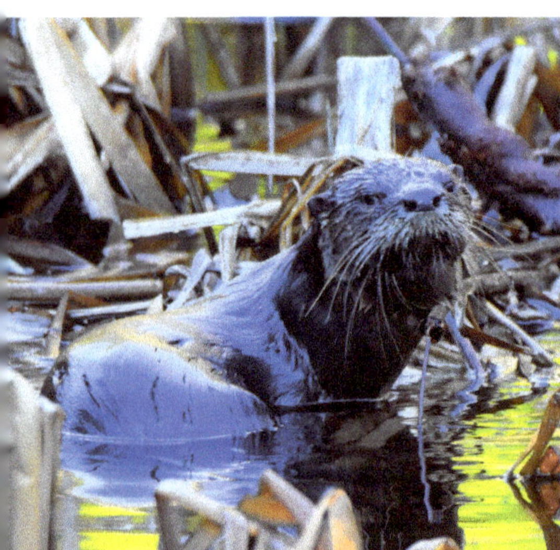
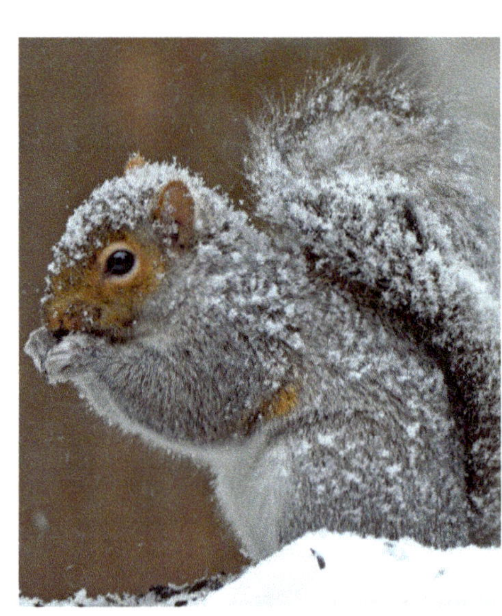
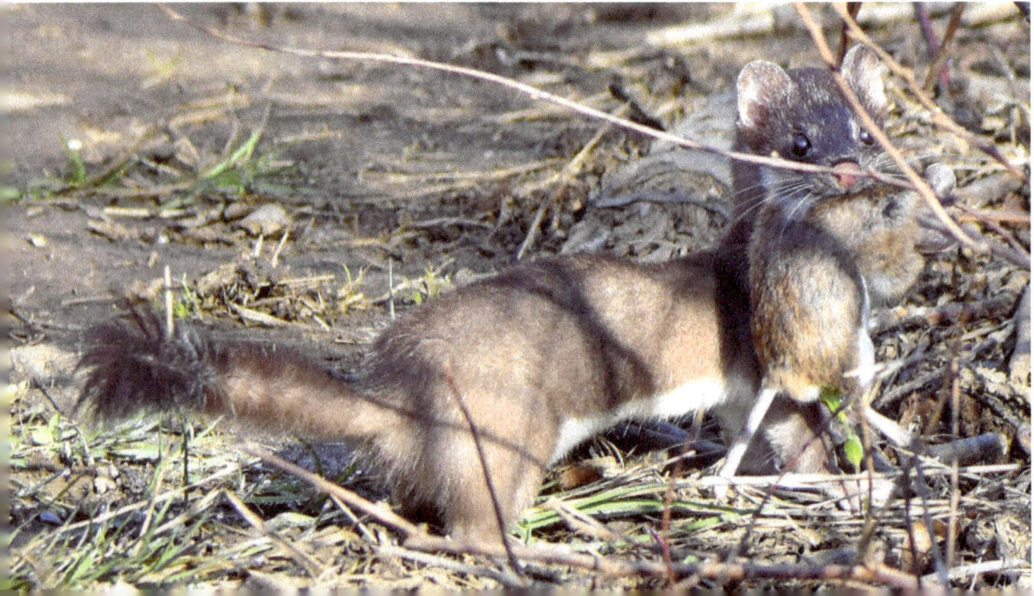

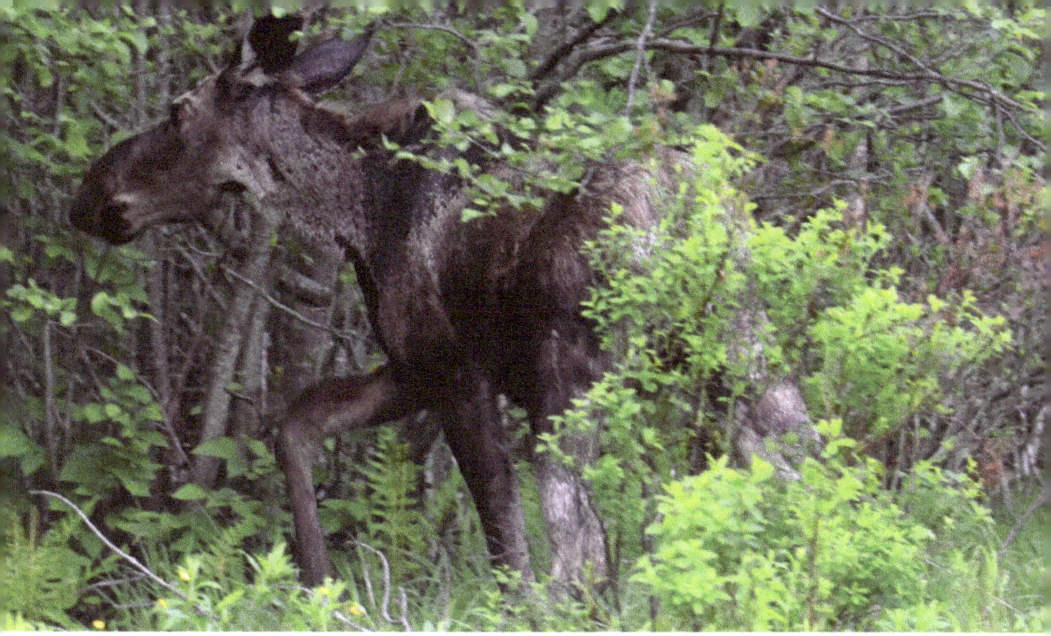

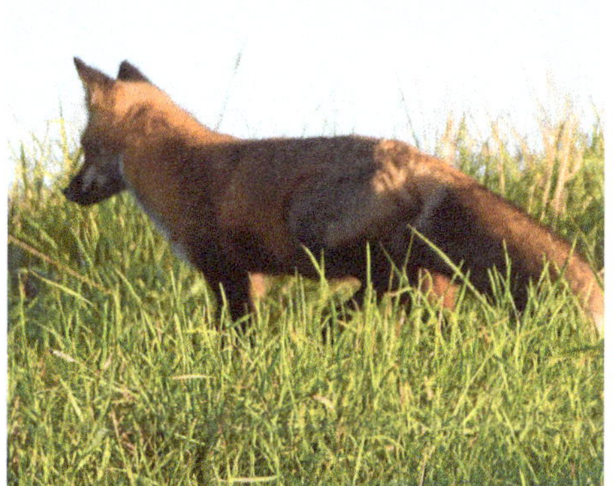

Mammals (cont.)

OPPOSITE
CLOCKWISE FROM TOP-LEFT
Porcupine
Flying Squirrels
Gray Squirrel
Short-tailed Weasel
River Otter

CURRENT
TOP Moose
CENTER Red Fox
BOTTOM White-tail Deer

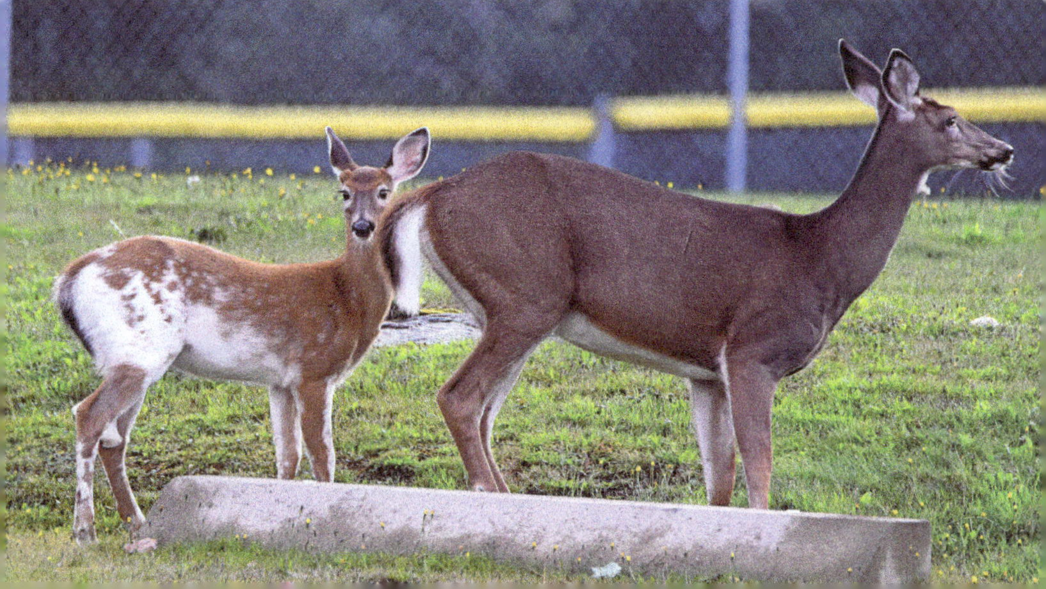

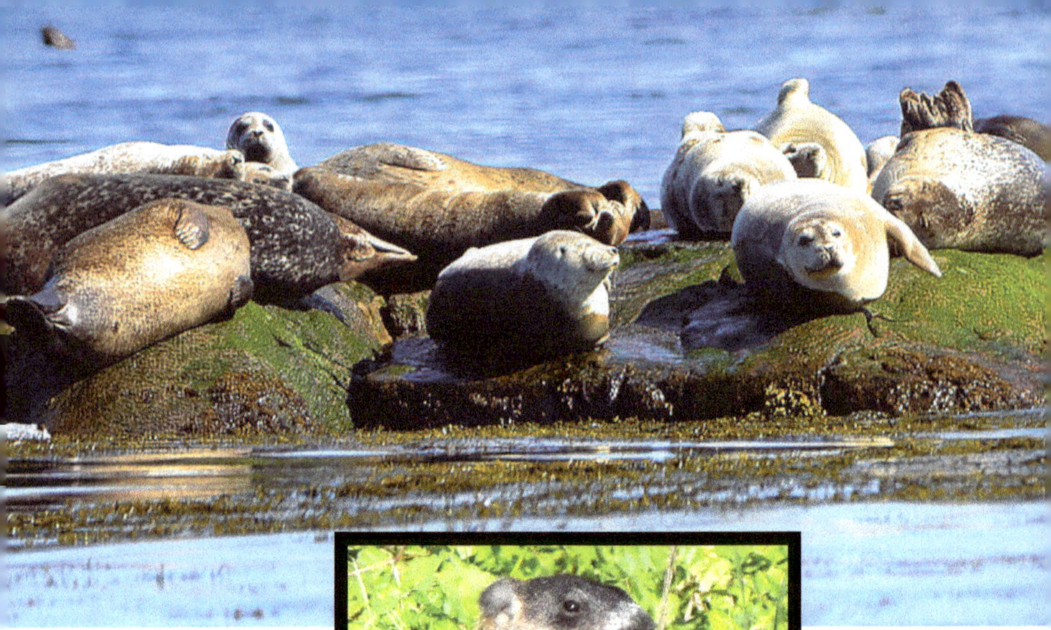

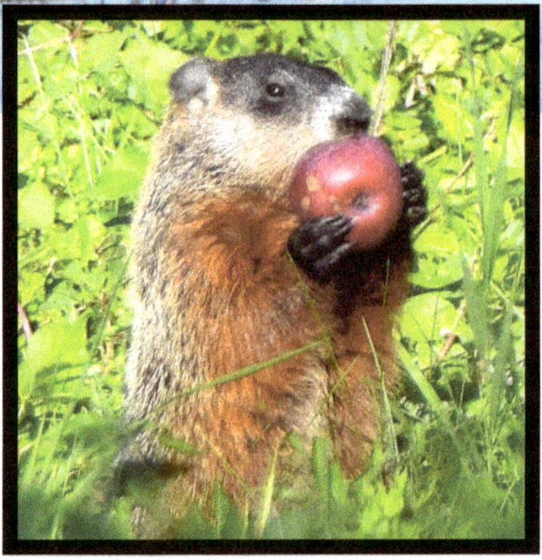

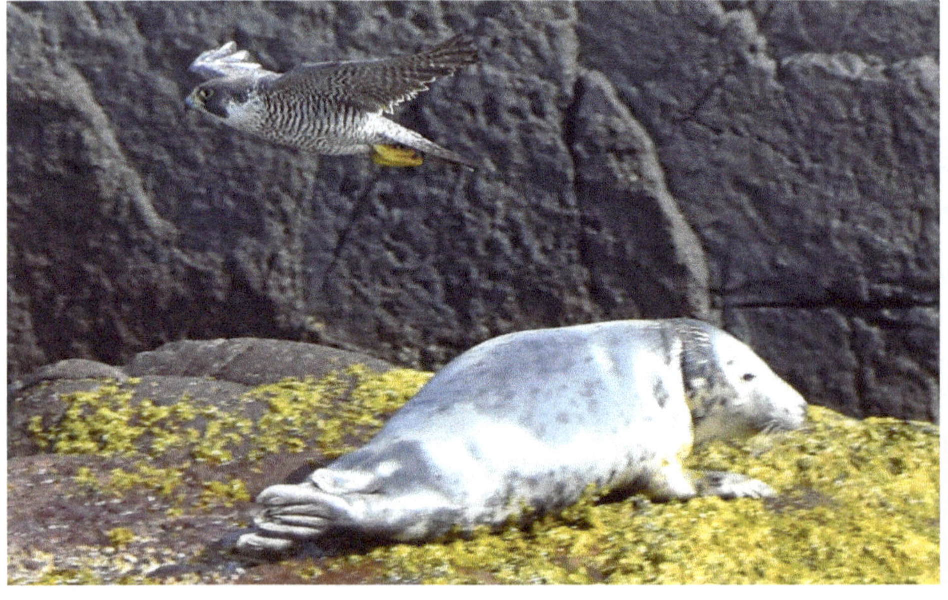

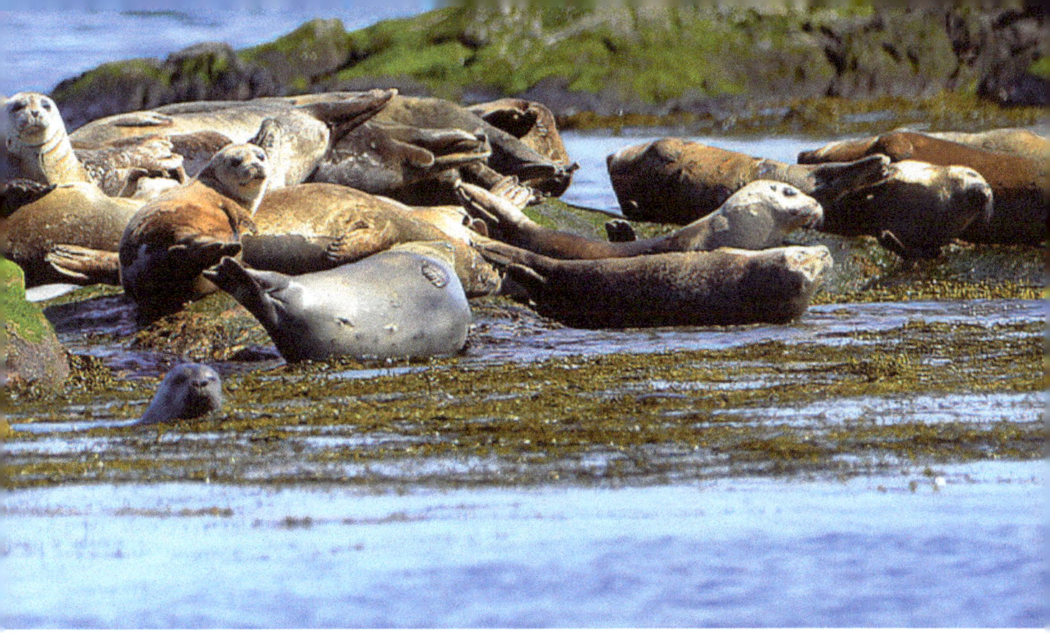

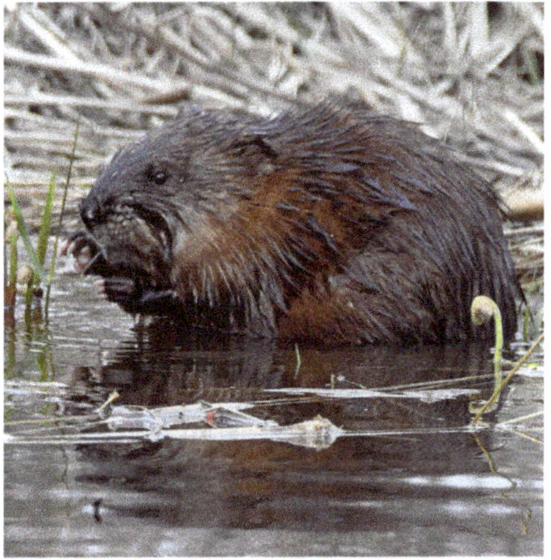

Mammals (cont.)

CLOCKWISE FROM TOP
Harbor Seals
Beaver
Muskrat
Eastern Red Bat
Gray Seal (and Peregrine Falcon)
Woodchuck

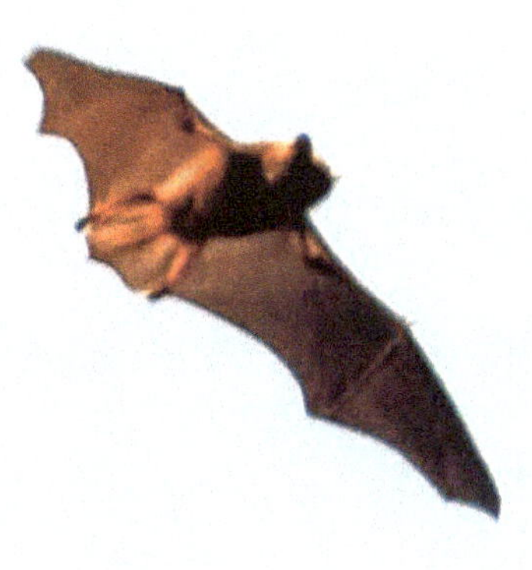

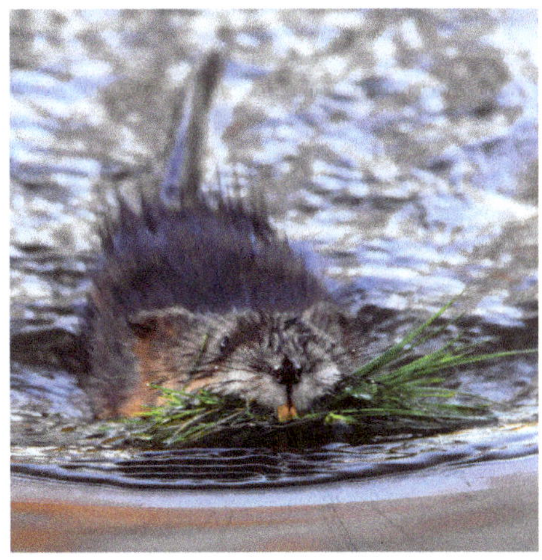

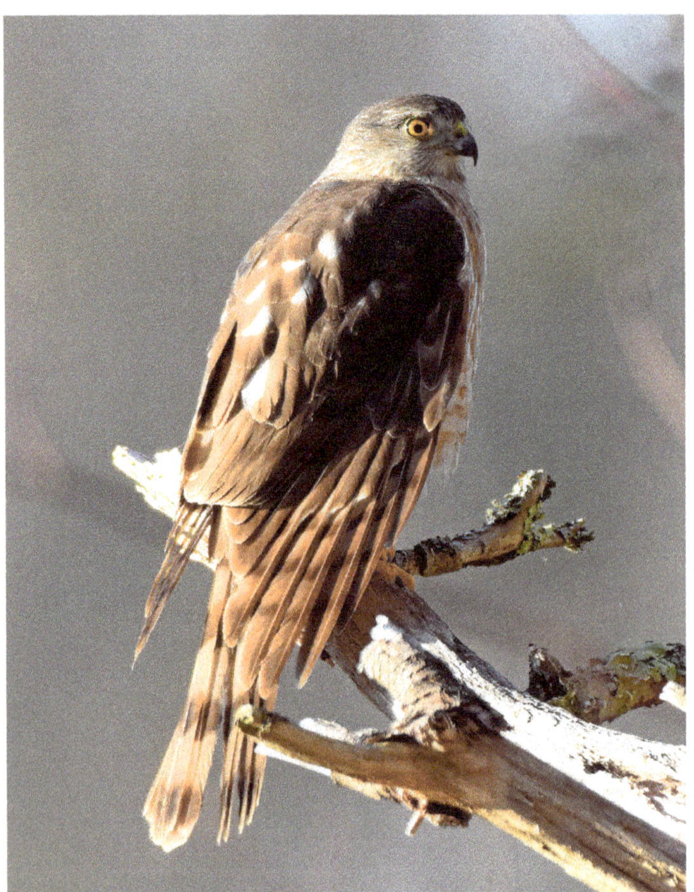

The two most common hawks in Maine are the Red-tailed and Cooper's Hawks. The former is the bird you see from the highway, perched high in an oak or pine tree. During the winter, Ingrid and I will count one every couple miles all the way from Kittery to our home in Wiscasset.

While a distinctive red-tail can be seen in flight, the best way to identify a sitting Red-tailed Hawk is by the wide belly band around its chest.

The call or scream of the Red-tailed Hawk is famous. Its *Cheeeeeeeewv* is used in seemingly every movie western ever made, often while showing an Eagle flying overhead, which drives birders crazy!!!!

If you see a hawk in the woods or on the edge of a field, acrobatically flying through the trees chasing songbirds, it's probably a Cooper's Hawk.

The Cooper's Hawk will fly with a flap-flap-glide cadence, even through the underbrush and when attacking. It often attacks from below, flying a few feet off the ground before rising up to its prey, sometimes using a rock or bush as a shield to surprise the target.

The Cooper's Hawk has a closely related and nearly identical relative, the Sharp-shinned Hawk. "Sharpies" are smaller, have a squarer tail and a tiny round head, but it is difficult to tell them apart.

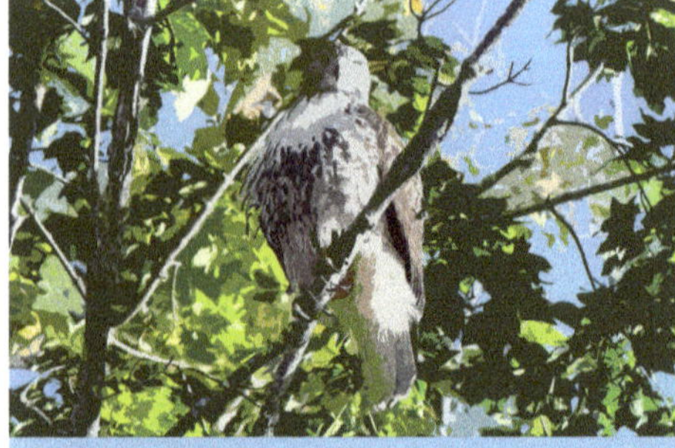

Hawks

TOP Cooper's Hawk (January 1)
OPPOSITE Red-tailed Hawk (January 1)

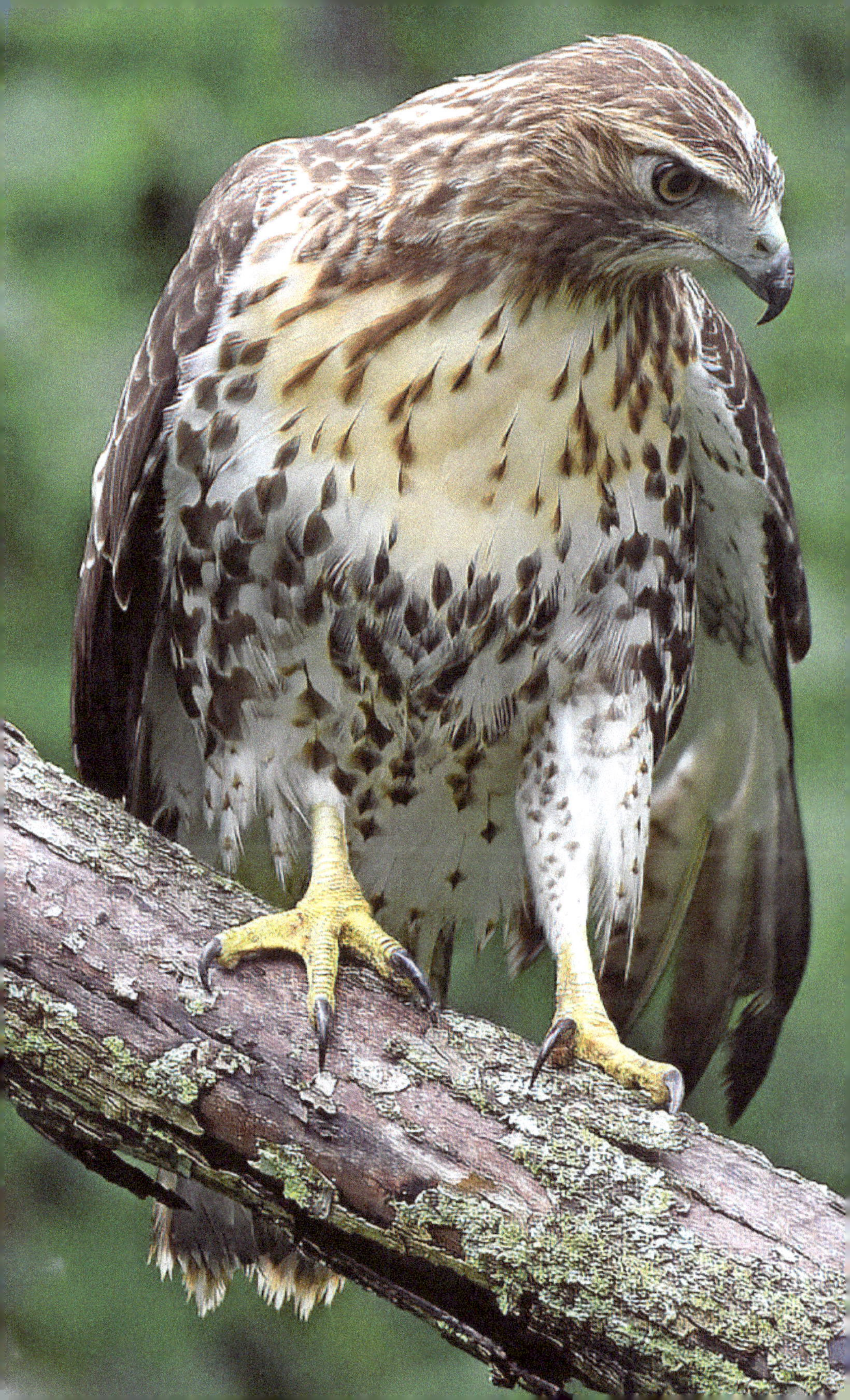

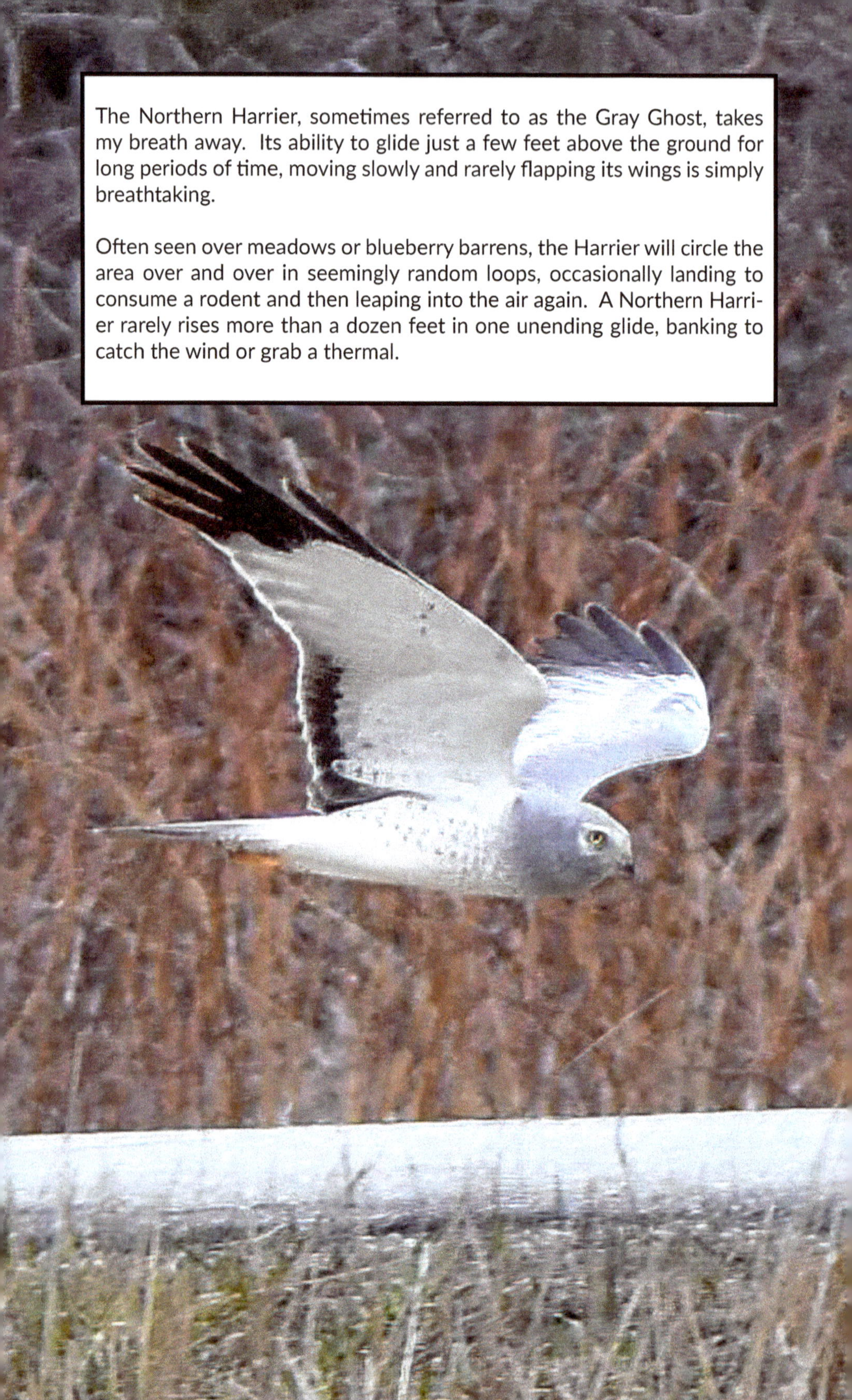

The Northern Harrier, sometimes referred to as the Gray Ghost, takes my breath away. Its ability to glide just a few feet above the ground for long periods of time, moving slowly and rarely flapping its wings is simply breathtaking.

Often seen over meadows or blueberry barrens, the Harrier will circle the area over and over in seemingly random loops, occasionally landing to consume a rodent and then leaping into the air again. A Northern Harrier rarely rises more than a dozen feet in one unending glide, banking to catch the wind or grab a thermal.

Hawks (cont.)

OPPOSITE Northern Harrier (January 11)

CURRENT
TOP Sharp-shinned Hawk (January 1)
MIDDLE Rough-legged Hawk (January 8)
BOTTOM Northern Goshawk (Jan 13)

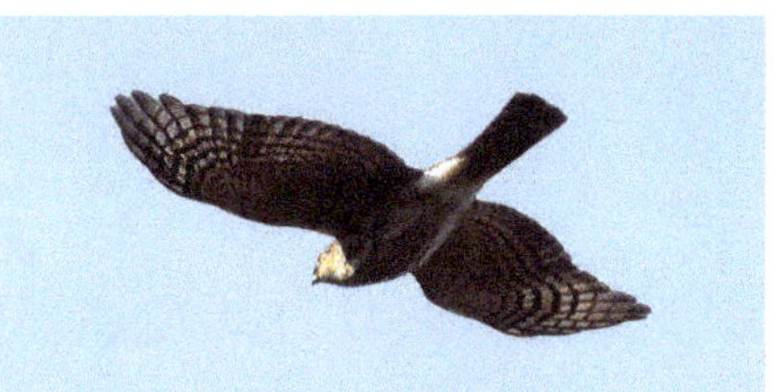

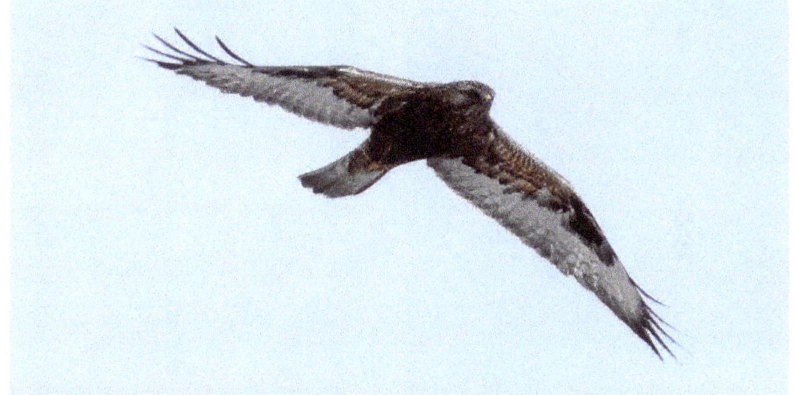

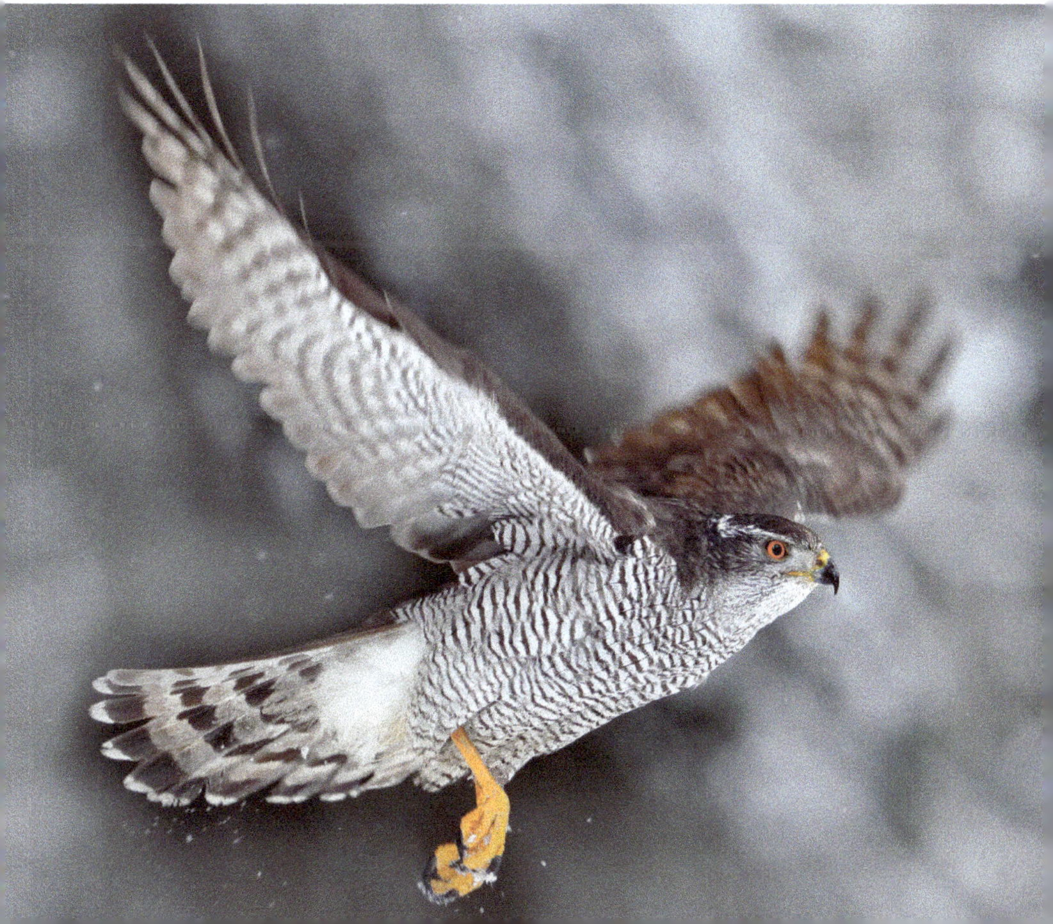

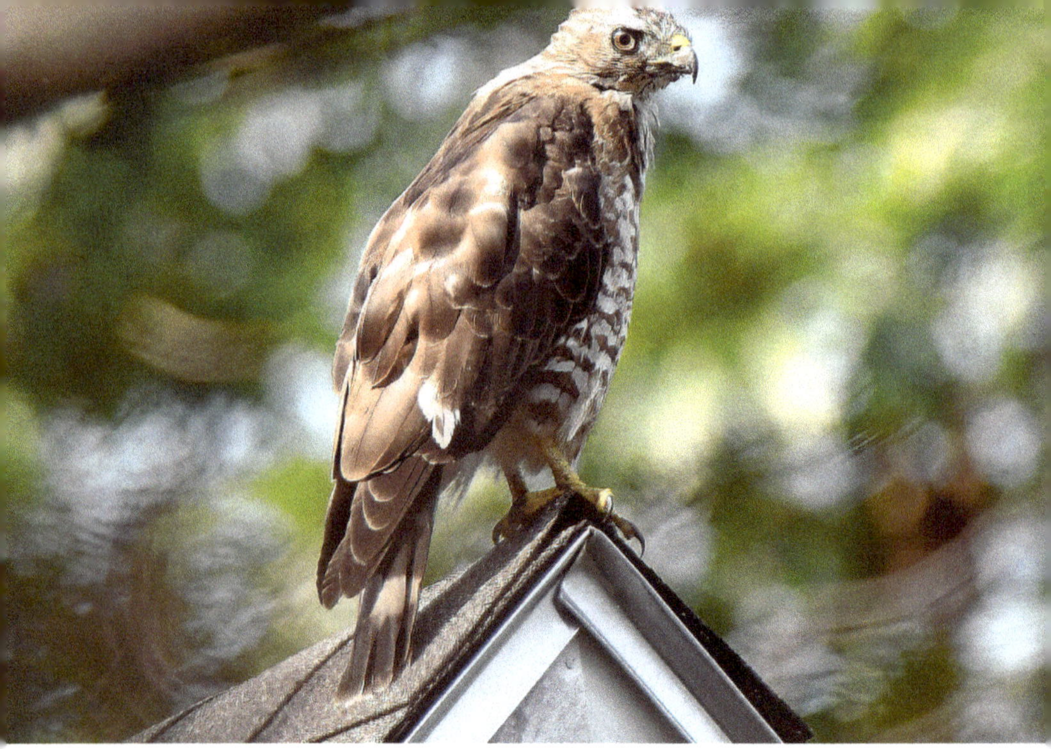

The Bradbury Mountain Hawk Watch takes place each spring atop an enormous granite uplift in Pownal. Visitors are treated to a 280 degree view of the surrounding towns and the nearby ocean. An official counter is joined by volunteers to scan the skies for raptors moving north to their breeding territories.

At Bradbury in late April, Ingrid and I observed a spectacular migration of Broad-winged Hawks soaring on thermals as they moved north.

Most raptors migrate as individuals, but Broad-wingeds move in small groups or even large flocks.

We picked the perfect day to visit Bradbury Mountain as the number of birds jumped 400% from previous week and we saw Bald Eagles, Ospreys, Turkey Vultures, Sharp-shinned Hawks and especially Broad-winged Hawks.

An estimated 30 Broad-wingeds flew by in 90 minutes, and many of them came quite close to us.

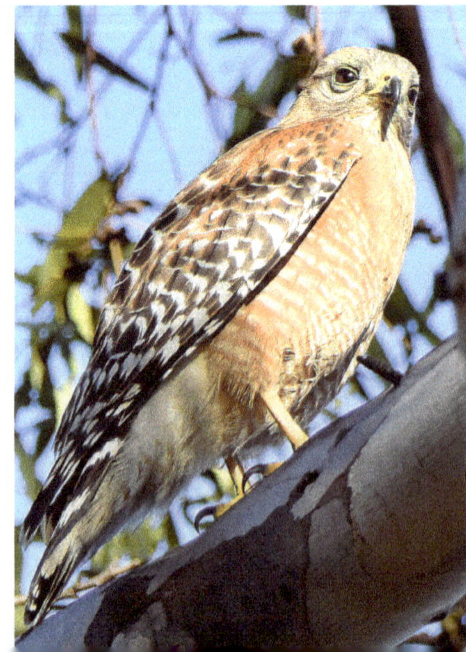

Hawks (cont.)

LEFT Broad-winged Hawk (March 22)
BOTTOM Red-shouldered Hawk (January 7)

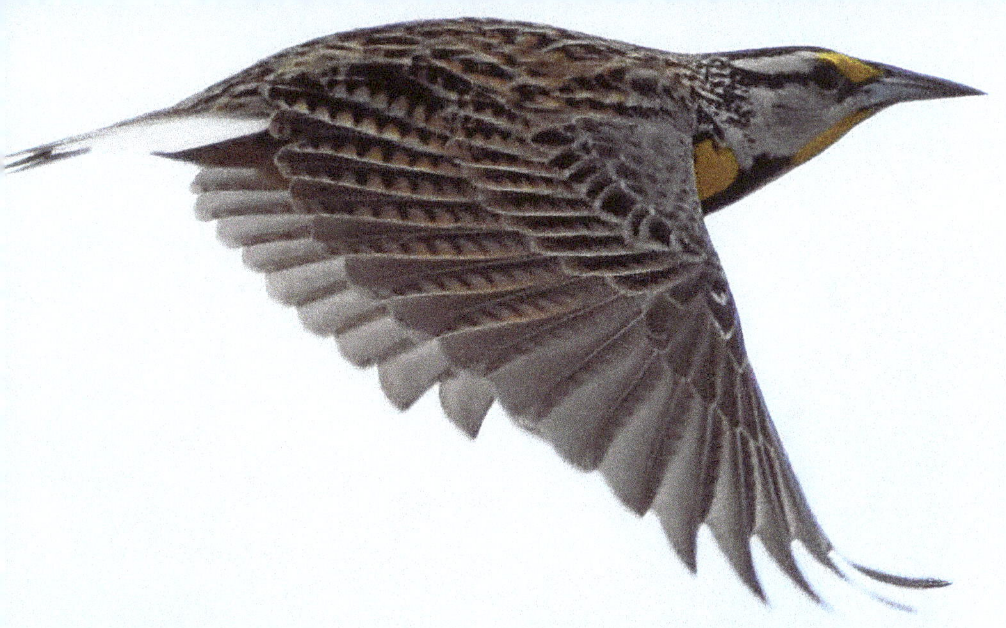

Before humans began to dominate the continent, natural fires would burn a forest to the ground. In the ashes, grasses and small pine trees would quickly arise, and a number of birds evolved to depend on this habitat.

Over the last few centuries, humans have stepped in to extinguish these fires, putting the birds that need grassland habitat in peril.

The Captain William Fitzgerald Conservation Area in Brunswick, California Fields in Poland and Kennebunk Plains Preserves are burned periodically to mimic this once natural environment. These "artificial" grassland habitats are a great place to see birds rarely seen anywhere else.

In these locations you'll find: Eastern Meadowlarks, Vesper, Field, Grasshopper and Clay-colored sparrows; Prairie Warblers; Bobolinks, and Eastern Towhees.

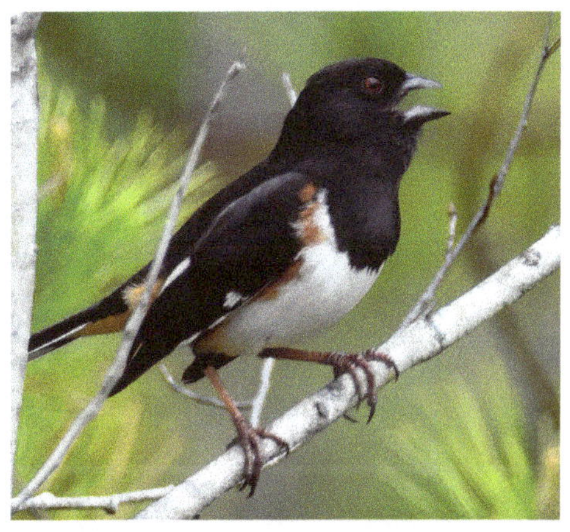

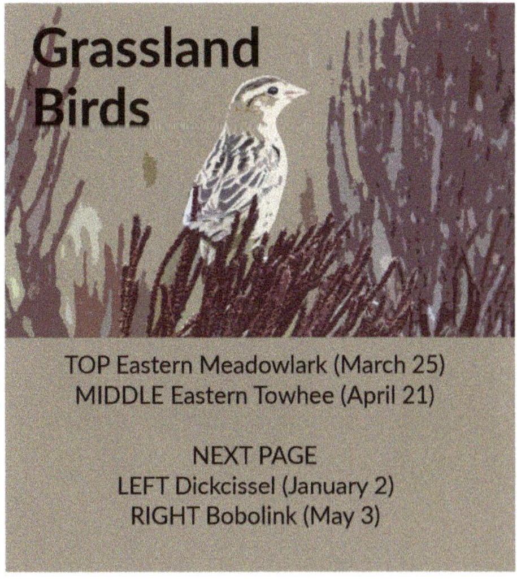

TOP Eastern Meadowlark (March 25)
MIDDLE Eastern Towhee (April 21)

NEXT PAGE
LEFT Dickcissel (January 2)
RIGHT Bobolink (May 3)

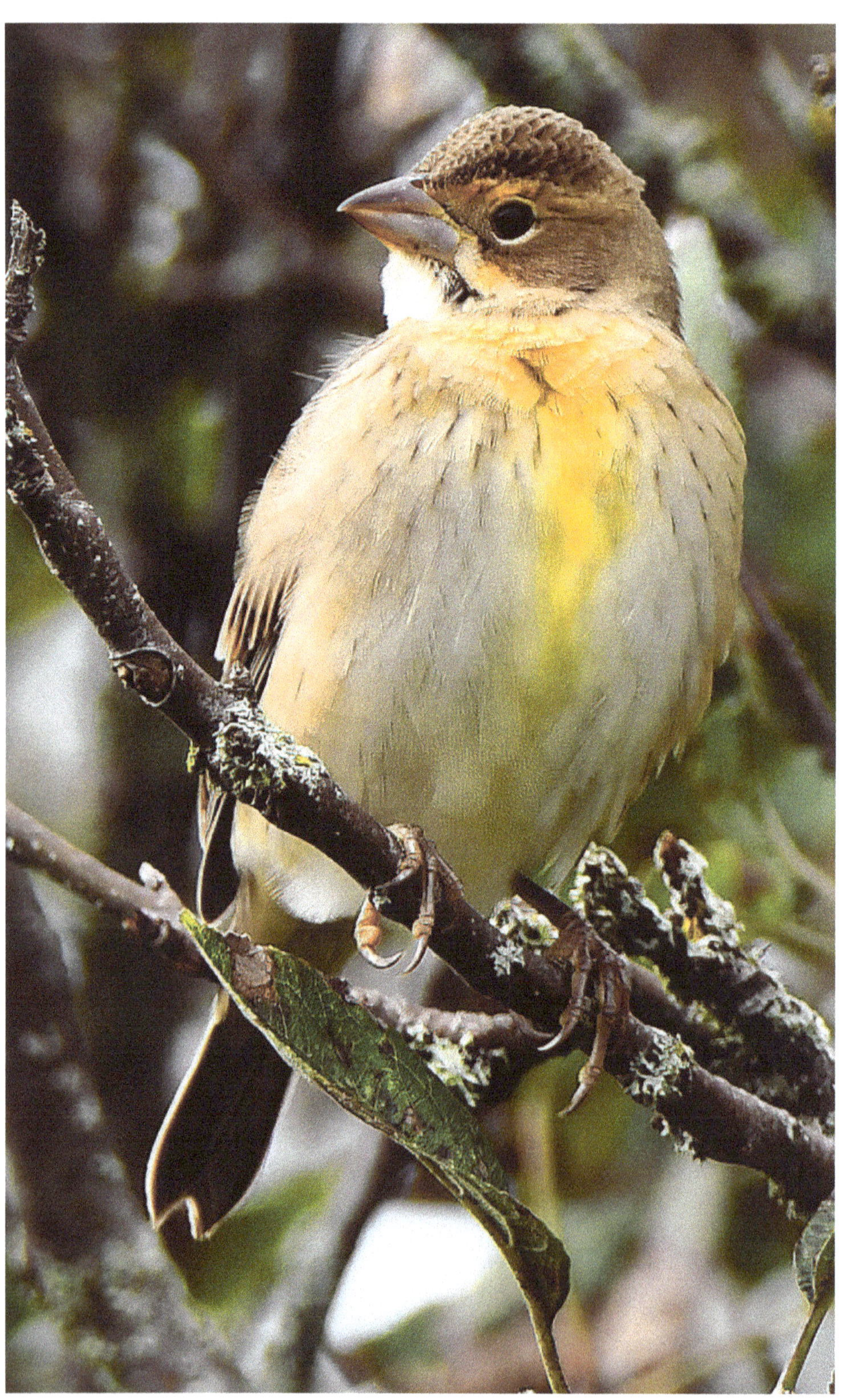

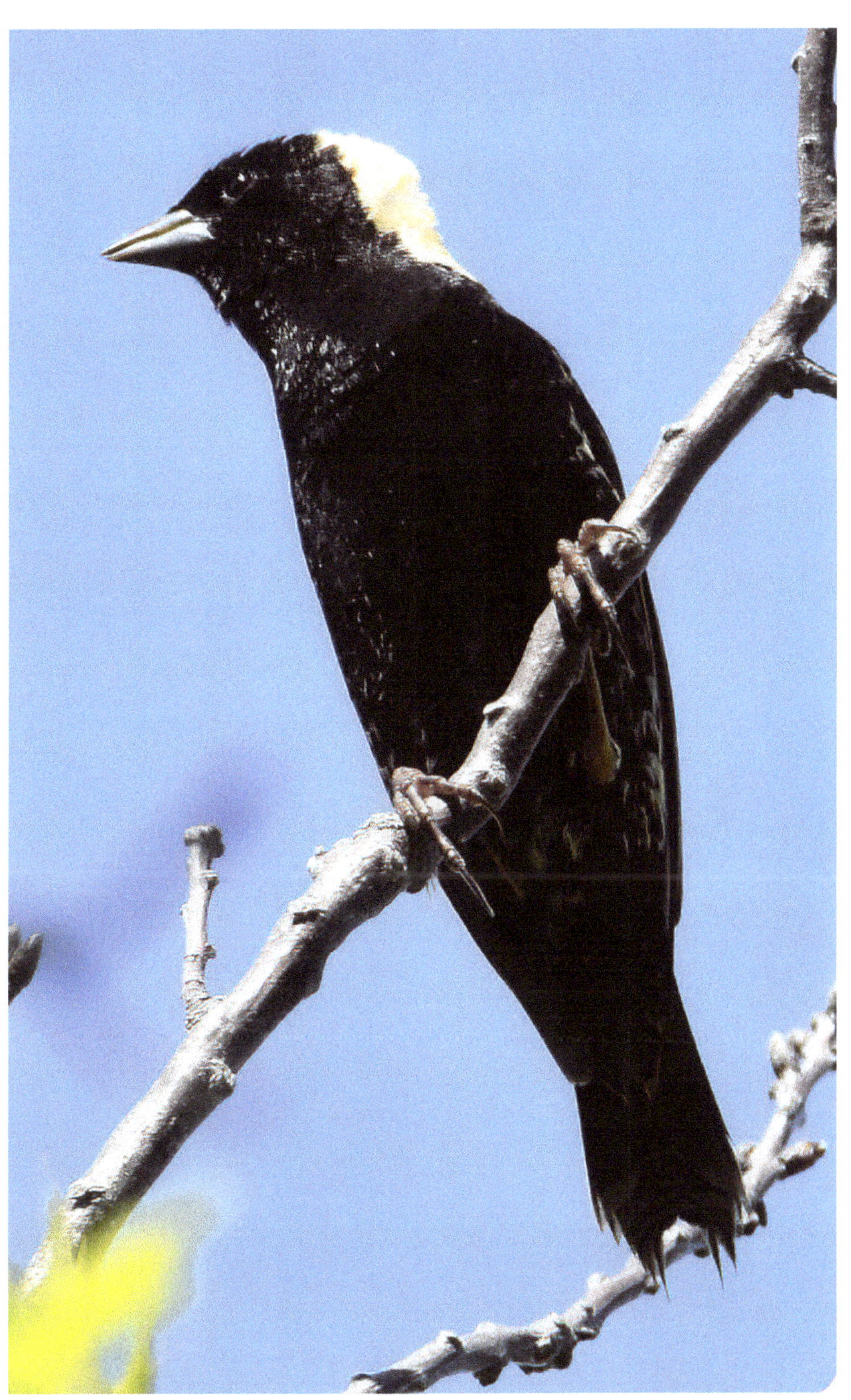

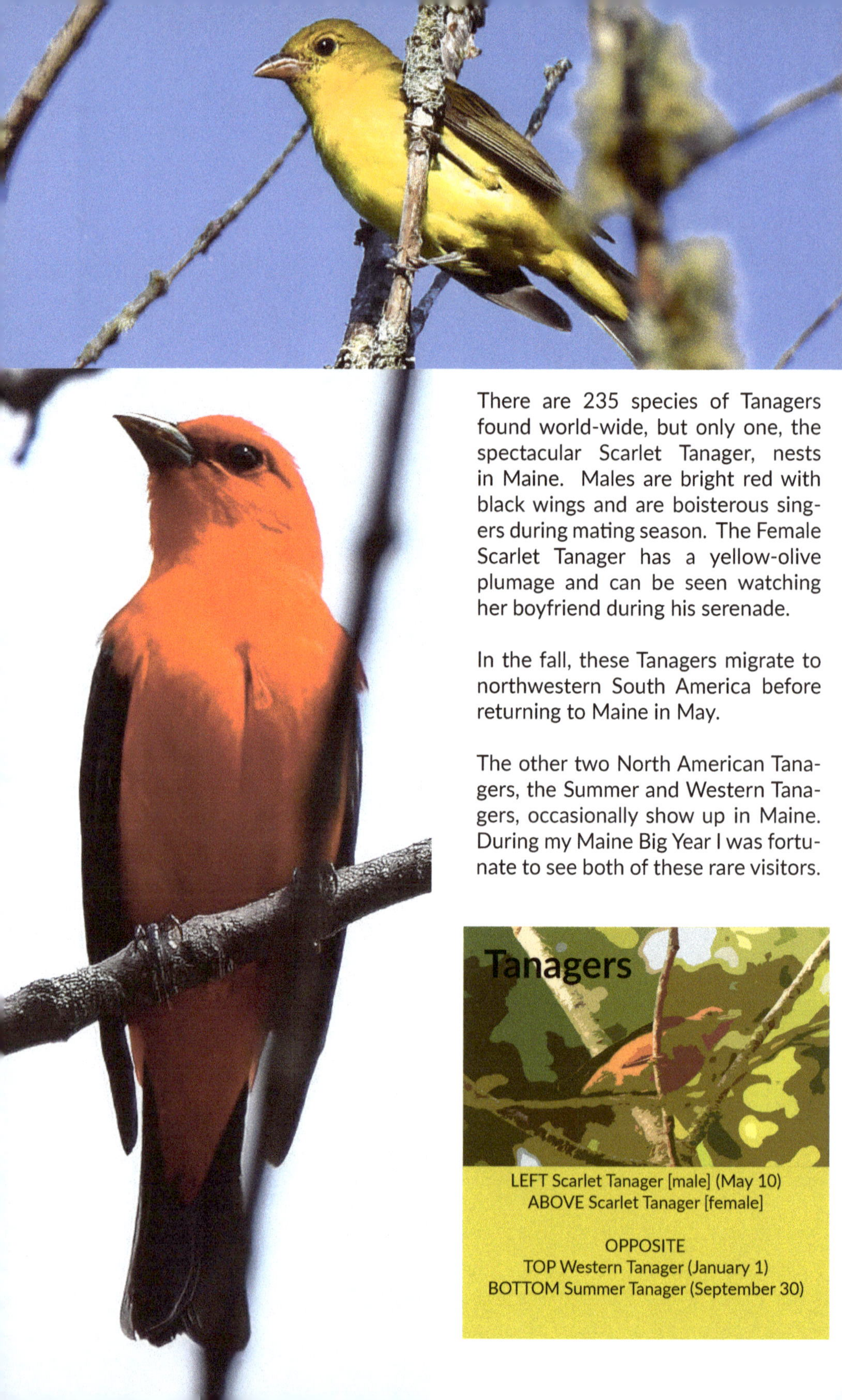

There are 235 species of Tanagers found world-wide, but only one, the spectacular Scarlet Tanager, nests in Maine. Males are bright red with black wings and are boisterous singers during mating season. The Female Scarlet Tanager has a yellow-olive plumage and can be seen watching her boyfriend during his serenade.

In the fall, these Tanagers migrate to northwestern South America before returning to Maine in May.

The other two North American Tanagers, the Summer and Western Tanagers, occasionally show up in Maine. During my Maine Big Year I was fortunate to see both of these rare visitors.

Tanagers

LEFT Scarlet Tanager [male] (May 10)
ABOVE Scarlet Tanager [female]

OPPOSITE
TOP Western Tanager (January 1)
BOTTOM Summer Tanager (September 30)

In December of 2020, there was a report of a juvenile female Western Tanager at the Cliff House, a premier resort in Cape Neddick. I was a good 90 minutes away and I'd only have about 45 minutes of daylight once I arrived.

After parking the car in the Cliff House lot, it was already getting dark with no other birders around.

Rushing down the trail where the bird was sighted that afternoon, I was horrified to come upon a wedding (tuxedos, gowns, etc). I waited 10 minutes for the wedding to end as tromping around the ceremony with my camera, boots and binoculars might be a little tacky.

Once the last guest left, I continued

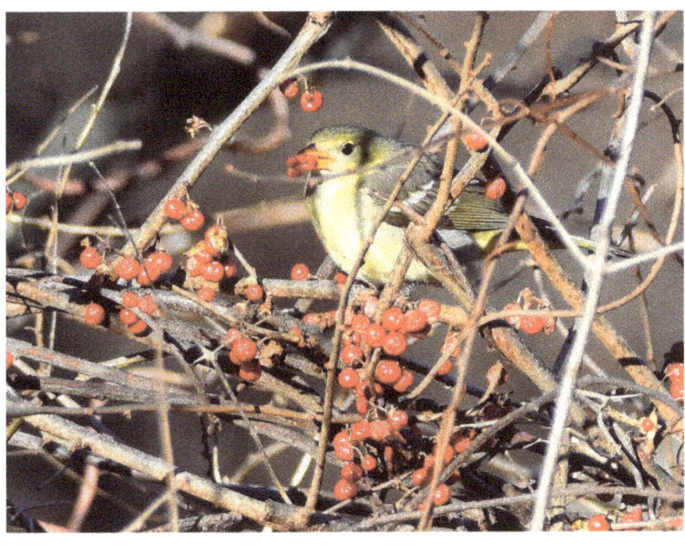

down the trail. Five minutes later, the Western Tanager came into view for a few rather dark photos.

Ingrid and I had seen Western Tanagers before while birding out West, but sighting one east of the Mississippi is quite exciting.

The same bird was still at the Cliff House on January 1, a nice start for the Maine Big Year!!!

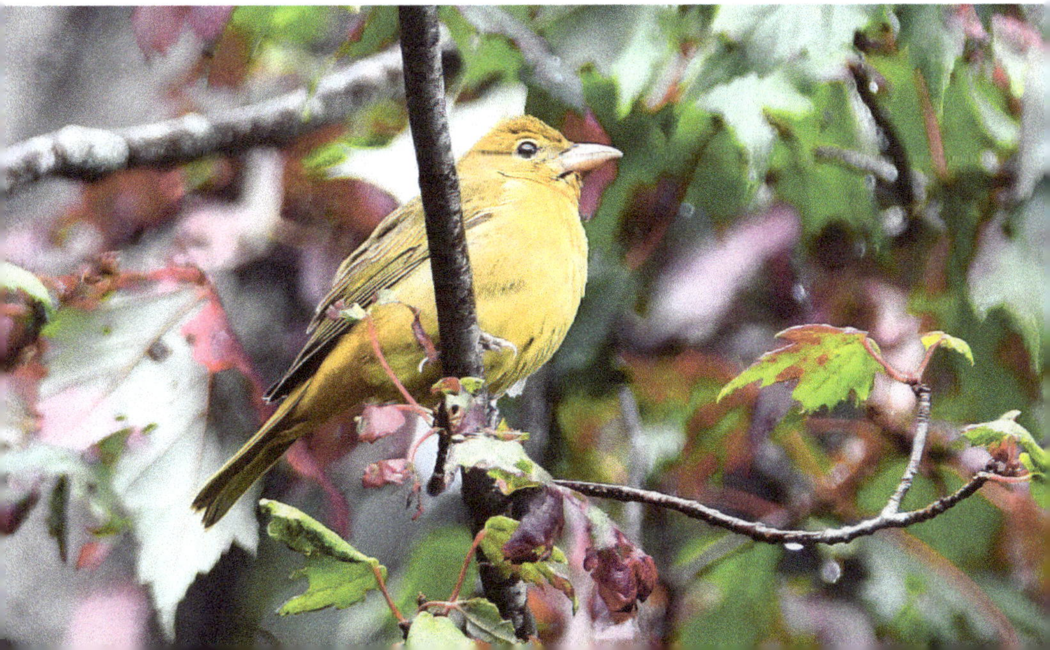

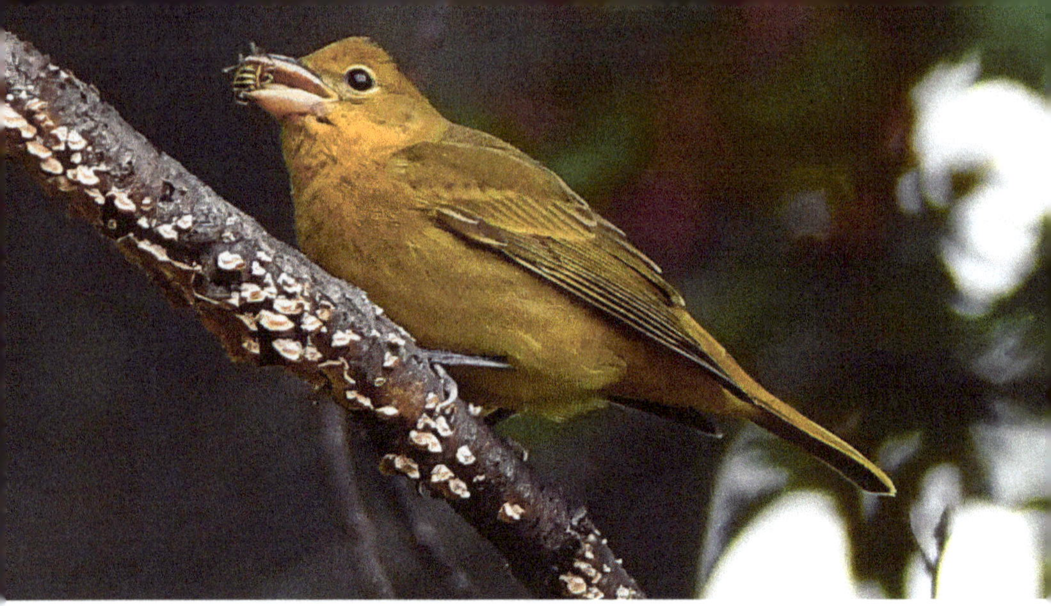

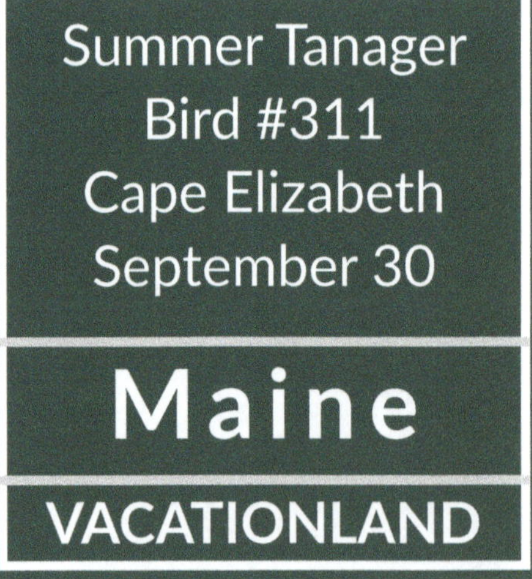

A Big Year is 25% planning, 25% skill, 25% execution and 90% luck. I know the math doesn't work, but the events of September 30 made me realize how big a role luck actually plays.

I was in the field at dawn and had spent six hours looking for birds in Cape Elizabeth and Biddeford Pool. I observed some really great species but nothing new.

Arriving home mid-afternoon, I made myself a salad for lunch (ok it was a ham and cheese sandwich), sat in my recliner and flipped on the TV to catch up on the day's events.

Suddenly, some movement from the trees outside the window caught my eye, something yellow. At first I thought it was a Baltimore Oriole, but the color was wrong. I grabbed some binoculars and noticed the bird's huge bill. This was a Summer Tanager!!!

Summer Tanagers are common summer birds across the American South, but are a rarity in Maine.

I grabbed my camera, ran outside in my stocking feet and took as many photos as I could.

I texted Ingrid and she rushed home. Fortunately, school was over for the day, or I fear Ingrid might have put one of her 4th graders in charge of her class and left anyway.

It took about 20 minutes for us to relocate the bird, but when we did, the Summer Tanager put on quite a show. It flew from tree to tree in the backyard and appeared to be feeding on yellow jackets.

That day, I drove and hiked all over the state of Maine and then found a true rarity while watching television at home.

That's all luck.

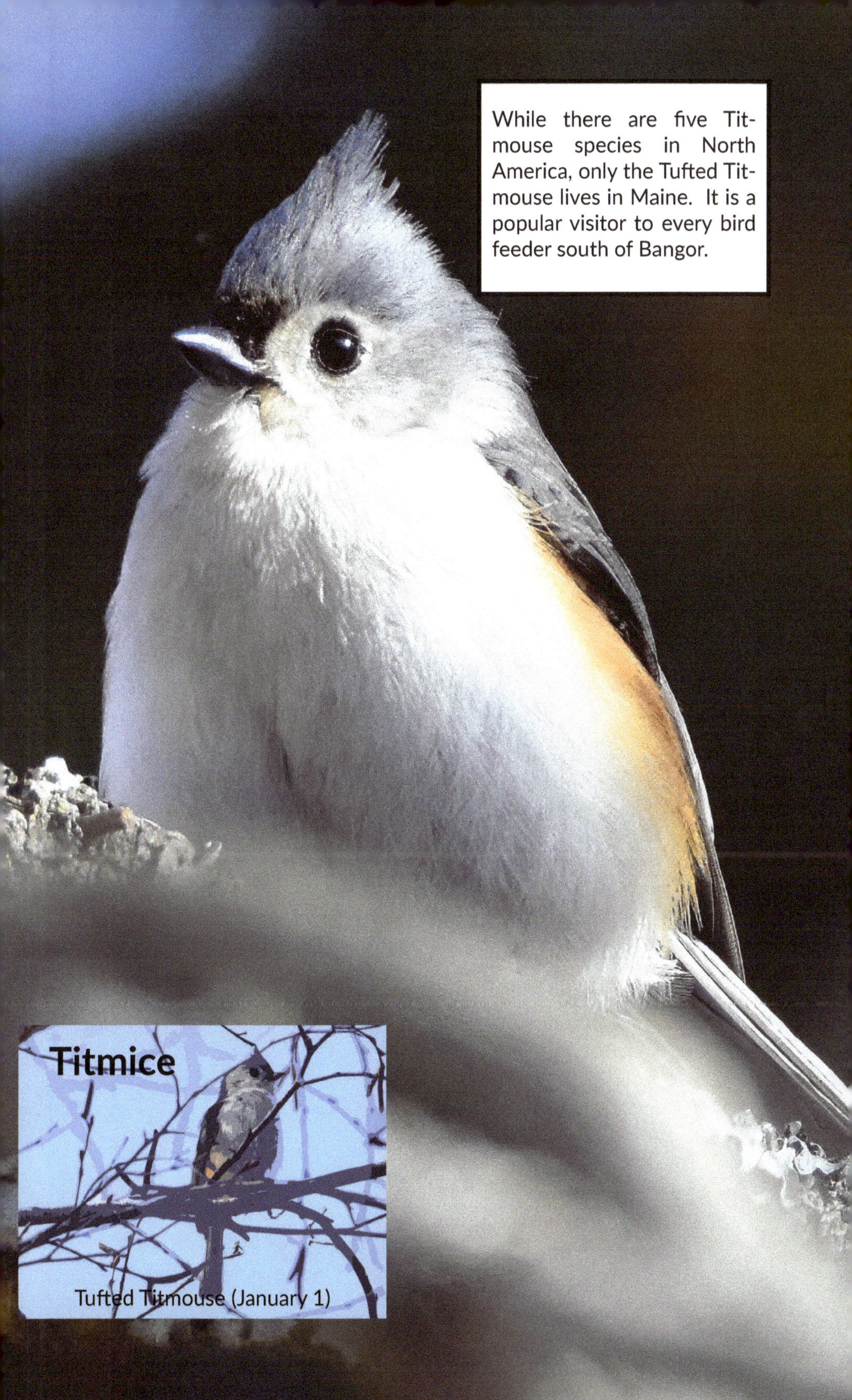

While there are five Titmouse species in North America, only the Tufted Titmouse lives in Maine. It is a popular visitor to every bird feeder south of Bangor.

Titmice

Tufted Titmouse (January 1)

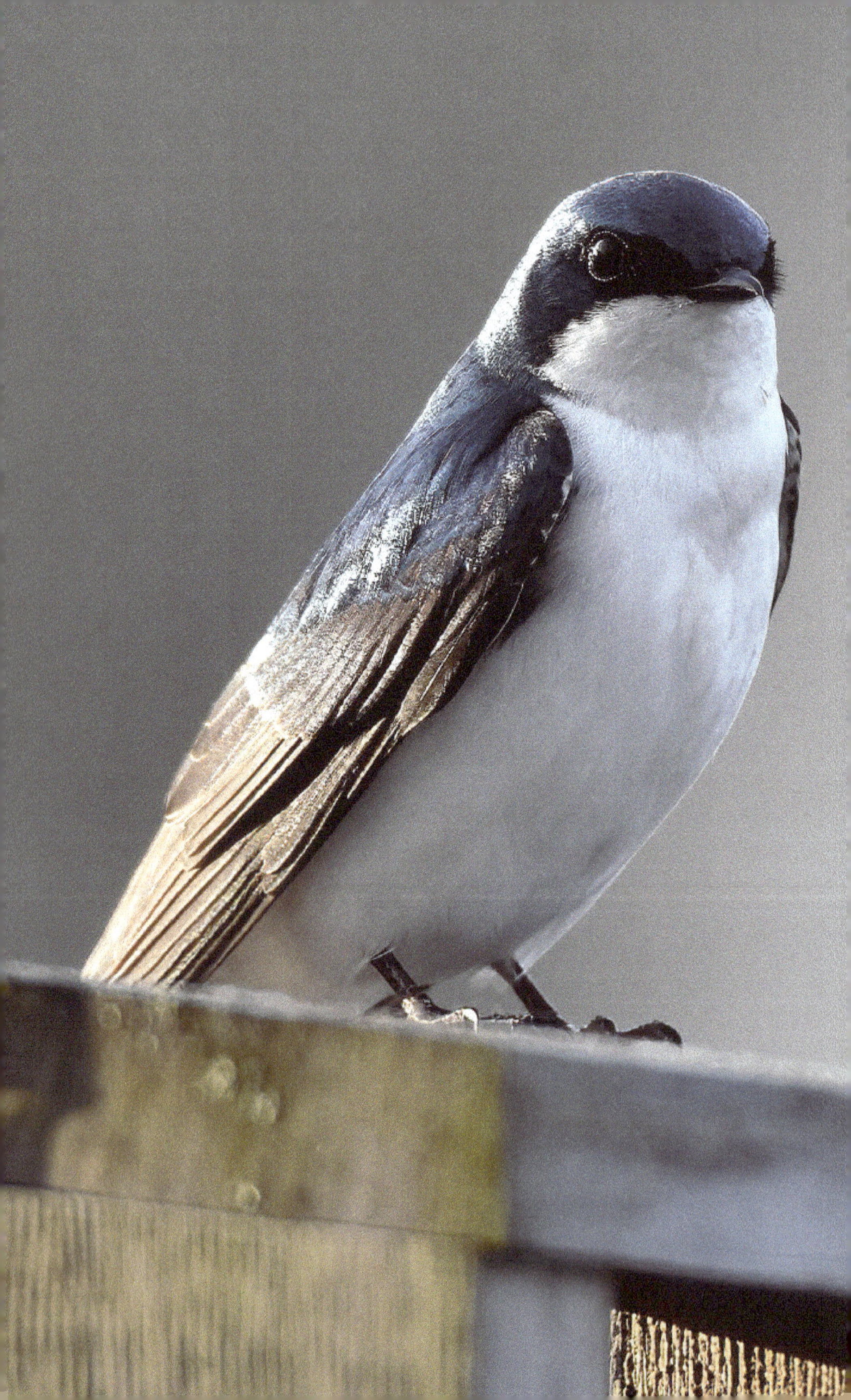

As a kid, I spent a lot of time at my grandparents' farm in Mt. Vernon, a small rural agricultural community northwest of Augusta, Maine.

I remember vividly the Barn Swallows flying in and out of the hayloft. Little did I know that fifty years later those same Swallows and the other Swallows on the family homestead would be such a help on my Maine Big Year.

Down by the pond behind the farmhouse I found the greenish Tree Swallow and a brown Rough-Winged Swallow.

A stream leading to the pond produced Bank Swallows, flying in and out of holes just above the waterline.

A classic bird condo at a home across from the farmhouse sported Purple Martins.

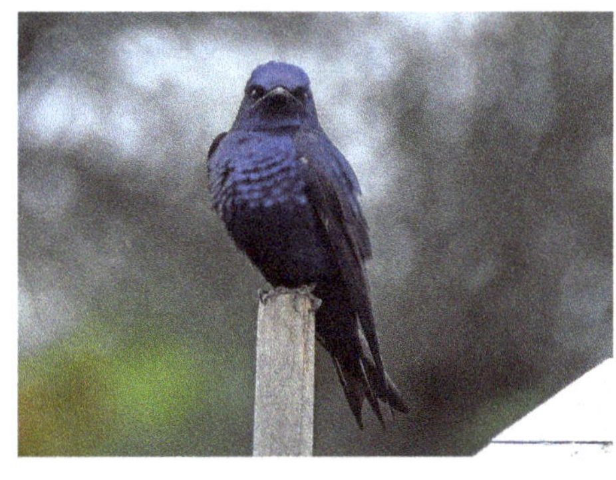

And five miles down the road, I got a Cliff Swallow at the Belgrade Boat launch.

All five Maine Swallow species, and all at or near my family's farm.

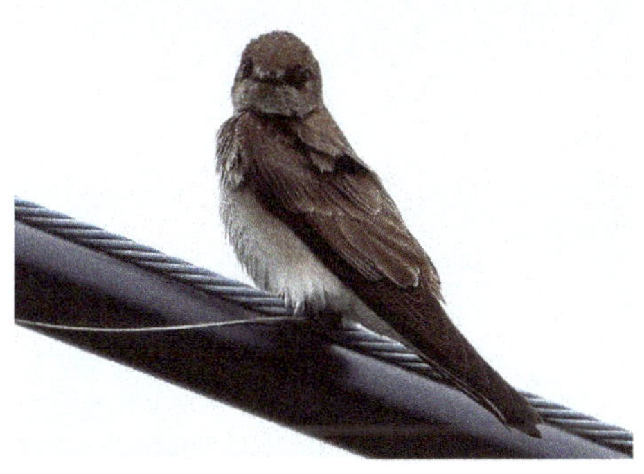

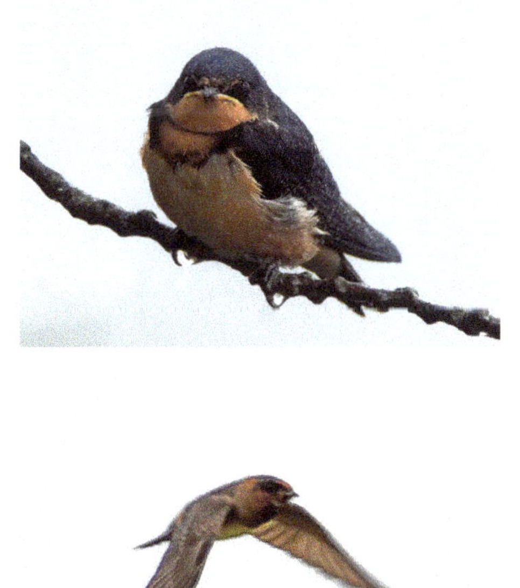

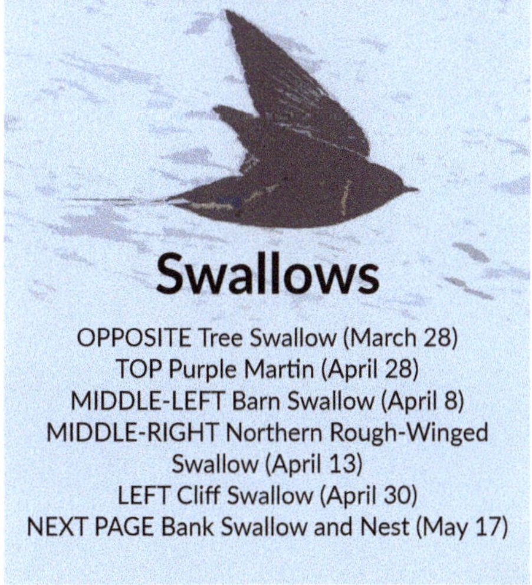

Swallows

OPPOSITE Tree Swallow (March 28)
TOP Purple Martin (April 28)
MIDDLE-LEFT Barn Swallow (April 8)
MIDDLE-RIGHT Northern Rough-Winged
Swallow (April 13)
LEFT Cliff Swallow (April 30)
NEXT PAGE Bank Swallow and Nest (May 17)

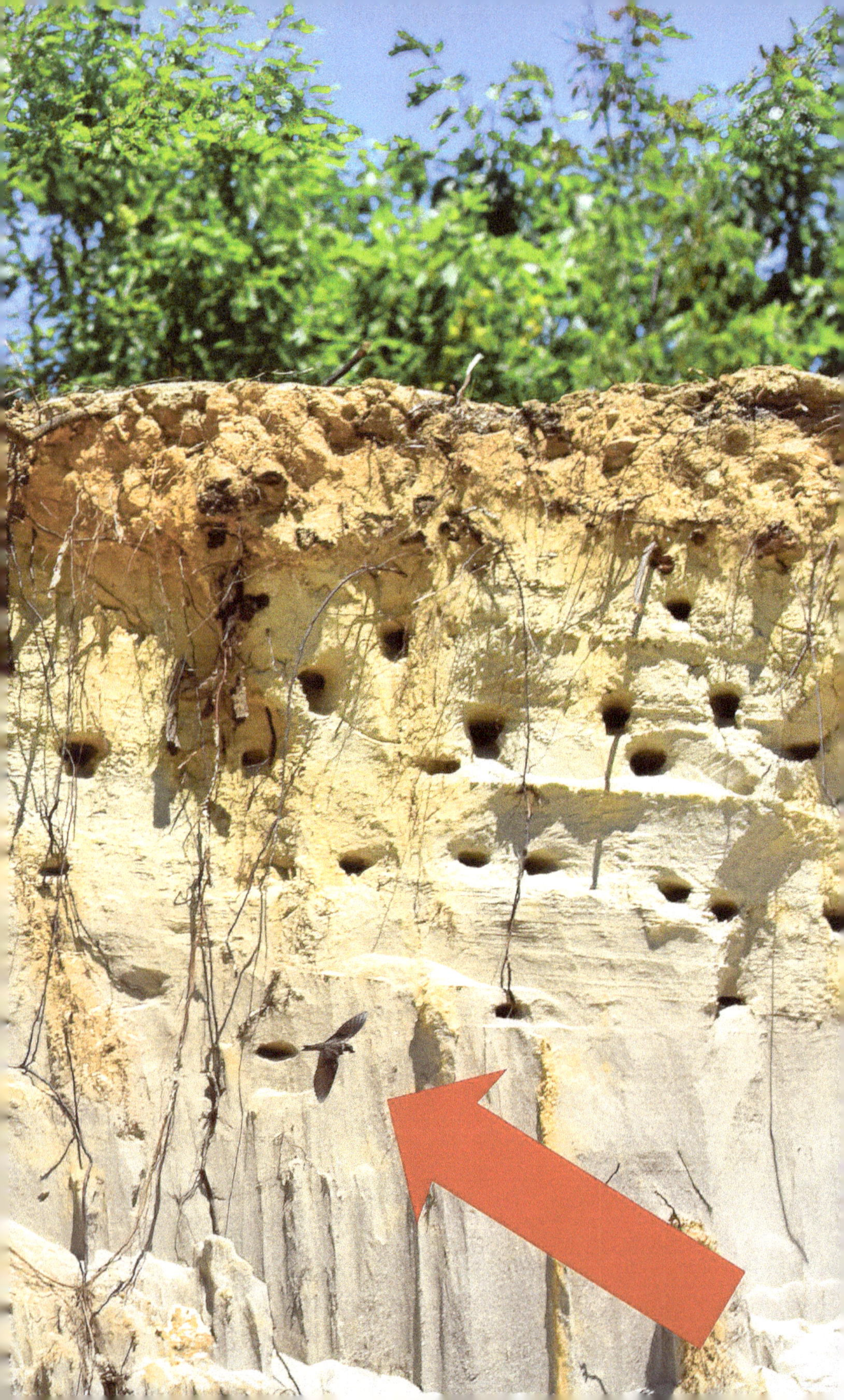

I'm sitting in the stands looking out at a football field. Someone is shouting: "He's at the 30", "He's at the 35", "The 40", "The 45", "Across Midfield"!!!!

No, I didn't give up birding for the day to attend a high school football game. I was watching a rare Barnacle Goose weave through the opposition (Canada Geese) on Wasgett Field, the gridiron home of the Oceanside High School Mariners.

The Barnacle Goose breeds each summer on the east coast of Greenland before migrating to the United Kingdom for the winter. Obviously, this particular bird's GPS wasn't working properly, and he landed on a Mid-coast Maine football field.

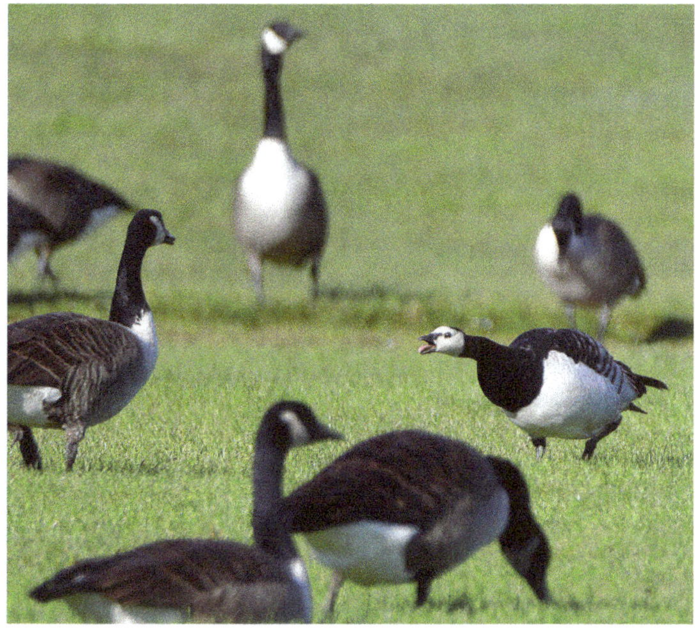

A Barnacle Goose is about half the size of a Canada Goose. Barney, as I dubbed him, was still pretty aggressive toward his bigger cousins, giving chase several times when one got too close.

Maine Big Year Bird # 317, which tied the Maine State Record!!!!

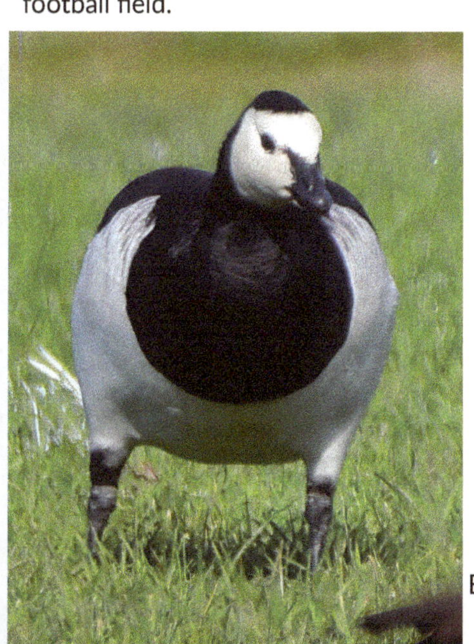

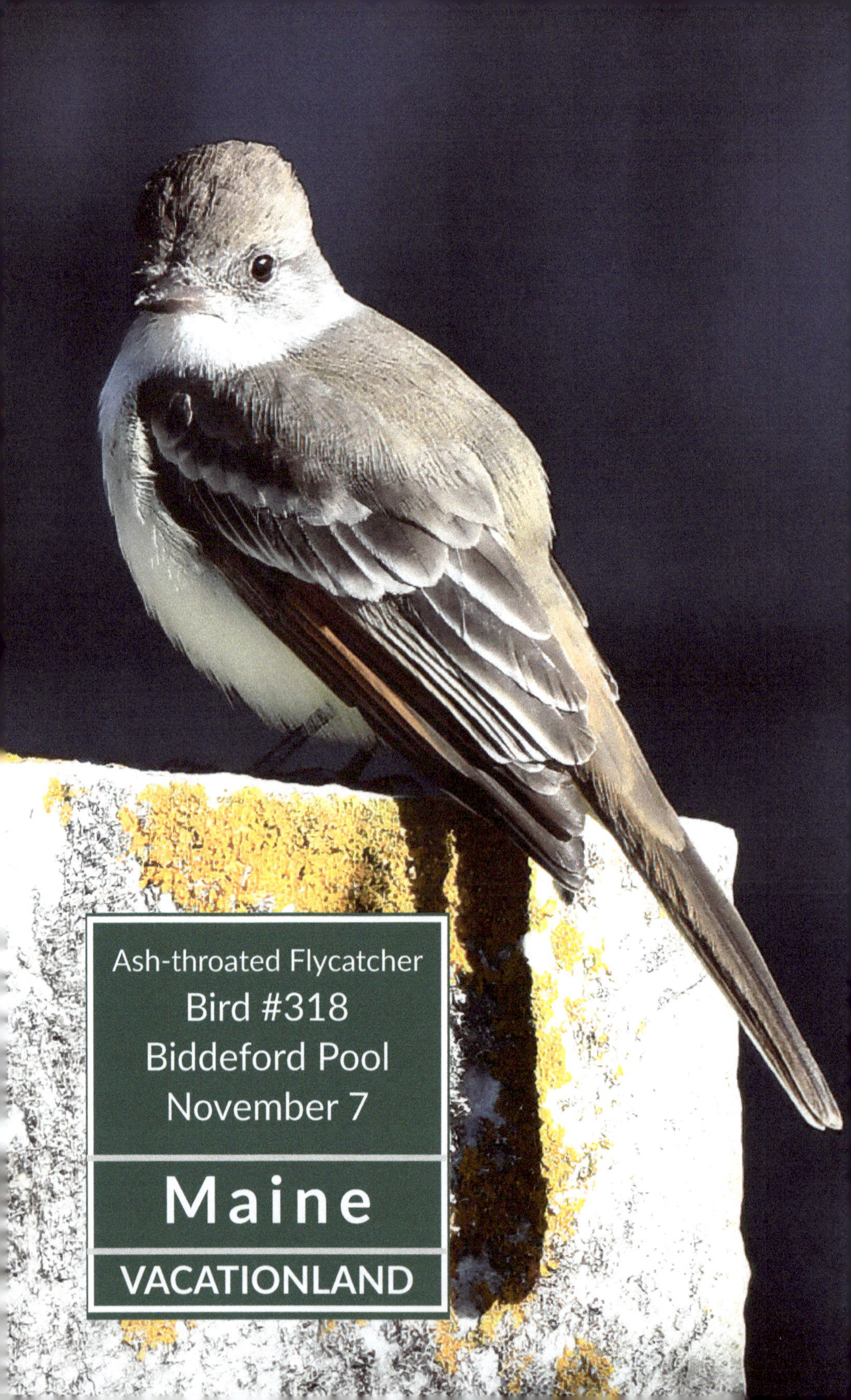

Ash-throated Flycatcher
Bird #318
Biddeford Pool
November 7
Maine
VACATIONLAND

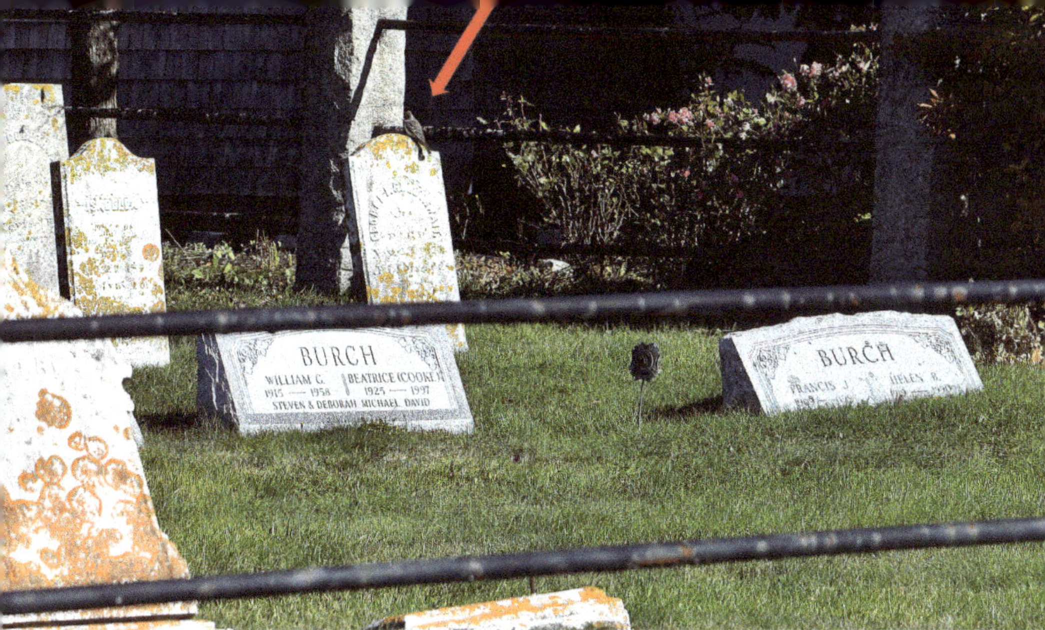

"It's right there."

"Where?"

"Right there on the gravestone."

"Still not seeing it."

"It's close to the fence by the church."

"I see it!!!!"

That's how fellow birder Leon Mooney helped me get my eyes on Maine Big Year Bird #318, an Ash-throated Flycatcher.

Ninety minutes earlier, I had received my first text message about the Flycatcher from Doug Hitchcox, Maine Audubon's staff naturalist.

Soon I got a text from Matthew Gilbert.

Then Charles Duncan.

Then Marian Zimmerman.

Big Years are a community effort and my birding friends were making sure I knew about this bird.

Ingrid and I had only seen an Ash-throated Flycatcher once before, in Southeast California. To see one in Maine, thousands of miles outside its range, made this the perfect bird on which to set a new record.

St. Martin's in the Field is a picturesque Episcopal church, complete with cemetery, located in the middle of a golf course. Leon and I arrived at the same time and walked together along the edge of the fairway watching out for errant golf balls as we made our way to the cemetery.

It was then that Leon saw the bird and graciously pointed it out.

Ingrid was in Washington DC visiting her daughter. She has been so supportive and patient through the whole Big Year adventure, I wish she could have seen the record bird with me. But she called immediately to congratulate me. I'm a very lucky man!!!

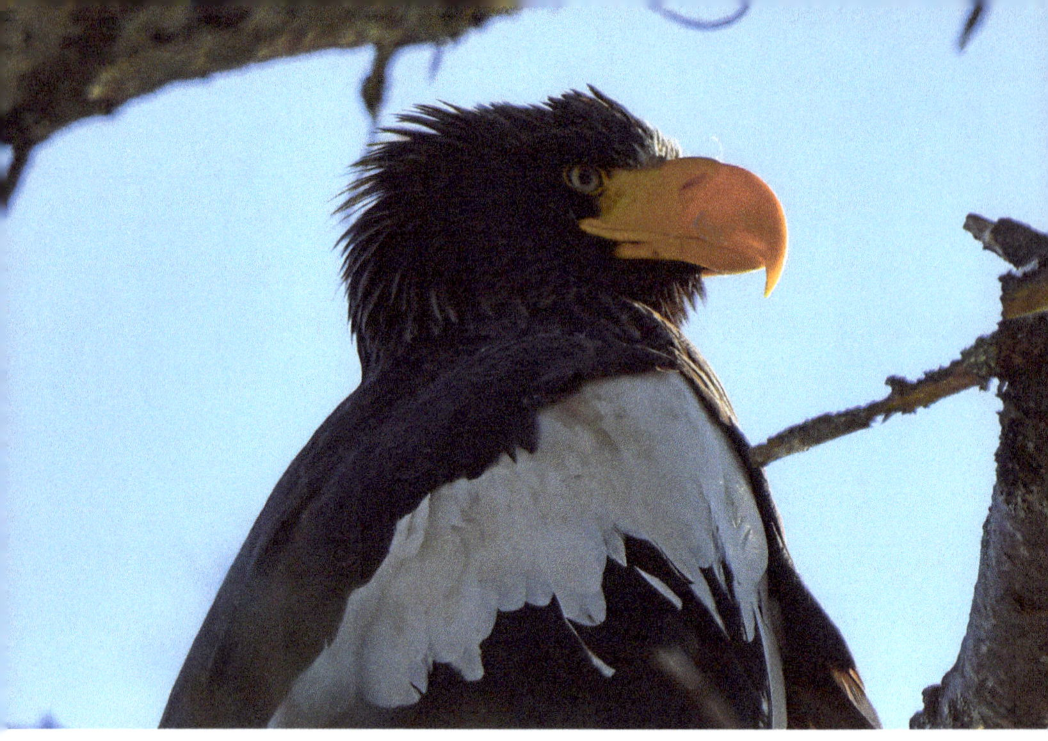

The Steller's Sea Eagle is one of the world's largest and rarest raptors. A glacial relict, it evolved over several ice ages, breeding along the east Russian coast and wintering in Korea, Japan and northern China. Occasionally one is seen over Alaska's Aleutian Islands, but this is an Asian bird of the Russian ice.

On March 10, 2021, just south of San Antonio, Texas, a Steller's Sea Eagle was photographed on a snag by a creek.

This is analogous to a Polar Bear taking a bath in the Rio Grande. Birders searched the area for days, but the bird was gone.

A few months later, in August, the same bird showed up in eastern Alaska for a few days. It then reappeared in New Brunswick for a few more. Next it was seen in Nova Scotia in November and then in Massachusetts after Christmas.

Throughout the fall, fellow birders commented that the wayward Steller's Sea Eagle would be the coming through Maine, but no one really believed it.

Late in the afternoon on December 30th, an incredible thing happened. A couple looked out the window of their Five Islands home in Georgetown (just south of Reid State Park) and saw the Steller's Sea Eagle perched in a tree.

Ingrid and I rushed down to Five Islands, but it was too dark and foggy to do much searching.

On December 31st, the last day of my Maine Big Year, I was searching Westport Island for the Eagle when my phone rang. It was Matthew Gilbert, a High School Senior from Cumberland.

"We've got it!!!" he exclaimed and sent me the GPS coordinates. I was only a mile away as the crow flies and 45 minutes by car.

I swung through Wiscasset and picked up Ingrid. We then drove a consistent 20 mph over the posted speed limit, and arrived in time to see the enormous Steller's Sea Eagle at the end of an icy road. We were soon joined by at least a hundred birders from all over the Northeast. Folks were exchanging hugs, fist bumps and high-fives. The rarest bird ever seen in Maine!!!

What a thrilling way to end the Maine Big Year!!!

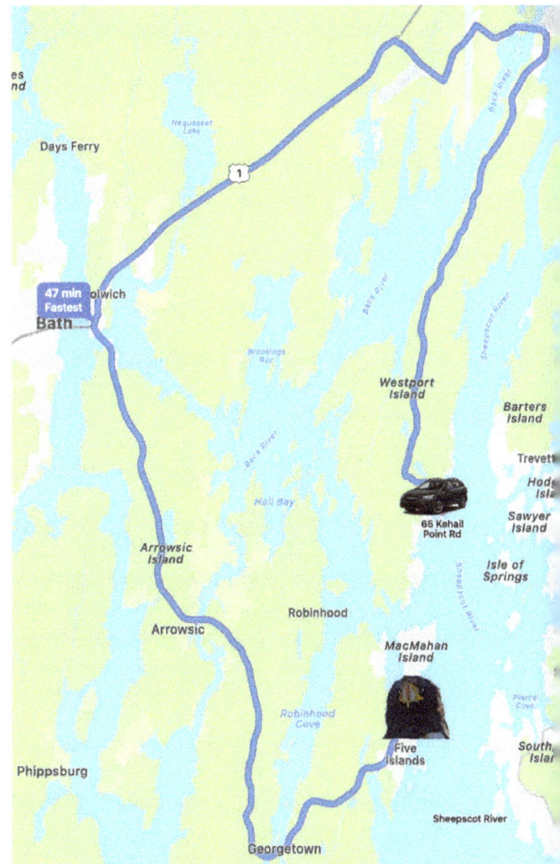

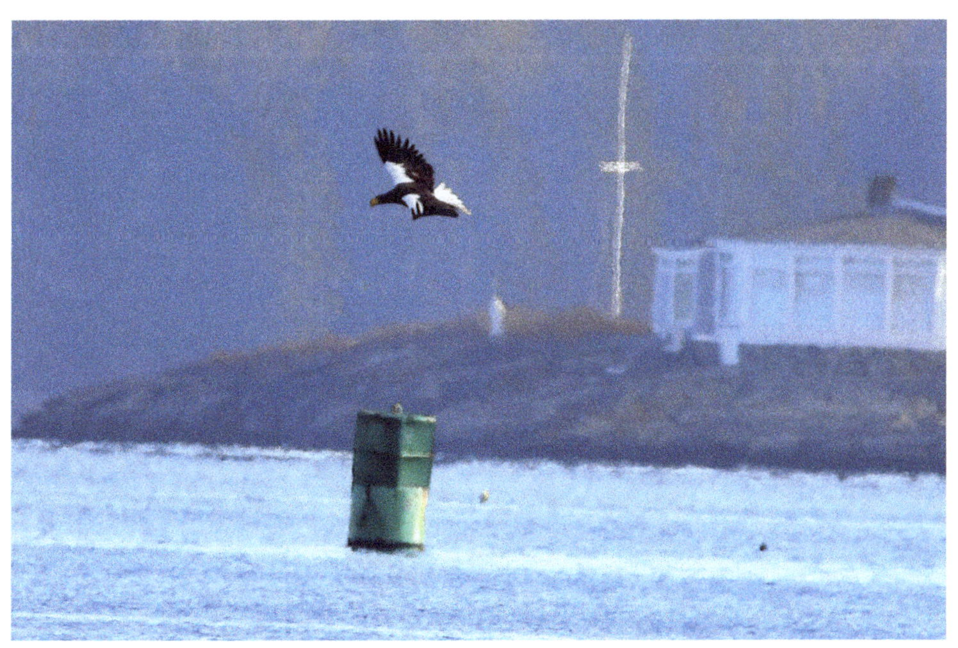

Maine Big Year - 2021

After seeing a Gray Kingbird on December 3 at Fortunes Rock Beach in Biddeford, the final four weeks of the Maine Big Year were bird free until the amazing Steller's Sea Eagle appeared on December 31.

Thanks to the Russian Eagle, the year ended with a bang instead of a whimper.

November was a really good month, with seven rarities coming through the state, all within binocular range.

Theses final nine birds from November through December, brought my Maine Big Year Total to 324, eclipsing Josh Fecteau's 2017 record of 317.

Josh is a much more knowledgeable birder than I am, and he helped me several times throughout the year to locate and identify birds. Like so many Maine Birders, Josh was gracious and helpful, a real gentleman.

The Steller's Sea Eagle was also Ingrid's 303rd bird of the year. She ended up the 8th birder and 2nd woman to hit 300. Amazing, considering her less than flexible 4th grade teaching schedule. She, didn't really start birding aggressively until May and still ended the year with the 7th highest total of all-time.

When I climbed into my 2019 Subaru Crosstrek before dawn on January 1, my odometer read 28,000. Twelve months later it read 90,000 miles. I put over 60,000 miles on my car and only left the State of Maine twice.

I made twenty-two boat excursions, including whale and pelagic trips out of Boothbay and Bar Harbor, numerous ferry trips to Monhegan and Peaks Is-

Western Kingbird
The One that Got Away

Every fall, one or two directionally challenged Western Kingbirds move through Maine as they migrate from their breeding zone west of the Mississippi toward Central America.

In earlier years I had no problem finding one, but when it really counted, during my Maine Big Year, the Western Kingbird became elusive.

Throughout September, October and November this bird was reported over and over on Monhegan Island, but would disappear whenever I trekked out on the ferry .

The Kingbird would reappear as soon as I returned to the mainland.

By the second week of December, the Western Kingbird reports ended, and I realized that this would be the bird that "got away".

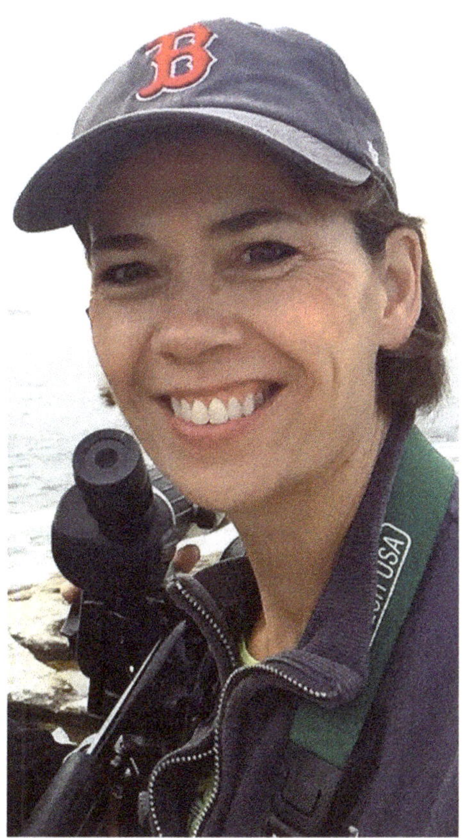

Gary Roberts, Ginny Bishop, Harry Wales, Howie Nielsen, Ian Carsen, Jeannette Lovitch, Jeff Cherry, Jeff Wells, Jennifer Long, Jessica Brainerd, John Aromando, John Drury, John Lorec, Jonah Levy, Josh Fecteau, Kathie Brown, Kevin Couture, Kevin Tolan, Kristen Linquist, Laura Blustein, Laura Robinson, Leon Mooney, Linda Cunningham, Linda Woodward, Louis Bevier, Magil Webber, Marian Zimmerman, Matthew Gilbert, Michael Boardman, Michael Good, Mike Fahay, Noah Gibb, Reed Robinson, Richard Garrigus, Rob Speirs, Robert Gundy, Robin Ohrt, Sean Hatch, Steve Mierzykopwski, Steven Gilchrist, Todd Abrahams, Tom Foley, Tova Mellen, Tracy Goupil, Travis Sparks, Turk Duddy, Weston Barker, Xander Vitarelli, and many others who all helped me along the way.

And of course thanks to Ingrid, my birding and life partner. She makes every day wonderful!!

lands, a chartered lobster boat to see the Red-billed Tropicbird and several more.

The 324 Maine Big Year Birds were identified in 82 different municipalities. The northern-most bird was a Pink-footed Goose in Limestone. The southern-most a Gray Catbird at Kittery Point. East and West were a Painted Bunting and a Brown Thrasher in Lubec and Fryeburg respectively.

Thanks to Andrew Magoun, Becky Marvil, Bill Sheehan, Bob Duchesne, Bud Heuer, Camden Martin, Carol Sue Cain, Charles Duncan, Charlie Nims, Chris Sayers, Craig Kesselheim, Derek Lovitch, Don Lima, Donna Cundy, Doug Hitchcox, Ed Jenkins, Eddy Edwards, Elaine Culleton, Gary Jarvis,

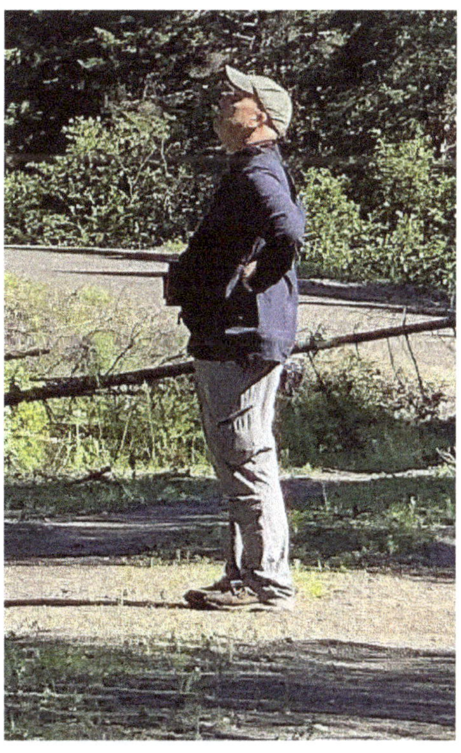

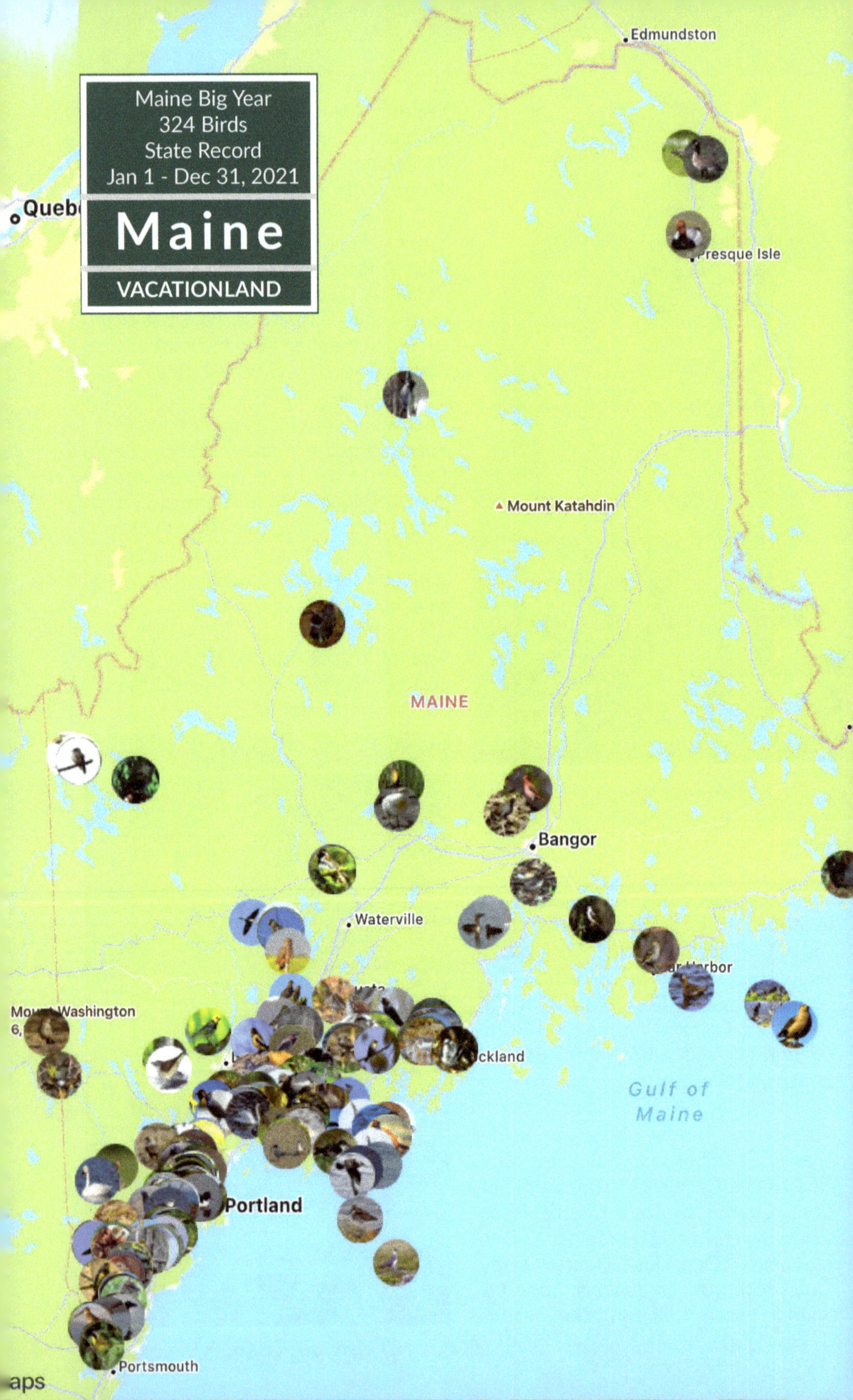

Maine Big Year
324 Birds
State Record
Jan 1 - Dec 31, 2021
Maine
VACATIONLAND
Edmundston
Quebec
Presque Isle
Mount Katahdin
MAINE
Bangor
Waterville
Mount Washington
6,
Portland
Rockland
Bar Harbor
Gulf of
Maine
Portsmouth
aps

Species by City or Town

City/Town	#	City/Town	#	City/Town	#
Andover	1	Jefferson	1	Rockport	3
Augusta	1	Kennebunk	4	Saco	2
Bangor	1	Kennebunkport	6	Sanford	5
Bath	3	Kittery	3	Scarborough	22
Belgrade	3	Kittery Point	7	Seal Island	1
Biddeford	23	Lewiston	1	Searsport	1
Birch Harbor	1	Lily Bay	1	Shirley Mills	1
Boothbay	1	Limestone	2	Sidney	4
Boothbay Harbor	2	Lubec	1	South Berwick	1
Bowdoin	1	Lyman	1	South Portland	21
Bristol	1	Monhegan	6	South Thomaston	4
Brownfield	1	Mount Vernon	1	Stockton Springs	1
Brunswick	10	Newcastle	1	Stratton	2
Cape Elizabeth	14	Newport	1	Thomaston	5
Cape Neddick	3	Nobleboro	3	Topsham	1
Clinton	8	Ogunquit	14	Trenton	1
Corinna	1	Old Orchard Beach	1	Union	1
Cumberland Foreside	2	Orland	1	Waldoboro	3
Dresden	10	Orono	2	Waterboro	1
Easton	2	Orrs Island	1	Wells	8
Falmouth	5	Pemaquid	1	Westport Island	1
Freeport	6	Phippsburg	5	Whitefield	1
Fryeburg	1	Poland	2	Windham	2
Gardiner	1	Portland	13	Wiscasset	7
Georgetown	6	Pownal	1	Woolwich	2
Gulf of Maine	12	Rangeley	4	York	9
Harpswell	1	Richmond	1		
Hollis Center	1	Rockland	7		
				Total Species	324

Index

Cape May Warbler 113
Chestnut-sided Warbler vi, 105
Common Yellowthroat 108
Louisiana Waterthrush 111
Magnolia Warbler 108
Mourning Warbler 114
Nashville Warbler 114
Northern Parula 105
Northern Waterthrush 111
Orange-crowned Warbler 34, 114
Ovenbird 111
Palm Warbler 113
Pine Warbler 108
Prairie Warbler 113
Prothonotary Warbler 114
Tennessee Warbler 114
Wilson's Warbler 113
Yellow-rumped Warbler 108
Yellow-throated Warbler 114
Yellow Warbler 105
Warbling Vireo 165
Waxwings
Bohemian Waxwing 32
Cedar Waxwing vi, 32
Western Kingbird 192
Western Sandpiper 154
Western Tanager 180
Whimbrel 147
White-breasted Nuthatch 43
White-crowned Sparrow 136
White-eyed Vireo 165
White-faced Ibis 86
White-rumped Sandpiper 152
White-tail Deer 169
White-throated Sparrow 136
White-winged Crossbill 47
White-winged Dove 74
White-winged Scoter 17
Wigeons
American Wigeon 22
Eurasian Wigeon 22
Wild Turkey 126
Willet 149
Willow Flycatcher 97
Wilson's Phalarope 162
Wilson's Snipe 149
Wilson's Storm-Petrel 120
Wilson's Warbler 113
Winter Fields
American Pipit 40
Horned Lark 40
Lapland Longspur 40
Snow Bunting 40
Woodchuck 171
Wood Duck 17
Woodpeckers
American Three-toed Woodpecker 38

Black-backed Woodpecker 38
Downey Woodpecker 37
Hairy Woodpecker 37
Northern Flicker 38
Pileated Woodpecker 37
Red-bellied Woodpecker 38
Red-headed Woodpecker 38
Yellow-bellied Sapsucker 38
Wood-Pewees
Eastern Wood-Pewee 98
Wood Thrush 79
Wrens
Carolina Wren 133
House Wren 133
Marsh Wren 133
Rock Wren 31, 133

Y

Yellow-bellied Flycatcher 97
Yellow-bellied Sapsucker 38
Yellow-billed Cuckoo 122
Yellow-breasted Chat 116
Yellow-crowned Night-Heron 73
Yellow-headed Blackbird 44, 92
Yellowlegs
Greater Yellowlegs 161
Lesser Yellowlegs 161
Yellow-rumped Warbler 108
Yellow-throated Vireo 165
Yellow-throated Warbler 114
Yellow Warbler 105

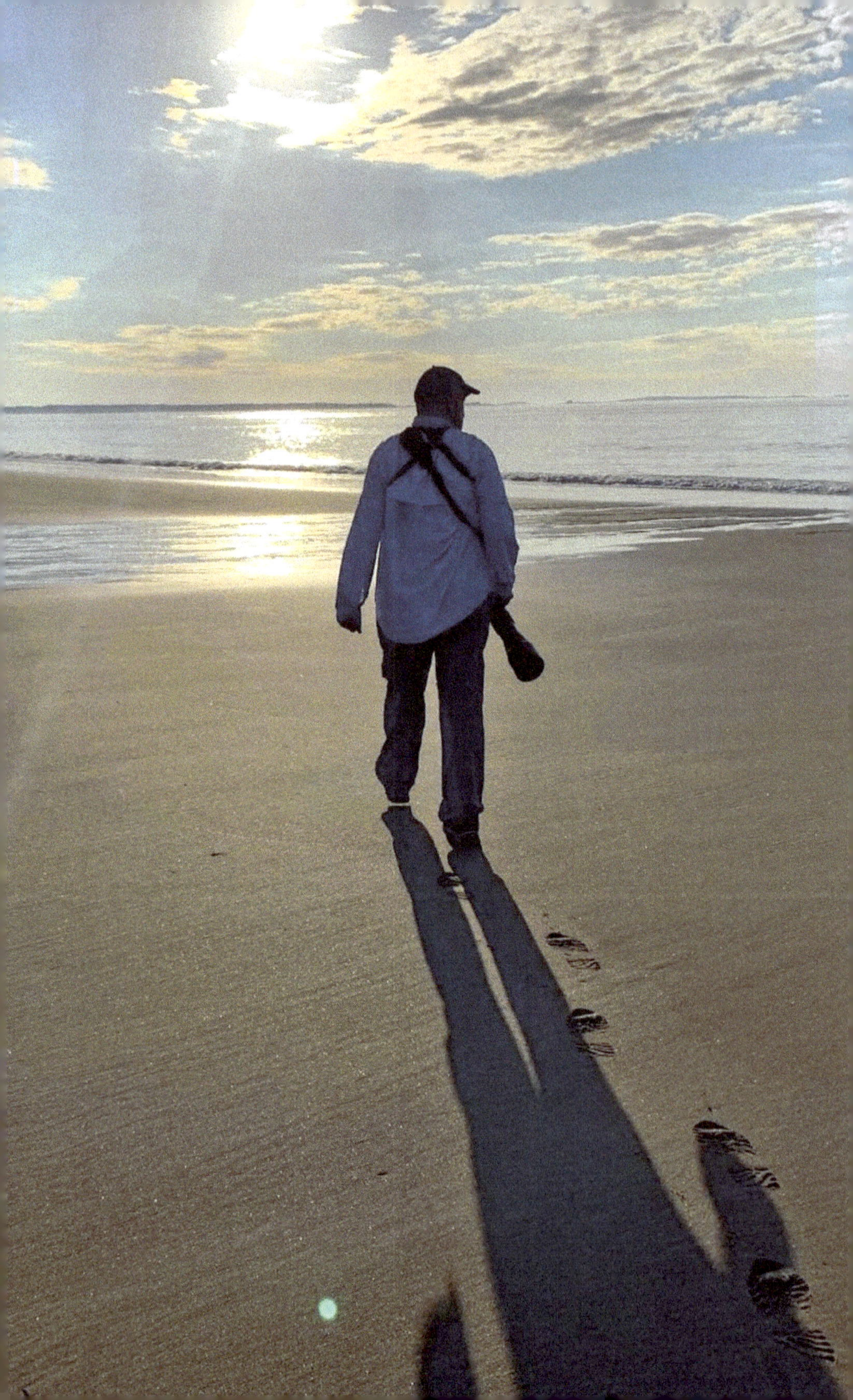